Studies in Empirical Economics

Aman Ullah /Ed.)
Semiparametric and Nonparametric Econometrics
1989. VII, 172 pp. Hard cover DM 120,–
ISBN 3-7908-0418-5

Walter Krämer (Ed.)
Econometrics of Structural Change
1989. X, 128 pp. Hard cover DM 85,–
ISBN 3-7908-0432-0

Wolfgang Franz (Ed.)
Hysteresis Effects in Economic Models
1990. VIII, 121 pp. Hard cover DM 90,–
ISBN 3-7908-0482-7

John Piggott and John Whalley (Eds.)
Applied General Equilibrium
1991. VI, 153 pp. Hard cover DM 98,–
ISBN 3-7908-0530-0

Baldev Raj and Badi H. Baltagi (Eds.)
Panel Data Analysis
1992. VIII, 220 pp. Hard cover DM 128,–
ISBN 3-7908-0593-9

Josef Christl
The Unemployment / Vacancy Curve
1992. XVI, 152 pp. Hard cover DM 98,–
ISBN 3-7908-0625-0

Jürgen Kaehler and Peter Kugler (Eds.)
Econometric Analysis of Financial Markets
1994. VII, 230 pp. Hard cover DM 98,–
ISBN 3-7908-0740-0

Klaus F. Zimmermann (Ed.)
Output and Employment Fluctuations
VI, 259 pp. Hard cover DM 128,–
ISBN 3-7908-0754-0

Jean-Marie Dufour
Baldev Raj (Eds.)

New Developments in Time Series Econometrics

With 28 Figures

Physica-Verlag
A Springer-Verlag Company

Editors
Prof. Jean-Marie Dufour
Director of the C.R.D.E.
(Centre de Recherche et Développement en Economique)
Université de Montréal
C.P. 6128, Succursale A
Montréal, Québec, Canada H3C 3J7

Prof. Baldev Raj
School of Business and Economics
Wilfrid Laurier University
Waterloo, Ontario, Canada

First published in "Empirical Economics"
Vol. 18, No. 4, 1993

ISBN 978-3-642-48744-6 ISBN 978-3-642-48742-2 (eBook)
DOI 10.1007/978-3-642-48742-2
CIP-Titelaufnahme der Deutschen Bibliothek

New developments in time series econometrics / Jean-Marie
Dufour ; Baldev Raj (eds.). – Heidelberg : Physica-Verl., 1994
(Studies in empirical economics)
ISBN 978-3-642-48744-6

NE: Dufour, Jean-Marie [Hrsg.]

Softcover reprint of the hardcover 1st edition 1994

2201/2202-543210 – Printed on acid-free paper

Contents

New Developments in Time Series Econometrics: An Overview[1]

JEAN-MARIE DUFOUR

C.R.D.E., Université de Montréal, C.P. 6128, succursale A, Montreal (Quebec) H3C 3J7, Canada

BALDEV RAJ

School of Business and Economics, Wilfrid Laurier University, Waterloo, Ontario, N2L 3C5, Canada

JEL Classification System-Numbers: C1, C22, C32, C52

Empirical data in economics are typically non-experimental, especially in finance and macroeconomics where researchers usually rely on time series gathered by official agencies or other investigators. This raises two basic problems for econometric modeling: first, to understand the dynamic structure of such series, both individually (e.g., stationarity and persistence properties) and jointly (dynamic relations between series); second, to use these series in order to identify and assess potential explanatory ("structural") models. Because such data are non-experimental, so that observations cannot be made independent and optimal experimental designs are not available, modeling and inference often require an exceptional degree of sophistication. Fortunately, in recent years, statistical methods for the analysis of time series have developed considerably and several remarkable innovations have been introduced.

The eleven articles in this special issue provide empirical applications as well as theoretical extensions of some of the most exciting recent developments in time-series econometrics. Several leading econometricians have contributed to this collection. The papers have been grouped around three broad themes: (I) the modeling of multivariate time series (five papers); (II) the analysis of structural change (three papers); (III) seasonality and fractional integration (three papers). Of course, these themes are closely inter-related, and several other topics covered are worth stressing: vector autoregressive (VAR) models (Juselius; Palm, Peeters and Pfann; Perron and Campbell; Tiao, Tsay and Wang), cointegration and error-correction models (Ghysels, Lee and Siklos; Juselius; Kunst; Lütkepohl; Palm, Peeters and Pfann; Perron and Campbell; Quintos and Phillips; Tiao, Tsay and Wang), nonparametric methods in time series

[1] This work was supported by the Academic Development Fund of Wilfrid Laurier University, the Institut de Statistique (Université Libre de Bruxelles), the Intercollegiate Center for Management Sciences (Bruxelles), the School of Economics, Kwansei Gakuin University (Japan), the Social Sciences and Humanities Research Council of Canada, the Natural Sciences and Engineering Research Council of Canada, the Government of Québec (Fonds FCAR), and the Ontario-Québec Academic Exchange Program.

(Campbell and Galbraith), and fractionally integrated models (Chung and Baillie). Another interesting feature of these contributions is that the majority of the papers (9 over 11) are mostly empirical or contain empirical illustrations, while five of them contain new methodological results (Quintos and Phillips; Perron; Ghysels et al.; Perron and Campbell; Chung and Baillie). A brief overview of these contributions is presented below.

The five papers in the first section (Tiao et al.; Juselius; Palm et al.; Perron and Campbell; Campbell and Galbraith) deal with relatively general issues relevant to the modeling of multivariate time series, especially in the context of VARMA and VAR models. In particular, the concept of cointegration, which provides a way of distinguishing between long-run equilibrium relations and short-run dynamics, plays a central role in these analyses. It is also interesting to note that the papers by Tiao et al., Juselius, and Palm et al. nicely illustrate increasing degrees of structural modeling, as opposed to a relatively model-free statistical analysis. Then the paper by Perron and Campbell makes an interesting theoretical contribution to the analysis of equilibrium relations (cointegration) in such systems, while the paper by Campbell and Galbraith shows how a finite-sample distribution-free technique can be useful in studying relationships between two time series.

More specifically, the article by George Tiao, Ruey Tsay and Tsychang Wang illustrates how several recently developed statistical techniques for analyzing multivariate time series from a relatively "atheoretical" standpoint can be fruitfully applied to economic time series. The authors have made important theoretical contributions to the development of several techniques used here, some of which have been little exploited by econometricians. The authors analyze the behaviour of three interest rates (on one-, three- and six-month deposits) in Taiwan (monthly, from 1961 to 1991). They study first whether these series have unit roots and whether they are cointegrated. To analyze cointegration, they use procedures proposed by Engle and Granger (1987), Johansen (1988), Stock and Watson (1988), and Chan and Tsay (1991), and conclude that the interest rates have unit roots but are not cointegrated. To analyze the dynamic relationships between the interest rates, the authors then employ the class of vector autoregressive moving average (VARMA) models and use the modeling approach proposed by Tiao and Box (1981). They find that a VAR(4) model appears to be appropriate. The aforementioned model is further improved and analyzed by using canonical correlation analysis (Box and Tiao, 1977). The results suggest a complex feedback system without any particular unidirectional relationship. Finally, the authors analyze the same series using the more recent technique of scalar component models (Tiao and Tsay, 1989), which can reduce the number of parameters to be estimated and reveal interesting underlying structures. The results suggest a VARMA (1, 1) model and indicate that the dynamic structure can be greatly simplified by transforming the series into (i) "an average component reflecting the general comovement of the data," and (ii) "two linear contrasts of the rates."

The second article, by Katarina Juselius, discusses general issues concerning the modeling of macroeconomic time series and presents an illustration of macroeconometric modeling which is intermediate between a purely statistical approach, such as the one illustrated by the preceding paper, and structural modeling. Juselius starts from the recent critical appraisal of "empirical macroeconomics" by Summers (1991) to emphasize the importance of distinguishing between two types of analysis: (i) the application of statistical methods to estimate the parameters of an economic model, and (ii) the analysis of a statistical model in view of economic questions of interest (Haavelmo, 1944). When data are obtained by passive observation (which is typically the case in macroeconomics), the latter activity then appears to be especially important to establish a link between observations and theory. She then describes how, in the context of nonstationary series, a strategy based on the analysis of cointegrating relationships and error-correction mechanisms (Engle and Granger, 1987) can provide insight into long-run (equilibrium) relationships and short-run dynamics. This strategy is illustrated by looking at Danish monetary data on money, real income, the price level and three interest rates (quarterly, 1969–1987). She identifies three long-run relations between these variables (a relation between the nominal interest rates and the inflation rate, a second one between real income, inflation and two interest rates, and a long-run "money demand" relation), analyzes the short-run dynamics, and finds the results to be both statistically and economically acceptable.

The article by Palm, Peeters and Pfann goes one step further by undertaking to formulate and estimate a model which is both derived from an explicit optimization model and is empirically acceptable. The authors study factor demand (for labor, structures and equipment) in U.S. manufacturing using a model that accounts for adjustment costs (Lucas, 1967) and gestation lags (Kydland and Prescott, 1982). While these two approaches are generally viewed as alternative explanations, the authors innovate by taking both elements into account in a model based on intertemporal optimization. The theoretical model so obtained has various implications concerning the time-series structure of the variables involved, including the presence of three cointegration relationships between factor quantities and prices. The authors then use quarterly data on the manufacturing industry in the U.S. (quantity used and price for each one of the three basic factors, 1960–1988) to assess whether the model is acceptable and study its properties. This is done first by analyzing the time-series properties of the data (order of integration, ARMA structure, cointegration), and then by estimating a "structural" VAR model that takes into account the restrictions implied by the theoretical model. Notable findings here include: the confirmation that three cointegration relationships appear to hold in the system considered (one for each factor demand with the factor prices), unidirectional Granger causality from production prices to production factors (another prediction of the theoretical model), and the fact that time-to-build considerations are at least as important as adjustment costs in the model.

In the following article, Pierre Perron and John Campbell consider the problem of testing the presence of r cointegrating relationships in a finite-order

VAR model when linear trends are present. They emphasize first the importance of distinguishing between "stochastic cointegration" and "deterministic cointegration", a distinction introduced by Ogaki and Park (1992). Stochastic cointegration is a weaker concept which allows cointegrating relationships to be stationary around a deterministic trend, while deterministic cointegration assumes that such trends are eliminated by the cointegration vectors. The authors argue that the hypothesis of stochastic cointegration is the one of most interest in empirical applications. Typical precedures for testing cointegration, however, such as those proposed by Johansen (1988, 1991), consider the more restrictive assumption of deterministic cointegration. The authors then show that not taking into account linear trends may lead to misleading inferences, e.g., with respect to causality properties. Finally, they propose a modified procedure for testing the hypothesis of r cointegrating relations, which is similar to the one of Johansen (1991), but allows for the presence of linear trends. They also provide a short table of asymptotic critical values.

The fifth article in this section, by Bryan Campbell and John Galbraith, applies recent finite-sample nonparametric techniques to test the expectations theory of the term structure of interest rates from Canadian and U.S. data (monthly 3- and 6-month interest rates, 1960–1989). Data on interest rates are delicate to analyze because they involve non-normal distributions and heteroskedasticity, so that standard parametric or non-robust statistical techniques can be very unreliable. Here, the authors use sign- and signed-rank tests which are especially well adapted to such situations because of their strong finite-sample validity and robustness properties (Campbell and Dufour, 1991; Dufour and Hallin, 1993). They conclude that the expectations theory is rejected for the U.S. but not for Canada. The authors also investigate the possibility of a time-varying risk premium. They find some evidence of systematic variability but conclude that it cannot be the primary source of deviation from the expectations theory.

The three articles in the second section (Quintos-Phillips; Perron; Lütkepohl) consider the more specific but important problem of detecting and taking into account structural change in the analysis of time series. Structural constancy is a perennial issue in time-series econometrics [see Lucas (1976) and Dufour (1982)], but an exceptional number of new developments in the econometrics of structural change have occurred in recent years.

The article by Carmela Quintos and Peter Phillips proposes tests of parameter constancy for a linear regression model where the regressors are integrated of order one. The alternative considered is one where the regression coefficients follow a random walk. So, in contrast with usual tests which consider the null hypothesis of no cointegration, the null hypothesis tested is the hypothesis of cointegration (which is the one of primary interest) against a special form of no cointegration. For this purpose, the authors consider LM-tests and establish the asymptotic distributions of the test statistics under the null hypothesis and for local alternatives. As usual, in such situations, the asymptotic distributions are non-standard and the authors provide tables of asymptotic critical values. The new procedures are applied to a number of specifications of the aggregate Australian consumption function (quarterly data, 1965–1988) and compared with those of other procedures. Though some of the results appear to conflict (due probably to the fact that alternative tests consider different null hypotheses), the authors conclude that cointegration appears to hold for a simple equation with consumption and disposable income.

The contribution of Pierre Perron illustrates the importance of taking into account structural breaks in the analysis of economic series. His purpose is to assess whether macroeconomic shocks are short-lived and, in particular, whether their effects are "hump-shaped" as the pre-Nelson-Plosser (1982) conventional wisdom suggested. For that purpose, Perron extends in two ways his well-known 1989 paper on structural breaks and unit roots. First, he applies to various macroeconomic series (GNP series, Nelson-Plosser data) the approach of Cochrane (1988) and Campbell-Mankiw (1987), which is based on estimating the spectral density of the first-differences of the series at the zero frequency [for related results, see also Raj (1992, 1993)]. The advantage of this method is that it is unaffected asymptotically by (non-repetitive) structural breaks. His results suggest that the effects of shocks vanish over long horizons, and thus tend to confirm his earlier findings. Second, he analyzes directly the stochastic structure of the series after they have been "detrended" using an appropriate "breaking trend". He then finds that the moving-average representation of these detrended series is hump-shaped.

In the third article of this section, Helmut Lütkepohl reconsiders the important question of money demand instability in the U.S. For that purpose, he uses "flexible least squares", a technique recently proposed by Kalaba and Tesfatsion (1989, 1990). Even though it is mainly descriptive, this technique can shed light on the pattern of parameter variation over time, and which coefficients are the most and least stable. The author applies it to an error-correction model of demand for M1 in the U.S. using quarterly data (1954–1987). He finds that the coefficients of long-run money demand are relatively stable: the instability of the relation is mainly associated with short-term dynamics, the coefficient of interest rate being the most unstable. These results appear consistent with a financial innovations explanation of money demand instability.

The third section contains contributions to the analysis of seasonal movements (Ghysels et al., and Kunst) and fractionally integrated models (Chung and Baillie). Many economic time series exhibit seasonal behaviour, which investigators either try to model or to eliminate by seasonal adjustment. Finding the right way of modeling seasonal behaviour and understanding the consequences of seasonal adjustment remains an important macroeconometric problem. The articles by Ghysels et al. and Kunst consider various aspects of this problem.

Eric Ghysels, Hahn Lee and Pierre Siklos consider two issues related to the problem of seasonal adjustment. First, they examine U.S. quarterly data on GNP, consumption and money (1946–1985) and study how various methods of eliminating seasonal fluctuations affect the univariate time-series properties of these series. The methods studied include seasonal differencing, X-11 and seasonal dummies. They find that these various methods produce series with widely different autocorrelations, so that the selection of a seasonal adjustment procedure can have an important impact on the analysis of dynamic properties. Second, they extend the procedure of Hylleberg, Engle, Granger and Yoo (HEGY, 1990) for analyzing seasonal unit roots in order to take into account the fact that selection of the order of the autoregressive process in the HEGY procedure is typically data-based. Then they apply the HEGY procedure to several U.S. macroeconomic series. They find little evidence of seasonal unit roots at the annual frequency but several roots at the biannual frequency. They conclude that none of the standard transformations captures the patterns suggested by the HEGY tests. Both seasonal dummies and seasonal unit roots appear to be required to model seasonal patterns appropriately.

The article by Robert Kunst considers the related idea of seasonal cointegration, introduced by Engle et al. (1989) and HEGY (1990), and tries to assess its value for prediction. By using both German and British macroeconomic data as well as a Monte-Carlo experiment, he finds that seasonal cointegration may be difficult to exploit to improve prediction. A misspecified VAR model in first differences which ignores the cointegration restriction can easily have a better predictive accuracy.

Finally, the paper by Ching-Fan Chung and Richard Baillie provides results on the estimation of fractionally integrated ARMA models (ARFIMA models). This class of processes, introduced by Granger (1980), Granger and Joyeux (1980) and Hosking (1981), exhibits autocorrelations which decay more slowly than those of ARMA models, even though they remain stationary. They may thus offer an attractive alternative to integrated processes which exhibit complete persistence. Such models, however, may be relatively difficult to estimate. The authors study by simulation the finite-sample properties of a relatively simple estimator suggested by Hosking (1984), the conditional sum-of-squares (CSS) estimator. They find that the CSS estimator can be a useful technique for estimating ARFIMA models in moderate to large samples, but the estimation of the mean can cause substantial bias in smaller samples (say, less than 150 observations).

Researchers and students interested in macroeconometrics and empirical finance will find in this collection a remarkably representative sample of recent work in this area. We are confident it will be a source of inspiration for many of them and lead to further research.

References

Box GEP , Tiao GC (1977) A canonical analysis of multiple time series. Biometrika 64:355–365

Campbell B, Dufour J-M (1991) Over-rejections in rational expectations models: A nonparametric approach to the Mankiw-Shapiro problem. Economics Letters 35:285–290

Campbell JY, Mankiw NG (1987) Are output fluctuations transitory? Quarterly Journal of Economics 102:857–880

Chan NH, Tsay RS (1991) On the use of canonical correlation analysis in testing common trends. Technical report, Department of Statistics, Carnegie Mellon University

Cochrane JH (1988) How big is the random walk in GNP? Journal of Political Economy 96:893–920

Dufour J-M (1982) Recursive stability analysis of linear regression relationships: An exploratory methodology. *Journal of Econometrics* 19:31–76

Dufour J-M, Hallin M (1993) Improved Eaton bounds for linear combinations of bounded random variables, with statistical applications. Journal of the American Statistical Association (forthcoming)

Engle RF, Granger CWJ (1987) Co-integration and error correction: representation, estimation and testing, Econometrica 55:251–276

Engle RF, Granger CWJ, Hallman JJ (1989) Merging short- and long-run forecasts: An application of seasonal cointegration to monthly electricity sales forecasting. Journal of Econometrics 40:45–62

Granger CWJ (1980) Long memory relationships and the aggregation of dynamic models. Journal of Econometrics 14:227–238

Granger CWJ, Joyeux R (1980) An introduction to long memory time series models and fractional differencing. Journal of Time Series Analysis 1:15–39

Haavelmo T (1944) The probability approach in econometrics. Econometrica 12 (supplement):1–118

Hosking JRM (1981) Fractional differencing. Biometrika 68:165–176

Hylleberg S, Engle RF, Granger CWJ, Yoo BS (1990) Seasonal integration and cointegration. Journal of Econometrics 44:215–238

Johansen S (1988) Statistical analysis of cointegration vectors. Journal of Economic Dynamics and Control 12:231–254

Johansen S (1991) Estimation and hypothesis testing of cointegration vectors in Gaussian vector autoregressive models. Econometrica 59:1551–1580

Kalaba R, Tesfatsion L (1989) Time-varying linear regression via flexible least squares. Computers and Mathematics with Applications 17:1215–1245

Kalaba R, Tesfatsion L (1990) Flexible least squares for approximately linear systems. IEEE Transactions on Systems, Man and Cybernetics. SMC-20:978–989

Kydland FE, Prescott EC (1982) Time to build and aggregate fluctuations. Econometrica 50:1345–1370

Lucas RE (1967) Adjustment costs and the theory of supply. Journal of Political Economy 75:321–334

Lucas RE (1976) Econometric policy evaluation. In: Brunner K, Meltzer AH (eds) Carnegie-Rochester Conference Series on Public Policy, Volume 1, Journal of Monetary Economics, supplement 19–46

Nelson CR, Plosser CI (1982) Trends and random walks in macroeconomic time series. Journal of Monetary Economics 10:139–162

Ogaki M, Park JY (1992) A Cointegration approach to estimating preference parameters. Technical Report, Department of Economics, University of Rochester

Perron P (1989) The great crash, the oil price shock and the unit root hypothesis. Econometrica 57:1361–1401

Raj B (1992) International evidence on persistence in output in the presence of episodic change. Journal of Applied Econometrics 7:281–293

Raj B (1993) The size of the random walk in macroeconomic time series. Journal of Macroeconomics 15:139–151

Stock JH, Watson MW (1988) Testing for common trends. Journal of the American Statistical Association 83:1097–1107

Summers LH (1991) The scientific illusion in empirical macroeconomics. Scandinavian Journal of Economics 93:129–148

Tiao GC, Box GEP (1981) Modeling multiple time series with applications. Journal of the American Statistical Association 76:802–816
Tiao GC, Tsay RS (1989) Model specification in multivariate time series. Journal of the Royal Statistical Society B51:157–213

Modelling of Multivariate Economic Time Series

Usefulness of Linear Transformations in Multivariate Time-Series Analysis

GEORGE C. TIAO and RUEY S. TSAY

Graduate School of Business, University of Chicago, 1101 E. 58th St., Chicago, Ilinois 60637, USA

TAYCHANG WANG

Department of Accounting, National Taiwan University, Taipei, Taiwan, R0C

Abstract: Much progress has been made in recent years in multivariate time-series analysis. In this paper we summarize some of the methodological developments that are particularly relevant to empirical economics and highlight especially the usefulness of linear transformations in analyzing multivariate time series. The topics considered include vector ARMA models, principal component analysis, scalar component models, canonical correlation analyses, co-integration, and unit-root tests. We illustrate the methods considered by an example using Taiwan's interest-rate series and provide critiques of these developments.

JEL Classification System-Numbers: C32, C51

1 Introduction

Interest rates (nominal) are the prices of credit with different maturities and varying risks. Their levels should be determined by the market in order to achieve efficiency if the market is perfect and competitive. But in many countries, interest rates have been controlled one way or another by governments and are regarded as important targets for monetary policies. Taiwan is no exception. However, due to the influence of other countries and the worldwide trend toward financial deregulation, it was officially recognized in Taiwan that financial liberalization is inevitable so that market efficiency and flexibility can be enhanced (Lee 1991). Since the process of financial deregulation there was gradual, it is therefore interesting to know how the interest rates evolved over time.

In this paper we shall focus on one-, three-, and six-month time-deposit interest rates. Although these series may not necessarily represent the characteristics of interest rates in general, they do have a long span of data, and time deposit has always been a major part of total deposits held by enterprises and individuals.[1] The main purposes of our analysis are

[1] The various deposits held by enterprises and individuals include checking deposits, passbook deposits, passbook-savings deposits, time deposits, time-savings deposits, foreign-currency deposits, foreign-exchange proceeds deposits, foreign-exchange trust funds, foreign-currency CDs. In the last twenty years, in terms of dollar amounts, the time deposits on average constitute approximately one-third of the total deposits made by enterprises and individuals. Maturities for the time deposits can be one-, three-, six-, nine-month, one-, two-, and three-year. The dollar amounts of the first three equal about half of the total time deposits. In Taiwan the money market and debt equity capital market are relatively new and have always been small in scale. Money and capital-market interest rates are meager in number of observations and poor in quality.

a) to examine the dynamics of and the relationships between the three time-deposit rates,
b) to explore possible transformations of the data that might have economic and financial implications, and to discuss the merits and weaknesses of the techniques used. The questions we address include the following:

1. Are the three financial series considered unit-root non-stationary? Are they co-integrated in the view of recent economic literature? To what extent can a study of co-integration reveal meaningful long-run links between interest rates in Taiwan?
2. Are there unidirectional or feedback relations among the three interest rates? What are the implications of such relationships?
3. Can we make linear transformations to obtain a simpler structure of the series? Does the simplifying structure have any economic interpretation which is hard to detect from direct modeling of the observed data?

We adopt the approach of Tiao and Box (1981) to model the series, the scalar component model (SCM) of Tiao and Tsay (1989) to seek simplifying structures and to reveal the non-stationary nature of the data, the canonical analysis of Box and Tiao (1977) to identify the most and the least "predictable" linear combinations of the series, and various unit-root tests to detect the existence of co-integrations. Our analysis reveals some interesting characteristics of the time-deposit interest rates in Taiwan. For instance, we find that prior to the lifting of the ceiling regulation on the deposit interest rates by the government in 1989 the simplified structure consisted of three meaningful transformed series. One of the transformed series measures the acceleration (or curvature) of the yield curve, another represents the slope (or first derivative) of the yield curve, and the third one depicts the general level of interest rates. The slope series is trending down towards zero, whereas the acceleration is relatively small in magnitude and varies within a small range of values. However, all three transformed series are nearly non-stationary, implying that the three interest-rate series considered are all nearly non-stationary but not co-integrated. This result is consistent with the results of various unit-root and co-integration tests.

On the other hand, the fact that one of the transformed series varies within a small range of values indicates the existence of a stable relationship among the interest rates. This feature is not reflected by the study of unit roots or co-integration, however. We feel that over-emphasis on the existence of unit roots overlooks other important features of a time-series. A more informative analysis is to consider directly the structure of the time series under study. This issue will be discussed and illustrated in detail.

2 Historical Background and the Data

We begin with some historical background on interest rates in Taiwan. Before July 1961 the ceilings of the bank-deposit interest rates were determined jointly by the Association of Banks and financial institutions, with the Bank of Taiwan serving as the acting authority of the Central Bank of China.[2] In July 1961 the Central Bank of China resumed its authority in overseeing interest-rate regulations. However, the same procedure as before was employed in setting the interest-rate ceilings, except that the Bank of Taiwan was replaced by the Central Bank.

In July 1975 a new Bank Act was promulgated which authorized the Central Bank to determine the ceilings on deposit rates by itself (Yuan 1984). Later, under the pressure of academics and the impact of financial deregulation in other countries, the Central Bank allowed the Association of Banks in November 1980 to propose changes in interest-rate ceilings. The ceilings must still be approved by the Central Bank, however.

In the early 1980s, Taiwan's huge trade surplus exerted immense pressure on the appreciation of the New Taiwan Dollar. To protect the economy from the adverse consequences of appreciation, the Central Bank kept purchasing foreign currencies that caused the money supply to soar. The conventional way of proposing ceiling changes by the Association of Banks was too slow to reflect market conditions. One might argue that since there was no regulation on the minimal rates of deposits, banks could choose whatever rates they preferred as long as they did not violate the ceilings. However, at that time the banks' customary practice was to adopt the ceilings as their deposit rates (Wei 1986a, b).[3] In January 1986 the Central Bank started to impose only one upper limit on interest rates for all deposits with one-, three-, six- and nine-month maturities instead of establishing different upper limits for different deposits. Consequently, the banks needed to set rates for different time deposits on their own.

In the late 1980s, the flux of deregulation was even more forceful. For instance, the exchange rate of the New Taiwan Dollar versus the US Dollar dropped from 40 to 28 in just two years. In July 1989 ceilings on all deposit rates were removed, according to the revised Bank Act. At the same time, new private banks were allowed to be incorporated, whereas before the number of banks in Taiwan was frozen and the government owned the majority of shares of all

---

[2] The Central Bank had not been administered since the communists took over Mainland China in 1949.

[3] Establishing high time-deposit rates was a standard policy advice to LDCs by external experts ranging from the visiting academic economists via the World Bank to emissaries of the IMF (Wijnbergen 1983, p.433). This is based on McKinnon's theory that higher time-deposit interest rates increase output and reduce inflation in the short-run and raise medium-term growth through higher savings rate (McKinnon 1973).

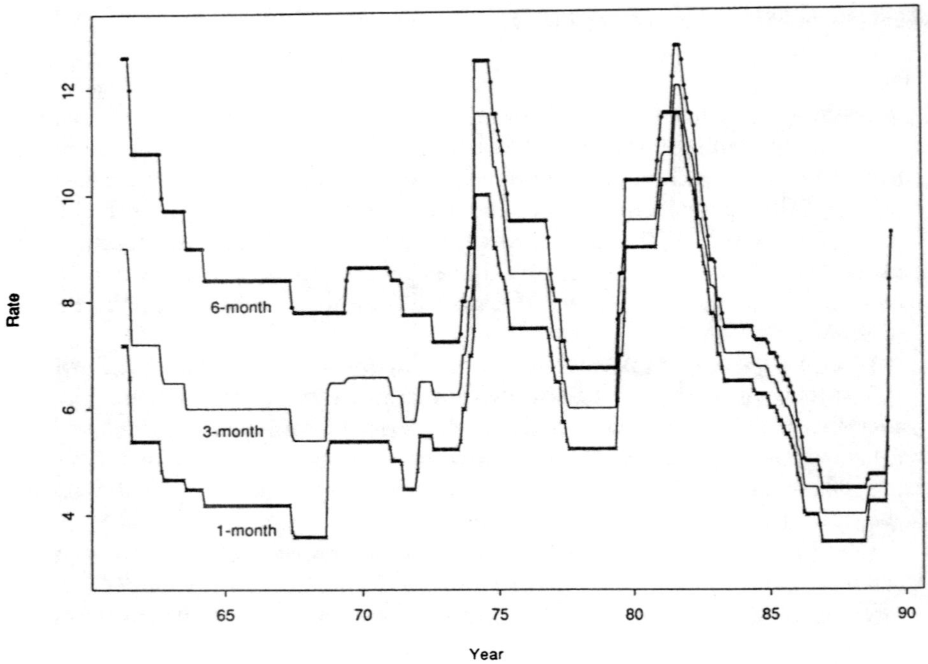

Fig. 1. Monthly time deposit interest rates in taiwan: 61.3–89.7

banks. These two factors substantially altered the operations of banks in Taiwan and moved the interest-rate market toward a competitive market.

The data used in this paper were obtained from the EPS database maintained by the Ministry of Education. There are 369 monthly observations from March 1961 to November 1991. The original data source was the "Financial Statistics Monthly: Taiwan District, The Republic of China" published monthly by the Economic Research Department, the Central Bank of China. Figure 1 shows time plots of the three series considered, namely one-, three- and six-month time deposit interest rates from March 1961 to July 1989. The observations represent the averages of the deposit rates offered by nine major banks.[4] Co-movements of these three series are clearly seen and, in general, interest rates on deposits are higher the longer the time to maturity, except for the last few observations, which may relate to the revision of the Bank Act. The two big swings are associated with the two recessions caused partially by the oil crises around 1973 and 1981. We categorize the data into the following different time spans according to the various stipulations mentioned in the preceding section:

[4] There were no interest payments for checking deposits in Taiwan.

Span	Time Period	Number of Observations
I.	1961:3–1975:7	172
II.	1961:3–1980:11	236
III.	1961:3–1986:1	298
IV.	1961:3–1989:7	340
V.	1961:3–1991:11	369

Our analyses focus on the data span from March 1961 to July 1989 with 340 observations. This data span is used because of the removal of ceiling regulation and the permission to establish new banks in July 1989. However, all five different data spans will be examined to study the stability of the relationships between these three variables over time.

3 Unit-Root and Co-Integration Tests

Let $Z_t = (Z_{1t}, Z_{2t}, Z_{3t})'$, where Z_{1t}, Z_{2t}, and Z_{3t} are, respectively, the time-deposit interest rate of one-, three- and six-month maturity at time index t with $t = 1, \ldots, 340$ corresponding to the period from March 1961 to July 1989. Figure 1 shows that the Z_{it}, $i = 1, 2, 3$, are apparently non-stationary. Indeed, the results of the augmented Dickey-Fuller (ADF) test and the $Z(\alpha)$ and $Z(t)$ tests of Phillips (1987) show that the three series are integrated processes of order 1, i.e. $I(1)$. Specifically, for a non-zero mean autoregressive AR(5) model, the ADF statistics are -2.17, -2.53 and -2.61, respectively, for one-, three- and six-month deposit. The values of $Z(\alpha)$ statistic are -5.68, -7.77 and -9.14 whereas that of $Z(t)$ statistic are -2.15, -2.69 and -3.18. Furthermore, for the first differenced data, all three tests reject the null hypothesis of a unit root.

Next, we adopt the methods of Engle and Granger (1987), Johansen (1988), Stock and Watson (1988), and Chan and Tsay (1991) to test for co-integration. These tests are designed to detect the existence of linear combinations of non-stationary series which are stationary, an idea proposed earlier by Box and Tiao (1977). The Engle-Granger test makes use of the difference in growth rates between stationary and non-stationary series. However, a minor complication arises in using this method because any component of the joint process can play the role of "dependent variable" in the test so that there are k test statistics for a k-dimensional process. Asymptotically, these k tests are equivalent. However, differences may exist in the finite sample case (see Dickey, Jansen and Thornton

Table 1. Results of some co-integration tests for time deposit rates

(a) Engle-Granger test	Dependent variable		
	Z_{1t} -2.48	Z_{2t} -2.70	Z_{3t} -2.93
5% critical value	3.78	3.78	3.78
(b) Johansen test	Number of Co-integrating Factors		
Non-zero-mean	$k = 0$	$k \leq 1$	$k \leq 2$
	21.04	10.27	2.14
5% critical value	35.07	20.17	9.09

1991). Critical values of this test are available in Engle and Yoo (1987). Johansen (1988) uses a likelihood ratio test and assumes that the process under study follows a finite-order Gaussian vector autoregressive (VAR) model. See also Johansen and Juselius (1990). The Stock-Watson test adopted in this paper does not make a strong model assumption, but it requires certain adjustments to handle the nuisance parameters. The Chan-Tsay test makes use of the asymptotic uncorrelatedness between the differenced series and the lagged original series. It is based on a canonical correlation analysis between the first differenced series ΔZ_t and Z_{t-1}. This test is easy to implement and is closely related to the canonical correlation analyses discussed later in the paper.

Because the levels of Z_{it} are non-zero, we shall use non-zero mean models in co-integration tests. The test statistic of Chan and Tsay is 16.11, which corresponds approximately to a p-value of 0.60, indicating the existence of three unit roots and, hence, no co-integration. The Stock-Watson test is $q(3, 2) = -14.55$, which is also insignificant at the 5% level. The results of the other tests are given in Table 1. These statistics were computed by using a VAR(5) model[5], the same order used in the unit-root tests. From Table 1, all the tests are consistent; they fail to reject the null hypothesis of three unit roots at the 5% level. Therefore, there is no evidence of co-integration in the three interest-rate series.

The preceding test results raise some interesting questions. First, the co-integration tests considered fail to reflect the apparent co-movements of the three interest-rate series shown in Figure 1. Second, from Figure 1, the spread between the three interest rates is diminishing, but the gap between the three- to one-month spread and the six- to three-month spread seems to be small and remains stable over time. These facts are not revealed by the co-integration tests,

[5] We have used other VAR models, but test results remain similar.

either. We believe that the inability of co-integration tests to describe the characteristics exhibited by the three interest rates is not an isolated case. On the contrary, these "failures" highlight the very nature of co-integration tests. The tests emphasize the existence of unit roots and the stationarity of linear combinations; they are invariant to the magnitudes of innovational noise. On the other hand, the variability of innovational noise should play an important role in empirical economics; they relate directly to the "stability" of a series. If co-integration is to be used as an indication of a long-run stable relation between economic variables, then the test statistics available in the literature fail to take into account the important role played by the innovational variance in determining such relations. It seems that co-integration tests are of theoretical interest rather than of practical value.

4 A Multivariate Model

The results of co-integration tests suggest that one may use the differenced series of time-deposit interest rates in a multivariate analysis of the three series. On the other hand, much of the study in finance on the term structure of interest rates, such as the yield curve, deals with levels directly. Furthermore, the results of Chan and Wei (1988) and Tsay and Tiao (1990) show that there is no need to apply the differencing operator in modeling unit-root non-stationary time series. Thus, in what follows we shall consider the three original interest-rate series.[6] Because interest rates are indicators of price of credit, they may conceivably be contemporaneously related, one series may lead the others or there may be feedback relationships. To study the dynamic relationships between the three interest rates, using data from March 1961 to July 1989, we employ the class of vector autoregressive moving average (VARMA) models and adopt the modeling approach of Tiao and Box (1981). This modeling procedure is iterative and consists of tentative specification, estimation, and diagnostic checking.

A VARMA model for Z_t can be written as

$$(I - \Phi_1 B - \cdots - \Phi_p B^p) Z_t = C + (I - \Theta_1 B - \cdots - \Theta_q B^q) a_t \ , \tag{1}$$

where $\{a_t\}$, $a_t = (a_{1t}, a_{2t}, a_{3t})'$, is a sequence of independent and identically distributed random vectors with mean zero and positive definite covariance matrix

---

[6] Of course, in this particular instance, one may choose to model the differenced series if desirable. The problem of taking difference, however, would become complicated when there is co-integration in the data.

Σ, I is a 3×3 identity matrix, C is a 3×1 constant vector, B is the usual back-shift operator such that $BZ_t = Z_{t-1}$, p and q are non-negative integers, and Φ_i's and Θ_j's are 3×3 real-valued matrices. We further assume that the two polynomial matrices $\Phi(B) = I - \Phi_1 B - \cdots - \Phi_p B^p$ and $\Theta(B) = I - \Theta_1 B - \cdots - \Theta_q B^q$ are left co-prime. Depending on the structure of $\Phi(B)$ and $\Theta(B)$, the VARMA model in (1) can give rise to various dynamic relationships between the components of Z_t. The model representation in (1), however, may encounter the problem of identifiability and requires further considerations in applications (see Tiao and Tsay (1989)). For general theory and methods of multivariate time-series analysis, see e.g., Hannan and Deistler (1988) and Lütkepohl (1991).

Tentative Specification: The objective here is to specify a low-order VARMA model in (1) for Z_t worthy of further study, and the basic tools used are the cross-correlation matrices and statistics associated with stepwise autoregressions. These tools are particularly useful in specifying VMA and VAR models.

Because the three series considered are highly auto- and cross-correlated, cross-correlation matrices are not helpful in model specification, and we rely instead on statistics of stepwise autoregressions. Table 2 shows the chi-squared statistics and Akaike's information criterion (Akaike, 1974) of stepwise autoregressions. The chi-squared statistic $M(l)$ is the likelihood ratio test statistic for testing the null hypothesis that Z_t is VAR$(l-1)$,

$$Z_t = C + \Phi_1 Z_{t-1} + \cdots + \Phi_{l-1} Z_{t-l+1} + e_t \ , \tag{2}$$

against the alternative hypothesis that Z_t is VAR(l),

$$Z_t = C + \Phi_1 Z_{t-1} + \cdots + \Phi_l Z_{t-l} + \varepsilon_t \ , \tag{3}$$

Under the null hypothesis,

$$M(l) = -\left(T - \frac{1}{2} - l \times k\right) \ln \frac{|S(l)|}{|S(l-1)|}$$

has asymptotically a chi-squared distribution with k^2 degrees of freedom, where T is the sample size, k is the dimension of Z_t, $|A|$ is the determinant of the matrix A, and $S(l)$ and $S(l-1)$ are the residual covariance matrices of the vector autoregressions in (3) and (2), respectively.

Akaike's Information Criterion (AIC) for a VAR(l) model is

$$\mathrm{AIC}(l) = -\ln(|S(l)|) + \frac{2lk^2}{T} \ ,$$

and one selects a model by searching for the minimum of the criterion among a set of candidate models. From Table 2, with a maximum order of 8, the AIC selects a VAR(2) model with VAR(4) as a close second whereas the $M(l)$ statistic chooses a VAR(4) model when the 5% critical value is used. Based on these results, we entertain a VAR(4) model for the three time-deposit interest rates.

Table 2. Summaries of stepwise autoregressions for time-deposit interest rates

Order	1	2	3	4	5	6	7	8
$M(l)$	3720.6	77.8	2.0	20.4	0.3	3.8	5.7	2.1
AIC	−13.31	−13.49	−13.45	−13.46	−13.41	−13.37	−13.33	−13.28

Estimation and Diagnostics: With a VAR(4) specification, we estimate the parameters by the least-squares method, which is asymptotically equivalent to the maximum likelihood method for a Gaussian AR model. Table 3(a) shows the results of fitting an un-constrained VAR(4) model. Obviously, such a model uses many parameters, most of which appear to be statistically insignificant. The residual cross-correlation matrices, however, show no model inadequacy.

Principal Component Analysis (PCA): To simplify the model, note that the estimated covariance matrix $\hat{\Sigma}$ of the innovation a_t shows that the components a_{it} are highly correlated. This is not surprising in view of the co-movements of the three deposit series shown in Figure 1. It is well known that such high correlations often contribute to high correlations among the parameter estimates of the autoregressive model. Thus, it will be helpful to consider linear transformations of Z_t by performing a PCA of $\hat{\Sigma}$. The eigenvalues δ_i and the corresponding normalized eigenvectors g_i of $\hat{\Sigma}$ are

$$\delta = \begin{bmatrix} \delta_1 \\ \delta_2 \\ \delta_3 \end{bmatrix} = \begin{bmatrix} .001 \\ .007 \\ .219 \end{bmatrix}, \quad G' = \begin{bmatrix} g_1' \\ g_2' \\ g_3' \end{bmatrix} = \begin{bmatrix} -.51 & .81 & -.30 \\ -.63 & -.12 & .77 \\ .58 & .58 & .57 \end{bmatrix}. \tag{4}$$

The transformed series $Z_t^* = (Z_{1t}^*, Z_{2t}^*, Z_{3t}^*)' = G'Z_t$ are shown in Figure 2. Given the transformation matrix G', the series Z_t^* will also follow a VAR(4) model,

$$Z_t^* = C^* + \Phi_1^* Z_{t-1}^* + \cdots + \Phi_4 Z_{t-4}^* + a_t^* , \tag{5}$$

where $C^* = G'C$, $\Phi_i^* = G'\Phi_i G$ for $i = 1, \ldots, 4$, $a_t^* = G'a_t$, and $\mathrm{Cov}(a_t^*) = \Sigma^* = G'\Sigma G$. The results of fitting the unconstrained VAR(4) model in (5) are given in Table 4(a). Inspection of the results clearly indicates that (i) these three transformed series are essentially uncorrelated (independent under normality), (ii) Z_{1t}^* and Z_{2t}^* individually follow AR(2) models, and (iii) Z_{3t}^* follows an AR(4) model. Table 4(b) shows the results of a constrained fit. Since the model for Z_t and Z_t^* are linked by the coefficient relations given in (5), we can readily calculate parameter estimates for Z_t from the constrained fit in Table 4(b). The results are shown in Table 3(b). By imposing equality constraints on the AR coefficients suggested by the pattern in Table 3(b), we obtain the final constrained model fit for Z_t given in Table 3(c). Apart from those in the covariance matrix Σ, this constrained model contains only 13 parameters, compared with 39 for the un-

Table 3. Estimation results of VAR(4) models for Z_t

	(a) Unconstrained Model						(b) Model From Z_t^*			(c) Constrained Model					
Par.	Estimates			St. Error			Estimates			Estimates			St. Error		
C'	.21	.22	.20	.07	.07	.07	−.06	.17	.13	.16	.17	.18	.06	.06	.06
Φ_1	1.31	−.05	.13	.31	.46	.22	1.28	.09	.06	1.23	.08	.08	.03	.02	—
	.16	1.08	.14	.31	.45	.22	.09	1.21	.08	.08	1.23	.08	—	.03	—
	.11	−.03	1.29	.31	.45	.22	.06	.08	1.23	.08	.08	1.22	—	—	.03
Φ_2	−.58	.25	−.14	.48	.69	.34	−.27	−.10	−.10	−.26	−.09	−.09	.04	.03	—
	−.38	.08	−.16	.47	.68	.33	−.10	−.26	−.10	−.09	−.26	−.09	—	.04	—
	−.34	.25	−.36	.47	.68	.33	−.09	−.10	−.27	−.09	−.09	−.25	—	—	.04
Φ_3	.58	−.46	.20	.48	.69	.34	.11	.11	.10	.10	.10	.10	.03	—	—
	.56	−.44	.22	.48	.68	.33	.11	.11	.10	.10	.10	.10	—	—	—
	.55	−.48	.26	.48	.68	.33	.10	.10	.10	.10	.10	.10	—	—	—
Φ_4	−.29	.23	−.20	.32	.46	.22	−.09	−.09	−.09	−.09	−.09	−.09	.02	—	—
	−.29	.21	−.20	.31	.45	.22	−.09	−.09	−.09	−.09	−.09	−.09	—	—	—
	−.29	.21	−.19	.31	.45	.22	−.09	−.09	−.08	−.09	−.09	−.09	—	—	—
Σ	.079	.077	.071				.080	.077	.072	.080	.077	.072			
	.077	.077	.074				.077	.078	.075	.077	.078	.074			
	.071	.074	.077				.072	.075	.078	.072	.074	.078			

Table 4. Estimation results of VAR(4) models for Z_t^*

	(a) Unconstrained						(b) Constrained					
Par.	Estimates			St. Error			Estimates			St. Error		
$(10C^*)'$	.05	−.04	3.63	.07	.21	1.19	.04	.03	2.95	.02	.09	1.05
Φ_1^*	1.21	.00	−.00	.06	.02	.00	1.12	—	—	.05	—	—
	.03	1.18	−.01	.17	.06	.01	—	1.17	—	—	.05	—
	.28	.03	1.38	.95	.31	.05	—	—	1.38	—	—	.05
Φ_2^*	−.17	−.00	.00	.08	.03	.01	−.16	—	—	.05	—	—
	−.01	−.23	.01	.26	.09	.02	—	−.18	—	—	.05	—
	.79	.15	−.46	1.44	.48	.10	—	—	−.45	—	—	.10
Φ_3^*	.02	−.00	.00	.08	.03	.01	—	—	—	—	—	—
	−.01	.04	.00	.26	.09	.02	—	—	—	—	—	—
	−1.29	−.23	.33	1.44	.48	.10	—	—	.31	—	—	.10
Φ_4^*	−.01	−.00	.00	.06	.02	.00	—	—	—	—	—	—
	−.01	.01	−.01	.17	.06	.01	—	—	—	—	—	—
	.68	.02	−.27	.96	.31	.06	—	—	−.26	—	—	.06
$10^2\Sigma^*$	.074	−.001	.111				.075	−.001	.108			
	−.001	.710	.053				−.001	.714	.047			
	.111	.053	22.5				.108	.047	22.7			

constrained results in Table 3(a). The estimated covariance matrices of these two models, shown in Tables 3(a) and 3(c), are nearly identical with determinant $.118 \times 10^{-5}$ and $.121 \times 10^{-5}$, respectively. The likelihood ratio statistic between the two models is 10.28, which is highly insignificant compared with a chi-squared distribution with 26 d.f. The constrained model is, therefore, adequate.

Interpretation and Discussion: The PCA of $\hat{\Sigma}$ not only helps achieve considerable parsimony in the parameterization of the VAR model for Z_t, but also reveals interesting and perhaps substantively meaningful features of the deposit rate data. First, the two transformed components Z^*_{1t} and Z^*_{2t} are linear contrasts of the three time-deposit interest rates. Let $S_{1t} = Z_{2t} - Z_{1t}$ be the spread between 3-month and 1-month rates and $S_{2t} = Z_{3t} - Z_{2t}$ be that between 6-month and 3-month rates. These spreads are approximations to the first derivative (or slope) of the yield curve. We can express Z^*_{1t} and Z^*_{2t} approximately as

$$Z^*_{1t} \approx 0.5(S_{1t} - 0.6S_{2t}) \; , \qquad Z^*_{2t} \approx 0.77S_{2t} + 0.63S_{1t} \; .$$

Therefore, Z^*_{1t} measures the second derivative of the yield curve and represents the acceleration (or curvature) of interest rates with respect to maturity; Z^*_{2t} corresponds to the first derivative of yield curve. The acceleration series Z^*_{1t} varies within a relatively small range throughout the data span with a sample

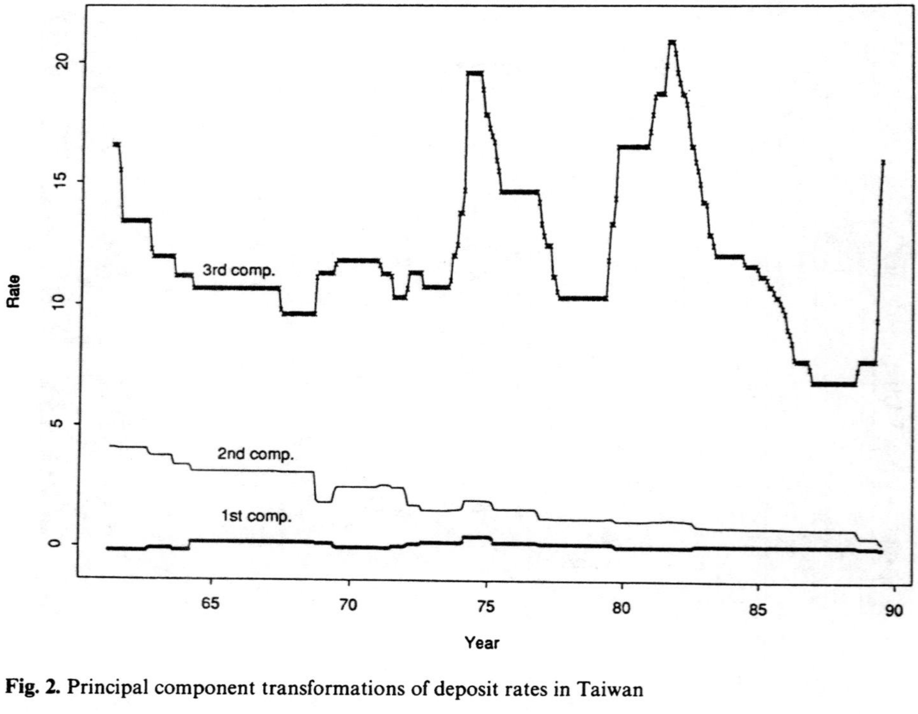

Fig. 2. Principal component transformations of deposit rates in Taiwan

mean 0.11 and sample range $[-0.16, 0.47]$; see Figure 2. This might reflect a policy of keeping the two spreads S_{1t} and S_{2t} in line with each other by the rate-setting institutions in Taiwan. From Figure 2, the first derivative series Z_{2t}^* is approximately a decreasing function of time and is approaching zero. Consequently, the yield curve of Taiwan interest rates is gradually approaching a constant. This phenomenon can also be seen from Figure 1 if one examines the plots carefully; the three interest rates moved closer together over time. The principal component transformation, on the other hand, highlights the features clearly. The third transformed series Z_{3t}^* is simply proportional to the average of the three interest-rate series and reflects the general level of the yield curve. The finding that Taiwan's interest rates can be transformed into level, first derivative, and curvature components is consistent with that of Litterman and Scheinkman (1988), who study the common factors of US bond returns.

Second, while the elements of Z_t^* are of the same scale we see, from the fitted model in Table 4(b), that the innovational variance of Z_{3t}^* is very much larger (by two orders of magnitude) than those of Z_{1t}^* and Z_{2t}^*. On the other hand, the AR polynomial for Z_{1t}^* contains a factor $(1 - .96B)$, that for Z_{2t}^* a factor $(1 - .99B)$ and that for Z_{3t}^* a factor $(1 - .92B)$ so that all three transformed series are nearly non-stationary. Although Z_{3t}^* is relatively the farthest from having a unit root, it has the appearance of being the most unstable of the three components because of its large innovational variance. This demonstrates clearly that the variability of innovations plays an important role in determining the stability of economic variables. As mentioned before, unit-root tests for cointegration do not consider such an important factor.

Third, return to the model in Table 3(c). It is clear that the behavior of the three interest-rate series is dominated by the movement of the transformed series Z_{3t}^*. In fact, the model can be written as

$$(1 - 1.16B - .17B^2)Z_{1t} = .164 + L(B)\bar{Z}_{t-1} + a_{1t}$$

$$(1 - 1.15B - .16B^2)Z_{2t} = .173 + L(B)\bar{Z}_{t-1} + a_{2t}$$

$$(1 - 1.14B - .15B^2)Z_{3t} = .175 + L(B)\bar{Z}_{t-1} + a_{3t}$$

where $L(B) = 3(.08 - .09B + .10B^2 - .09B^3)$ and $\bar{Z}_t = (Z_{1t} + Z_{2t} + Z_{3t})/3$ Thus, dynamically, each series depends on its own two past values as well as on a common factor involving lagged values of the average $\bar{Z}_t \approx 1.74Z_{3t}^*$. Therefore, the three interest rates form a feedback system and there is little evidence of any particular undirectional relationship among them. The dynamic structure here as well as the highly positive correlations among the innovations a_{1t}, a_{2t} and a_{3t} implies that the three interest rates are driven in a like manner by external economic (and perhaps political) forces. This finding suggests that the autoregressive index model of Reinsel (1983) might be helpful in modeling the data at hand. The uncovered dynamic structure also illustrates clearly that linear transformations are useful in multivariate time-series analysis.

5 Canonical Correlation Analysis

In the preceding section, the primary goal was to model the dynamic leading, lagging and feedback relationships between the observed series. After building an initial VAR(4) model for Z_t, it is seen that linear transformations based on a PCA of $\hat{\Sigma}$ can help achieve parsimony as well as reveal structures not easily discernible in direct analyses of the original data. In this and the next sections, we discuss two additional structural methods, one by Box and Tiao (1977) and the other by Tiao and Tsay (1989). While both methods make use of canonical correlation analysis, the first is a model-based approach and the second constitutes an integral part of model building.

The Box and Tiao canonical analysis aims at characterizing multivariate time-series in terms of the strength of their dynamic relation to past observations. For a stationary series, this dependent relation is measured by the canonical correlations between the series and their one-step ahead forecasts. More specifically, a linear multivariate time series Z_t can be written as

$$Z_t = \hat{Z}_{t-1}(1) + e_t \ , \tag{6}$$

where $\hat{Z}_{t-1}(1)$ is the minimum mean-squared error forecast of Z_t made at time $t-1$ and e_t is the associated forecast error. In practice, such a forecast can be computed from a specified model for Z_t. Note that $\hat{Z}_{t-1}(1)$ is the projection of Z_t onto the space generated by $\{Z_{t-i}|i > 0\}$. From the orthogonality between $\hat{Z}_{t-1}(1)$ and e_t, and stationarity, the covariance matrices of the variables in (6) satisfy the relation

$$\Gamma_z = \Gamma_z(1) + \Sigma \ . \tag{7}$$

Now, consider a non-zero linear combination $y_t = m'Z_t$. From (6) and (7), we have $y_t = m'\hat{Z}_{t-1}(1) + m'e_t$, and the variance decomposition of y_t is $\sigma_y^2 = \sigma_y^2(1) + \sigma_e^2$, where $\sigma_y^2 = \text{var}(y_t) = m'\Gamma_z m$, $\sigma_y^2(1) = m'\Gamma_z(1)m$ and $\sigma_e^2 = m'\Sigma m$. A natural measure of the dynamic dependence of y_t is therefore the ratio

$$\lambda_y = \frac{\sigma_y^2(1)}{\sigma_y^2} = [m'\Gamma_z m]^{-1}[m'\Gamma_z(1)m] \ , \qquad 0 \le \lambda_y < 1 \ ,$$

which shows the portion of variability in y_t that can be explained by $m'\hat{Z}_{t-1}(1)$, the concept of R^2 in linear regression analysis. Box and Tiao call λ_y a measure of "predictability" by past observations and seek to transform the series Z_t in terms of λ_y. Consequently, for the maximal "predictability," λ_y must be the largest eigenvalue of $[\Gamma_z]^{-1}\Gamma_z(1)$ and m is the corresponding eigenvector. Similarly, the smallest eigenvalue of $[\Gamma_z]^{-1}\Gamma_z(1)$ gives the least "predictable" series. These two eigenvalues are, respectively, the largest and smallest squared canonical correlations between Z_t and $\hat{Z}_{t-1}(1)$. In general, let $\lambda_1 \le \lambda_2 \le \cdots \le \lambda_k$ be the ordered eigenvalues of the matrix $[\Gamma_z]^{-1}\Gamma_z(1)$ and $m_1, \ldots, m_k$ be the corresponding eigenvectors, which can be normalized such that $\|m_i\| = 1$. Also, let $M = [m_1, \ldots, m_k]$ be the matrix of eigenvectors and $\Lambda = \text{diag}\{\lambda_1, \ldots, \lambda_k\}$ be the diagonal matrix of eigenvalues. Then, $\Gamma_z^{-1}\Gamma_z(1)M = M\Omega$ so that

$$M^{-1}\Gamma_z^{-1}\Gamma_z(1)M = (M'\Gamma_z M)^{-1}[M'\Gamma_z(1)M] = \Omega \quad (8)$$

and, in fact, $M'\Gamma_z M$ and $M'\Gamma_z(1)M$ are both diagonal matrices. Let $Y_t = (Y_{1t}, \cdots, Y_{kt})' = M'Z_t$ be the transformed series, $\hat{Y}_{t-1}(1) = M'\hat{Z}_{t-1}(1)$ and $d_t = M'e_t = (d_{1t}, \cdots, d_{kt})'$. Equation (6) implies $Y_t = \hat{Y}_{t-1}(1) + d_t$ and equations (7) and (8) show that

$$I = \Lambda + M^{-1}\Gamma_z^{-1}\Sigma M \equiv \Lambda + D \quad (9)$$

where D is necessarily a diagonal matrix.

The result of equation (9) highlights the characteristics of the canonical transformation. First, the transformed series Y_{1t} is the least predictable linear combination of Z_t and Y_{kt} is the most predictable linear combination of Z_t. The predictability of the Y_{it} series ranges from λ_1 to λ_k. If $\lambda_1 = 0$, $Y_{1t} = c_1 + d_{1t}$ where c_1 is a constant. In this case, Y_{1t} is a white-noise process with mean c_1 and a constant variance. Since Y_{1t} is a linear combination of Z_t, this implies that there exists a very stationary contemporaneous relationship among the k original series. By a stationary relation, we mean a relation which varies around a *fixed* level with a *constant* variance. On the other extreme, when $\lambda_k \to 1$, it can be shown that Y_{kt} will approach a series with a unit root in its model so that Z_t will contain a non-stationary component. Thus, one may also regard the λ_i's as measures of the stationarity of the transformed components, with small values signifying the existence of very stationary components and values close to unity, non-stationary components. The idea here is, of course, closely related to co-integration.

Next, the transformed series are not contemporaneously correlated. Finally, the forecast errors of the transformed series are not contemporaneously correlated, neither are they serially correlated. The latter property, however, is due to projection rather than canonical correlation analysis.

Empirical Results: Consider the three time-deposit interest rates of Taiwan. To apply the above canonical transformation, we adopt the constrained VAR(4) model of Z_t in Table 3(c) to produce the one-step ahead forecasts $\hat{Z}_{t-1}(1)$. Of course, the analysis applies to general VARMA models. The eigenvalues and eigenvectors of the estimated $\Gamma_z^{-1}\Gamma_z(1)$ are:

j	Eigenvalue λ_j	Eigenvector m_j'		
1	0.947	−0.529	0.803	−0.272
2	0.977	0.775	−0.375	0.508
3	0.994	−0.440	−0.361	0.822

The three eigenvalues correspond to canonical correlations of 0.973, 0.988 and

0.997, respectively, confirming that the serial dependence of the series is strong. We can make the following observations. First, the transformed series Y_{1t} and Y_{3t} are, to a close approximation, linear contrasts of the three deposit rates. In fact, Y_{1t} is essentially identical to Z_{1t}^* and Y_{3t} is very close to Z_{2t}^* discussed in the preceding section. See Equation (4). The second component Y_{2t} is approximately $.8Z_{1t} - .4Z_{2t} + .5Z_{3t} = .8Z_{1t} + .1Z_{2t} + .5S_{2t}$ and, hence, will tend to behave like Z_{1t}. The three transformed series are shown in Figure 3.

Next, it is interesting to consider the vector model of Y_t. The coefficient matrices of such a model can be computed directly from those of Z_t and the transformation matrix M', yielding

$$Y_t = C_y + \sum_{j=1}^{4} \varphi_j Y_{t-j} + d_t \tag{10}$$

where $\varphi_j = M'\Phi_j(M')^{-1}$, $\mathrm{Cov}(d_t) = \Sigma_d = M'\Sigma M$,

$$C_y = \begin{bmatrix} .005 \\ .151 \\ .009 \end{bmatrix}, \qquad \varphi_1 = \begin{bmatrix} 1.16 & .00 & .01 \\ .19 & 1.38 & .00 \\ -.00 & -.01 & 1.15 \end{bmatrix},$$

$$\varphi_2 = \begin{bmatrix} -.17 & .00 & -.01 \\ -.25 & -.46 & -.00 \\ .00 & .01 & -.16 \end{bmatrix}, \qquad \varphi_3 = \begin{bmatrix} .00 & .00 & .00 \\ .27 & .31 & .01 \\ .01 & .01 & .00 \end{bmatrix},$$

$$\varphi_4 = \begin{bmatrix} -.00 & -.00 & -.00 \\ -.22 & -.26 & -.01 \\ -.01 & -.01 & -.00 \end{bmatrix}, \qquad 10^2\Sigma_d = \begin{bmatrix} .075 & - & - \\ - & 6.198 & - \\ - & - & .645 \end{bmatrix}.$$

It is readily seen that, to a close approximation, the AR polynomial matrix $(I - \varphi_1 B - \cdots - \varphi_4 B^4)$ of the model (10) is divisible by the factor $(1 - B)$. This means that the model can be expressed in terms of the first differences $\Delta Y_{it} = (1 - B)Y_{it}$, $i = 1, 2, 3$, of the transformed series. For example, from (10), the model for Y_{1t} is $(1 - 1.16B + .17B^2)Y_{1t} = .005 + d_{1t}$, which has a root close to the unit circle (about 0.98). Thus, the series Y_{1t} can be regarded as unit-root non-stationary according to most of the unit-root tests, e.g. Dickey and Fuller (1979) and Phillips (1987). On the other hand, the canonical transformation shows that the range of variation of Y_{1t} is relatively small so that Y_{1t} could be regarded as "stable" for some practical purposes. This is in sharp contrast to the behavior of Y_{2t} the model of which is also nearly unit-root non-stationary. In this sense, we believe that there exist important differences between stability and unit-root non-stationarity. Using unit-root tests alone in economic and financial studies might overlook some important issues. The main source of our misgivings on unit-root tests stems from the fact that unit-root tests focus primarily on random level changes but do not take into account the magnitude of the changes.

Finally, it is worth noting that since the smallest eigenvalue $\lambda = .947$ is nearly unity, it follows that there exists no linear transformation of Z_t which will make

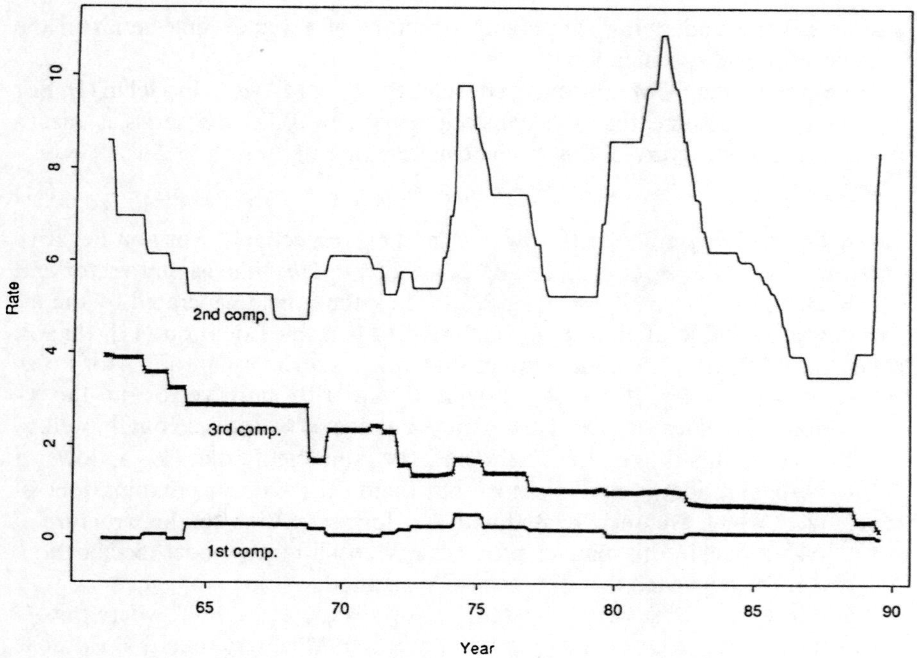

Fig. 3. Canonical transformations of deposit rates in Taiwan

the transformed series "very stationary." Again, this is the basic idea of co-integration.

6 Scalar Component Model

6.1 Methodology

The canonical analysis of the preceding section is a model-based analysis, because it requires that a vector model for Z_t is available. In practice, models are often built from the data. Further, for a given vector time-series Z_t, it is not a simple task to build an adequate VARMA model, especially when the dimension of Z_t is large. The main reason is that building a VARMA model may encounter the difficulties of (a) parameter explosion and (b) lack of unique model representation. It is therefore important to seek methods that can simplify the modeling process in analyzing multivariate time-series. To this end, Tiao and Tsay (1989) propose the scalar component model (SCM) approach which (a) can substantially reduce the number of parameters that require estimation and (b) can reveal the underlying simplifying structure of a vector time-series in the process of model specification.

To motivate the SCM approach, consider the VARMA(p, q) model in (1). For simplicity, we assume that the constant term $C = 0$, i.e. the series is mean-corrected. The structure of this model can be written as

$$Z_{it} - \Phi_{1,i.}Z_{t-1} - \cdots - \Phi_{p,i.}Z_{t-p} = a_{it} - \Theta_{1,i.}a_{t-1} - \cdots - \Theta_{q,i.}a_{t-q} \tag{11}$$

where $\Phi_{l,i.}$ and $\Theta_{l,i.}$ are the i-th row of Φ_l and Θ_l, respectively. For non-negative integers m and j, let $Z_{m,t} = (Z_t', \ldots, Z_{t-m}')'$ be a $(m+1)k$-dimensional vector and $F_{t-j} = \sigma\{a_{t-j}, a_{t-j-1}, \ldots\} = \sigma\{Z_{t-j}, Z_{t-j-1}, \ldots\}$, the σ-field generated by the information available at time $t-j$ (inclusive). Then, by Equation (11), that Z_t follows a VARMA(p, q) model implies that $v'Z_{p,t}$ is orthogonal to F_{t-j} for $j > q$, where $v' = (u_i', -\Phi_{1,i.}, \ldots, -\Phi_{p,i.})$ with u_i the i-th unit vector in the k-dimensional Euclidean space. This orthogonal property applies equally well to all the components of Z_t. Therefore, the statement that Z_t follows a VARMA(p, q) model is equivalent to that there exist k linear combinations of $Z_t, \ldots, Z_{t-p}$ which are uncorrelated with F_{t-j} for $j > q$. Viewing the structure of a VARMA model in this manner provides new insight into model specification, and this is the approach taken by the SCM method.

For a $(r+1)k$-dimensional constant vector $v = (v_0', v_1', \ldots, v_r')'$, where the v_i's are k-dimensional vectors and v_0 is not a null vector, we say that $x_t = v_0'Z_t$ has a *scalar component model* of order (r, s) if $v'Z_{r,t}$ is orthogonal to F_{t-j} for $j > s$. Denote such an SCM by $x_t \sim \text{SCM}(r, s)$. The above definition says that x_t, a linear combination of Z_t, follows an SCM of order (r, s) if there exist r k-dimensional vectors $v_1, \ldots, v_r$ such that the scalar process

$$x_t + \sum_{i=1}^{r} v_i'Z_{t-i} = \sum_{i=0}^{r} v_i'Z_{t-i} \tag{12}$$

is uncorrelated with the past values Z_{t-j} for all $j > s$. Obviously, for a VARMA(p, q) model, each component Z_{it} is an SCM of order (p, q). The idea of SCM, however, is more powerful than just a simple way to describe the structure of Z_{it}. Since the vector v_0 is an arbitrary non-zero vector, SCM enables us to seek linear combinations of Z_t that can substantially simplify the model structure of the system. For instance, there is no reason that each component Z_{it} of a VARMA(p, q) model must be an SCM of order (p, q) because some of the component orders can be lower than (p, q).

Suppose that for $i = 1$ and 2, $x_{it} \sim \text{SCM}(p_i, q_i)$ with $x_{it} = v_{i,0}'Z_t$. We say that x_{1t} and x_{2t} have linearly independent SCMs if $v_{1,0}$ and $v_{2,0}$ are linearly independent k-dimensional real vectors. It is then easily seen that for a k-dimensional time-series Z_t, k linearly independent SCMs determine a VARMA model for Z_t. More specifically, suppose that $x_{it} \sim \text{SCM}(p_i, q_i)$ for $i = 1, \ldots, k$ such that $x_{it} = v_{i,0}'Z_t$ and they are linearly independent. Then, for a given i, there exist p_i k-dimensional vectors $v_{i,1}, \ldots, v_{i,p_i}$, such that

$$x_{it} + \sum_{l=1}^{p_i} v_{i,l}'Z_{t-l} = v_{i,0}'Z_t + \sum_{l=1}^{p_i} v_{i,l}'Z_{t-l} \tag{13}$$

is orthogonal to F_{t-j} for $j > q_i$. Since the scalar process in (13) is in F_t to which F_{t-j} is a subspace for $j > 0$, it follows, from the uncorrelatedness of a_t, that the scalar process in (13) must be in the subspace generated by $\{a_t, \ldots, a_{t-q_i}\}$. Consequently, we have

$$v_{i,0}' Z_t + \sum_{l=1}^{p_i} v_{i,0}' Z_{t-l} = v_{i,0}' a_t + \sum_{j=1}^{q_i} h_{i,j}' a_{t-j} \tag{14}$$

where $h_{i,j}$ are k-dimensional vectors. Note that the coefficient of a_t is also $v_{i,0}$, because Z_t is a linear process which can be written as $Z_t = a_t + \sum_{i=1}^{\infty} \Psi_i a_{t-i}$ where Ψ_i are functions of Φ_l and Θ_j in (1).

Let $p = \max\{p_i\}$ and $q = \max\{q_i\}$. For $l = 0, \ldots, p$, let $V_l = [v_{1,l}, \ldots, v_{k,l}]'$ be a $k \times k$ matrix where it is understood that $v_{i,l} = O$ if $p_i < l \le p$. Similarly, for $j = 1, \ldots, q$, define $H_j = [h_{1,j}, \ldots, h_{k,j}]'$, where $h_{i,j} = O$ if $q_i < j \le q$. By (14), we have

$$V_0 Z_t + V_1 Z_{t-1} + \cdots + V_p Z_{t-p} = V_0 a_t + H_1 a_{t-1} + \cdots + H_q a_{t-q} , \tag{15}$$

which is a VARMA(p, q) model. This model has certain features that are particularly useful in model-building. For instance, $\sum_{i=1}^{k} [(p - p_i) + (q - q_i)]$ rows of V_i and H_j are zero. Such a reduction in the number of parameters can substantially simplify the task of parameter estimation. Another feature is that the SCMs might have substantive meanings in real applications; at least they point out linear combinations of the system that have simple structures. For example, if $p_i = q_i = 0$, this implies that the linear combination $v_{i,0}' Z_t$ is a white-noise process whatever the nature of the original Z_t process is.

Let $X_t = (x_{1t}, \ldots, x_{kt})' = V_0 Z_t$ be the transformed series. By inserting $V_0^{-1} V_0$ in the front of Z_{t-i} and a_{t-j} and letting $b_t = V_0 a_t$, the model in (15) becomes

$$X_t - \sum_{l=1}^{p} \Phi_l^* X_{t-l} = b_t - \sum_{j=1}^{q} \Theta_j^* b_{t-j} \tag{16}$$

where $\Phi_l^* = -V_l V_0^{-1}$ and $\Theta_j^* = -H_j V_0^{-1}$. Since post-multiplication does not affect the zero rows of a matrix, the coefficient matrices Φ_l^* and Θ_j^* have the same zero-row structure as V_l and H_j, respectively. Thus, the number of zero rows in (16) is $\sum_{i=1}^{k} [(p - p_i) + (q - q_i)]$. Clearly, we must keep the order (p_i, q_i) of x_{it} as low as possible in order to achieve the maximal simplification in modeling Z_t. It turns out that to obtain a canonical model specification for Z_t via SCM, we require that the two quantities

$$NR(X_t) = \sum_{i=1}^{k} (p_i + q_i) \qquad \text{and} \qquad R(X_t) = \sum_{i=1}^{k} \max\{p_i, q_i\} \tag{17}$$

of X_t are as small as possible among all collections of k linearly independent SCMs (see Tsay 1991). The first quantity $NR(X_t)$ is the number of non-zero rows in model (16), whereas the second quantity $R(X_t)$ ensures that we can remove all the "redundant parameters" in the non-zero rows of (16). By "redundant parameters," we mean those coefficients which play the same role in the autoregressive and the moving-average parts of (16). For details, see Tiao and Tsay (1989).

The remaining problem in using the SCM method is to identify k linearly independent SCMs from the data that satisfy the two requirements in (17). We employ a canonical correlation analysis between $Z_{m,t}$ and $Z_{m,t-j-1}$ for $m, j = 0, 1, \ldots$ to identify SCMs. The idea behind this approach is to make use of the orthogonal property between an SCM and the σ-field F_{t-l} in (12). For instance, existence of an SCM(r, s) in Z_t implies that a linear combination of $Z_{r,t}$ is orthogonal to F_{t-l} for $l > s$. This in turn implies that a linear combination of $Z_{r,t}$ is orthogonal to $Z_{r,t-j-1}$ for all $j \geq s$. Thus, there is a zero canonical correlation between $Z_{r,t}$ and $Z_{r,t-j-1}$ for $j \geq s$. In practice, the number of zero canonical correlations can be tested using an asymptotic chi-squared statistic. However, some further analysis is needed in order to identify a "genuine" SCM, because an SCM(r, s) is also an SCM(p, q) if $p \geq r$ and $q \geq s$. Consequently, one needs to eliminate the SCMs that are already found in the searching process. To satisfy the two requirements in (17), we can take a direct approach by starting the search process with $m + j$ to be as small as possible. For those m and j satisfying $m + j = c$, a constant, we follow the sequence $m = 0, 1, \ldots, c$ based on computational consideration. For further properties of SCM, methods of eliminating duplicated SCMs and other details, see Tiao and Tsay (1989).

In summary, the SCM method adopted in this paper works as follows: (a) Perform canonical correlation analysis between $Z_{m,t}$ and $Z_{m,t-j-1}$ for $m, j = 0, 1, \ldots$. (b) For each canonical correlation analysis, test for the number of zero canonical correlations. A zero canonical correlation implies existence of an SCM of order (m, j) and the corresponding canonical vector gives the linear combination of that SCM, up to a scaling factor. (c) Considering the SCMs found at the order (m, j), delete those which are equivalent to SCMs found prior to (m, j). Any remaining SCMs are new SCM of order (m, j). (d) The search process is terminated when k linearly independent SCMs are found. (e) Finally, use the k linearly independent SCMs to specify a VARMA in (16). A corresponding VARMA model for Z_t, of course, can be obtained by (16) and the transformation matrix V_0.

We remark here that, in practice, a stable (dynamic) relation between economic variables means that a linear combination of the variables is close to a white-noise series. From the SCM view point, this implies that a linear combination has essentially the SCM(0, 0) representation. Because the SCM approach is designed to search for simple structure in the data, it can directly reveal co-integrations if they exist.

6.2 *Empirical Results*

We apply in this subsection the SCM approach to the three Taiwan interest rates of Figure 1. Table 5 summarizes the results of canonical correlation analy-

Table 5. Results of canonical correlation analyses for scalar component models. Data used are time-deposit interest rates of Taiwan from 61.3 to 89.7

m	j	Eigenvalue	Chi-Square	d.f.	p-value
0	0	.947	993.83	7	0.00
		.976	2249.71	16	0.00
		.993	3945.41	27	0.00
0	1	.880	717.11	4	0.00
		.929	1612.41	10	0.00
		.984	3009.63	18	0.00
1	0	.026	8.74	7	0.27
		.041	22.98	16	0.11
		.212	103.04	27	0.00
0	2	.814	568.66	1	1.00
		.878	1279.20	4	1.00
		.975	2521.80	9	0.52
1	1	.000	0.04	4	0.00
		.001	0.28	10	0.00
		.081	28.74	18	0.00
		.948	1026.47	28	0.00
		.979	2330.70	40	0.00
		.994	4031.82	54	0.00

ses between $Z_{m,t}$ and $Z_{m,t-j-1}$ for $(m, j) = (0, 0)$, $(0, 1)$, $(1, 0)$, $(0, 2)$ and $(1, 1)$. The search process was terminated at $(m, j) = (1, 1)$ because the third linearly independent SCM was found here.

The chi-squared statistic in Table 5 is a cumulative test such that the l-th test at the order (m, j) is to test that the l smallest eigenvalues are zero, and d.f. denotes degrees of freedom of the associated chi-squared statistic. From the table, it is clear that based on the usual 5% or 1% criterion (a) there are no SCMs found at $(m, j) = (0, 0)$ or $(0, 1)$; (b) there are two SCMs found at $(m, j) = (1, 0)$; (c) no SCM is detected at $(m, j) = (0, 2)$; and (d) three SCMs exist at the order $(m, j) = (1, 1)$. Obviously, the two SCMs found at the order $(m, j) = (1, 0)$ are "genuine" SCMs. The eigenvectors associated with the two zero eigenvalues are given in Part (a) of Table 6. From these two eigenvectors, we obtain the SCMs $x_{1t} = (-.465, .811, -.355)Z_t$ and $x_{2t} = (-.811, .372, .452)Z_t$.

On the other hand, since $(1, 0)$ is a submodel of $(1, 1)$, among the three SCMs found at $(1, 1)$, only one is "genuine." To identify this new SCM, we consider the associated eigenvectors given in Part (b) of Table 6. Let F^* be the space generated by these three eigenvectors. Without loss of generality, we pick the new SCM as the one that is in F^*, but is orthogonal to the subspace generated by the two eigenvectors at $(m, j) = (1, 0)$. It turns out that this orthogonal vector is $(.582, .557, .593, -.568, -.594, -.525)$, which in turn gives the third SCM $x_{3x} = (.582, .557, .593)Z_t$.

Table 6. Eigenvectors associated with zero eigenvalues of Table 5

Eigenvalue	Eigenvector					
(a) $(m, j) = (1, 0)$						
0.26	−.465	.811	−.355	.450	−.786	.345
.041	−.811	.372	.452	.799	−.359	−.454
(b) $(m, j) = (1, 1)$						
.000	−.263	.797	−.545	.247	−.767	.532
.001	−.667	.739	−.093	.647	−.708	.082
.081	−.399	.890	.223	.386	−.877	−.204

Using the three identified SCMs, we specify a tentative VARMA(1, 1) model for the transformed series

$$X_t = \begin{bmatrix} x_{1t} \\ x_{2t} \\ x_{3t} \end{bmatrix} = \begin{bmatrix} -.46 & .81 & -.36 \\ -.81 & .37 & .45 \\ .58 & .56 & .59 \end{bmatrix} Z_t \; . \tag{18}$$

The model is

$$X_t - \varphi^* X_{t-1} = C_x + b_t - \Theta^* b_{t-1} \tag{19}$$

where C_x is a constant vector, φ^* is a full matrix, but Θ^* has non-zero elements only in the last row. In other words, the first two rows of Θ^* in (19) are zero, a saving of 6 parameters in estimation. The estimation results of model (19) are given in Table 7(a), which shows all the off-diagonal elements in Φ^* and Θ^* are statistically insignificant. Table 7(b) shows the results of a constrained model by deleting all off-diagonal elements in (19). However, residual analysis of this model shows some serial correlation at lag-1 of x_{1t} and x_{2t}. Following the iterative modeling procedure, we further refine the model by considering these serial correlations. The refined VARMA(1, 1) model is given in Table 7(c), which shows that all the three transformed series are uncorrelated and follow a univariate ARMA(1, 1) model. The moving-average parts of x_{1t} and x_{2t} are statistically significant but relatively weak. The first five residual cross-correlation matrices of the refined model are shown in Table 8. The model appears to be reasonable. All the cross-correlations are small except the 3rd diagonal element of the lag-3 cross-correlation matrix. The value of .16 is roughly three times the estimated standard deviation of $1/\sqrt{340} = .05$ based on the assumption of a white-noise vector process for b_t. If desirable, a further improvement can be made for the component x_{3t} by fitting the model

$$(1 - \varphi_{33}^* B) x_{3t} = c_3 + (1 - \theta_{33}^{(1)} B)(1 - \theta_{33}^{(3)} B^3) b_{3t} \; . \tag{20}$$

Table 7. Estimation results of VARMA(1, 1) models for transformed time-deposit rates. The numbers in parentheses are standard error

	C	φ^*			Θ^*			$\Sigma_b \times 10^2$		
(a)	.00(.01)	.97(.01)	−.00(.00)	−.00(00)	—	—	—	.078	−.001	.018
	−.01(.02)	−.01(.03)	.99(.01)	.00(.00)	—	—	—	−.001	.510	−.111
	.39(.17)	.11(30)	−.05(.06)	.98(.01)	.48(94)	−.06(.37)	−.44(.05)	.018	−.111	23.98
(b)	−.00(.00)	.97(.01)	—	—	—	—	—	.078	−.001	.013
	−.00(.01)	—	1.0(.01)	—	—	—	—	−.001	.511	−.103
	.32(.15)	—	—	.97(.01)	—	—	−.44(.05)	.013	−.103	24.13
(c)	−.00(.00)	.97(.01)	—	—	−.16(.05)	—	—	.077	−.001	.018
	.00(.01)	—	.99(.01)	—	—	−.19(.05)	—	−.001	.494	−.099
	.32(.15)	—	—	.97(.01)	—	—	−.44(.05)	.018	−.099	24.13

Table 8. Residual cross-correlations matrices of the model in part (c) of table 7

Lag-1			Lag-2			Lag-3			Lag-4			Lag-5		
.00	−.01	−.01	.00	.00	.00	.00	.00	.02	.01	.00	−.02	−.01	.02	.03
.00	.00	−.03	−.01	−.01	.00	.00	−.01	.04	.00	−.01	.00	.01	−.01	.02
−.01	.00	.01	.03	.05	.08	−.02	.01	.16	.00	.00	.04	.00	.03	.03

The estimates are

	c_3	φ_{33}^*	$\theta_{33}^{(1)}$	$\theta_{33}^{(3)}$	$10^2 \times \sigma_{33}$
Estimate	.37	.97	−.40	−.19	23.4
Stand. Err.	.18	.01	.05	.06	

Diagnostic checks of residuals show no further evidence of model inadequacy.

Interpretation and Discussion: From (18), we see that x_{1t} and x_{2t} are two linear contrasts of the deposit interest rates and x_{3t} is proportional to the average of the rates. Compared with Z_t^* of Section 4 based on PCA of $\hat{\Sigma}$, x_{1t} is roughly the same as Z_{1t}^*, measuring the curvature of the yield curve, and x_{3t} is virtually identical to Z_{3t}^*, representing the general level of the three series. In terms of the two spreads S_{1t} and S_{2t}, we can write x_{2t} as $x_{2t} \approx .8S_{1t} + .5S_{2t}$, which is a weighted average of the spreads and is, again, an approximation to the first derivative of the yield curve. Thus, the behavior of x_{2t} will be similar to that of Z_{2t}^*. Further, since (x_{1t}, x_{2t}) and (Z_{1t}^*, Z_{2t}^*) are linear functions of S_{1t} and S_{2t} only, they are also linear functions of each other, not involving the third component $x_{3t} \approx Z_{3t}^*$. Now, the model in Table 3(c) for Z_t^* is in the form of a VAR(4) whereas that for X_t via the SCM approach assumes the mixed VARMA form

$$(I - \varphi^* B)X_t = C + (I - \Theta_1^* B)(I - \Theta_3^* B^3)b_t \ . \tag{21}$$

By expanding the MA part of (21) in an AR form, it can be readily checked that the two fitted models are in fact approximately equivalent.

In summary, based on the PCA of Section 4, the canonical correlation analysis of Section 5, and the SCM approach to model-building, the structure of the three interest-rate series can be greatly simplified by transforming the series into (i) an average component reflecting the general co-movement of the data, and (ii) two linear contrasts of the rates. One of the contrasts is a weighted average of the two spreads S_{1t} and S_{2t} representing the first derivative of the yield curve and the other is essentially a contrast of the spreads providing a measure of the curvature of the yield curve. The two contrasts are uncorrelated with the average. The curvature measure moves within a small range throughout the data span, whereas the first derivative shows a decreasing trend towards zero. The component representing the average of the rates dominates the variation of the three series. While these features of the interest-rate series are noticeable in Figure 1, they are clearly brought out by the transformations considered. We note that the three kinds of linear transformation of the data considered are designed for different goals. Specifically, the PCA focuses on innovations driving the system, the canonical transformation on strength of linear dynamic relation, and the SCMs on row rank of the AR and MA parameter matrices. It is interesting that for the interest-rate series considered they all lead to very similar results.

While the results of unit-root and co-integration tests in Section 3 are largely consistent with the analyses presented in Sections 4–6, we believe that some cautionary remarks are in order. As mentioned earlier, unit-root tests are basically designed to test for random level shifts, normalized to be independent of the magnitude of the noise. Thus, one needs to be careful in interpreting the test results in application. Consider, for example, again the components Z^*_{1t} and Z^*_{3t} in Section 4. These two components have essentially the same units of measurement. Both will pass unit-root tests (of having a unit root) but their behavior is vastly different (see Figure 2). A key reason is, of course, that the variance of a^*_{3t} is over 300 times of that of a^*_{1t}. Thus, one should not draw the conclusion that since both components have a unit root, they are equally unstable. The same caution should be applied to co-integration tests. Consider the component Y_{1t} ($\approx Z^*_{1t}$) from the canonical analysis in Section 5. It has the minimal eigenvalue $\lambda_1 = .947$, implying that there is essentially no co-integration. Again, the λ's are measures independent of the magnitude of the noise driving the system. Since the variance of Y_{1t} is very small, it may be regarded as very stable from a practical point of view in spite of the fact that it is nearly unit-root non-stationary. Finally, from Figure 1, the three time-deposit rates apparently move in tandem, yet the co-integration tests considered fail to show any common source of the co-movement. We feel that over-emphasis on the existence of unit roots might overlook some important practical implications in economic and financial studies. On the other hand, linear transformations such as those considered in the paper may reveal more about the structure of the time-series and merit further study.

6.3 Sensitivity of SCM Analysis

In Section 2 we categorized the data into five different time spans according to the data history. An immediate concern is whether the models built, including the results of SCM analysis, are sensitive to the data period we chose in the previous analysis. To investigate this issue, we redid the SCM analysis for each of the other four dominions, using 1% criterion for the chi-squared statistics. The resulting SCMs and their orders are summarized in Table 9. From the table, we make the following observations: (a) the first SCM, which measures acceleration, is stable for all time spans; (b) the second SCM, which measures the first derivative of the interest-rate yield curve, is stable until July of 1989; (c) the last SCM, which is the average of the three deposit rates, is stable in Spans II, III and IV; (d) the overall VARMA(1, 1) model is also consistent for Spans II to IV. The overall model becomes VAR(1) in Span I and VARMA(3, 2) in Span V; (e) the striking changes in SCMs from Span IV to Span V indicate a structure change in the system after July 1989. Thus, lifting the ceilings on the time-deposit rates had a great influence on the behavior of interest rates in Taiwan.

Table 9. SCM analysis of time-deposit rates for different data spans. T is the sample size

Identified SCM			Order
(a) Time Span: 61.3–75.7, $T = 172$			
−.585	.768	−.263	(1, 0)
−.267	−.535	.801	(1, 0)
−.436	.895	−.096	(1, 0)
(b) Time Span: 61.3–80.11, $T = 236$			
−.518	.797	−.311	(1, 0)
−.694	−.042	.719	(1, 0)
.539	.572	.619	(1, 1)
(c) Time Span: 61.3–86.1, $T = 298$			
−.530	.798	−.288	(1, 0)
−.589	−.212	.780	(1, 0)
.588	.520	.619	(1, 1)
(d) Time Span: 61.3–89.7, $T = 340$			
−.465	.811	−.355	(1, 0)
−.811	.372	.452	(1, 0)
.582	.557	.593	(1, 1)
(e) Time Span: 61.3–91.11, $T = 369$			
−.176	.771	−.612	(1, 0)
−.046	.594	.804	(1, 1)
−.371	.532	.761	(3, 2)

In summary, even though there were several revisions of the Bank Act in Taiwan, the SCM analysis indicates that the basic structure of the interest rates in Taiwan was stable before July 1989. However, the new Bank Act in July 1989 drastically changed the features of the interest rates. It is conceivable that recisions of ceilings on time-deposit rates and of restrictions on the incorporation of new banks intensified competitions among the banks, which, in turns, altered their rate-setting policy.

Acknowledgement: This research was supported in part by NASA, NSF, the Graduate School of Business, the University of Chicago, and a grant from National Taiwan University, Taipei, Taiwan, R.O.C. We wish to thank Baldev Raj and Victor Zarnowitz for helpful comments.

References

Akaike H (1974) A new look at the statistical model identification. IEEE Transaction of Automatic Control AC-19:716–723

Box GEP, Tiao GC (1977) A canonical analysis of multiple time series. Biometrika 64:355–366.

Chan NH, Tsay RS (1991) On the use of canonical correlation analysis in testing common trends. Technical Report, Department of Statistics, Carnegie Mellon University

Chan NH, Wei CZ (1988) Limiting distribution of Least squares estimates of unstable autoregressive processes. Annals of Statistics 16:367–401

Dickey DA, Fuller WA (1979) Distribution of the estimators for autoregressive time series with a unit root. Journal of the American Statistical Association 74:427–431

Dickey DA, Jansen DW, Thornton DL (1991) A Primer on co-integration with application to money and income. Federal Reserve Bank of St. Louis Review 73:58–78

Engle RF, Granger GWJ (1987) Co-integration and error correction: representation, estimation and testing. Econometrica 55:251–276

Engle RF, Yoo BS (1987). Forecasting and testing in co-integrated systems. Journal of Econometrics 35:143–159

Hannan EJ, Deistler M (1988) The statistical theory of linear systems, New York John Wiley

Johansen S (1988) Statistical analysis of cointegration vectors. Journal of Economic Dynamics and Control 12:231–254

Johansen S, Juselius K (1990) Maximum likelihood estimation and inference on co-integration—with applications to the demand for money. Oxford Bulletin of Economics and Statistics 52: 109–210

Lee SY (1991) Issues of financial liberalization in Taiwan. Asia Pacific Journal of Management 8:55–70

Litterman R, Scheinkman J (1988) Common factors affecting bond returns. Working Paper, Goldman Sachs

Lütkepohl H (1991) Introduction to multiple time series analysis. New York, Springer-Verlag

McKinnon R (1973) Money and capital in economic development, Brookings Institution. Washington, DC

Phillips PCB (1987) Time series regression with a unit root. Econometrica 55:227–301

Reinsel GC (1983) Some results on multivariate autoregressive index models. Biometrika 70:145–156

Stock JH, Watson MW (1988) Testing for common trends. Journal of the American Statistical Association 83:1097–1107

Tiao GC, Box GEP (1981) Modeling multiple time series with applications. Journal of the American Statistical Association 76:802–816

Tiao GC, Tsay RS (1989) Model specification in multivariate time series Journal of the Royal Statistical Society B 51:157–213

Tsay RS (1991) Two canonical forms for vector ARMA processes. Statistica Sinica 1:247–269

Tsay RS, Tiao GC (1990) Asymptotic properties of multivariate non-stationary processes with applications to autoregressions. Annals of Statistics 18:220–250

Wei JL (1986a) Liberalization of deposit interest rate and trend of bank management in Taiwan. Taiwan Economics and Finance Monthly, February 2–8 in Chinese

Wei JL (1986b) A study of the effects of interest rate deregulation in Taiwan. Taiwan Economics and Finance Monthly October 2–13 in Chinese

Wijnbergen S Van (1983) Interest rate management in LDC's. Journal of Monetary Economics 12:433–452

Yuan YS (1984) The evolution of interest rate management in Taiwan. Bank of Taiwan Quarterly 35:81–92 in Chinese

VAR Modelling and Haavelmo's Probability Approach to Macroeconomic Modelling[1]

KATARINA JUSELIUS

Institute of Economics, University of Copenhagen, Studiestraede 6, 1455 Copenhagen K, Denmark

Abstract: Some recent developments in the macroeconometric analysis of time series are discussed in the light of Haavelmo (1944). Experimental design in econometrics is discussed and related to the case of passive observation. The general ideas are illustrated with a analysis of the long-run and short-run structure in Danish monetary data.

Key Words: Haavelmo; macroeconometric time-series modelling; multivariate cointegration; non-stationary time series.

JEL Classification System-Number: B23

1 Introduction

Summers (1991) discusses what he calls "the scientific illusion in empirical macroeconomics." He begins by observing that applied econometric work in general has exerted little influence on the development of economic theory and generated little new insight into economic mechanisms. To illustrate he discusses two widely different approaches to applied econometric modelling: (i) the representative agent's approach, where the final aim of the empirical analysis is to estimate a few deep parameters characterizing preferences and technology, and (ii) the use of sophisticated statistical techniques, exemplified by Sim's VAR-models, to "identify" certain parameters on which inference to the underlying economic mechanisms is based.

Summers concludes that less formal examination of empirical observations, the so-called stylized-facts approach, has generally resulted in more fruitful economic research. This is a very pessimistic view of the usefulness of formal econometric modelling, and therefore has to be challenged by the profession. The paper below discusses some shortcomings in applied econometric work and shows how recent advances provide powerful tools for analyzing complicated macroeconomic phenomena.

Because the formal link between economic theory and empirical modelling lies in the field of statistical inference, the focus here is on statistical aspects. In

[1] This paper has benefitted from useful comments from Søren Johansen, Claus Va strup and John Muellbauer, and in particular, from two unknown referees. Financial report from the joint committee of the Nordic Social Science Research Council is gratefully acknowledged.

particular, the discussion will focus on what could be called the economist's approach and the statistician's approach to macroeconomic modelling, and a distinction will be made between the role of an economic model and the role of a statistical model. Economists frequently formulate an economically well-defined model as the empirical model and *apply statistical methods* to estimate its parameters. In contrast, statisticians might formulate a statistically well-defined model for the data and *analyze the statistical model* to answer the economic questions of interest. The difference may not seem fundamental, but it is probably of the utmost importance. In the first case, statistics are used passively as a tool to get some desired estimates, and in the second case, the model is taken seriously and used actively as a means of analyzing the underlying generating process of the phenomenon in question.

The general principle of analyzing models instead of applying methods can be traced back to R.A. Fisher. It was introduced into econometrics by Haavelmo (1944) [hereafter Haavelmo] and operationalized and further developed mainly by Hendry and Richard (1983), Hendry (1983, 1987) and Ericsson, Campos, Tran (1990). Haavelmo's influence on modern econometrics has been discussed in Hendry, Spanos, and Ericsson (1989) and Anderson (1992), among others.

The organization of this paper is as follows. Section 2 goes back to Haavelmo's work and questions whether "the scientific illusion in empirical macroeconomics" can be largely explained by the failure to follow the principles expressed in the monograph. Section 2 focuses on empirical macroeconomic modelling. In section 3, the notion of experimental design in econometrics when data are collected by passive observation is discussed with reference to Hendry and Richard (1993). Section 4 extends the general framework of section 3 to include recent developments in the analysis of non-stationary data. These ideas are illustrated in sections 5 and 6 with an empirical analysis of aggregate monetary behavior based on Danish data. Section 7 summarizes the findings.

2 On the Choice of Economic Versus Empirical Models

This section discusses three issues from Haavelmo that are often overlooked in empirical macroeconomics: (i) the link between theoretical, true and observed variables, (ii) the distinction between testing a hypothesis and testing a theory, and (iii) the formulation of an adequate design of experiment.

An aggregate money-demand relation illustrates these issues. Before the above questions are tackled in more detail, the motivation for investigating such a relation will be briefly examined.

2.1 Economic Motivation

Monetarist theories motivate an interest in money demand. According to them, the inflation rate can be directly related to expansions in the (appropriately defined) supply of money at a rate greater than that warranted by the growth of the real productive potential of the economy. The policy implication is that the aggregate supply of money should be controlled in order to control the inflation rate. The optimal control of money, however, requires knowledge of the "non-inflationary level" of aggregate demand for money at each point of time, defined as the level of money stock, m^*, at which there is no tendency for the inflation rate to increase or decrease. Thus, on a practical level, the reasoning is based on the assumption that there exists a stable aggregate demand-for-money relation, $m^* = f(x)$, that can be estimated. What, then, can be learned from the available economic theories about the form of such a relation, and what are the crucial determinants?

There are three distinct motives for holding money: the transactions motive (the need to hold cash for handling everyday transactions); the precautionary motive (the need to hold money to be able to meet unforeseen expenditures); and the speculative motive (agents' wishes to hold money as part of their portfolio). Since all three motives are likely to affect agents' needs to hold money, let the initial assumption be that $m = f(y, c)$, which means that money holdings, m, is a function of the level of income which is assumed to determine the volume of transactions and precautionary money, and the cost of holding money, c.

Further assumptions leading to optimizing behavior are needed in order to derive a formal model for agents' willingness to hold money balances. Among the available theories two different approaches can be discernible: (i) theories treating money as a medium of exchange for transaction purposes, so that minimizing a derived cost function leads to optimizing behavior, (ii) theories treating money as a good-producing utility, so that maximizing the utility function leads to optimizing behavior.

Only the first approach will be discussed here, specifically the theoretical model suggested by Baumol (1952), which is still frequently referred to in this context. The model, strongly influenced by inventory theory, has the following basic features. Over a certain time period $t_1 - t_2$, the agent will pay out T units of money in a steady stream. Two different costs are involved, the opportunity cost of the forgone investment measured by the interest rate r, and the so-called "brokerage" cost b. It is also assumed that liquid money does not yield interest. The optimal value of cash withdrawn from investment can now be found as:

$$C = \sqrt{2bT/r} \tag{1}$$

so that the cost-minimizing agent will demand cash in proportion to the square root of the value of his transactions. Taking the logarithms of (1) gives a transactions elasticity of 0.5 and an interest elasticity of -0.5. These have been the prior hypotheses of many empirical investigations based on aggregated data, and estimates supporting this have been found, for instance, in Baba, Hendry and Starr (1992).

2.2 *Theoretical, True and Observable Variables*

If Baumol's theoretical model is tested against data, more precise statements of what is meant by the theoretical concepts C, b, T and r will be needed. Haavelmo suggests how they should be measured in an ideal situation, and introduces in this context the concepts of true and theoretical variables as opposed to observable variables. According to Haavelmo, p. 5:

We may express the difference [between the "true" and the theoretical variables] by saying that the "true" variables (or time functions) represent our ideal as to accurate measurements of reality "as it is in fact" while the variables defined in theory are the true measurements that we should make if reality were actually in accordance with our theoretical model.

For instance, say that a careful analysis of the above example shows that the true measurements are the average holdings of cash and demand deposits by private persons in private banks, postal banks or similar institutions (building societies, etc.) measured at closing time each trading day of a month. The theoretical variable C as defined by Baumol's model would then correspond to the true measurements, given that *i*) no interest is paid on this liquid money, ii) transactions are paid out in a steady stream over successive periods, iii) the brokerage cost and interest rate r are well-defined, iv) no cash and demand deposits are held for speculative or precautionary motives, and so on.

Needless to say, the available measurements from official statistics are very far from the definitions of the true variables. Even if it were possible to obtain measurements satisfying the above definition of the true measurements, it seems obvious that these would not correspond to the theoretical variables[2].

Nevertheless, if the purpose of the empirical investigation is to test a theory, a prerequisite for valid inference from reality to the theoretical model is a close correspondence between the observed variables and the true variables, or in the words of Haavelmo:

It is then natural to adopt the convention that a theory is called true or false according as the hypotheses implied are true or false, when tested against the data chosen as the "true" variables. Then we may speak interchangeably about testing hypotheses or testing theories.

---

[2] It should be pointed out that Baumol does not claim any such correspondence. In fact, he gives a long list of reasons why this cannot be the case.

Examples of violation of this principle are easy to find in macroeconomic applications. The many unit-root tests of GDP time-series to discriminate between different real growth theories can be mentioned in this respect.

Though data collected by passive observation do not generally qualify for the purpose of testing "deep" theoretical models, most empirical macroeconomic models are based on such data. The reason for this can be a general reluctance for collecting data by experimental design, but more probably because of a genuine interest in the macrodata as such. Since "data seldom speak by themselves," theoretical arguments are very much needed to understand the variation in these data. But the role of these arguments should be modified if the correspondence between the theoretical and observed variables is rather weak. This leads to the second issue to be discussed here, the distinction between testing a hypothesis and testing a theory.

2.3 Testing a Theory as Opposed to a Hypothesis

When the arguments of the theory do not apply directly to the empirical model, one compromise is to be less ambitious about testing theories as such. Instead, specific hypotheses derived from the theoretical model can be tested in empirical models that do not contain all aspects of the underlying theory. For instance, the hypotheses that the elasticity of the transactions demand for cash $e^c = 0.5$ and of the interest rate $e^r = -0.5$ have frequently been tested within empirical models that do not include all aspects of Baumol's theoretical model. Other popular hypotheses that have been widely tested include long-run price and income homogeneity, the sign of first derivatives, zero restrictions, and the direction of causality. "Sophisticated statistical techniques" have often been used in this context. But, according to Summers, the outcomes of these exercises have not been convincing or interesting enough to change economists' views. Two explanations why empirical results are often considered unpersuasive are given here.

i) *Not Enough Care is Taken to Ensure that the Specification of Empirical Models Mimics the General Characteristics of the Data*
In such cases the validity of the empirical outcome cannot be assessed and the test results remain unpersuasive. Therefore, the additional concept of a statistically well-defined model that accounts for all basic features of the data is required. Valid test procedures can then be derived from the analysis of the likelihood function and inferences about the specified hypotheses are valid. Nevertheless, inference about the theory as such depends on the strength of the correspondence between the observed and the true and the theoretical variables.
ii) *Not Enough Attention is Paid to the Crucial Role of the Ceteris Paribus Assumption*

In particular, if the effects of institutional changes, such as interventions, regulations, deregulations, are not properly accounted for, the structural parameters of interest are likely to be poorly estimated.

These issues will be further discussed below and illustrated with an empirical application to Danish monetary data. Before the discussion can proceed further, the concept of "a design of experiment" in econometrics as discussed by Haavelmo has to be clarified.

2.4 Experimental Design in Macroeconometrics

As discussed above, the link between the true variables suggested by the theory and the actual measurements taken from official statistics is, in most cases, too weak to justify valid inference from the empirical model to the theory. High-quality, reasonably long aggregate series are difficult to obtain because definitions change, new components have entered the aggregates and new regulations have changed the behavior. The end result is the best set of measurements in the circumstances; but still quite far from the true measurements obtainable in an ideal situation. This problem is discussed in terms of a "design of experiment" in Haavelmo, p. 14.

If economists would describe the experiments they have in mind when they construct the theories they would see that the experiments they have in mind may be grouped into two different classes namely, (1) experiments that we should like to make to see if certain real economic phenomena – when artificially isolated from other influences – would verify certain hypothesis and (2) the stream of experiments that nature is steadily turning out from his own enormous laboratory, and which we merely watch as passive observers.... In the first case we can make agreements or disagreements between theory and facts depend on two things: the facts we choose to consider and our theory about them.... In the second case we can only try to adjust our theories to reality as it appears before us. And what is the meaning of a design of experiment in this case. It is this: We try to choose a theory and a design of experiments to go with it, in such a way that the resulting data would be those which we get by passive observation of reality. And to the extent that we succeed in doing so, we become masters of reality – by passive agreement.

Since the interest here is the case of passive observations, one possible formalization of a "design of experiment" for this case will be discussed. What is needed is a set of assumptions which are general enough to ensure a statistically valid description of typical macroeconomic data, and a common modelling strategy to allow questions of interest to be investigated in a consistent framework. Since controlled experiments are not usually possible within a single macroeconomy, one has to rely on the "experiment" provided by other countries or regions that differ in various aspects with regard to the investigated economic problem. For instance, if the question of interest is whether in general an expansion of money supply increases the inflation rate, it is probably a good idea to examine this using similar data from countries that differ in terms of the economic policy pursued.

A *structural* VAR procedure will be suggested here as *one possibility* of a common modelling strategy because the time-series properties can be utilized in a straightforward way to define structural components that can be given an economic interpretation. This procedure is less pretentious about the *prior* role of an economic model, and investigates the time-series structure of the chosen data against the background of not just one but a variety of relevant theories.

The set of assumptions leading to the VAR model was discussed at length by Hendry and Richard (1983). For the sake of completeness, their basic arguments will be given in section 3, with the purpose of arriving at an adequate experimental design that could produce data for which the VAR model would be an adequate description.

3 An Experimental Design for the "Institutional" VAR Model

Let us assume that the chosen economic theories suggest classification into y_t, the economic variable(s) of primary interest and x_t, the main determinants of y_t. For instance, in the money-demand example, y_t could be private holdings of transaction money, and the vector x_t could contain the volume of transactions, the price level, its own interest rate and the bond interest rate. The sample consists of time-series observations from $t = 1$ to T, where at each point of time t there is just one realization from the underlying stochastic process. A time graph will immediately reveal that successive observations are highly time-dependent, and that most of the series reveal trend-like behavior. Since all variables are assumed to be stochastic, a specification of a full statistical model is motivated, although in the economic sense, y is the variable of interest whereas the other variables have been chosen because they are assumed to be the main determinants.

Therefore, in line with Hendry and Richard (1983), it will be assumed that the observed data are realizations of a sequence of random vectors $Z_t = \{z_1, \ldots, z_t\}$, where $z_t = \{y_t, x_t\}$, with a joint density function $P(z_1, \ldots, z_t; Z_0, \theta)$, where $Z_0 = \{z_{-k}, \ldots, z_0\}$ is a matrix of initial values and θ is the parameter taking values in the parameter set Θ. The strong time dependence in economic data makes it natural to investigate the conditional process $\{z_t | Z_{t-1}; Z_0\}$. In addition, it is often necessary to include in the conditioning set a vector of deterministic variables D_t. This vector contains the extra facts that have caused such systematic variation in the data that cannot be explained by the information given by previous realizations of the process z_t. These variables are often related to political and economic interventions and are needed to account for institutional differences.

A tentative formulation can be obtained by assuming that the conditional process $\{z_t|Z_{t-1}D_t; Z_0\}$ is multivariate normal (μ_t, Σ), where $\mu_t = A_1 z_{t-1} + \cdots + A_t z_1 + A_0 + \phi D_t$ and Σ is positive definite. Assuming that $A_{k+i} \simeq 0$, for $i = 1, \ldots, t-k$, produces the conditional vector autoregressive model as a statistical model for the data-generating process.

$$z_t = \sum_{i=1}^{k} A_i z_{t-i} + a_0 + \phi D_t + \varepsilon_t \,, \qquad \varepsilon_t \sim \mathrm{NIID}_p(0, \Sigma) \tag{2}$$

where a_0 is a vector of constants and $\theta = \{A_1, \ldots, A_k, a_0, \phi, \Sigma\}$ varies unrestrictedly. It is multivariate, time-dependent and based on the three assumptions: (i) conditional normality, (ii) linearity and (iii) the order of truncation k, all of which are testable assumptions.

As discussed in Hendry and Richard (1983) data for which (2) is an appropriate description could have been generated by economic agents that are rational in the sense that they learn by past experience and adjust their behavior accordingly. In particular, the "design of experiment" consistent with (2) is based on the assumption that the unexpected components given the chosen information set behave as in a multivariate normal innovation process. This implies that agents' contigency plans z_t^p are given by the conditional expectations $E(z_t|Z_{t-1}, D_{t-1})$, and that the variables in D_t have an additive effect, such that $z_t - z_t^p - \phi(D_t)$ is multivariate normal.

Hence, the empirical adequacy of the stochastic specification is the only available check on the appropriateness of the assumed "design of experiment." If the residuals do not pass the check, or parameter non-constancy is detected, the "design of experiment" has to be reconsidered. Frequent reasons for mis-specification are that: (i) all relevant information has not been accounted for, either in the form of theoretical variables or "other facts," (ii) an intervention might have multiplicative instead of additive effects, or (iii) the speed of adjustment differs as regards negative and positive (as well as large and small) deviations from steady-states. What we can do in these cases is to adjust our theories and the assumed "design of experiment" to include this evidence. The final success of the empirical analysis therefore relies crucially on the choice of a sufficient and relevant information set and the skillfulness of the investigator to extract economically interesting results from this information.

4 Non-Stationarity and Macroeconomic Modelling

When data are non-stationary, there is the additional possibility that the process $\{z_t\}$ contains information about (i) the equilibrating forces that make the process adjust towards long-run steady states and (ii) the driving forces that push the economy out of equilibrium. The first aspect can best be investigated in the autoregressive representation (see, for instance, Engle and Granger, 1987, Johansen, 1988 and 1991). The second aspect is best investigated in the moving average representation (see, for instance, Stock and Watson, 1988, Johansen, 1991 and Mellander, Vredin and Warne, 1991).

4.1 The Role of Cointegration

For reasons of simplification, the subsequent discussion will be restricted to first-order non-stationary processes, and it will be assumed that $k = 2$ in (2). Rewriting (2) in the error-correction form produces:

$$\Delta z_t = \Gamma_1 \Delta z_{t-1} + \Pi z_{t-1} + a_0 + \phi D_t + \varepsilon_t \,, \qquad \varepsilon_t \sim \mathrm{Niid}_p(0, \Sigma) \tag{3}$$

where $\Gamma_1 = -A_2$ and $\Pi = -(I - A_1 - A_2)$. It is obvious from (3) that all terms except Πz_{t-1} are stationary by definition. The well-known first-order non-stationarity hypothesis is formulated as:

$$\Pi = \alpha\beta' \text{ is reduced rank} \tag{4}$$

and

$$\alpha'_\perp (I - \Gamma_1)\beta_\perp \text{ is a full rank matrix} \tag{5}$$

where α and β are $p \times r$ matrices, $\alpha_\perp$, $\beta_\perp$ are orthogonal complements of α and β of dimension $p \times p - r$, and $0 \leq r \leq p$, (Johansen, 1991). The second condition (5) is needed to check whether z_t is actually $I(1)$ and not $I(2)$. The first-order multivariate cointegration model in the autoregressive representation can now be defined as:

$$\Delta z_t = \Gamma_1 \Delta z_{t-1} + \alpha\beta' z_{t-1} + a_0 + \phi D_t + \varepsilon_t \,, \qquad \varepsilon_t \sim \mathrm{Niid}_p(0, \Sigma) \tag{6}$$

and in the corresponding moving-average representation as:

$$z_t = z_0 + C \sum_{i=1}^{t} \varepsilon_i + C \sum_{i=1}^{t} D_i + C\mu t + C^*(L)(\varepsilon_t + D_t) \tag{7}$$

where $C = \beta_\perp(\alpha'_\perp(I - \Gamma_1)\beta_\perp)^{-1}\alpha_\perp$ and C^* is a non-singular matrix function of θ, (Johansen, 1991).

What additional economic insight can be gained from the data using the property of non-stationarity? By investigating (6), it is easy to see that the component $\alpha\beta' z_{t-1}$ is directly related to the non-stationarity in the data. Since this component contains information about the force of adjustment α to some long-run relations $\beta' z_t$, it can be inferred that, if there is cointegration in the data and $\beta' z_t$ is time correlated, the reality under discussion can generally be understood in a theoretical model that assumes adjustment behavior to some extent. This implies that the great bulk of theoretical models of economic behavior derived under the assumption of static equilibrium cannot be used *as such as* a basis for most empirical models for trending data.

Model (6) can be directly interpreted in terms of backward-looking adjustment behavior, whereas the forward expectations hypothesis is generally consistent with a model of the same form but with non-linear parameter restrictions. Generally, forward expectations hypotheses can be formulated as sub-models of the unrestricted VAR model such that likelihood ratio testing is straightforward. Even though structural backward-looking adjustment models postulate less sophisticated agents, they often seem to provide a more adequate description of the actual data-generating process than the forward-looking models (see, for instance, Ericsson and Hendry (1989), Juselius (1992), Brodin and Nymoen (1992), Ripatti (1992)). These results stand up as quite strong evidence against the Lucas critique.

The next section concerns the connection between the statistically oriented multivariate cointegration model and the multivariate error-correction model, interpreted in terms of economic adjustment behavior.

4.2 *Cointegration and Error-Correction*

The multivariate cointegration model (6) is given in the error-correction form, but it is essentially a statistical description of the data. It is therefore of some interest to compare the statistical formulation with an error-correction model specified on the basis of economic considerations. When there is cointegration in (6), the linear combinations corresponding to the estimated cointegration vectors $\beta' z_t$ can in some cases have a *direct* interpretation as long-run economic relationships. Since any linear combination of the r cointegration relations is also a stationary relation, a direct interpretation of the cointegration vectors as meaningful economic relations is generally not possible. Therefore, if $r > 1$, identifying restrictions should be imposed on the cointegration space.

For illustrative purposes, assume that restrictions are imposed on the parameters of model (6), motivated by prior economic hypotheses such that the system of structural error-correction models becomes:

$$A_0(\theta)\Delta z_t = A_1(\theta)\Delta z_{t-1} + a(\theta)\{b(\theta)' z_{t-i}\} + a_0(\theta) + \phi D_t + \varepsilon_t \tag{8}$$

where $\operatorname{diag}(A_0) = \operatorname{diag}(I)$ and the parameters A_0, A_1, a_0 and a and b are functions of $\theta \in \Theta$ chosen such that they are economically well defined. The number of assumed steady-state relations is f.

The correspondence between (6) and (8) can now be investigated, and it is easily seen that, for $A_0 = I$, $A_I = \Gamma_1$ and $ab' = \alpha\beta'$, the economic formulation coincides with the statistical formulation. In most cases, the two models would differ in certain respects, for instance $A_0 \neq I$, $r \neq f$ and $A_1 \neq \Gamma_1$. The matrices a and b usually have many zero restrictions motivated by economic considerations, whereas α and β are unrestricted parameters defined by the statistical model using the non-stationarity property of the data vector. In Hendry and Mizon (1992), the statistical adequacy of the reduction from (6) to (8) is formally investigated in the encompassing framework.

As discussed in section 2.4., a modelling strategy for macroeconomic data should in the ideal case allow a variety of questions to be investigated in a consistent framework. A few examples of general questions that can then be asked within the structural VAR model are given below:

The number of steady-state relations and driving trends. As far as the money relation is concerned, it seems likely that an economist would assume *a priori* just one steady-state relation describing aggregate money holdings, and therefore that $f = 1$. However, if two of the assumed exogenous variables, namely the two interest rates, were themselves cointegrating, the statistical analysis would reveal that the cointegration rank is two and not one, such that there are two cointegrating relations, one between money and income and the other between bond rate and deposit rate, say. In this case, the statistical evidence for two cointegration relations would provide some new insight into the system. Nevertheless it could be consistent with the prior economic hypothesis of one long-run steady-state money relation, as a linear combination of the two cointegrating relations. Whether the rank is equal to one or two is clearly not uninteresting. The latter case implies the presence of two driving common trends, such as the real growth of the economy and the development of nominal interest rates in the financial sector. The former, on the other hand, implies the presence of three driving trends, say a real trend and two financial trends, one from the banking sector and the other from the bond market.

Actual behavior versus intention. An important aspect of a data-based procedure like the one discussed here is the economic interpretability of estimated coefficients. In model framework (6), it seems straightforward to ask two different types of questions, one concerning agents' intentions, the other concerning the actual behavior. By distinguishing between short-run behavior, i.e., how agents change their behavior in response to unanticipated changes in certain important determinants, and long-run behavior, i.e., how agents would behave for given values of the determinants in an imaginary steady-state economy, it is possible to answer both questions within the structural VAR framework. This does not exclude the possibility that the short-run behavior is fully intentional, though theories explaining satisfactorily such behavior do not yet seem to be widely available.

Interactive behavior. Suppose, as in the example here, that the system of equations contains a quantity variable, aggregated money holdings, and a price variable, the average yield on money holdings, such that the first cointegration relation describes a demand-for-money relation and the second a supply-of-money relation. In such a system, it could be of interest to ask what effect a deviation from optimal money holdings in the private sector has, not just on money holdings, but also on the interest rates offered by the banks, as well as on the other determinants of the system. For instance, in a situation with positive excess money, one would expect banks to be more inclined to lower the interest rate offered and the private sector to be inclined to get rid of excess liquidity, whereas it is more disputable whether prices or real income will tend to rise.

The general ideas expressed above will now be illustrated in terms of an empirical analysis of long-run and short-run behavior using Danish monetary data. In line with the discussion in section 2.4., the results of the empirical analysis can be interpreted as being generated by the Danish experiment. In the ideal case, they should be compared with other countries results using a similar modelling approach. For the present, such examples can be found in Ripatti (1992) for Finnish data, in Durevall and Meuller (1993) for Swedish data, in Bårdsen and Klovland (1993) for Norvegian data, in Juselius and Hargreaves (1992) and Johansen and Juselius (1993) for Australian data, and in Hendry and Mizon (1992) for UK data.

5 An Empirical Example

This section analyses the data-generating properties of a statistically well-defined VAR model. It will be demonstrated that a careful statistical analysis of the chosen model provides valuable insight about the time-series structures of the data, which can point to possible improvement in model specification. The empirical analyses below can be seen as an extension of the empirical work in Johansen and Juselius (1990) and Juselius (1993a). Only those results which are relevant to the discussion in this paper will be briefly reported.

5.1 The Choice of Observed Variables

In Johansen and Juselius (1990), a long-run money demand relation was estimated based on the basic data vector $z_t = [m_t, y_t, i_{b_t}, i_{d_t}]$ where $m_t = m_t^n - p_t$, m^n is the log of the average level of demand and time deposits in private banks, p_t is the log of the implicit price deflator of domestic demand, y_t is the log of real domestic demand, i_b is the effective yearly bond rate, and i_d is the average yearly deposit rate in private banks.

A detailed examination of the measurements reveal that essentially all the usual problems plague the data. For instance, new components have entered the aggregate, banking technology has changed, the time interval between the measurements is too broad, and so on. Referring to the discussion in section 2.2, it seems very hard to justify inference to Baumol's specific transactions demand-for-money theory.

The main reason these variables were selected is simply because they were being used by the Central Bank of Denmark as a basis for its policy analysis. In that sense, the data have been collected *not only* because of their closeness to some theoretical counterparts, but because of an interest in the variables for their own sake. This choice does not exclude the possibility that the empirical investigation will suggest other measurements which might be more useful for policy analysis. It has recently been demonstrated in LaCour (1993) using an extended sample period that a weighted average of components of different liquidity measures seems to be preferable to the money-stock variable used here.

Johansen and Juselius (1990) showed that only one cointegration relation between the four variables existed, which implied that m and y did not co-integrate by themselves, and neither did i_b and i_d. In Juselius (1993a), the implicit long-run price homogeneity assumption in Johansen and Juselius (1990) was tested and accepted using results of the statistical analysis of $I(2)$ processes. By imposing long-run price homogeneity the data were brought back to the $I(1)$ case. However, short-run price homogeneity did not seem to be present, and therefore the analysis was performed on the extended data vector $z_t = [m_t, y_t, \Delta p_t, i_{b_t}, i_{d_t}]$. For this vector, the hypothesis of linear trends in the data was rejected, and two cointegration vectors were found. The estimates showed that one of the vectors could be interpreted as a relation for money holdings, whereas the other seemed to have the properties of an incompletely specified real aggregate demand relation. A third relation which was not considered stationary, although quite close to acceptance levels, seemed to have the properties of a price-setting relation for the private banks.

This short overview illustrates one aspect of the suggested strategy worth mentioning. Contrary to the principle of "general to specific" in the general VAR model, it seems more useful to follow the principle of "specific to general" in the choice of information set. If the number of variables is initially very large, as is therefore the number of cointegrating relations, it is often quite difficult to separate feasible stationary relations from each other. The number of possible combinations is simply too large. If, instead, more information is gradually added to the analysis, it is possible to build on previous results, thereby not as easily losing track. However, just as the initial lag-specification of the VAR model should not be too large, the initial information set should not be too small to invalidate the identification of the relevant cointegrating relations.

In line with this, the information set analyzed below is extended by one variable, the loan interest rate of the private banks i_{l_t}, to examine whether it is possible to improve the empirical identification of the previously incompletely specified relations. With this extension, z_t becomes:

$$z_t = [m_t, y_t, \Delta p_t, i_{b_t}, i_{d_t}, i_{l_t}] \qquad \text{for } t = 1974{:}2, \ldots, 1987{:}3 \; .$$

In addition to the variables in z_t are the conditioning variables in D_t which, as discussed in section 3, are not modelled:

$$D'_t = [\text{s1}_t, \text{s2}_t, \text{s3}_t, \text{con}_t, \text{D74:3}_t, \text{uip83}_t]$$

where s1, s2 and s3 are orthogonalized seasonal dummies, $\text{con}_t = 1$ for all t, D74:3 is a dummy variable accounting for the effect of the transitory removal of value added tax, and uip83 is a measure of the deviation from uncovered interest-rate parity between Denmark and West Germany.[3] It becomes effective in the model from 1983 onwards to account for the effect of the abolition of capital control.

5.2 *Empirical Adequacy*

The unrestricted model (2) was estimated for z_t and D_t as given above. As a general test of the adequacy of the statistical model specification, the following residual tests were performed: the Box-Pierce residual autocorrelation test based on the estimates of the first 13 autocorrelation coefficients, the ARCH test for residual heteroskedasticity of order two, and the Jarque-Bera test for normality, based on the deviation of the third and fourth moments from the mean. The results are presented in Table 1 for the lag order $k = 2$. The mis-specification test statistics indicate that model (2) can be considered a satisfactory description of the DGP and thus the assumed "design of experiment" as defined in section 3 is acceptable.[4]

Since the requirement of a statistically well-defined model is fulfilled, it is straightforward to test hypotheses of specific interest. The outcome of the previously mentioned money-demand studies prompted the following questions for consideration later on in the empirical analysis:

Is there a stable aggregate money relation for the chosen observed variables? Is the velocity of money stationary? Is money stock endogenously or exogenously determined? Should money stock or interest rates be used as monetary instruments? Is the interest-rate differential stationary? Are interest rates exogenously or endogenously given? Does money matter for real aggregate income? Does an expansion of money stock in exccess of the real productive level in the

---

[3] In order to justify the classification of uip83 in the conditioning set D_t an assumption of strong exogeneity is needed.

[4] The calculations of the cointegration analyses of sections 5 and 6 were made using the computer package CATS in RATS (Juselius, 1991). Extensions to this package for calculating the recursive results were kindly provided by Henrik Hansen and Hans Christian Kongsted, Economics department, University of Copenhagen.

Table 1. Residual mis-specification tests of model (2)

eq.	σ_ε	$\eta_1(11)$	$\eta_2(2)$	skewness	ex. kurt.	$\eta_3(2)$
Δm	.0153	6.0	1.8	0.51	−0.21	2.32
Δy	.0159	8.4	0.6	−0.11	0.20	0.20
$\Delta^2 p$	.0056	9.1	0.1	0.42	−0.33	1.74
Δi_b	.0069	14.0	0.5	0.02	0.18	0.08
Δi_d	.0045	7.7	6.1	0.15	0.39	0.52
Δi_l	.0058	7.5	1.4	0.62	0.69	4.36

where $\eta_1(v)$ is the Box-Pierce test statistic for residual autocorrelation, $\eta_2(v)$ is the ARCH test for heteroskedastic residuals, $\eta_3(v)$ the Jarque-Bera test for normality. All test statistics are appr. distributed as χ^2 with v degrees of freedom

economy permanently increase real income, or is the final effect only an increase in the inflation rate? In asking these questions, it should be remembered that the answer can only be interpreted given the chosen information set, and not directly in terms of an underlying theoretical model. As exemplified in Juselius and Hargreaves (1992), with different choices of measurements of the selected variables, the answers are likely to be different as well.

5.3 *The Order of Integration and Cointegration*

The first step in the analysis is to determine the order of integration of the process $\{z_t|D_t\}$. This consists of testing the two hypotheses (4) and (5). The $I(2)$ reduced-rank hypothesis was strongly rejected,[5] whereas the hypothesis (4) could not be rejected, implying that the process can be considered $I(1)$. The next step is to determine the order of cointegration. Because the asymptotic distribution of the rank test statistics is not necessarily a close approximation in small samples, the choice of r is often difficult. Additional information in this respect can, however, be obtained from the recursively calculated test statistics, since test statistics corresponding to non-zero eigenvalues should grow linearly with t (see Hansen and Johansen, 1992). The graphs of the test statistics and the eigenvalues calculated recursively over the period 1983:Q2–1987:Q3 are reported in Figure 1. It appears that only the first three eigenvalues seem to grow with time, which is an indication that $r = 3$. This choice is also supported by the trace test statistics given in Table 2.

As appears from Table 2, the fourth vector v_4, though not acceptable as stationary, seems to suggest quite an interesting relation describing the spread

[5] To save space, the test results are not given here. They may be obtained from the author on request.

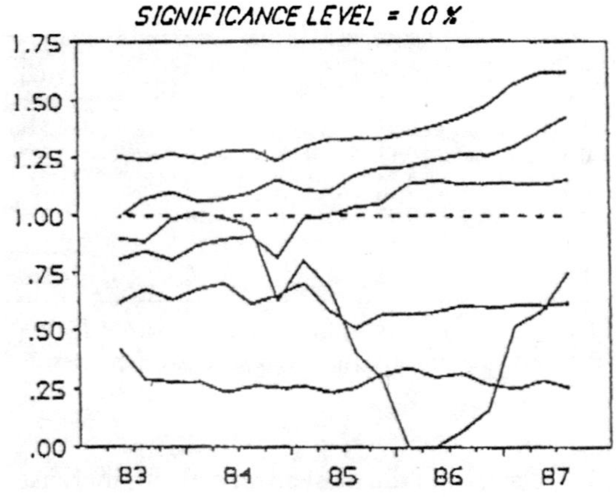

Fig. 1. The recursively calculated trace-tests

between the deposit rate and the loan rate as a negative function of excess money stock in private banks. The quite large fluctuations of the first three recursively calculated trace-tests in Figure 1 indicate that the rejection of stationarity of the fourth vector might be due to instability over time in this relationship.

5.4 *The Unrestricted Cointegration Space*

The unrestricted estimates of the three stationary eigenvectors β_i and the corresponding loadings are given in Table 2. To facilitate the interpretation of the results, test statistics for long-run exclusion and weak exogeneity are presented

Table 2. The estimated eigenvectors and the corresponding weights in the transformed model

				The eigenvalues are test statistics:					
$\hat{\lambda}_i$		.682	.572	.422	.200	.064	.038		
$Q(r)$		149.3	89.7	45.6	17.1	5.5	2.0		
				The eigenvectors:					
var.	$\hat{\beta}_1$	$\hat{\beta}_2$	$\hat{\beta}_3$	$\hat{v}_4$	eq.	$\hat{\alpha}_1$	$\hat{\alpha}_2$	$\hat{\alpha}_3$	$\hat{w}_4$
m	−.00	.01	1.00	.08	Δm	−.30	6.84	−.21	−.31
y	−.01	−.02	−.79	−.07	Δy	3.69	6.22	.13	.30
Δp	−.27	−.17	2.43	.11	$\Delta^2 p$	3.00	.80	.02	−.26
i_b	.22	−.05	15.20	.06	Δi_b	−.05	−.08	.00	−.01
i_d	1.00	−1.27	−36.24	.48	Δi_d	−.44	.01	.02	−.08
i_l	−.88	1.00	18.19	1.00	Δi_l	−.18	−.53	.02	−.12
const	.12	.02	−7.63	−.58					

Table 3. The likelihood ratio test statistics of hypotheses about the long-run structure

Long-run exclusion					Long-run weak exogeneity				
Var	$Q(\beta_1)$	$Q(\beta_2)$	$Q(\beta_3)$	Q_β	eq.	$Q(\alpha_1)$	$Q(\alpha_2)$	$Q(\alpha_3)$	Q_α
m	.33	1.77	12.29	14.39	Δm	0.99	3.86	11.89	16.74
y	1.67	7.81	9.64	19.12	Δy	1.74	4.59	4.75	11.09
Δp	10.21	14.70	16.75	41.75	$\Delta^2 p$	11.23	2.35	0.76	14.33
i_b	7.01	0.43	16.92	24.92	Δi_b	.05	.08	.39	.52
i_d	4.66	11.13	16.86	32.65	Δi_d	5.29	.00	7.58	12.87
i_l	5.81	13.50	16.35	35.67	Δi_l	.47	2.93	5.64	9.05

in Table 3 (for discussion about these tests see Juselius and Hargreaves, 1992). Since the unrestricted cointegration estimates are not necessarily interesting from an economic point of view, as discussed in section 5.2., the analysis of the unrestricted estimates should only be considered the first step in the search for an economically meaningful structure.

The first cointegration relation can be tentatively interpreted as a relation between nominal interest rates and the inflation rate,[6] according to the significant values in column $Q(\beta_I)$ that correspond to these variables. Similarly, the test statistics in column $Q(\alpha_1)$ can be used to infer that the first cointegration vector primarily affects the inflation rate and the deposit rate, whereas there does not seem to be much feedback effect to the bond and the loan interest rates. The second cointegration relation seems to be a relation between real income, the inflation rate and the two domestic interest rates, with feedback effects primarily to real income. The third relation is similar to the previously estimated long-run money relation, as discussed in Juselius (1993), with feedback effects to money stock, real income and domestic interest rates.

The joint tests of the long-run exclusion, $\beta_{i.} = 0$, $i = 1, \ldots, 6$ and weak exogeneity, $\alpha_{i.} = 0$, $i = 1, \ldots, 6$ suggest that all variables are relevant in the three-dimensional cointegration space, but that only the bond interest rate is weakly exogenous for the long-run parameters.

5.5 *The Moving-Average Representation*

As discussed in section 3, the moving-average representation (7) of the statistical model provides some complementary information about the driving forces of the system. Table 4 shows the estimates of matrix C in (7), which describes how the individual variables have been affected by the stochastic trends measured by

6 Note that the coefficients of the yearly interest rates have been multiplied by 0.25 to make them comparable with the inflation rate, which is measured as a quarterly rate.

Table 4. An estimate of the impact matrix C in the MA-representation

	$\Sigma\varepsilon_m$	$\Sigma\varepsilon_y$	$\Sigma\varepsilon_{inf}$	$\Sigma\varepsilon_{ib}$	$\Sigma\varepsilon_{id}$	$\Sigma\varepsilon_{il}$
m	.19	.13	.04	−3.93	−.11	1.52
y	.09	.55	−1.41	−.29	−1.93	1.43
Δp	−.00	−.03	.09	.06	.11	−.08
i_b	.23	.08	.04	1.11	−.62	.83
i_d	.31	.01	.36	.49	−.39	1.11
i_l	.40	.05	.39	.84	−.63	1.47

the cumulative innovations, defined by the information set $\{Z_{t-1}, D_t\}$. Note, however, that the interpretation of the common trends as given below is not invariant to changes in the information set. The estimated results can nevertheless provide useful complementary information about the process, but should not be given a structural interpretation.

The significance of the coefficients in Table 4 cannot be directly assessed, since measures of dispersion have not yet been calculated. But the logarithmic transformation of the data should guarantee that the magnitude of the coefficients is comparable. The first row indicates that the long-run component in real money stock is primarily determined by the financial trends, i.e., the development of the bond interest rate and the loan interest rate. The second row indicates that the long-run component in real income is primarily determined by the stochastic trend in the inflation rate and the two bank interest rates and, to some extent, by the long-term component of leal money stock. The inflation rate is quite close to a stationary variable, which explains the numerically small coefficients in this row. The long-run component of both the bond and the loan rates is dominated by its own stochastic trend, indicating that it is primarily exogenously given, which is consistent with the weak exogeneity results shown in Table 3. Finally, the deposit interest rate seems to be affected by the stochastic trend primarily of the loan rate, but also to some extent of the bond and inflation rates. Altogether, the estimates point to the dominant role of the financial variables as driving forces in this system, whereas the long-run component in real money stock and real income seems to play a much more modest role in this context.

6 The Identification of a Structural Economic Model

Since the statistical analysis showed that the data were non-stationary and strongly autocorrelated, an estimable economic model consistent with this information should be based on adjustment. An attempt will be made to identify a structural model that belongs to the family of multivariate error-correction models. This involves the identification of both the long-run as well as the short-run structure (Johansen and Juselius, 1993). For the purpose of the subsequent discussion, it will be useful to partition the total parameters of the structural error-correction model (16) into the long-run parameters $\lambda_l = [\beta]$ and the short-run parameters $\lambda_s = [A_0, A_1, a, \phi, \Omega]$. First, identifying restrictions will be imposed on β, and then the short-run structure will be estimated, given the estimated long-run structure.

6.1 *The Long-Run Structure*

In section 5.3, the statistical model was used to determine the order of integration of the time-series process $\{z_t|D_t\}$. Here, the properties of the statistical model will be used to analyze the time-series properties of the individual variables and combinations of them. The test results are presented in Table 5, where the hypotheses being tested are expressed as hypotheses about a restricted vector in the space spanned by the first three cointegration vectors. The likelihood ratio test statistic $Q(v)$ comparing the restricted model with the unrestricted one is approximately distributed as χ^2 with v degrees of freedom. In addition, the eigenvalue λ_r, corresponding to the restricted vector is reported to provide a measure of how strongly the restricted vector is correlated with the stationary process. The hypotheses put forward in Table 5 are classified in three groups; in the first, the stationarity of the inflation rate and each of the interest rates is

Table 5. Testing stationarity hypotheses about the cointegration space

Hypothesis	λ^r	LR statistic
H^1: $[0, 0, 1, 0, 0, 0, *]' \in Sp(\beta)$	.214	Q(3) = 26.01
H^2: $[0, 0, 0, 1, 0, 0, *]' \in Sp(\beta)$	.085	Q(3) = 24.48
H^3: $[0, 0, 0, 0, 1, 0, *]' \in Sp(\beta)$	.084	Q(2) = 24.19
H^4: $[0, 0, 0, 0, 0, 1, *]' \in Sp(\beta)$	.074	Q(3) = 25.19
H^5: $[1, -1, 0, 0, 0, 0, *]' \in Sp(\beta)$	.070	Q(3) = 24.88
H^6: $[0, 0, 1, -1, 0, 0, *]' \in Sp(\beta)$	.322	Q(3) = 21.99
H^7: $[0, 0, 1, 0, -1, 0, *]' \in Sp(\beta)$	.318	Q(3) = 22.26
H^8: $[0, 0, 1, 0, 0, -1, *]' \in Sp(\beta)$	.313	Q(3) = 22.40
H^9: $[0, 0, 0, 1, -1, 0, *]' \in Sp(\beta)$	.156	Q(3) = 20.35
H^{10}: $[0, 0, 0, 1, 0, -1, *]' \in Sp(\beta)$	.281	Q(3) = 14.74
H^{11}: $[0, 0, 0, 0, 1, -1, *]' \in Sp(\beta)$	.122	Q(3) = 25.53
H^{12}: $[0, 0, 1, -.78, 0, 0, *]' \in Sp(\beta)$	.364	Q(2) = 21.72
H^{13}: $[0, 0, 1, 0, -1.3, 0, *]' \in Sp(\beta)$	.321	Q(2) = 21.27
H^{14}: $[0, 0, 1, 0, 0, -.80, *]' \in Sp(\beta)$	.325	Q(2) = 22.70
H^{15}: $[0, 0, 0, 1, -2.1, 0, *]' \in Sp(\beta)$	.269	Q(2) = 12.48
H^{16}: $[0, 0, 0, -.76, 0, 1, *]' \in Sp(\beta)$	.340	Q(2) = 10.98
H^{17}: $[0, 0, 0, 0, 1, -.60, *]' \in Sp(\beta)$	.380	Q(2) = 14.35

tested; in the second, the stationarity of velocity and of real interest rates, as given by the nominal interest rate minus the actual inflation rate, as well as all combinations of interest-rate differentials, is tested; finally, in the third group, hypotheses regarding whether a freely estimated combination of each interest rate and inflation rate, or a combination of two interest rates, cointegrate, are tested and the estimated coefficients are given in the table. All stationarity hypotheses are rejected at the 0.5% level. This result can be understood by noting that in the present sample, the deposit and the loan rates were more controlled by the monetary authorities than the bond rate. In the more recent period the convergence between the interest rates is in fact much more pronounced than in the whole sample. For this paper, the results imply that combinations of at least three variables are needed to find cointegration.

The unrestricted coefficients β_{ij} and α_{ij} are uniquely defined up to a non-singular $r \times r$ transformation matrix. This means that, in general, $r - 1$ exactly identifying restrictions, plus a normalizing coefficient on each cointegration vector, can be imposed without changing the likelihood function, whereas further restrictions involve testing. Here the following identifying restrictions were imposed on the cointegration space β:

$$H^{18}\colon \beta = \{H_1\psi_1, H_2\psi_2, H_3\psi_3\} \tag{9}$$

where

$$H_1 = \begin{bmatrix} 1 & 0 & 0 \\ -1 & 0 & 0 \\ 0 & 0 & 0 \\ 0 & 1 & 0 \\ 0 & -1 & 0 \\ 0 & 0 & 0 \\ 0 & 0 & 1 \end{bmatrix}, \quad H_2 = \begin{bmatrix} 0 & 0 & 0 & 0 \\ 1 & 0 & 0 & 0 \\ 0 & 1 & 0 & 0 \\ 0 & 0 & 0 & 0 \\ 0 & 0 & 1 & 0 \\ 0 & 0 & -1 & 0 \\ 0 & 0 & 0 & 1 \end{bmatrix} \quad \text{and}$$

$$H_3 = \begin{bmatrix} 0 & 0 & 0 \\ 0 & 0 & 0 \\ 0 & 0 & 0 \\ 1 & 0 & 0 \\ 0 & 1 & 0 \\ 0 & -1 & 0 \\ 0 & 0 & 1 \end{bmatrix}$$

The corresponding restricted estimates are given in Table 6. Two restrictions were imposed on the first two vectors and one on the third, which gives 5 degrees of freedom in the LR test. The test statistics were 3.35 and hypothesis (9) was clearly acceptable. The freely estimated coefficients are significant, implying empirical identification in the sense defined in Johansen and Juselius (1993). Therefore, only the question of economic identification remains, i.e., whether the estimated coefficients are plausible from an economic point of view.

The first relation has the property of a long-run money relation, for which the opportunity cost of holding money is primarily measured by the interest-rate differential between the bond and the deposit rates. The second relation describes a very strong negative association between real income and the inflation rate, and the spread of the two domestic bank rates. The third relation indicates the spread between domestically determined deposit and loan rates as a function of the internationally determined bond rate. Both the signs and the magnitudes of the estimated coefficients seem plausible.

But before the estimated relations can qualify as candidates for a meaningful long-run structure, some sort of constancy in parameters has to be demonstrated. Figure 2 records the graphs of the recursively estimated coefficients of the long-run structure, calculated as conditional on the full sample estimates of the short-run structure (see Johansen, 1993).[7] For the purpose of this paper, the results are acceptable, and attention will now turn to the estimation of the short-run structure conditional on the estimated long-run structure.

Table 6. A structural representation of the cointegration space

The eigenvectors and the adjustment coefficients:							
var.	$\hat{\beta}_1$	$\hat{\beta}_2$	$\hat{\beta}_3$	eq.	$\hat{\alpha}_1$	$\hat{\alpha}_2$	$\hat{\alpha}_3$
m	1.0	0.0	0.0	Δm	−.11	−.05	−4.45
y	−1.0	1.0	0.0	Δy	.16	−.11	−3.80
Δp	0.0	16.1(1.1)	0.0	$\Delta^2 p$	.02	−.06	1.92
i_b	22.5(1.6)	0.0	0.30(.02)	Δi_b	.00	.00	−.08
i_d	−22.5	8.5(3.1)	1.0	Δi_d	.02	.01	−.74
i_l	0.0	−8.5	−1.0	Δi_l	.01	.01	.00
Const.	−6.2	−6.1	.0				

6.2 The Short-Run Structure

Because $\hat{\beta}_i' z_t$ ($\approx \beta_i' z_t$) is stationary, (3) can be formulated in terms of stationary variables. This has the advantage that standard distributional results apply, and the interpretation of the estimated coefficients becomes easier. Therefore, the question whether hypothetical restrictions on the short-run coefficient matrices A_0, A_1, a and Ω are identifying or not can be investigated using the conventional rank and other condition. However, in order to keep the length of this paper within reasonable limits, the full exercise of short-run identification[7] as discussed in Johansen and Juselius (1993) will not be carried out. Instead, the technically less demanding causal chain procedure will be used to identify the

[7] This includes testing for parameter stability as an essential part of the analysis.

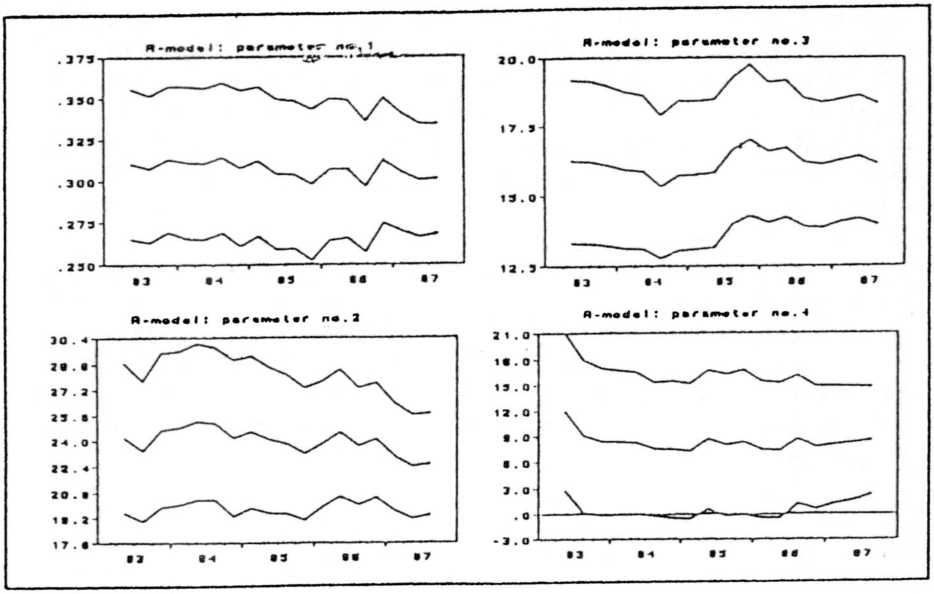

Fig. 2. Recursively calculated estimates of the freely estimated parameters in β

short-run structure. In this case, the empirical model can be represented as a recursive system:

$$\Delta z_{1t} = E(\Delta z_{1t} | \Delta z_{2t}, \ldots, \Delta z_{pt}, \Delta z_{t-1}, \beta' z_{t-1}) + u_{1t}$$

$$\Delta z_{2t} = E(\Delta z_{2t} | \Delta z_{3t}, \ldots, \Delta z_{pt}, \Delta z_{t-1}, \beta' z_{t-1}) + u_{2t}$$

$$\vdots$$

$$\Delta z_{pt} = E(\Delta z_{pt} | \Delta z_{t-1}, \beta' z_{t-1}) + u_{pt}$$

The causal chain model is just identified because the off-diagonal elements of the covariance matrix Ω and the lower triangular elements of A_0 are restricted to zero. One drawback of the triangular representation is the arbitrariness associated with the choice of ordering. Because of the difficulty of suggesting one choice criterion that *a priori* can be asşumed to be more objective than another, the ordering will be based on the results of the moving-average analysis and the long-run weak exogeneity tests discussed above.

From Table 3, it appears that the bond rate can be considered weakly exogenous in this system. Besides, the loan rate could almost be accepted as weakly exogenous. Therefore, the bond rate has been placed at the bottom of the of the chain, followed by the loan rate. Table 4 indicates that the long-run component in real money stock seems to be generated primarily by the stochastic trends of the other determinants in the system. Almost the same can be said about real domestic income. This can be taken as an indication that real money stock should be on the top of the causal chain, followed by real income. The third place is given to the deposit rate, since it seems to be affected by the stochastic trends of the loan rate, as well as the inflation rate and the bond rate. Table 3 indicates that there appear to be feedback effects from the loan rate and the bond rate to the inflation rate. These considerations taken together resulted in the following causal ordering:

$$\Delta i_{b_t} \rightarrow \Delta i_{l_t} \rightarrow \Delta^2 p_t \rightarrow \Delta i_{d_t} \rightarrow \Delta y_t \rightarrow \Delta m_t$$

and the corresponding triangular system of error-correction equations:

$$A_0 \Delta z_t = A_1 \Delta z_{t-1} + a\hat{\beta}' z_{t-1} + \phi D_t + u_t \qquad (10)$$

where A_0 is an upper triangular matrix for $z_t = [m, y, i_d, \Delta p, i_l, i_b]$ and $\beta' z = [\hat{\beta}_1' z, \hat{\beta}_2' z, \hat{\beta}_3' z,]$ is defined by the estimated eigenvectors of the identified long-run structure given in Table 6.

The parameter estimates of the short-run structure chosen are given in Table 7. To increase readability, insignificant coefficients have been restricted to zero.[8] Since the estimates of the short-run structure are tentative in the sense that they have not been subject to sensitivity analysis, stability tests and more demanding identification procedures, the individual estimates will not be commented upon in great detail. Instead, three general results that appear interesting and robust will be discussed.

First of all, it appears that the short-run adjustment to the long-run steady-states are of prime importance for understanding the actual changes of the

Table 7. The estimates of the short-run structure represented as a casual chain system: $A_0 \Delta z_t + A_1 \Delta z_{t-1} + a\hat{\beta}' z_{t-1} + \phi D_t + u_t = 0$

$$\begin{bmatrix} -1 & 0 & 0 & -1.22 & 0 & -1.41 \\ & -1 & 0 & -1.77 & 0 & 0 \\ & & -1 & .03 & .68 & 0 \\ & & & -1 & 2.02 & 0 \\ & & & & -1 & 0 \\ & & & & & -1 \end{bmatrix} \begin{bmatrix} \Delta m_t \\ \Delta y_t \\ \Delta i_{d_t} \\ \Delta^2 p_t \\ \Delta i_{l_t} \\ \Delta i_{b_t} \end{bmatrix} + \begin{bmatrix} 0 & 0 & 0 & 0 & 0 & 0 \\ .55 & -.21 & .66 & 0 & 0 & 0 \\ -.13 & 0 & 0 & 0 & -.13 & 0 \\ 0 & 0 & 0 & 0 & 0 & 0 \\ .04 & 0 & .27 & 0 & 0 & .28 \\ 0 & 0 & 0 & 0 & 0 & .29 \end{bmatrix} \begin{bmatrix} \Delta m_{t-1} \\ \Delta y_{t-1} \\ \Delta i_{d_{t-1}} \\ \Delta^2 p_{t-1} \\ \Delta i_{l_{t-1}} \\ \Delta i_{b_{t-1}} \end{bmatrix}$$

$$+ \begin{bmatrix} .49 & .04 \\ -.72 & .03 \\ .04 & .002 \\ -.22 & -.03 \\ 0 & 0 \\ -.07 & 0 \end{bmatrix} \begin{bmatrix} \text{UIP83}_{t-1} \\ \text{D75.4}_t \end{bmatrix} + \begin{bmatrix} -.12 & -.11 & 0 \\ .16 & -.17 & 0 \\ .007 & .003 & -.70 \\ 0 & -.08 & 1.62 \\ .008 & .013 & 0 \\ 0 & 0 & 0 \end{bmatrix} \begin{bmatrix} \beta_1' z_{t-1} \\ \beta_2' z_{t-1} \\ \beta_3' z_{t-1} \end{bmatrix}$$

$\hat{\beta}_1' z = m - y + 22.5(i_b - i_d) - 6.18$ $\qquad$ $\hat{\beta}_2' z = y + 16.1\Delta p + 8.5(i_d - i_l) - 6.14$

$\hat{\beta}_3' = i_d - i_l + .30 i_b + .007$

---

8 It should be noted, however, that this means that the identifying restrictions of the off-diagonal elements of Ω are now only approximately valid.

determinants of the equation system. Interpreting $\hat{\beta}_1' z_{t-1}$ as measuring excess money and $\hat{\beta}_2' z_{t-1}$ as excess aggregate demand, it can be noticed that both of them seem to be important determinants to changes in real money stock and real domestic demand. It is interesting to note that excess money primarily affects money holdings (the error-correction effect), but also real domestic demand and, to some extent, the deposit and loan rates, but has no effect on the inflation or the bond rates. This is consistent with the empirical results in Juselius (1992) which, based on a much larger information set, showed that monetary shocks can only explain a very small part of inflation-rate behavior in the Danish economy. The small, but significant, coefficients of excess money and excess aggregate demand in the interest-rate equations can be understood since the interest-rate differentials $i_b - i_d$ and $i_d - i_1$ enter the long-run relations with large coefficients. Allowing for the combined effect of the three cointegration relations shows that the deposit rate primarily follows the bond rate, whereas the loan rate primarily follows the inflation rate and the bond rate. The third cointegration relation $\hat{\beta}_3' z_{t-1}$ measures a relation between the domestic bank rate and the bond rate. It is interesting to note that the inflation rate seems to increase when the yield on money and bonds is above their steady-state value.

Secondly, the results show that the two "institutional" variables are very important as explanatory variables. The lifting of capital control at the beginning of 1983 clearly had an impact on all variables except the loan rate, whereas the transitory removal of value added tax in 1975:Q4 had a transitory effect on money stock, domestic demand, the deposit rate and price inflation (almost by definition). This is an illustration of the importance of accounting for important institutional or political interventions which have short-run additive effects on the behavior of the process which cannot be explained directly by the information set $\{Z_{t-1}\}$.

Thirdly, estimates of the short-run adjustment to current and lagged changes of the process itself do not seem to be of crucial importance, though clearly each equation has its own interesting pattern. In this context, it is clear that lagged changes in real money stock seem to affect real domestic demand, but not directly the inflation rate.

To summarize, the short-run estimates seem quite reasonable in the sense that essentially all signs correspond to the expected ones, and the order of magnitude of the coefficients is plausible, which, all in all, must be considered quite a good result.

6.3 Summary Results

At the end of section 5.2., several questions of empirical interest were formulated. As a summary of the empirical analysis, an attempt will be made to provide an answer to each of them. The recursive graphs in section 6.1 seem to lead to the conclusion that the estimated long-run money relation is quite stable. However, the velocity of money was not found to be stationary by itself; the opportunity cost of holding money has to be added to the relation to obtain stationarity. Money stock as defined in this paper is clearly not exogenously determined, the implications being that it is not an optimal choice as a monetary policy instrument. This conclusion is also supported by the modest role money seems to play as a determinant of the inflation rate. The only variable that is found to be exogenously given is the bond rate. It is, however, doubtful whether the central bank can exert any significant control on the level of this variable. Since the deposit rate and the loan rate, which in principle might be easier to control, are strongly dependent on the bond rate, the scope for using interest rates as monetary instruments seems limited indeed. The results presented in Table 7 suggest that money matters for real aggregate income, defined as aggregate domestic demand, both in the long run and the short run. However, a different definition of real income might very well give a different answer. The results described in section 6.2. seem to indicate that the inflation rate is very modestly, if at all, influenced by monetary expansions. Instead, it is rather strongly influenced by interest rates, a finding that is supported by the empirical results in Juselius (1993a and 1993b).

7 Discussion

As a response to Summers' highly critical views on macroeconomic modelling this paper discusses possible shortcomings in empirical work and suggests a structural VAR procedure in which the choice of information set plays a crucial role. The statistical analysis of the VAR model was shown to facilitate distinction between and analysis of different aspects of reality such as: (i) short- and long-run behavior, (ii) actual behavior and intentions, (iii) feedback behavior and exogenous behavior, (iv) steady-state relations and common trends, (v) different degrees of permanence in economic behavior. One important aspect in this respect is that the investigation usually starts with a certain number of prior hypotheses and ends with some associated results. In addition, it produces a number of new results which were not thought of at the beginning of the analysis. These new results can then be the starting hypotheses of the next analysis, based on a new data set, for instance, from another country. By applying the same methodological approach to different data sets, it should be possible to make a comparison of similarities and dissimilarities between different countries/regions, and most importantly to investigate whether the dissimilarities can be understood in terms of institutional differences. This is probably the closest one can come to the ideal of a controlled experiment in macroeconomics. However, to be successful, each country's data has to be seriously analyzed by accounting for institutional and country-specific features, and not, as is often done, by forcing one simplified model onto several data sets as if just one data-generating process existed for all countries, originating from one theoretical explanation.

Within the modelling approach discussed here, the success of an empirical investigation should be judged by the stability of the estimated parameters, by the interpretability of its short- and long-run structure, as well as by the interpretability of the pulling forces of the long-run steady-state relations and the pushing forces of the driving trends. To the extent that we succeed in understanding all these aspects of the empirical problem, I believe, in Haavelmos' words, "that we become masters of reality – by passive agreement."

The purpose of the empirical example was to illustrate that the time-series properties of the data can be used to structure the observed variation, such that different aspects of the empirical problem can be highlighted. In the example discussed here, we have focused on the statistical aspects, whereas the economic aspects have been given a secondary role. It is worth mentioning that the former can be highly sample-dependent and, therefore, care should be taken when associating the statistical result with an economic interpretation.

In the ideal case, the interplay between theory and stylized facts should lead to a progression of analyses, where at each stage a better understanding of the different aspects of the empirical problem can be achieved.

References

Anderson TW (1991) Trygve Haavelmo and the simultaneous equation models. Scandinavian Journal of Statistics

Baba Y, Hendry DF, Starr RM (1992) The demand for M1 in the USA, 1960–1988. Review of Economic Studies 59:1, 25–61

Baumol J (1952) The transactions demand for cash: An inventory theoretic approach. Quarterly Journal of Economics 66:545–556

Brodin PA, Nymoen R (1991) Wealth effects and exogeneity: The norwegian consumption function 1966 (1)–1989 (4). Oxford Bulletin of Economics and Statistics 54, 3:431–454

Bårdsen G (1992) Dynamic modelling of the demand for narrow money in Norway. Journal of Policy Modelling 14:363–393

Bårdsen G, Klovland JT (1983) Finding a nominal indicator: The stability of cointegration between money, credit, and income in Norway. Discussion Paper, Norwegian School of Economics and Business Administration

Durevall D, Meuller L (1993) Money demand and transmission effects in Sweden. Discussion Paper, Department of Economics, University of Gothenburg

Engle RF, Granger CWJ (1987) Cointegration and error correction: Representation, estimation and testing. Econometrica 55:251–276

Ericsson NR, Campos J, Tran H-A (1990) PC-GIVE and David Hendry's econometric methodology. Revista de Econometria 10, 1:7–117

Ericsson NR, Hendry DF (1989) Encompassing and rational expectations: How sequential corroboration can imply refutation. International Finance Discussion Paper No 354, Board of Governors of the Federal Reserve System, Washington D.C

Granger C. (1991) Developments in the nonlinear analysis of economic series. Scandinavian Journal of Economics 93, 2:129–148

Haavelmo T (1944) The probability approach in econometrics. Econometrica 12 (supplement): 1–118

Hansen H, Johansen S (1993) Recursive estimation in cointegrated Var-models. Discussion Paper, Institute of Mathematical Statistics, University of Copenhagen

Hendry DF (1979) Predictive failure and econometric modelling in macroeconomics: The Transactions Demand for Money, Chapter 9. In: Ormerod P (ed.) Modelling the Economy, London, Heinemann Education Books 217–242

Hendry DF (1983) Econometric modelling: The 'consumption function' in retrospect. Scottish Journal of Political Economy 30, 3:193–220

Hendry DF (1987) Econometric methodology: A personal perspective. Ch. 10 in Advances in Econometrics (ed) T Bewley (Econometric Society Fifth World Congress)

Hendry DF (1988a) The encompassing implications of feedback versus feedforward mechanisms in econometrics. Oxford Economic Papers 40:132–149

Hendry DF, Mizon GE (1992) Evaluating econometric models by encompassing the VAR. In Models, Methods and Applications of Econometrics (Phillips PC Ed) Basil Blackwell

Hendry DF, Richard J-F (1983) The econometric analysis of economic time series (with discussion). International Statistical Review 51:111–163

Hendry DF, Spanos A, Ericsson NR (1989) The contributions to econometric in trygve haavelmo's: the probability approach in econometrics. Socialøkonomen 43, 11:12–17

Johansen S (1988) Statistical analysis of cointegration vectors. Journal of Economic Dynamics and Control 12:231–254

Johansen S (1991) Estimation and hypothesis testing of cointegration vectors in Gaussian vector autoregressive models. Econometrica 59:1551–1580

Johansen S (1993) Identifying restrictions in linear equations. Forthcoming in the Journal of Econometrics

Johansen S, Juselius K (1990) Maximum likelihood estimation and inference on cointegration – with applications to the demand for money. Oxford Bulletin of Economics and Statistics 52, 2:169–210

Johansen S, Juselius K (1992) Structural tests in a multivariate cointegration analysis of the PPP and UIP for UK. Journal of Econometrics 53:211–244

Johansen S, Juselius K (1993) Identification of the long-run and the short-run structure. Forthcoming in the Journal of Econometrics

Juselius K (1991) CATS in RATS. A manual to Cointegration Analysis. Institute of Economics, University of Copenhagen

Juselius K (1992) Domestic and foreign effects on prices in an open economy. Journal of Policy Modeling

Juselius K (1993a) On the duality between long-run relations and common trends in the $I(1)$ versus the $I(2)$ model. An Application to Aggregate Money holdings. Forthcoming in Econometric Reviews

Juselius K (1993b) Do the purchasing power parity and the uncovered interest rate parity hold in the long run? – An example of likelihood inference in a multivariate time-series model. Forthcoming in the Journal of Econometrics

Juselius K, Hargreaves C (1992) Long-run relations in Australian monetary data. In: Hargreaves (ed) Modelling the Long Run. Edward Elgar

Kongsted HC (1993) Exogeneity and long-run parameter constancy in a cointegrated VAR model of manufactured exports. Discussion Paper, University of Copenhagen

LaCour L (1993) Divisia monetary aggregates for Denmark: Theory, construction and empirical performance. PhD. thesis, Economics Department, University of Copenhagen

Mellander E, Vredin A, Warne A (1993) Stochastic trends and economic fluctuations in small open economies. Journal of Applied Econometrics 7:369–394
Ripatti A (1992) Econometric modelling of the demand for money in Finland. Licenciate thesis, University of Helsinki
Stock JH, Watson MW (1988) Testing for common trends. Journal of the American Statistical Association 83:1097–1107
Summers LH (1991) The scientific illusion in empirical macroeconomics. Scandinavian Journal of Economics 93, 2:129–148

Inference in Expectations Models of the Term Structure: A Non-parametric Approach

BRYAN CAMPBELL

Department of Economics, Concordia University,
1455 De Maisonneuve Blvd., Montreal Quebec H3G 1M8, Canada

JOHN W. GALBRAITH[1]

Department of Economics, McGill University,
855 Sherbrooke St. W., Montreal Quebec H3A 2T7, Canada

Abstract: Recent research has examined apparent deviations from the expectations theory of the term structure detectable in regression tests, which may be interpreted as efficiency tests. Efficiency is rejected in many studies. Inference is complicated, however, by the non-normality of regression residuals, invalidating standard parametric test procedures. The present paper examines these rejections using robust diagnostic methods and non-parametric tests. We find some evidence against the expectations theory of the term structure in U.S. data, but not in Canadian. We also investigate the possible explanation of a link between forecast error and the yield spread through models of time-variation in the liquidity premium.

JEL Classification System-Numbers: E43, C14

1 Introduction

The expectations theory of the term structure of interest rates states that differences in yields at different maturities – the yield curve – can be explained by agents' expectations about future interest rates. Long-term rates are set to equal the expected return from a series of short-term bonds, plus a premium for risk or liquidity (see, for example Cox, Ingersoll and Ross, 1981; Shiller, Campbell and Schoenholtz, 1983). Promising as this theory seemed, the results of empirical tests have typically not been consistent with the strict form of the theory, in which the risk premium is constant (for example, Mankiw and Summers, 1984; Mankiw, 1986).

As Mankiw and Miron (1986) note, a number of economic explanations have been offered, most of which seem most plausible as explanations of anomalies in the relationship between yields on very long and very short bonds. In particu-

[1] Campbell acknowledges the financial support of Concordia University's FRPD; Galbraith thanks *Fonds* FCAR and SSHRC for financial support. Both authors thank Jean-Marie Dufour and an anonymous referee for valuable comments on earlier versions of the paper.

lar, Modigliani and Sutch (1966) suggested that different classes of investor prefer different maturities, and that they must be encouraged to hold other maturities through higher holding yields. Cox, Ingersoll and Ross (1981) modified the hypothesis to make the preferences for different maturities dependent upon differing degrees of risk aversion. By examining three- and six-month yields, however, we hope to have abstracted from any such effects; the Modigliani and Sutch argument suggests that two short maturities such as these would not attract substantially dlfferent types of investor.

Empirical evidence against the expectations theory persists even in this relationship between the yields on otherwise-identical three- and six-month bonds. Shiller *et al.* (1983) and Mankiw and Summers (1984), for example, find strong evidence against the expectations theory (augmented with a strict form of the rational expectations hypothesis to describe market forecasts); Mankiw and Miron (1986) find similar results, albeit with limited support (although still rejecting in formal tests) for the theory on earlier data sets.

These tests rely, however, on parametric inference based on the normal distribution for equation errors, which we find to be invalid. In the present paper, we re-examine this time-series evidence, using statistical techniques appropriate to the analysis of relationships with errors having an unknown distribution. We ask whether the rejections of the strict form of the expectations theory can be attributed to outliers in the data, and whether the rejections appear in non-parametric tests which are robust to the non-normality of errors. As by-products of this analysis, we find more precise estimates of the size of the liquidity premium (if constant) than appear in the existing literature.

The next section of the paper introduces the notation, hypotheses, data and standard parametric regression results, together with some mis-specification testing appropriate to these models. Section 3 uses diagnostics robust to non-normality and the presence of large outliers to investigate the possibility that the standard results are affected by the failure of distributional assumptions underlying the regression model. In section 4 we apply traditional non-parametric tests based on signed ranks, as well as a permutation *t*-test using bounds given by Dufour and Hallin (1992), which require no assumptions about the form of the distribution of the underlying errors. We find some evidence against the expectations theory of the term structure in U.S. data, but not in Canadian. Section 5 takes up the issue of a time-varying risk premium by modelling the time variability and investigating its effect on regression estimates. The sixth and final section offers some conclusions.

2 Hypotheses and Data

The expectations theory of the term structure states that a two-period yield will be equal to the sum of the current one-period yield and the expected one-period yield in the next period, plus a premium for risk and reduced liquidity. We will focus entirely on a period of three months; letting r_t^3 and r_t^6 be the yields on three- and six-month bonds sold at time t, we have the linear approximation[2]

$$r_t^6 = \theta + \tfrac{1}{2}r_t^3 + \tfrac{1}{2}\hat{r}_{t+1:t}^3 . \tag{1}$$

where θ is the risk and liquidity premium (taken as constant by the strict form of the theory), and $\hat{r}_{t+1:t}^3$ is the market forecast at time t of r_{t+1}^3. The weights of 1/2 on each of the left-hand side variables reflect the fact that we are considering data expressed as annual yields. If r_{t+1}^3 were known, r_t^6 would simply be equal to the average yield over the sub-periods, plus a liquidity premium.

As a test of the expectations theory, most investigators relax (1) to write

$$r_t^6 = \theta + \beta_1 r_t^3 + \beta_2 \hat{r}_{t+1:t}^3 , \tag{2}$$

so that the expectations theory is represented by the hypothesis H_0: $(\theta, \beta_1, \beta_2) = (\theta, 1/2, 1/2)$. Next, if we let ε_{t+1} be the forecast error,

$$r_{t+1}^3 = \hat{r}_{t+1:t}^3 + \varepsilon_{t+1} ; \tag{3}$$

substituting into (2) from (3) and re-arranging gives

$$(r_{t+1}^3 - r_t^6) = -\theta\beta_2^{-1} - \beta_1\beta_2^{-1}r_t^3 + (1-\beta_2)\beta_2^{-1}r_t^6 + \varepsilon_{t+1} \tag{4a}$$

$$\equiv \gamma_0 + \gamma_1 r_t^3 + \gamma_2 r_t^6 + \varepsilon_{t+1} . \tag{4b}$$

Because $\hat{r}_{t+1:t}^3$ is not observed, most empirical investigators (Campbell *et al.*, Mankiw and Summers, Mankiw and Miron) impose the simplest form of rational expectations, whereby ε_{t+1} is orthogonal to all information observable at t. Normality of this forecast error is typically assumed for finite-sample hypothesis testing.

The hypothesis H_0 given above comprises two linear restrictions, which could also be written, for example, as H_0: $\{\gamma_1 = -\gamma_2, \gamma_1 = -1\}$.[3] Mankiw and Summers's (1984) formulation can now be seen as a special case of (4a) or (4b), wherein the first restriction ($\beta_1 + \beta_2 = 1$ in (4a), or $\gamma_1 + \gamma_2 = 0$ in (4b)) alone is imposed, yielding a model with a constant and one other explanatory variable:

$$(r_{t+1}^3 - r_t^6) = -\theta(1-\lambda)^{-1} + \lambda(1-\lambda)^{-1}(r_t^6 - r_t^3) + \varepsilon_{t+1} . \tag{5}$$

We have set $\lambda = \beta_1$ and $(1-\lambda) = \beta_2$ (both equal to 1/2 under H_0) so that this formulation implies

$$r_t^6 = \theta + \lambda r_t^3 + (1-\lambda)\hat{r}_{t+1:t}^3 . \tag{6}$$

---

[2] See Cox *et al.* (1981) for a precise treatment of the implications of the theory. Equation (1) embodies a linearizatlon which was checked on the data used below and found to have had little effect.

[3] We write the restrictions in this form because the first of these is not at odds with most of our samples; in the form $\gamma_1 = -1$, $\gamma_2 = 1$, each restriction would be rejected.

We may also re-write this model in the form appropriate to an efficiency test. Subtracting $r_t^6 - r_t^3$ from both sides,

$$(r_{t+1}^3 - 2r_t^6 + r_t^3) = -\theta(1-\lambda)^{-1} + [\lambda(1-\lambda)^{-1} - 1](r_t^6 - r_t^3) + \varepsilon_{t+1} \tag{7a}$$

$$\equiv \delta_0 + \delta_1(r_t^6 - r_t^3) + \varepsilon_{t+1}\,. \tag{7b}$$

Finally note that under H_0, re-arranging (1) gives the implied forecast

$$\hat{r}_{t+1:t}^3 = 2r_t^6 - 2\theta - r_t^3\,,$$

and the expectational error $r_{t+1}^3 - \hat{r}_{t+1:t}^3$ can be written as

$$r_{t+1}^3 - 2r_t^6 + 2\theta + r_t^3\,,$$

so that under H_0 the regressand in (7) is the forecast error, up to a (constant) risk/liquidity premium, and $\delta_1 = 0$.

Ordinary least-squares estimates of the model (4) or the more restricted models (5) or (7) are sufficient to display the apparent departure from the strict expectations theory which has been observed in a number of data sets. We report results on both U.S. and Canadian data. The models (5) and (7) are equivalent, being linear transformations of one another; we use (7) because of the convenient interpretation just given.

The data sets consist of monthly observations on 3- and 6- month Treasury Bill rates, expressed as annual yields. Because the models describe relationships between interest rates at different periods, where each period is three months long, the monthly data are treated as three subsets of observations taken at three-month intervals. Briefly, the monthly data are separated into three distinct samples of quarterly data by choosing the ith month (i = 1, 2, 3) in each quarter as representing one sample. We label these three sub-samples as S_1, S_2 and S_3 respectively, for both the U.S. and Canadian full samples; the samples extend from 1960:2 to 1989:4.[4] If the sample were not divided in this way, then the period covered by r_t^3 and r_{t+1}^3 would not be the same as that covered by r_t^6, as required by the relationships above. As well, our procedure generates these quarterly samples such that under the null the disturbance terms are not serially correlated.

It is clear from Table 1 that these *OLS* estimates and associated tests on δ_1 typically reject (the exception is the first Canadian sample) the strict form of the expectations theory, even at these short maturities. The restriction that $\gamma_1 = -\gamma_2$ in (4b) is typically not rejected, and we will use the model (7b) hereafter. Recursive estimates of the parameter δ_1 (not reproduced in this version) indicate the evolution of the parameter across the sample.[5] It is interesting to record that the three U.S. samples are quite similar, with zero outside the two-standard-

[4] Data sources: Canadian, Bank of Canada Review, selected volumes, series B14007, B14008; U.S., OECD *International Financial Statistics.*

[5] Graphs of the recursive parameter estimates on each of the six samples, as well as plots of the data, are available from the authors.

Table 1a. Canadian data: *OLS* estimates of simple term-structure models. $T = 119$, Samples: 1960:2 to 1989:4

Unrestricted Model			
		Data set	
Model and parameters	S_1	S_2	S_3
γ_0 (std err) in (4b)	0.05 (0.27)	0.16 (0.28)	0.43 (0.28)
γ_1 in (4b)	−0.64 (0.46)	0.10 (0.42)	0.61 (0.43)
γ_2 in (4b)	0.61 (0.46)	−0.13 (0.43)	−0.67 (0.43)
$\Sigma\hat{\varepsilon}_t^2$	156.839	157.294	182.890
Restricted Model			
		Data set	
Model and parameters	S_1	S_2	S_3
δ_0 (std err) in (7b)	−0.22 (0.13)	−0.09 (0.12)	−0.01 (0.13)
δ_1 in (7b)	−0.30 (0.45)	−1.01 (0.41)	−1.52 (0.43)
$\Sigma\hat{\varepsilon}_t^2$	158.542	158.665	187.254
(Diagnostics)			
Autocorrelation (LM: χ_4^2)	5.32	2.16	23.29
Functional form (RESET: χ_1^2)	2.56	0.06	0.12
Residual normality (Jarque-Bera: χ_2^2)	46.41	113.51	250.24
Heteroskedasticity (LM: χ_1^2)	0.57	2.32	1.63
Test of H_0: $\{\gamma_1 = -1, \gamma_2 = -\gamma_1\}$ on model (4b) ($F_{2,116}$)	0.85	3.53	7.80
Test of restriction (4b) to (7b) ($F_{1,116}$)	1.26	1.01	2.77

error bands for δ_1 at most points in all three. By contrast, zero lies within the bands throughout the first Canadian sample, and for most of the other two; only on the third is $\delta_1 = 0$ consistently rejected after a certain point. Note, also, from Table 1, that a zero risk/liquidity premium is not rejected on any of the six samples.

These parametric t-tests require normality of the errors in finite samples, which is overwhelmingly rejected on all samples. Moreover, a visual examination of the data suggests the possibility that the apparent negative relation between the forecast error and the spread may be accounted for by a few influential outliers, particularly those with large spread and large negative forecast error or large negative spread and large positive forecast error. Upon closer inspection, therefore, these standard results no longer appear compelling.

In the following section, we pursue this suggestion and, by using several techniques to detect influential sample points, we address first the possibility that influential outliers account for the negative results previously derived.

Table 1b. U.S. data: *OLS* estimates of simple term-structure models. $T = 119$, Samples: 1960:2 to 1989:4

Unrestricted Model			
		Data set	
Model and parameters	S_1	S_2	S_3
γ_0 (std err) in (4b)	0.35 (0.28)	0.38 (0.29)	0.59 (0.34)
γ_1 in (4b)	0.70 (0.48)	0.63 (0.43)	0.53 (0.50)
γ_2 in (4b)	−0.76 (0.49)	−0.69 (0.44)	−0.62 (0.52)
$\Sigma\hat{\varepsilon}_t^2$	119.330	135.154	196.049
Restricted Model			
		Data set	
Model and parameters	S_1	S_2	S_3
δ_0 (std err) in (7b)	−0.07 (0.12)	−0.07 (0.13)	−0.10 (0.15)
δ_1 in (7b)	−1.45 (0.46)	−1.43 (0.42)	−1.24 (0.49)
$\Sigma\hat{\varepsilon}_t^2$	122.163	138.744	204.531
(Diagnostics)			
Autocorrelation (LM: χ_4^2)	1.81	15.91	19.29
Functional form (RESET: χ_1^2)	2.85	0.13	0.50
Residual normality (Jarque-Bera: χ_2^2)	239.83	194.09	887.65
Heteroskedasticity (LM: χ_1^2)	0.002	0.27	0.19
Test of H_0 on model (4b) ($F_{2,116}$)	6.46	7.46	5.75
Test of restriction (4b) to (7b) ($F_{1,116}$)	2.75	3.08	5.02

We also examine a regression technique based on minimizing median residuals rather than mean as in *OLS*, and which should as a result be less subject to influence by outliers. Next, we return to the issue of the distributions of the test statistics for the hypothesis that $\delta_1 = 0$, and offer two non-parametric tests robust to the non-normality evident in these samples.

3 Robustness of Rejections of the Null Hypothesis

Influential data diagnostics are methods designed to isolate systematically those points which make particularly large contributions to determining the overall parameter estimates. One natural approach is to exclude points singly, or in groups, in order to assess the changes in estimated coefficients, covariance matrix, and fit of the regression line. Belsley, Kuh and Welsch (1980) give a thorough review of methods of isolating influential points. The following is a summary of the basic diagnostic tools:

i) Leverage and the "hat matrix": define $H = X(X'X)^{-1}X'$; h_i is a leverage point if $h_i > 2k/T$, where there are k regressors and T sample points.
ii) Studentized residuals: define $e_i^* = e_i/(s(i)(1-h)^{1/2})$, where e_i is the ith residual and

$$s(i) = \left[\frac{(n-k)s^2 - e_i^2/(1-h_i)}{(n-k-1)}\right]^{1/2}.$$

iii) Change in coefficients when the ith data point is dropped: define $b_j(i)$ as the value of the jth least-squares coefficient, so that $b_j(i) = b_j - c_{ij}e_i/(1-h_i)$, where $C = (X'X)^{-1}X'$. A scaled measure of change can then be calculated, and the point deemed influential if this exceeds $2/\sqrt{T}$.
iv) Change in fit at point i when the ith point is dropped. Another scaled measure of fit can be established, and the point is deemed influential if this exceeds $2(k/T)^{1/2}$.
v) Change in the variance-covariance matrix when the ith point is dropped: the ratio of the determinants of the covariance matrix associated with the two regressions is compared, and ratios far from unity signal influential points.

Detailed reportage of the results of such an exercise is necessarily bulky, and is therefore omitted. However, the results may be summarized as follows. The candidate points for elimination were chosen on the basis of the measure of leverage and the other diagnostic measures. We then examined the coefficients when each of the possible combinations of three or more of the selected points was in turn omitted. With six points, this yielded 42 combinations, and for each one the regression model (7b) was fitted to the sample omitting these points. Overall, the results are not very sensitive to the exclusion of most of these groups of points. It *is* possible to find sets of points which, when eliminated, reduce the estimated coefficient δ_1 to insignificance at the 5% level on the typical sample; nonetheless, the rejection in the t-test is clearly a reasonably robust result. The typical outcome is a test statistic with a p-value in a near neighbourhood of the full-sample *OLS* statistic on the same data set. It is clearly *not* true that the *OLS* results are governed by a few influential sample points without which the results change radically.

A second means of checking the robustness of the results of section 2 to outliers in the data is to use a robust regression technique. We use one of the simplest of these, the *least median of squares* (LMS) estimator (see Rousseeuw and Leroy (1987) for an exposition). Least median of squares regression minimizes the median of squares of residuals,[6] rather than the average, which is

---

6 Algorithms to approximate the LMS line typically operate by enlightened trial and error, checking full-sample medians for parameters estimated by *OLS* on many sub-samples. See Rousseeuw and Leroy (1987, 197 ff.).

Table 2. *LMS* estimates of simple term-structure models

a: Canadian data $T = 119$

Model and parameters	Data set S_1	S_2	S_3
(7b) δ_0	−0.06	−0.08	0.28
(7b) δ_1	−0.92	−0.99	−2.04
median $\hat{\varepsilon}_t^2$	0.1750	0.1518	0.1767
median of *OLS* residuals	0.2152	0.1561	0.2350
median with $\delta_1 \equiv 0$	0.2809	0.3025	0.2601

b: U.S. data $T = 119$

Model and parameters	Data set S_1	S_2	S_3
(7b) δ_0	0.09	0.09	−0.04
(7b) δ_1	−1.66	−1.21	−0.64
median $\hat{\varepsilon}_t^2$	0.1075	0.1273	0.1112
median of *OLS* residuals	0.1653	0.1686	0.1787
median of $\delta_1 \equiv 0$	0.2916	0.3844	0.2704

minimized by *OLS*. In doing so it provides an estimator less sensitive to influence by a few unusual observations.

Table 2 records the LMS estimates of model (7b) on each of the three Canadian and three U.S. samples. The movement to a more robust estimation technique does not produce very large movements in the parameter of interest; while standard errors are unfortunately not available, the cluster of estimated values of δ_1 remains. Moreover, imposing the null value of zero for δ_1 leads to a large jump in the median squared residual on all samples. Again, therefore, a robust method suggests the insensitivity of the original rejections to changes in the influence of outliers.

4 Non-parametric Tests of Efficiency

Again, the implied forecast error under the maintained hypothesis of the rational expectations interpretation of the term structure at the short end is given by:

$$\xi_{t+1} = r_{t+1}^3 - 2r_t^6 + r_t^3 + 2\theta,$$

where θ is the liquidity premium and $\xi_{t+1} \equiv r_{t+1}^3 - \hat{r}_{t+1:t}^3$ is the forecast error at time $t + 1$. A testable implication of the theory is that the forecast error is independent of any information available to the market at the time the long rate was determined; in particular the forecast error should be uncorrelated with the spread, $S_t \equiv r_t^6 - r_t^3$. Non-parametric tests for such examples of conditional stochastic independence based on ranks have recently been introduced by Campbell and Dufour (1991a, b) as analogues to the t-test associated with the usual regression considered in this context. The tests are provably exact – *i.e.*, they reject at their nominal levels – in the presence of non-normal disturbances and heteroskedasticity, and simulation results indicate that they have good power relative to the t-test, particular in the presence of outliers. A non-parametric methodology which incorporates these tests in a general assessment of the adequacy or, more controversially, the rationality of survey forecast data, is presented in Campbell and Ghysels (1992).

The non-parametric procedures adopted in these papers could be applied directly to our problem if θ were known; in that situation the following statistics would be of interest:

$$S_0 \equiv \sum_{t=1}^{T} u(\xi_{t+1} S_t), \qquad W_0 \equiv \sum_{t=1}^{T} u(\xi_{t+1} S_t) R_t^+ ,$$

where $u(z) \equiv 0$ if $z \geq 0$ and $\equiv 1$ otherwise, and R_t^+ is the rank (*i.e.* position) of $Z_t \equiv |\xi_t|$ in the $T \times 1$ vector Z. Under the null and the assumption that the true forecast errors have median 0, S_0 has the binomial distribution with number of trials T and probability of success 0.5; under the further assumption that the errors are symmetric around zero, W_0 is distributed as a Wilcoxon signed-rank variate of size T (*i.e.*, as $W = \sum_{t=1}^{T} tB_t$ with the B_t independent Bernoulli variates) in situations where the true forecast errors are symmetric around 0. An important feature of the non-parametric approach is that under the null the distributions of the statistics S_0 and W_0 are robust to heteroskedasticity. For further details see the papers previously cited.

Where θ is unknown we modify the simultaneous inference procedure of Dufour (1990), which treats a similar problem involving a nuisance parameter, but in an entirely different context. The procedure involves two steps. In our environment the primary idea is to estimate the liquidity premium via non-parametric procedures under the maintained hypothesis that the errors are centered at 0. Accordingly, we find a 97.5% non-parametric confidence interval for the centre of the sequence $r_{t+1}^3 - 2r_t^6 + r_t^3$; we denote the interval by I and its mid-point by a_0; according to this procedure, $-(1/2)a_0$ is the non-parametric estimate of the liquidity premium. For each $a \in I$, the estimate of the forecast error contingent upon the related estimate of the liquidity premium can be written ξ_t^a.

We can now use this confidence interval to introduce sign and signed-rank tests analogous to those defined above for the case where the liquidity premium was assumed known:

$$S_a \equiv \sum_{t=1}^{T} u(\xi_t^a S_{t-1}^c), \qquad W_a \equiv \sum_{t=1}^{T} u(\xi_t^a S_{t-1}^c) R_t^+$$

where $a \in I$, R_t^+ is the rank (position) of $Z_t^a \equiv |\xi_t^a|$ in the $T \times 1$ vector Z^a, and where $S_t^c \equiv S_t - t^{-1} \sum_{i=1}^{t} S_i$ represents the distance of the current spread from a centering of the spread using a restricted sample (*n.b.*, some centering manoeuvre is required to assure that the tests have power; only past information may be used, in order to preserve the level).

Two general approaches to testing the null may be associated with these statistics. On the first – a generalized bounds procedure based on a .973 confidence interval for the liquidity premium – the null of the conditional independence of the forecast error is rejected if $S_a(W_a)$ is significant at the 2.7% level for every $a \in I$, and the null is not rejected if the infimum of the p-values associated with the $S_a(W_a)$ is greater than .075; otherwise the test is inconclusive (see Dufour (1990, Proposition 2) for details). This approach has the property that the probability of rejection under the null is bounded by .05. However, simulation studies for a variety of standard specifications indicate that this approach may lead to tests which are quite conservative. The studies (available upon request) do indicate that if a test is based solely on the statistic $S_{a_0}(W_{a_0})$, its level will still be .05; accordingly, we will also consider the results of non-parametric tests based on the median estimate of the nuisance parameter.

When the simultaneous inference procedure is applied to the U.S. and Canadian data, the results of the first step – given in Table 3 – indicate strongly that there is a statistically significant and positive liquidity premium in the neighbourhood of 12 basis points embodied in the six-month rate. This conclusion appears to hold for both data sets, with perhaps a marginally smaller premium in the Canadian sample. Recall that the parametric estimates in section 2 were not significant.

Table 4 presents the results of the second step in the simultaneous inference procedure. For each data set, the largest and smallest p-values are given for S_a and W_a, $a \in I$, along with the p-values associated with the statistics derived from the midpoint of I. It is apparent, and interesting, that the results contrast some-

Table 3. Non-parametric estimate of the liquidity premium[1]

	Lowest $X_{(1)}$	$L_{(.973)}$ $X_{(47)}$	Median $X_{(60)}$	$U_{(.973)}$ $X_{(72)}$	Highest $X_{(119)}$
Canadian data					
Sample 1	−4.28	−0.35	−0.26	−0.06	3.97
Sample 2	−5.63	−0.36	−0.23	−0.08	4.05
Sample 3	−6.18	−0.32	−0.15	−0.00	4.92
USA data					
Sample 1	−4.70	−0.45	−0.27	−0.14	3.56
Sample 2	−4.67	−0.48	−0.28	−0.16	4.04
Sample 3	−7.79	−0.40	−0.20	−0.07	4.62

[1] $X_{(k)}$ is the kth order statistic of the sample $X_t \equiv r_t^3 - (2r_{t-1}^6 - r_{t-1}^3)$; $(X_{(47)}, X_{(72)})$ gives a 97.3% confidence interval for the median; the estimate of the liquidity premium is given by −.5a for every a in the interval.

Table 4. Non-parametric orthogonality tests[1]

	Largest p-value Sign	Wilcoxon	Smallest p-value Sign	Wilcoxon	Mid-point p-value Sign	Wilcoxon
Candian data						
Sample 1	.71	.69	.14	.44	.36	.57
Sample 2	.85	.58	.46	.50	.58	.53
Sample 3	.85	.99	.20	.74	.20	.86
USA data						
Sample 1	.04	.01	.00	.00	.02	.00
Sample 2	.99	.99	.19	.35	.36	.73
Sample 3	.20	.08	.00	.00	.07	.02

[1] Smallest and large p-values are given for S_a and W_a, $a \in I$, and for S_a and W_a corresponding to the mid-point of I.

what with the previous regression assessment of the expectations hypothesis. First, the hypothesis is not rejected on the Canadian data for any of the samples, and it is rejected in only the first U.S. sample for all estimates of the liquidity premium falling within the appropriate confidence interval. When this admittedly conservative procedure is relaxed to consider solely the median estimate, there is some indication that the hypothesis is rejected by the third U.S. sample.

The second non-parametric test is based on Dufour and Hallin (1992), and uses a bound on tail-area probabilities of linear combinations of independent, bounded random variables. The variables need not be identically distributed. As with the previous non-parametric procedure, the resulting critical values are conservative. The particular test applied is a permutation t-test, which is again directed at a univariate regression model; see section 4(b) of Dufour and Hallin (1992). Our treatment of the risk premium in the model is similar to that in the previous tests, based on signed ranks: we first remove a non-parametric estimate of the intercept in (7b) from the independent variable, taking the estimate from the 97.3% confidence interval reported in Table 3. We then use the Dufour-Hallin univariate regression and calculate a p-value for the permutation t-statistic corresponding to the particular estimate of the risk premium. According to this two-step procedure, we reject the null at significance level bounded by $\alpha\%$ if the supremum of the Dufour-Hallin p-values is less than or equal to $(\alpha - 2.7)\%$.

The bounds on the critical values are non-uniform: that is, they are dependent upon the regressand as well as the moments of the regressors. We therefore report the p-values of the test statistic under the null, rather than the test statistic itself, using bounds for $T = 120$ from Table 3 of Hallin and Dufour. Table 5 reports the range of p-values for each sample, as well as the p-value at the median estimate (from Table 3) of the intercept term.

Two points concerning Table 5 are espeically noteworthy. First, the conservative test (maximum p-value) does not allow a rejection on any sample; however, as in the results of the Campbell-Dufour test, there is somewhat more evidence

Table 5. Nonparametric univariate regression tests[1]

	Largest p-value	Smallest p-value	p-value at median
Canadian data			
Sample 1	0.5*	0.5*	0.5*
Sample 2	0.5*	0.24	0.5*
Sample 3	0.5*	0.15	0.31
U.S. data			
Sample 1	0.5*	0.01	0.06
Sample 2	0.5*	0.03	0.12
Sample3	0.5*	0.04	0.13

[1] These are marginal significance levels (p-values) in two-tailed tests of the null hypothesis, interpolated from the critical values given by the Dufour-Hallin procedure. The heading "p-value at median" refers to the p-value in the test conducted at the median value of the non-parametrically estimated liquidity premium, given in Table 3. "0.5*" indicates a p-value exceeding 0.5.

against the null in the U.S. data than in the Canadian (based on the smallest p-values and p-values at the median estimates of the intercepts). The second point is that the differences in the marginal significance levels across different samples from either country tend to be less marked in the Dufour-Hallin test results.

5 Time-Varying Behaviour in the Risk Premium

A next step in examining these data is to examine the time-varying component to the liquidity premium. It has already been noted (Mankiw and Summers, 1984) that variability in the liquidity premium will tend to lead to a downward bias in the coefficient on the spread, the null being otherwise valid. If we retain the hypothesis of orthogonality between expectational errors and observable data, the rejection of the null embodied in (1) suggests just such a time-varying liquidity premium. Such a possibility has been discussed a good deal in the existing literature on the behaviour of the term structure.

A related approach is that of Engle, Lilien and Robins (1987), who find evidence that changes in volatility can usefully be modelled as implying an increase in the liquidity premium, captured through ARCH in mean (ARCH-M). Engle *et al.* find, however, that the use of an ARCH-M model does not entirely remove the apparent effect of the spread or the forecast error (in our formulation); see, for example, their equation (22) ff. The spread remains, in fact, a significant determinant of the forecast error at the 5% level in their (parametric) tests incorporating an ARCH-M model of the premium.

Variability of the term premium can be, of course, modelled in a number of ways. A natural question, which is the basis of this section, is whether a model of variation in the liquidity premium can be found such that, when this effect is accounted for, the apparent effect of the spread is removed. Since the ARCH-M model does not eliminate the effect, we consider here models from the ARMA class. Evidence of autocorrelation in several of the tests recorded in Table 1 also suggests the omission of some autocorrelated effect from the simple models, which could be accounted for by a time-varying premium, and which in any event may fruitfully be modelled by an ARMA process.

A time-varying liquidity premium in (7b) can be viewed as a constant (the mean liquidity premium) plus an autocorrelated component which appears in the equation error (if this component were not autocorrelated, its addition to the original error would not affect the validity of *OLS* estimation, and there would be no reason to expect a bias in the coefficient on the spread term). We therefore model the process followed by the deviation of the liquidity premium from its mean by a model from the AR or ARMA class, and re-estimate the model to incorporate this effect, using the general *GLS* method for estimation of regression models with ARMA errors proposed by Zinde-Walsh and Galbraith (1991), and the semi-recursive estimator for this model as described by Galbraith and Zinde-Walsh (1992). The well-known Cochrane-Orcutt and Prais-Winsten estimators for the AR(1) cases are special cases of the former method.

To model the time-series process characterizing the risk premium, we use first a simple AR(1) model, and second a model from the ARMA(p, q) class with p,

Table 6. *GLS* estimates from models with autocorrelated error processes

a: Canadian data

	Data set		
	S_1	S_2	S_3
AR(1) model:			
coefficient on spread	−0.01	−1.06	−1.45
standard error	0.44	0.39	0.38
ARMA model:			
coefficient on spread	0.03	−1.01	−1.68
standard error	0.44	0.40	0.28

b: U.S. data

	Data set		
	S_1	S_2	S_3
AR(1) model:			
coefficient on spread	−1.64	−1.64	−1.89
standard error	0.42	0.38	0.39
ARMA model:			
coefficient on spread	−1.52	−1.58	−1.84
standard error	0.57	0.37	0.40

$q \leq 3$, selected by comparing results of the estimation of the various models in that class. Table 6 reports full-sample *GLS* estimates and standard errors for each of the six samples, for the AR(1) case and the case of a preferred model (which differs from sample to sample) within the ARMA class.

It is clear from Table 6 that the incorporation of an autoregressive element estimated from the residuals of (7b) does not lead to a substantial change in the coefficient of interest (δ_1) in that equation. While the estimation of autocorrelated error processes does give evidence of processes that can be modelled within the ARMA class, it is equally important that such models do not clearly account for the deviations from the null hypothesis.

Both the ARCH-M and ARMA classes, then, find evidence of some systematic variability in the deviations from the null hypothesis, which we may attribute to variability in the risk premium. However, the view that varying term premia are the primary source of the deviations from the pure expectations theory that are observed in efficiency tests is not supported by these results.

6 Concluding Remarks

This paper has attempted to re-evaluate the standard conclusion that the expectations hypothesis of the term structure is untenable, even at the short end. Simple *OLS* regression analysis of Canadian data, as with U.S. data, does tend to confirm the view that the forecast implicit in six-month rates does not efficiently exploit the information available in the spread between three- and six-month rates; this result holds in five of our six samples. However, we have noted that the regression residuals are apparently non-normal in all samples, and, accordingly, we have undertaken more robust estimation procedures to guard against the possibility that the usual test statistics will have perverse distributions in small samples.

The presence of outliers in the samples investigated here is reflected in the positive readings of various regression diagnostics. Using these diagnostic measures, we isolate a small set of influential sample points; it is in fact possible, by eliminating these points from the sample, to overturn the rejection of efficiency according to standard tests. Of course, such manipulation in itself provides little evidence in favour of the expectations hypothesis, but serves to underscore the need for more robust procedures. Nonetheless, the results of such procedures are somewhat mixed. Least median of squares estimates of the crucial slope coefficient are actually greater in absolute value than their *OLS* counterparts in four of the samples considered; only in the third U.S. sample does the coefficient estimate move considerably towards the hypothesized value of zero.

However, non-parametric efficiency tests based on signs and signed ranks do tend to run contrary to these rejection results: according to these procedures there is clear-cut rejection of efficiency in only one sample, and a strong indication of inefficiency in one other. To elaborate, the marginal significance levels of these tests applied to the Canadian data are quite high across all three subsamples. The contrary evidence is supplied by the first and third U.S. samples. These results are borne out, broadly, by the third non-parametric test that we consider; again, such evidence against the null that we find appears only in the U.S. data.

Up to this point, we have emphasized that the non-parametric procedures have suggested a difference between the Canadian and the U.S. data that was not revealed by the previous regression-based studies. Moreover, while our decision to split the sample into three sub-samples was dictated by the requirement that we avoid autocorrelation in the errors when applying the sign and signed-rank statistics, this approach has also shown that proximate sub-samples can display strikingly different characteristics. Both of these observations merit further attention.

References

Belsley DA, Kuh E, Welsch RE (1980) Regression diagnostics: Identifying influential data and sources of collinearity. Wiley. New York

Campbell B, Dufour J-M (1991a) Over-rejections in rational expectations models: A nonparametric approach to the Mankiw-Shapiro problem. Economics Letters 35:285–290

Campbell B, Dufour J-M (1991b) Nonparametric orthogonality and random walk tests. Mimeo

Campbell B, Ghysels E (1992) Is the outcome of the federal budget process unbiased and efficient? A nonparametric assessment. Mimeo

Cox JC, Ingersoll JE, Ross SA (1981) A re-examination of traditional hypotheses about the term structure of interest rates. Journal of Finance 36:769–799

Dufour J-M (1990) Exact tests and confidence sets in linear regression with autocorrelated errors. Econometrica 58:475–495

Dufour J-M and Hallin M (1991) Nonuniform bounds for nonparametric t-tests. Econometric Theory 7:253–263

Dufour J-M, Hallin M (1992) Improved Eaton bounds for linear combinations of bounded random variables, with statistical applications. Working paper, CRDE, Université de Montréal. Forthcoming, Journal of the American Statistical Association

Engle RF, Lilien DM, Robins RP (1987) Estimating time-varying risk premia in the term structure: the ARCH-M model. Econometrica 55:391–407

Galbraith JW, Zinde-Walsh V (1992) The *GLS* transformation matrix and a semi-recursive estimator for the linear regression model with ARMA errors. Econometric Theory 8:95–111

Hettmansperger TP (1984) Statistical inference based on ranks. Wiley, New York

Mankiw NG (1986) The term structure of interest rates re-visited. Brookings Papers on Economic Activity I:61–107

Mankiw NG, Miron JA (1986) The changing behavior of the term structure of interest rates. Quarterly Journal of Economics 101:211–228

Mankiw NG, Summers LH (1984) Do long-term interest rates over-react to short-term interest rates? Brookings Papers on Economic Activity I:223–247

Modigliani F, Sutch R (1966) Innovations in interest rate policy. American Economic Review 55:178–197

Rousseeuw PJ, Leroy AM (1987) Robust regression and outlier detection. Wiley, New York

Shiller RJ, Campbell JY, Schoenholtz KL (1983) Forward rates and future policy: Interpreting the term structure of interest rates. Brooking Papers on Economic Activity 173–217

Zinde-Walsh V, Galbraith JW (1991) Estimation of a linear regression model with stationary ARMA(p, q) errors. Journal of Econometrics 47:333–357

Adjustment Costs and Time-To-Build in Factor Demand in the U.S. Manufacturing Industry

Franz C. Palm, H.M.M. Peeters and G.A. Pfann[1]

Faculty of Economics and Business Administration, Department of Quantitative Economics, Tongersestraat 53, 6211 LM Maastricht, The Netherlands

Abstract: In order to explain cyclical behavior of factor demand, the static neoclassical model of the firm has been extended to include either adjustment costs (e.g. Lucas (1967)) or time-to-build considerations as in Kydland and Prescott (1982). This paper presents an intertemporal factor demand model which accounts for adjustment costs and gestation lags. The closed form solution of the model is a highly restricted vector ARMA-process that is estimated using quarterly data for the manufacturing industry in the U.S., 1960–1988.

The main conclusion is that both sources of dynamics of factor demand are identifiable and found to be empirically of importance.

Key Words: factor demand models, adjustment costs, gestation lags.

JEL Classification System-Numbers: C32, C5, E22

1 Introduction

In order to explain cyclical behavior of factor demand, the static neoclassical model of the firm has been extended along two alternative lines. Adjustment costs proposed by Lucas (1967) and time-to-build considerations as in Kydland and Prescott (1982) lead to factor demand models which have different dynamic properties. A large number of theoretical and empirical analyses of factor demand uses the adjustment costs approach. A survey is presented in Palm and Pfann (1990). Since the pioneering contribution of Kydland and Prescott (1982), some authors have included time-to-build considerations in their models, usually in a general equilibrium real business cycle framework.

The two approaches have generally been presented as alternative explanations of the dynamics of factor demand. For instance, Rossi (1988) develops Bayesian posterior odds to compare an adjustment-cost model of factor demand with a gestation-lag model as non-nested hypotheses.

This paper presents an intertemporal optimization model for labor, structures and equipment demand which accounts for adjustment and gestation lags in factor demand. A similar approach in a general equilibrium model has been

[1] This research was sponsored by the Economics Research Foundation, which is part of the Netherlands Organization for Scientific Research (NWO) and by the Royal Netherlands Academy of Arts and Sciences (K.N.A.W.).

adopted by Park (1984). The aim of this study is to investigate to what extent gestation lags and adjustment costs are needed to explain the dynamics of factor demand in a partial equilibrium model. While adopting a partial equilibrium framework we test if the main determinants of factor demand are indeed parametric for the decision makers in the model in which case a partial equilibrium analysis becomes legitimate. Investment flows are modeled instead of capital stock series because the latter series have been constructed from investment series without taking into account time-to-build considerations. The model is estimated using quarterly data for the manufacturing industry in the U.S., 1960–1988. The analyses have been carried out along the lines of a modeling approach which integrates time series and econometric analyses of a dynamic model derived from intertemporal optimizing behavior.

The main features of the approach are as follows. Economic theory is used to specify a dynamic model for the series to be analyzed. Adding the process generating the exogenous variables, the model is completed. In line with the Simplicity Principle, we start with a linear-quadratic optimization model for which the first order necessary conditions are linear and derive a forward-looking closed-form solution for the demand for labor, structures and equipment. Univariate time series methods are used to investigate the properties of the initial theoretical model. In particular, the order of integration, the serial correlation properties and the distribution of the series are analyzed.

As mentioned above when adopting a partial equilibrium approach, Granger-causality of the conditioning variables plays a crucial role in the intertemporal optimization models. The directions of causality between factor input and factor prices are examined. Non-stationarity is modeled jointly with other dynamic features in the series instead of being eliminated prior to the econometric analysis.

The implications of the optimization model for the presence of cointegrating regressions are also investigated. The reduced form of the joint model is estimated and model specification tests are performed. The structural parameters are computed from the reduced form parameter estimates using a minimum distance estimator. This methodology iterates into a model that is theoretically sensible and in agreement with the information in the data. Finally, plots of the impulse response functions for the endogenous variables give additional insights in the dynamics of the model.

The paper is organized as follows. In section 2, an econometric specification for the dynamic factor demand model is derived using linear-quadratic approximations. Section 3 describes the results of the empirical analysis. Finally, in section 4 some concluding remarks are made and further extensions are discussed. Some technical derivations, data definitions and results for additional tests are given in appendices.

2 An Intertemporal Model of Factor Demand

A firm is assumed to maximize its real present value of profits over an infinite horizon. It employs labor N_t, uses capital in the form of structures K_t^s and equipment K_t^e. Decisions to change inputs are costly.

The technology assumes that time is required to build structures. The firm operates under uncertainty. In order to determine the optimal level of the variables N_t, K_t^s and K_t^e, the firm uses all the relevant information available up to time t. Current factor prices are part of the information set. Real factor costs, that is factor prices deflated by the price of output, are assumed to be given to the firm in the sense that they are not Granger-caused by factor demand. The production technology obeys the usual regularity conditions ($\partial Q_t/\partial X_t > 0$, $X_t' = [N_t, K_t^s, K_t^e]$ and Q_t denotes real output per time period; the Hessian matrix is negative definite) and is locally approximated by a quadratic function

$$Q_t = (\alpha + \lambda_t)' X_t - \tfrac{1}{2} X_t' A X_t \ , \tag{2.1}$$

where α is a (3×1)-vector with constant coefficients α_i $(i = 1, 2, 3)$, λ_t denotes a (3×1)-vector of exogenous stochastic shocks to the marginal productivity of the inputs and A is a positive definite matrix. Adjustment costs (AC) are assumed to be quadratic in net changes in labor and capital stocks

$$AC_t = \tfrac{1}{2} \Delta X_t' \Gamma \Delta X_t \ , \tag{2.2}$$

where Δ denotes the first differences and Γ a positive definite matrix. Structures and equipment depreciate at the rates κ^s and κ^e respectively. The law of motion for equipment yields

$$K_t^e = (1 - \kappa^e) K_{t-1}^e + I_{t-1}^e \ , \qquad 0 < \kappa^e < 1 \ , \tag{2.3}$$

where I_t^e denotes gross investment in equipment.

Contrary to equipment, structures need to be built. Following Kydland and Prescott (1982), structures with fixed plans are specified by

$$K_t^s = (1 - \kappa^s) K_{t-1}^s + S_{1,t-1} \ , \qquad 0 < \kappa^s < 1 \tag{2.4a}$$

$$S_{j,t} = S_{j+1,t-1} \ , \qquad j = 1, 2, \ldots, J - 1 \tag{2.4b}$$

$$I_t^s = \sum_{j=1}^{J} \delta_j S_{j,t} \tag{2.4c}$$

and

$$\sum_{j=1}^{J} \delta_j = 1 \ , \qquad 0 \leq \delta_j < 1 \ , \tag{2.4d}$$

where $S_{j,t}$ are the total expenditures of structure projects j periods from completion at period t and J denotes the total time to build structures.

New investment projects initiated in period t are denoted by $S_{J,t}$ and equation (2.4b) implies that the expenditures necessary to complete these projects do not change during the gestation. From equation (2.4a) it follows that finished time-to-build capital $S_{1,t-1}$ is added to linearly depreciating structures, so that at time t productive structures are K_t^s. During the gestation period, J, expenditures to current structure projects are given by $\delta_J, \delta_{J-1} \ldots \delta_1$, where the production stage j ($j = J, J-1, \ldots, 1$) indicates the number of periods a project is away from completion. Equation (2.4d) implies that for all time-to-build structure projects the distribution of investments as well as the gestation J are assumed to be the same. Gross investments at time t, I_t^s, consist of investments in all current structure projects ($S_{1,t}, S_{2,t} \ldots S_{J,t}$) with $\delta_j S_{j,t}$ ($j = 1, 2 \ldots J$) being the amount of investment in each project (equation (2.4c)). Notice that if $J = 1$ the structure accumulation equation (2.4a) is similar to equation (2.3).

Variable costs are defined as

$$VC_t = Y_t' P_t \ , \tag{2.5}$$

with $Y_t' = [N_t, I_t^s, I_t^e]$ and $P_t' = [W_t, C_t^s, C_t^e]$ being the vector of factor inputs and real factor prices respectively.

The firm's objective is to maximize its real value of current and future profits (PV) at time t,

$$PV_t = \lim_{H \to \infty} E_t \sum_{h=0}^{H} \beta^h [Q_{t+h} - VC_{t+h} - AC_{t+h}], \qquad 0 < \beta < 1 \ , \tag{2.6}$$

where β is the constant real discount factor and $E_t(\cdot) = E(\cdot|\Omega_t)$ with Ω_t being the available information set at time t.

Substitution of (2.4b) into (2.4a) and then into (2.4c) yields

$$S_{j,t} = S_{1,t+j-1} = K_{t+j}^s - (1 - \kappa^s) K_{t+j-1}^s \ , \qquad j = 1, 2, \ldots, J \ , \tag{2.7}$$

and

$$I_t^s = \sum_{j=1}^{J} \delta_j (K_{t+j}^s - (1 - \kappa^s) K_{t+j-1}^s) = \sum_{j=0}^{J} \phi_j K_{t+j}^s \ , \tag{2.8}$$

with

$$\phi_0 = (\kappa^s - 1)\delta_1$$

$$\phi_j = \delta_j + (\kappa^s - 1)\delta_{j+1} \ , \qquad j = 1, 2, \ldots, J - 1$$

$$\phi_J = \delta_J \ .$$

Notice that gross structures investments are the sum of current and future net structures investments and depreciation ($\Delta K_{t+j}^s + \kappa^s K_{t+j-1}^s$, $j = 1, 2 \ldots J$) weighted by the time-to-build parameters (δ_j, $j = 1 \ldots J$).

Variable factor costs can then be expressed as

$$VC_t = W_t N_t + C_t^s \left[\sum_{j=0}^{J} \phi_j K_{t+j}^s \right] + C_t^e [K_{t+1}^e + (\kappa^e - 1) K_t^e] \ . \tag{2.9}$$

At period t decisions are made concerning labor N_t, and the new capital projects $S_{J,t}$ and investment I_t^e that determine K_{t+J}^s and K_{t+1}^e respectively. The criterion function (2.6) is maximized with respect to the decision variables N_{t+h}, K^s_{t+J+h} and K^e_{t+1+h} ($h = 0, 1 \ldots$). First order necessary conditions for maximization of (2.6) consist of the set of Euler equations and a pair of transversality conditions assuring the finiteness of the process. We further assume absence of interrelations in the production- and adjustment cost-functions, that is the matrices A and Γ are diagonal with i-th ($i = 1, 2, 3$) diagonal elements denoted by a_{ii} and γ_{ii} respectively. This assumption substantially simplifies the derivation of the solution.

The Euler equations for N_t, K^s_{t+J} and K^e_{t+1} can be written as

$$\alpha_1 + \lambda_{1t} - \alpha_{11} N_t - W_t - \gamma_{11} \Delta N_t + \beta \gamma_{11} E_t \Delta N_{t+1} = 0 \tag{2.10a}$$

$$\beta^J [\alpha_2 + E_t \lambda_{2,t+J} - a_{22} K^s_{t+J}] - \sum_{j=0}^{J} \beta^j \phi_{J-j} E_t C^s_{t+j} - \beta^J \gamma_{22} \Delta K^s_{t+J} + \beta^{J+1} \gamma_{22} E_t \Delta K^s_{t+J+1} = 0 \tag{2.10b}$$

$$\beta[\alpha_3 + E_t \lambda_{3,t+1} - a_{33} K^e_{t+1}] - C^e_t - \beta(\kappa^e - 1) E_t C^e_{t+1} - \beta \gamma_{33} \Delta K^e_{t+1} + \beta^2 \gamma_{33} E_t \Delta K^e_{t+2} = 0 \; . \tag{2.10c}$$

The transversality conditions are satisfied if each variable has an exponential order less than $1/\sqrt{\beta}$. Defining $X^d_t = [N_t, K^s_{t+J}, K^e_{t+1}]'$ and using the method of Blanchard and Kahn (1980) the solution of the Euler equations can be expressed as follows

$$X^d_t = F_1 X^d_{t-1} - \sum_{i=0}^{\infty} (\beta F_1)^{i+1} D E_t(Z_{t+i}) \; . \tag{2.11}$$

Z_t contains the observed variables W_t, C^s_t, C^e_t and the unobservable variables λ_{1t}, $E_t \lambda_{2,t+J}$, $E_t \lambda_{3,t+1}$, $E_t C^s_{t+k}$ ($k = 1, 2, \ldots, J$) and $E_t C^e_{t+1}$. A derivation and description of the matrices F_1 and D can be found in appendix I.

Since we use investment data for the empirical analysis we rewrite the second and third equation in (2.11) in terms of gross investment. The first equation remains unaltered. From (2.8) it follows that:

$$I^s_t = \sum_{j=0}^{J} \phi_j K^s_{t+j} \qquad \text{and} \qquad \sum_{j=0}^{J} \phi_j = \kappa^s \sum_{j=1}^{J} \delta_j = \kappa^s \; . \tag{2.12}$$

Defining $[\cdot]_2$ as the second row of the matrix in square brackets, the second equation in (2.11) together with (2.12) then gives

$$K^s_{t+J} = f_2 K^s_{t+J-1} - \sum_{i=0}^{\infty} (\beta f_2)^{i+1} [D]_2 E_t(Z_{t+i}) \qquad \Leftrightarrow$$

$$\sum_{j=0}^{J} \phi_j K^s_{t+j} = f_2 \sum_{j=0}^{J} \phi_j K^s_{t+j-1} - \sum_{j=0}^{J} \phi_j \sum_{i=0}^{\infty} (\beta f_2)^{i+1} [D]_2 E_{t+j-J}(Z_{t+i+j-J}) \qquad \Leftrightarrow$$

$$I^s_t = f_2 I^s_{t-1} - \sum_{j=0}^{J} \phi_j \sum_{i=0}^{\infty} (\beta f_2)^{i+1} [D]_2 E_{t+j-J}(Z_{t+i+j-J}) \; . \tag{2.13a}$$

Defining $\phi^e_0 = \kappa^e - 1$ and $\phi^e_1 = 1$, the third equation is obtained in the same way

$$I_t^e = f_3 I_{t-1}^e - \sum_{j=0}^{1} \phi_j^e \sum_{i=0}^{\infty} (\beta f_3)^{i+1} [D]_3 E_{t+j-1}(Z_{t+i+j-1}) \ . \tag{2.13b}$$

Reminding that $Y_t' = [N_t, I_t^s, I_t^e]$, the system of equations (2.11) becomes

$$Y_t = F_1 Y_{t-1} + \sum_{j=0}^{J} D_j \sum_{i=0}^{\infty} (\beta F_1)^{i+1} D E_{t-j}(Z_{t+i-j}) \ , \tag{2.14}$$

where

$$D_0 = \begin{bmatrix} -1 & 0 & 0 \\ 0 & -\boldsymbol{\phi}_J & 0 \\ 0 & 0 & -1 \end{bmatrix}, \quad D_1 = \begin{bmatrix} 0 & 0 & 0 \\ 0 & -\boldsymbol{\phi}_{J-1} & 0 \\ 0 & 0 & (1-\boldsymbol{\kappa}^e) \end{bmatrix},$$

$$D_k = \begin{bmatrix} 0 & 0 & 0 \\ 0 & -\boldsymbol{\phi}_{J-k} & 0 \\ 0 & 0 & 0 \end{bmatrix}, \quad k = 2, 3, \ldots, J \ .$$

Contrary to productive capital (K_t^s and K_t^e) the gross investments of capital (I_t^s and I_t^e) depend on realized real prices for the total gestation period due to the fact that gross investments are a weighted sum of investment projects that were initiated during the period $t - J$ and t. For example K_t^s in (2.13a) depends on C_{t-J}^s but not on $C_{t-J+1}^s, \ldots, C_{t-1}^s, C_t^s$, whereas I_t^s depends on all these prices because $K_{t+1}^s, K_{t+2}^s \ldots K_{t+J}^s$ are included.

In order to obtain a model which relates the decision variables Y_t to observed exogenous variables, we have to specify the processes that generate the exogenous variables. We assume that the productivity shocks and the first differences of factor prices are generated by first order vector-autoregressions

$$\lambda_t = R\lambda_{t-1} + \varepsilon_t^\lambda \ , \quad \text{with } E_t\varepsilon_t^\lambda = 0 \ , \quad E_t\varepsilon_t^\lambda \varepsilon_t^{\lambda'} = \Sigma^\lambda \ , \quad E_t\varepsilon_t^\lambda \varepsilon_s^{\lambda'} = 0 \ , \quad t \neq s \tag{2.15}$$

R being a diagonal matrix with typical diagonal element ρ_{ii} ($i = 1, 2, 3$), and

$$\Delta P_t = \overline{M} \Delta P_{t-1} + \varepsilon_t^p \quad \text{with } E_t\varepsilon_t^p = 0 \ , \quad E_t\varepsilon_t^p \varepsilon_t^{p'} = \Sigma^p \ , \quad E_t\varepsilon_t^p \varepsilon_s^{p'} = 0 \ , \quad t \neq s \tag{2.16}$$

and a typical element of $\overline{M}$ being denoted by μ_{ij}. These assumptions are permissive and will be tested in the empirical analysis.

As described in appendix I, along the lines of Pfann (1990) from (2.15) and (2.16) one can obtain an expression for the expected future values of the exogenous variables and substitute it into (2.14). After applying a Koyck transformation to eliminate the serial correlation in the unobservable technology components λ_t, the forward-looking linear decision rules for the production factors yield

$$Y_t = C + (F_1 + R) Y_{t-1} - RF_1 Y_{t-2} + \sum_{j=0}^{J+2} M_j P_{t-j} + \boldsymbol{\varepsilon}_t^y \ , \tag{2.17}$$

where C, M_j ($j = 0, 1, \ldots, J+2$) and ε_t^y are defined in appendix I. The process of prices (in (2.16)) which can be written as

$$P_t = (I + \overline{M})P_{t-1} - \overline{M}P_{t-2} + \varepsilon_t^p \ , \tag{2.18}$$

and the system (2.17) form the model for factor demand and factor prices which we complete by assuming that

$$\varepsilon_t = \begin{bmatrix} \varepsilon_t^y \\ \varepsilon_t^p \end{bmatrix} \sim N(0, \Sigma) \ , \qquad \text{where } \varepsilon_t^y = \begin{bmatrix} \varepsilon_{1t}^y \\ \varepsilon_{2t}^y \\ \varepsilon_{3t}^y \end{bmatrix}, \qquad \varepsilon_t^p = \begin{bmatrix} \varepsilon_{1t}^p \\ \varepsilon_{2t}^p \\ \varepsilon_{3t}^p \end{bmatrix},$$

$$\mathrm{Cov}(\varepsilon_t^y, \varepsilon_{t-k}^p) = 0 \qquad \text{for all } k$$

and

$$\begin{aligned}
\mathrm{Cov}(\varepsilon_{1t}^y, \varepsilon_{1s}^y) &= 0 && t \neq s \\
\mathrm{Cov}(\varepsilon_{2t}^y, \varepsilon_{2,t-k}^y) &= \sum_{j=0}^{J-k} \phi_j \phi_{j+k} [\Sigma^{\lambda^*}]_{22} && k = 1, 2, \ldots, J \\
&= 0 && k > J \\
\mathrm{Cov}(\varepsilon_{3t}^y, \varepsilon_{3,t-k}^y) &= (\kappa^e - 1)[\Sigma^{\lambda^*}]_{33} && k = 1 \\
&= 0 && k > 1 \\
\mathrm{Cov}(\varepsilon_{it}^p, \varepsilon_{is}^p) &= 0 && t \neq s \quad i = 1, 2, 3,
\end{aligned}$$

where $[\Sigma^{\lambda^*}]_{ij}$ is the (i, j)-th element of covariance matrix Σ^{λ} multiplied by a constant. Notice that these assumptions imply that technology shocks can not instantaneously influence production prices (and vice versa).

The subsystem (2.17) is a multivariate linear dynamic regression model with diagonal autoregressive matrices because of the diagonality of both R and F_1. The matrices M_i $(i = 4 \ldots J + 2)$ only have non-zero elements in the second row. M_3 has zero restrictions in the first row, whereas M_0, M_1 and M_2 are unrestricted.

System (2.17) is a trivariate ARMAX-model. The equations for labor, structures and equipment are ARX(2, 2), ARMAX(2, J + 2, J) and ARMAX(2, 3, 1) processes with the figures between parentheses indicating the order of the AR part, the number of lagged factor prices and the degree of the MA part respectively. The contemporaneous correlations among the three disturbances ε_{1t}^y, ε_{2t}^y, ε_{3t}^y are unrestricted.

In system (2.17) the first lagged dependent variable appears because of the adjustment cost assumption. The lagged prices P_{t-1} and P_{t-2} are included in all equations due to the first order autoregressive process of price differences. The second equation in system (2.17) contains the largest number of lags. Gross investment of structures is a weighted sum of current capital projects. Current projects were started during periods $t - J$ up to t. The information set in this model includes the technology shocks and prices of all production factors. Prices realized during the periods $t - J - 2$ to t appear as explanatory variables. Technology shocks realized during the periods $t - J$ to t are unobserved. Their influence is found in the model as the persistent part (R) and the transitory part (ε_t^{λ}). The persistent part is represented by the last lagged dependent variable and the last lagged vector of prices, present in all equations in (2.17). The transitory part of technology shocks is represented by the moving average disturbance with weights ϕ_j ($j = J, J-1, \ldots, 0$). The interpretation is as follows. At time $t-J$, structure project $S_{J,t-J}$ is initiated, a decision that is influenced by the technology disturbance $\varepsilon^{\lambda}_{2,t-J}$ but only by the part ϕ_J which is invested in that period. During the gestation time $t-J, t-J+1, \ldots, t$ this decision has an impact that can not be changed due to the fixed investment plan assumption. The impact of the disturbance $\varepsilon^{\lambda}_{2,t-J}$ on gross investments is $\phi_J\varepsilon^{\lambda}_{2,t-J}, \phi_{J-1}\varepsilon^{\lambda}_{2,t-J}, \ldots, \phi_0\varepsilon^{\lambda}_{2,t-J}$. Gross investments at time t, building up $K^s_t, K^s_{t+1}, \ldots, K^s_{t+J}$ are thus influenced by the random part of the technology shocks by the amounts $\phi_0\varepsilon^{\lambda}_{2,t-J}, \phi_1\varepsilon^{\lambda}_{2,t-J+1}, \ldots, \phi_J\varepsilon^{\lambda}_{2,t}$. In a similar way the matrices M_i ($i = 0, 1, \ldots, J+2$) bear the time-to-build parameters.

The structural parameters are the parameters of the production technology, of the adjustment cost functions, the time-to-build coefficients, the depreciation rates, the real discount factor and the parameters in the processes for P_t and λ_t. The structural parameters are subject to nonlinear restrictions. There are also cross-equations restrictions between the parameters of the subsystems (2.17) and (2.18). In appendix I, it is shown that the structural parameters are all identified from the reduced form estimates of (2.17) and (2.18) and the additional restrictions (see appendix I (A.6) and (2.4d)).

Given that the parameters of the decision rules (2.17) and of the process for P_t in (2.18) are functionally related, one cannot expect P_t to be weakly exogenous with respect to the parameters in (2.17) (see Engle et al. (1983)). Therefore, P_t cannot be superexogenous either which is a different way of stating the Lucas' critique; structural changes which affect the conditional mean of P_t and/or λ_t will also affect the parameters in the factor demand system (2.17) in a way that can be predicted. Although the economic model implies absence of weak and superexogeneity, it relies on the assumption of no Granger-causality from Y_t to P_t and λ_t.

With respect to the non-stationarity of P_t, λ_t and Y_t, a number of interesting features can be mentioned. For instance, λ_t can be interpreted as the impact of technological change on production or as total factor productivity (the so called Solow residual). If λ_t is assumed to be generated by a random walk, i.e. if $R \equiv I$, conditional on the past of P_t, the autoregressive part of the model for Y_t has also roots on the unit circle. A random walk for λ_t is consistent with the idea that technical change is a cumulative process of generating knowledge, a point which has been forcefully argued by Lippi and Reichlin (1990) among others. As λ_t is not directly observed, the random walk hypothesis has to be tested indirectly. For instance, an estimate of R which is close to I is evidence in favor of the random walk hypothesis on λ_t. Alternatively, if both P_t and Y_t are found to be integrated of order one, cointegration tests can be used to check whether the non-stationarity of Y_t can be fully accounted for by the non-stationarity of P_t. This discussion also illustrates that non-stationarities in economic series can be and in our view should be investigated and interpreted within the framework of a theoretical model.

One can estimate the complete model as a reduced form model without imposing the nonlinear restrictions and analyze its dynamic specification. The adjustment cost model and the pure time-to-build model are nested in the model (2.17). Without time-to-build considerations (i.e. $J = 1$), the second equation reduces to a ARMA(2, 1) with three lagged prices as explanatory variables. Alternatively, if adjustment costs are absent (i.e. if $\Gamma = 0$), the second autoregressive term disappears in all three equation. The general set-up of the model (2.17) allows us to investigate the appropriateness of adjustment costs and gestation lags for explaining the dynamics of factor demand.

3 Empirical Analysis

In this section we apply the model for dynamic factor demand to quarterly U.S. manufacturing industry data for the period 1960–1988. A description of the data and the sources are given in appendix II.

Section 3 is divided into three parts. The first part reports the results of the time series properties of the data and relates them to assumptions underlying the theoretical model. In the second part a comparison of the adjustment cost specification and the gestation lag dynamics with the reduced form model given in (2.17) and (2.18) is carried out. Finally, the third part presents the parameter estimates of the reduced form and the structural model. It should be noted that quarterly dummies are included in the model to take account of the presence of seasonality in the data.

3.1 *Integration, Order Selection and Cointegration*

An important issue in time series analysis is the determination of the order of integration of the individual series. In model (2.18), it is assumed that the variables in the vector P_t are integrated of order 1. Under the assumption that the innovations λ_t are stationary, the elements of vector Y_t in (2.17) are integrated of order 1 as well . If technology shocks λ_t are $I(1)$ as one might expect, factor demand and factor prices in (2.17) will not be cointegrated.

In table I, we report the values of Fuller's $\hat{\tau}_\mu$ and $\hat{\tau}_\tau$ statistics for the six variables in the system. The results in the upper part of table I indicate that with the exception of N_t and I_t^s the null hypothesis of a unit root cannot be rejected at the conventional 5% significance level. The inclusion of additional lags (see the last rows of table I) does not affect this conclusion for labor and structures either. The hypothesis of second order integration is strongly rejected for all

Table I. Tests for integration

	N_t	I_t^s	I_t^e	W_t	C_t^s	C_t^e
Fuller's $\hat{\tau}_\mu$	−3.37*	−3.74*	−2.11	−2.14	−1.31	−1.63
Adjusted R^2	0.62	0.67	0.37	0.11	0.21	0.23
Fuller's $\hat{\tau}_\tau$	−3.38	−3.83*	−3.03	−2.00	−1.78	−3.06*
t-value trend	0.85	−1.10	2.35*	0.14	1.20	−2.71*
Adjusted R^2	0.62	0.67	0.39	0.11	0.21	0.27
Fuller's $\hat{\tau}_\mu$	23.17*	51.20*	23.82*	16.46*	23.71*	26.81*
Fuller's $\hat{\tau}_\mu$	−3.07	−2.00	−2.11	−2.23	−1.16	−1.11
Fuller's $\hat{\tau}_\tau$	−3.11	−2.18	−3.2	−2.14	−1.56	−2.21

Model: $\Delta V_t = u_0 + u_1 t + u_2 V_{t-1} + u_3 \Delta V_{t-1} + u_4 \Delta V_{t-2} + \varepsilon_t^v$ with $V_t \in \{N_t, I_t^s, I_t^e, W_t, C_t^s, C_t^e\}$
The first row gives the statistics for the hypothesis H_0: $u_2 = 0$ while $u_1 = u_4 = 0$. The third row gives the statistics for the hypothesis H_0: $u_2 = 0$ while $u_4 = 0$. The fourth row gives the t-value of u_1. The sixth row gives the same statistics as the first row where the variables V_t in the model are differenced once more. The seventh and eighth rows give the statistics for the hypothesis H_0: $u_2 = 0$ while $u_1 = 0$ and H_0: $u_2 = 0$ respectively.
* Significant at the 5% level.

series. Thus according to these results all variables are assumed to be integrated of order 1. Labor and structures seem to be on the verge of stationarity and non-stationarity possibly due to the fact that they have risen until the mid sixties and did not rise significantly during the seventies and eighties (see also the graphs in appendix II). Also from the differences between the $\hat{\tau}_\mu$ and $\hat{\tau}_\tau$ statistics and from the t-values of the linear trend, it appears that including a linear trend significantly improves the fit of the investment and price process of equipment. The signs of the trends suggest that equipment investments have risen whereas prices have fallen during the time period under analysis.

Next, we identify the order of the dynamics of ΔP_t from information in the data. Estimated autocorrelations and partial autocorrelations for each time series suggest a first order univariate autoregressive model for ΔW_t, ΔC_t^s and ΔC_t^e. The results of order selections for the trivariate system are presented table II.

The cross-correlation matrices and the Schwarz (1978) criterion suggest a first order trivariate autoregression for ΔP_t. This finding and the outcomes of the unit roots tests in table I corroborate the first order VAR specification for the process of ΔP_t in (2.18) and the implied order of integration of Y_t in (2.17). The χ^2 and the Akaike criteria however suggest a higher order autoregressive process. Notice that the Schwarz criterion is also at the high (conservative) end of the acceptable range of penalty terms in certain model selection settings (see Potscher (1989)). Assuming a higher order autoregressive process for prices would entail including longer lags for prices in (2.18). We shall come back to this point in section 3.2.

Finally, we investigate whether the variables Y_t and P_t in (2.17) and (2.18) are cointegrated. Under the assumption that the productivity shocks are stationary, the theoretical model implies that there exist three cointegration rela-

Table II. Order selection for the trivariate process of factor prices

Lag j	1	2	3	4	5
Schwarz(j)	−26.22	−26.12	−25.92	−25.63	−25.35
AIC	−26.44	−26.56	−26.58	−26.51	−26.45
CHI²(j)	54.27	31.43	20.23	10.75	11.56

$\text{Schwarz}(j) = \ln|\Sigma| + (9j^* \ln(T))/T$ $j = 1, 2, \ldots, 5$ $T = 110$
$\text{AIC}(j) = \ln|\Sigma| + (18j)/T$ $j = 1, 2, \ldots, 5$
$\text{CHI}^2(j) = T(\ln|\Sigma_{j-1}| - \ln|\Sigma_j|) \sim \chi^2_{0.05}(9) = 16.92$ $j = 1, 2, \ldots, 5$

Cross-correlation matrices of $\Delta P_t' = [\Delta W_t, \Delta C_t^s, C_t^e]$

	ΔW_{t-1}	ΔC_{t-1}^s	ΔC_{t-1}^e	ΔW_{t-2}	ΔC_{t-2}^s	ΔC_{t-2}^e	ΔW_{t-3}	ΔC_{t-3}^s	ΔC_{t-3}^e
ΔW_t	0.22*	0.37*	0.34*	0.16	0.15	0.18	0.18	0.09	0.21*
ΔC_t^s	0.34*	0.45*	0.33*	0.25*	0.09	0.04	0.16	0.07	0.00
ΔC_t^e	0.29*	0.27*	0.49*	−0.08	0.01	0.06	−0.10	0.22*	−0.06

* Significant cross-correlations, i.e. larger than $2/\sqrt{T} \approx 0.189$ ($T = 112$)

tionships between factor demand and factor prices as then the disturbance vector of (2.17) is stationary [see Nickell (1985) and Palm and Pfann (1991) for a discussion of the relationship between intertemporal optimization models and cointegration]. Rejecting cointegration points towards the nonstationarity of technological shocks and/or other explanatory variables that have not been included in the model.

In order to test for the number of cointegrating relationships, we adopt the approach put forward by Johansen and Juselius (1990) and estimate the following unrestricted VAR model by ordinary least squares

$$\Delta Z_t = \mu_0 + \tau t + \Gamma_1 \Delta Z_{t-1} + \Gamma_2 \Delta Z_{t-2} + \Gamma_3 \Delta Z_{t-3} + \Pi Z_{t-4} + \varepsilon_t^z , \qquad (3.1)$$

where $Z_t' = (Y_t', P_t')'$ and μ_0 and τ are two 6×1 vectors and Γ_i ($i = 1, 2, 3$) and Π are 6×6 matrices with constant coefficients. The residuals of system (3.1) are analyzed. The results are presented in table III. Both the skewness and the excess kurtosis of the residuals do not deviate significantly from those of a normal distribution. The LM-statistics (see Jarque and Bera (1980)) do not reject normality either. Using the Box-Pierce test, the hypothesis of zero residual autocorrelation in (3.1) is not rejected at the conventional significance levels either. The results for Hosking's (1980) multivariate portmanteau test show that serial cross-correlation is not significant when more than ten lags are taken. This result is not unsatisfactory in view of the fact that the number of lags is less than 10 percent of the total sample and therefore the approximation of the asymptotic χ^2-distribution still holds.

We use the trace based likelihood ratio (LR) statistic $-2\ln LR(H_1|H_0) = -T\sum_{j=r+1}^{n} \ln(1 - Eig(j))$ to test H_0: the rank of Π is $r < n$ against H_1: Π has full rank n with $Eig(j)$ denoting the maximum likelihood estimate of the j-th eigenvalue of Π. No cointegrating relations were found when the linear trend was not included in (3.1), which is possibly due to the fact that labor and struc-

Table III. Test statistics for the normality and zero disturbance serial correlation and for cointegration in the model (3.1)

	N	I^s	I^e	W	C^s	C^e
Skewness (SK)	−0.16	0.42	−0.32	0.39	0.25	−0.21
Excess Kurtosis (EK)	1.01	0.36	0.42	0.54	−0.22	0.08
Normality (NORM)	5.24	3.88	2.75	4.28	1.40	0.83
Autocorrelation $Q(10)$	7.64	6.22	5.85	10.50	7.09	9.46

s	HQ	$\chi^2_{0.05}(36.s-144)$
5	99.15*	53.94
10	263.90*	258.11
11	290.93	297.38
12	316.59	336.42
13	347.93	375.28
14	374.86	413.98
15	416.02	452.54

H_0	i	Eig(i)	Lambda$_{max}$-test $U(i)$	Trace-test $CU(i)$
$r \leq 5$	6	0.053	6.09	6.09
$r \leq 4$	5	0.072	8.38	14.47
$r \leq 3$	4	0.132	15.86	30.33
$r \leq 2$	3	0.175	21.60	51.93
$r \leq 1$	2	0.232	29.63	81.56
$r = 0$	1	0.342	46.82	128.38*

* Significant at the 5% level
$\text{NORM} = (\text{SK}^2 + \text{EK}^2/4)/6 \sim \chi(2)$
$Q(10) = T\sum r_i^2 \ (i = 1, 2, \ldots, 10) \sim \chi(10)$
$\text{HQ} = T\sum_{r=1}^{s} \text{trace}(C_r' C_0^{-1} C_r C_0^{-1})'$, with $C_r = (1/T)\sum_{t=1}^{T} \varepsilon_t^{z} \varepsilon_t^{z'} \sim \chi^2(36 \cdot (s-4))$
$U(i) = -T\ln(1 - \text{Eig}(i))$
$CU(i) = \sum_{j=i}^{6} U(j)$

tures are close to stationarity, whereas the other series are not. Comparing the outcomes of the trace test statistics with the critical values given by Johansen (1991) table (V) suggests that the null hypothesis of $r \leq 1$ is not rejected whereas the null hypothesis of $r = 0$ is rejected at the 5 percent level, implying that the number of cointegrating regressions is one, a finding that suggests that the technological shocks are non-stationary. However, the same analysis for model (3.1) with five lagged dependent variables (the results are not given here) suggests that there exist three cointegration relationships.

Therefore we also test for cointegration between the variables in subsets which include one series on factor demand and the three price series. Because the matrices R and F in (2.17) are diagonal, if λ_t is stationary, at least one cointegrating relationship per subsystem should be found. If R is nondiagonal, because of interrelation more than one longrun relationship can hold for each subsystem. The results are presented in table IV. In almost all cases, normality of the residuals of the cointegration relations is not rejected. Only for labor, the residuals seem to be leptokurtic. This result can possibly be explained by the near stationarity of labor and the nonstationarity of the three prices and the linear trend. The results for autocorrelation, both univariate and multivariate, corroborate the model due to the fact that in each subsystem up to four lags of the dependent variable were included. The conclusion from the cointegration tests is that for each subsystem of a production factor and factor prices one equilibrium relationship is found. We also investigated model (3.1) for the three factor prices only. The results are given in the bottom part of table IV and suggest that no cointegration relationship among prices exists.

In summary, the existence of no cointegration relationship among prices and of one cointegration relationship per subsystem is predicted by the theoretical model presented in section 2. The empirical results do not deny that this is consistent with the information in the data.

3.2 Reduced Form Tests

In order to estimate the restricted VAR model (2.17) and (2.18) the length of the time to build structures has to be determined. For the mid fifties Mayer (1960) investigated the length of time required to complete investment projects by individual U.S. firms, and found that the average construction time to complete plants equals 11 months. In line with this finding, we assume J to be equal to 4 quarters. Imposing only exclusion restrictions, model (2.17)–(2.18) can be estimated as a system of seemingly unrelated ARMAX equations. In table V we give the log-likelihood values of several variants model (2.17)–(2.18). Three quarterly seasonal dummies and a linear trend (as a consequence of the cointegration test results) were included in each equation. The number of variables given in table V does not include these variables.

When the joint model is compared with the model without adjustment costs (see table V, part A), which is a model with only one lagged dependent variable in (2.17), the likelihood ratio (LR) statistic is 49.77. As it is much larger than the $\chi^2_{0.01}(3)$-value of 11.34, the null hypothesis $\Gamma = 0$ is rejected. The same conclusion holds for the exclusion of the time-to-build aspect, that is the exclusion of the lagged factor prices P_{t-i} ($i = 4, 5, 6$) and the moving average part $\varepsilon_{2,t-j}$ ($j = 2, 3, 4$) for which we have a likelihood ratio statistic of $36.85 > \chi^2_{0.01}(12) = 26.217$.

The technology process in the model was assumed to be a first order autoregressive process with a diagonal autoregressive matrix R in (2.15).

If interrelations in the form of a non-diagonal matrix R are allowed for, the matrices $R + F$ and $-RF$ in the autoregressive part of (2.17) are no longer diagonal. The likelihood ratio statistic for the test of the model with diagonal matrix R against that with an unrestricted matrix R is 27.66 (see table V, part

Table IV. Test statistics for the normality and zero disturbance serial correlation and for cointegration in subsystems

Labor	N	W	C^s	C^e
Skewness (SK)	0.15	0.14	0.10	−0.13
Excess Kurtosis (EK)	2.45*	0.41	0.36	−0.00
Normality (NORM)	28.32*	1.18	0.78	0.33
Autocorrelation Q(10)	5.70	3.70	7.43	8.71

Structures	I^s	W	C^s	C^e
Skewness (SK)	0.37	0.06	0.21	−0.12
Excess Kurtosis (EK)	0.57	−0.24	−0.29	−0.33
Normality (NORM)	4.00	0.33	1.22	0.74
Autocorrelation Q(10)	11.10	6.20	7.51	12.10

Equipment	I^e	W	C^s	C^e
Skewness (SK)	−0.26	0.23	0.24	−0.02
Excess Kurtosis (EK)	−0.03	−0.13	−0.06	−0.19
Normality (NORM)	1.26	1.06	1.05	0.17
Autocorrelation Q(10)	7.56	5.02	6.90	8.34

Hosking test

s	Labor	Structures	Equipment	$\chi^2_{0.05}(16.s-64)$
5	33.37*	36.75*	35.71*	28.33
6	53.59*	46.72	48.17	48.98
7	71.09*	58.24	55.99	68.52
8	85.81	78.56	77.57	87.51
9	100.55	97.37	107.20	106.14
10	121.63	111.47	118.03	124.51
15	189.90	174.61	195.21	214.14

H_0	i	Labor CU(i)	Structures CU(i)	Equipment CU(i)	Prices CU(i)
$r \leq 3$	4	4.80	7.23	3.64	
$r \leq 2$	3	15.24	19.63	14.43	7.44
$r \leq 1$	2	34.84	35.95	36.09	17.52
$r = 0$	1	66.15*	67.30*	68.63*	38.34

Prices	W	C^s	C^e	s	Hosk.	$\chi^2_{0.05}(9.s-36)$
SK	0.03	−0.00	−0.01	5	13.84	18.50
EK	0.20	0.14	0.21	6	27.58	31.02
NORM	0.21	0.09	0.22	7	32.06	42.69
Q(10)	5.25	7.26	12.4			

* Significant at the 5% level.

Table V. Reduced form tests[+]

A) Adjustment costs, time-to-build and technology (1961.IV–1988.IV)			
Model (2.17)	$-2\cdot$loglik.	Number of variables	LR-statistic
with $J = 4$	1188.42	59	—
without adjustment costs	1238.19	56	49.77**
without time-to-build ($J = 1$)	1225.27	47	36.85**
with R unrestricted	1160.76	71	27.66**
B) Granger-causality (1962.III–1988.IV)			
Process of prices	AR(2)	AR(4)	AR(5)
Wald	24.57**	21.37*	20.72**
LR	23.06**	22.49**	21.76*
C) Dynamics of (2.17) implied by the order of the process for P_t (1962.III–1988.IV)			
	LR-statistic		Degrees of freedom
Process of prices is ARI(3, 1)	52.73**		18
Process of prices is ARI(4, 1)	64.65**		27
D) The length of the time-to-build (J) in model (2.17) (1962.I–1988.IV).			
J	2	3	4
LR-statistic			
H_0: J against			
H_1: $J + 1$	11.96*	14.39**	0.01
Degrees of freedom	4	4	4

[+] The models are estimated using the computer package SCA from Liu et al. (1986). The likelihood values are all "exact".
* Significant at the 5%-level (using the table for the χ^2-distribution).
** Significant at the 1%-level.

A). The number of degrees of freedom involved is 12 and the test is significant at the conventional level of 5%. The assumption of a non-diagonal R has also implications for the moving average part of (2.17) (R^* and D_j in (A.14) in appendix I are no longer interchangeable and as a consequence a vector Koyck-transformation is required). Although a more general technology process seems reasonable according to the above test, the exact implications of this extension are not obvious. Notice however that when R is nondiagonal, capital stock is included in each Euler equation. The implied model for gross investment has a moving average part in each equation.

A crucial assumption in the specification of the theoretical model is the unidirectional causality relationship between real production prices and production factors. If an individual entrepreneur could affect factor prices by varying factor demand, the assumption (2.18) should also include lagged production factors (Y_{t-i}, $i > 0$) and the closed-form solution (2.17) should be extended with price decision equations. In table V, part B we estimate a system of factor price equations

$$P_t = \sum_{j=1}^{p} \overline{M}_j P_{t-j} + DY_{t-1} + \varepsilon_t^p$$

including an intercept, seasonal dummies and a linear trend and test the hypothesis $H_0: D = 0$ against the hypothesis $H_1: D \neq 0$. The number of degrees of freedom involved is 9.

The number of lagged prices (prices are expressed in levels for reason of comparison with the factors in levels) is taken to be 2, 4, 5 respectively as suggested by the order selection criteria reported in table II. However, as shown by Toda and Phillips (1991), the conventional causality tests are valid asymptotically as χ^2-criteria only when there is sufficient cointegration with respect to the variables whose causal effects are being tested. When this cointegration condition fails to hold, the limit distribution involves a mixture of a χ^2-distribution and a non-standard distribution, which generally involves nuisance parameters. Simulation results obtained by Toda and Phillips (1991) indicate that the rejection frequency associated with the conventional Wald test is usually much larger than the nominal size of 5%. Therefore, our finding of Wald and LR-values in the range between 20.72 and 24.57 for the complete system are too low to be taken as evidence in favor of the existence of Granger causality from demand to prices. A natural extension would be concerned with analyzing the causality structure between the subvectors P_t and Y_t in the framework of the vector ARMA process (2.17)–(2.18) along the lines of Boudjellaba et al. (1992), a point left for future research.

The test results in table II, concerning the order of the autoregressive process of prices is reconsidered in table V, part C. The order of 3 and 4 for the autoregressive part, suggested by the Akaike and the χ^2-criteria implies longer lags in prices in the system of factor demand equations (2.17). For instance, if the process of prices is ARI(3,1) then up to eight lagged prices should be included in (2.17) with 18 additional non-zero elements. When compared with model (2.17) with P_t being ARI(1, 1), this extension of the model (2.17) is significant according to the LR-test. A LR-test of the implications for (2.17) of an ARI(4, 1) process for prices is also significant when it is compared with the ARI(1, 1) model. However, the ARI(4, 1) model is not significant when it is compared with the ARI(3, 1) model. Testing the time-to-build assumption within the extension of model (2.17) when the process for prices is ARI(3, 1) and ARI(4, 1) give the LR-statistic 23.36 and 22.69 that are still significant ($\chi^2_{0.05}(12) = 21.03$), implying that even in this extended model time-to-build is found to be relevant. Moreover, the Schwarz criterion leads us to select an ARI(1, 1) process for P_t whereas the AIC tends to overestimate the order of the process, we prefer to stick to the low order process for P_t.

To test whether the findings of Mayer (1960) about the length of the time-to-build are consistent with the findings for our model, we vary the length of the time-to-build up to five quarters. The results are given in the lower panel of table V. The specifications with four quarters gestation lags ($J = 4$) are significantly different from those with a gestation of two or three quarters. According to these results, the extension to a gestation period from four to five quarters is not significant. Therefore, the length of the gestation period in model (2.17) is consistent with the survey findings of Mayer.

3.3 *Reduced and Structural Form Estimates*

In table VI the reduced form estimates of model (2.17)–(2.18) subject to exclusion restrictions implied by the theoretical specification are given.

The following conclusions emerge from the estimation results for the reduced form in table VI. The parameters of the AR matrices $F_1 + R$ and $F_1 R$ and of the MA matrices Φ_i, $i = 1, \ldots, 4$ are highly significant. The deterministic trend appears to be relevant only in the demand equation for labor.

Table VII contains diagnostic tests for the labor, structures and equipment equations in (2.17). The first statistics show that the assumption of normality can only be rejected for the labor-residuals. The LM-statistic is significant because of the presence of leptokurtosis. A similar result was also found when testing for cointegration (see table III) with a VAR(4) model. The ARCH-statistics in table VII are not significant. No univariate autocorrelation is found as the Box-Pierce statistic Q is not significant. Hosking's multivariate autocorrelation indicates that there is significant cross-correlation in the residuals of the model (2.17)–(2.18).

In the lower panel of table VII, the same test statistics are reported for the model in (2.17)–(2.18) estimated without restricting R to be diagonal as suggested by the empirical findings in table V, part A. Even in this extended model a very high order multivariate autocorrelation is found. Notice that in this case the autocorrelation is also caused by autocorrelation of the residuals of the equipment equation.

The theoretical model (2.17)–(2.18) contains 68 reduced form parameters, whose estimates are given in table VI. These parameters are functions of the structural parameters, that can be estimated using the method of Asymptotic Least Squares (see for example Kodde et al. (1990)). Estimates of the structural parameters are given in table VIII. The estimates for the matrix of the process of prices are identical with the reduced form estimates.

The discount rate (β) and both depreciation rates (κ^s and κ^e) are not identified. The discount rate is assumed to be 0.96. According to depreciation rates used by the OECD when calculating capital stock ("Flows and Stocks of fixed capital", see appendix II) it is assumed that $\kappa^s = 0.0125$ and $\kappa^e = 0.025$. The estimates of the structural coefficients of the production function, the adjustment cost function, the technology process and the time-to-build parameters are conditional on these values. As the data have been seasonally adjusted using dummies, the parameter vector α in the production function cannot be identified from the intercept. The time-to-build parameters δ_1, δ_2, δ_3 are identified from

Table VI. Reduced form estimates (Standard errors within parentheses)

$$C = \begin{bmatrix} -0.91\ (0.35) \\ -0.50\ (0.69) \\ -0.12\ (0.03) \end{bmatrix} \qquad \tau = \begin{bmatrix} 0.02\ (0.01) \\ 0.01\ (0.01) \\ 0.00\ (0.00) \end{bmatrix}$$

$$F_1 + R = \begin{bmatrix} 1.20\ (0.08) & 0 & 0 \\ 0 & 1.80\ (0.05) & 0 \\ 0 & 0 & 1.70\ (0.10) \end{bmatrix} \qquad -F_1 \cdot R = \begin{bmatrix} -0.37\ (0.08) & 0 & \\ 0 & -0.84\ (0.05) & 0 \\ 0 & 0 & -0.78\ (0.10) \end{bmatrix}$$

$$M_0 = \begin{bmatrix} 0.15\ (0.17) & -0.26\ (0.26) & 0.19\ (0.84) \\ -0.16\ (0.57) & 1.09\ (0.88) & 6.43\ (3.01) \\ -0.01\ (0.02) & -0.01\ (0.03) & 0.13\ (0.10) \end{bmatrix} \qquad M_1 = \begin{bmatrix} 0.32\ (0.22) & -0.16\ (0.30) & 1.07\ (1.32) \\ 0.05\ (0.64) & -1.43\ (0.89) & -7.87\ (4.14) \\ 0.01\ (0.03) & -0.00\ (0.04) & -0.28\ (0.19) \end{bmatrix}$$

$$M_2 = \begin{bmatrix} -0.20\ (0.19) & 0.04\ (0.24) & -1.76\ (0.84) \\ 1.39\ (0.69) & 0.26\ (0.95) & 2.15\ (3.85) \\ -0.00\ (0.03) & -0.00\ (0.04) & 0.16\ (0.18) \end{bmatrix} \qquad M_3 = \begin{bmatrix} 0 & 0 & 0 \\ -1.29\ (0.64) & -0.68\ (0.90) & 1.32\ (3.56) \\ 0.01\ (0.02) & -0.00\ (0.02) & -0.04\ (0.08) \end{bmatrix}$$

$$M_4 = \begin{bmatrix} 0 & 0 & 0 \\ -0.42\ (0.61) & -2.34\ (0.89) & -5.38\ (3.50) \\ 0 & 0 & 0 \end{bmatrix} \qquad M_5 = \begin{bmatrix} 0 & 0 & 0 \\ 1.79\ (0.59) & -0.17\ (0.76) & 4.39\ (3.37) \\ 0 & 0 & 0 \end{bmatrix}$$

$$M_6 = \begin{bmatrix} 0 & 0 & 0 \\ -0.01\ (0.57) & 1.23\ (0.69) & -0.28\ (2.31) \\ 0 & 0 & 0 \end{bmatrix}$$

$$\Phi_0 = I_3 \qquad \Phi_1 = \begin{bmatrix} 0 & 0 & 0 \\ 0 & -0.18\ (0.10) & 0 \\ 0 & 0 & 0.53\ (0.15) \end{bmatrix}$$

$$\Phi_2 = \begin{bmatrix} 0 & 0 & 0 \\ 0 & 0.41\ (0.09) & 0 \\ 0 & 0 & 0 \end{bmatrix} \qquad \Phi_3 = \begin{bmatrix} 0 & 0 & 0 \\ 0 & 0.38\ (0.08) & 0 \\ 0 & 0 & 0 \end{bmatrix} \qquad \Phi_4 = \begin{bmatrix} 0 & 0 & 0 \\ 0 & 0.39\ (0.10) & 0 \\ 0 & 0 & 0 \end{bmatrix}$$

$$\overline{M} = \begin{bmatrix} -0.05\ (0.15) & 0.36\ (0.20) & 0.23\ (0.14) \\ -0.07\ (0.11) & 0.34\ (0.12) & 0.10\ (0.14) \\ 0.05\ (0.11) & 0.13\ (0.15) & 0.48\ (0.11) \end{bmatrix}$$

$$\Sigma^{\lambda} = \begin{bmatrix} 0.41 & & \\ 0.44 & 3.42 & \\ 0.02 & 0.06 & 0.01 \end{bmatrix} \qquad \Sigma^{p} = \begin{bmatrix} 0.0002 & & \\ 0.00008 & 0.00013 & \\ 0.00008 & 0.00006 & 0.00018 \end{bmatrix}$$

The following model was estimated after seasonal adjustment:

$$Y_t = C + \tau t + (F_1 + R) Y_{t-1} - RF_1 Y_{t-2} + \sum_{j=0}^{J+2} M_j P_{t-j} - \sum_{i=0}^{J} \Phi_i \varepsilon_{t-i}^{\lambda} \tag{2.17}$$

$$\Delta P_t = \overline{M} \Delta P_{t-1} + \varepsilon_t^p \tag{2.18}$$

Assumption: $J = 4$
Number of observations = 109 (1961:IV, 1988:IV)
2.loglik = 1188.42

Table VII. Tests on the residuals (see table V)

A. R diagonal (table VI)	Labor	Structures	Equipment
SKEW	0.34	0.05	0.03
EX.KURT.	1.19*	−0.22	−0.06
LM	12.22*	0.27	0.04
ARCH			
1	0.85	1.35	0.99
2	3.50	2.15	1.92
3	5.29	2.33	2.39
4	7.28	2.45	5.22
5	7.52	2.77	7.26
Q(10)	13.5	10.6	13.0
s	Hosking	$\chi^2_{0.05}(9.s-53)$	
10	99.84*	55.17	
15	139.18*	108.44	
20	169.87*	159.60	
25	204.55	209.72	
30	234.89	259.21	
40	309.02	356.95	

B. R unrestricted	Labor	Structures	Equipment
SKEW	0.38	0.02	0.11
EX.KURT.	1.42*	−0.23	0.50
LM	11.75*	0.25	1.32
Q(10)	13.6	10.5	21.3*
s	Hosking	$\chi^2_{0.05}(9.s-65)$	
8	67.15*	15.49	
9	79.53*	28.33	
10	83.74*	40.14	
15	118.82*	94.53	
20	149.73*	146.08	
25	183.68	196.43	
30	215.75	246.06	
40	287.71	343.99	

* Significant at the 5% level.

the moving average parameters of the structures equation. The value of δ_4 can then be determined from (2.4d), that is from the assumption that the δ's add up to one.

Given these time-to-build parameters, the coefficients f_1, f_2, f_3, ρ_1, ρ_2, ρ_3 and γ_{11}, γ_{22}, γ_{33} can be determined from the six parameters of the autoregressive part and all the parameters of M_0, thereby imposing all restrictions on M_0 (see (A.11) and (A.12)). The value of f_4, f_5 and f_6 then follows from (A.6a). Finally, the production coefficients a_{11}, a_{22} and a_{33} can be obtained from (A.6b) and the restrictions on b_i (see the expression below (A.1)). Notice that by only taking

Table VIII. Structural form estimates (ALS) (Standard errors within parentheses)

Assumptions: $\beta = 0.96$
$\kappa^s = 0.0125$
$\kappa^e = 0.025$

	Labor	Structures	Equipment
Production function	$a_{11}: 2.64$ (2.51)	$a_{22}: 0.006$ (0.017)	$a_{33}: 0.58$ (1.83)
Adjustment costs	$\gamma_{11}: 12.19$ (11.56)	$\gamma_{22}: 0.35$ (0.93)	$\gamma_{33}: 27.60$ (86.60)
Technology	$\rho_1: 0.47$ (0.35)	$\rho_2: 0.86$ (1.10)	$\rho_3: 0.96$ (0.67)
Eigenvalues	$f_1: 0.64$ (0.29)	$f_2: 0.89$ (1.06)	$f_3: 0.88$ (0.57)
	$f_4: 1.63$ (0.73)	$f_5: 1.17$ (1.39)	$f_6: 1.18$ (0.77)

Process of prices

$$\overline{M} = \begin{bmatrix} -0.05\ (0.15) & 0.36\ (0.20) & 0.23\ (0.14) \\ -0.07\ (0.11) & 0.34\ (0.12) & 0.10\ (0.14) \\ 0.05\ (0.11) & 0.13\ (0.15) & 0.48\ (0.11) \end{bmatrix}$$

Time-to-build

$\phi_3/\phi_4: 0.18$ (0.10)	$\phi_2/\phi_4: -0.41$ (0.09)	$\phi_1/\phi_4: -0.38$ (0.08)	$\phi_0/\phi_4: -0.39$ (0.10)
$\delta_1: 0.114$ (0.063)	$\delta_2: 0.237$ (0.083)	$\delta_3: 0.360$ (0.074)	$\delta_4: 0.289$ (0.054)

Number of reduced form parameters = 68
Number of structural parameters = 27

into account M_0, the restrictions of M_1 to M_6 are not considered. Imposing all restrictions on this highly overidentified model is complicated. As a result of ignoring some restrictions, the estimates of the structural parameters in table VIII are not fully efficient.

As can be seen from table VIII, almost all time-to-build parameters are significant at the 5% level. These estimates imply a hump-shaped distribution of investments during the gestation period. Most other coefficients in table VIII are not significant, the reason being, the insignificance of many coefficients of M_0 in table VI. The value of the Wald statistic associated with the restriction imposed when estimating the structural parameters from the reduced form parameters using asymptotic least squares equals 1.09 ($<\chi^2_{0.05}(1) = 3.84$). As a consequence, the restriction imposed between ϕ_i/ϕ_4, $i = 0, 1, 2, 3$ and δ_i, $i = 1, 2, 3$ is not rejected.

A high persistence of technological shocks in the equipment and structures equations with estimates of ρ_1 and ρ_2 of 0.86 and 0.96 respectively is found. Other factors of persistence (f_i) in the reduced form depend on the adjustment costs coefficients γ_{ii} and the production function coefficients a_{ii} (see the equation for b_i below (A.1) and (A.6b)). There is obviously a trade-off between the eigenvalues and the adjustment costs provided the marginal productivity is kept constant.

From the estimation results for the structures and equipment equations, it can be concluded that f_2 and f_3 are almost equal, whereas adjustment costs and marginal productivity for these production factors are quite different. A possible explanation of this finding is the time-to-build for structures.

Finally, again we want to stress the fact that care has to be taken when interpreting these results. More precise estimates could be obtained when all restrictions implied by the theoretical model were imposed on the structural coefficients.

3.4 *The Dynamics of the Model*

In order to study the dynamic properties of the different models we computed the moving average representation (MAR) for the first differences of the variables I_t^s, I_t^e and N_t. The results are given in the figures 1–15. The figures presenting the impulse response of ΔI^s to a shock in the productivity $\varepsilon_{3t}^{\lambda}$ and that of ΔI^s and ΔI^e to a shock in $\varepsilon_{1t}^{\lambda}$ are not reported, as these responses are zero (see also expression (A.9) in the appendix I with Γ being diagonal). The MAR has been obtained from the reduced form estimates of the models with respectively time-to-build and adjustment costs (t.t.b. and a.c.), time-to-build only (t.t.b.) and adjustment costs only (a.c.) and $J = 4$. The estimates for the model with time-to-build and adjustment costs are given in table VI. The contemporaneous covariance matrix of the technology and factor price shocks Σ has been decomposed such that in the recursive form the variables are ordered as follows C_t^s, C_t^e, W_t, I_t^s, I_t^e, N_t with C_t^s appearing in all six equations, C_t^e appearing in five equations (with the exception of the equation for C_t^s) and so on. The size of the impulse is equal to one standard deviation of the associated shock.

Several features emerge from the impulse responses in the figures 1–15. First there is no evidence of persistence in the impact of the shocks on the first differences of factor demand. Second, the shortrun dynamics of the different models differ in several respects. The model allowing for time-to-build dynamics only exhibits in general a fairly smooth monotonic response pattern. Adjustment costs instead lead to cyclical patterns in the impulse response function with peaks and troughs generally appearing between quarters 4 and 12. The model with time-to-build and adjustment costs exhibits the largest fluctuations in the impulse response. Third, the response of N_t to the different shocks is hardly sensitive to the choice of the specification for the dynamics. Fourth, the reaction of the model with time-to-build only has immediately the expected sign. A positive technology shock leads to an increase in ΔI^s and ΔI^e, whereas price shocks imply a decrease in the change of I^s and I^e. Fifth, the response of ΔI^s and ΔI^e to respectively $\varepsilon_{2t}^{\lambda}$ and $\varepsilon_{3t}^{\lambda}$ is hump-shaped for the models with adjustment costs included. Notice that Park (1984) also finds a hump-shaped response in the change of gross private domestic fixed investment using U.S. quarterly data for the period 1948–1981. Sixth, the positive reaction of ΔI^s and ΔI^e quickly after the shocks ε_{2t}^{p} and ε_{3t}^{p} respectively for the model with time-to-build only, resembles that found by Park (1984) for the change in gross private domestic investment in the U.S. While, because of sampling errors some care has to be taken when interpreting these findings, one can conclude that the specification of the dynamics strongly affects the shape of the estimated response function.

Finally, notice that our findings cannot be directly compared with the simulation results in Rouwenhorst (1991) where the impulse response of the capital stock is reported instead of that of investment. The figures 1–15 represent impulse responses of ε shocks in a partial equilibrium model of factor inputs. Real business cycle models describe economies instead of demand or supply functions only.

4 Conclusions

In this paper, we formulated a dynamic factor demand model which incorporates adjustment costs and time-to-build considerations and derived the closed form solution for the demand for labor, structures and equipment. The inclusion of time-to-build features for structures adds – beside the adjustment costs of all production factors – another dynamic dimension to the model. Both sources of dynamics can be identified from the information in the data. Given the processes for the exogenous variables the factor prices and technology, the dynamics and the nonstationarity of factor demand are completely determined by the theoretical model.

The model was analyzed using quarterly data U.S. manufacturing industry data for the period 1960.I–1988.IV. The findings of the univariate time series and the econometric analyses were interpreted in the framework of the initial optimization model. The joint model performs reasonably well when it is applied to quarterly U.S. manufacturing data. In particular, assumptions on the order of integration, on the number of cointegration relationships were found to be supported by the information in the data. Tests on assumptions concerning the process of technology indicate that the theoretical model could be extended by a more general specification where interrelations between production factors arise.

When accounting for the fact that in the presence of integrated regressors, the Wald statistic has a non-standard distribution, the results from LR-tests

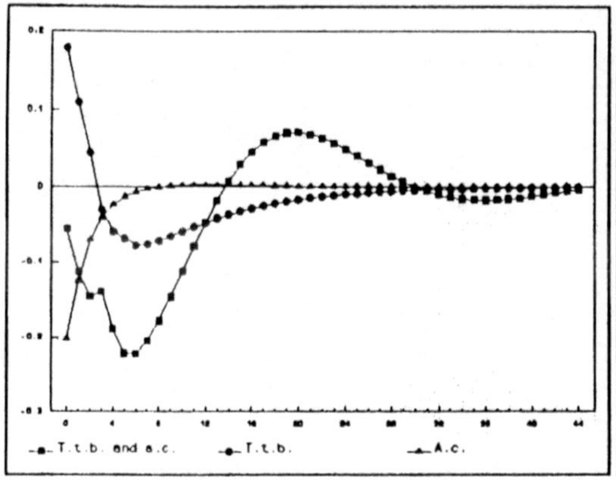

Fig. 1. Impulse from ε^p_{2t} to I^s

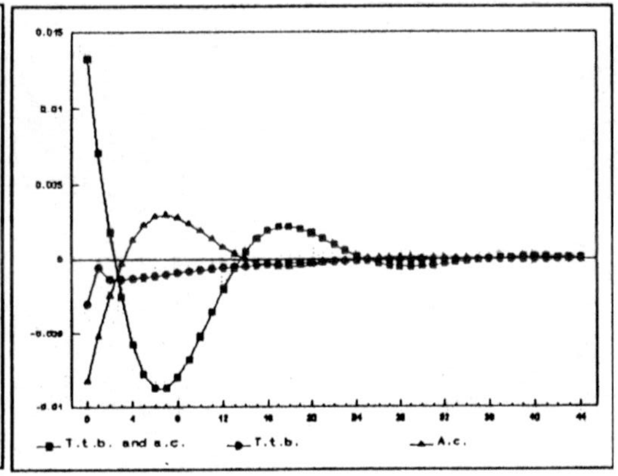

Fig. 2. Impulse from ε^p_{2t} to I^e

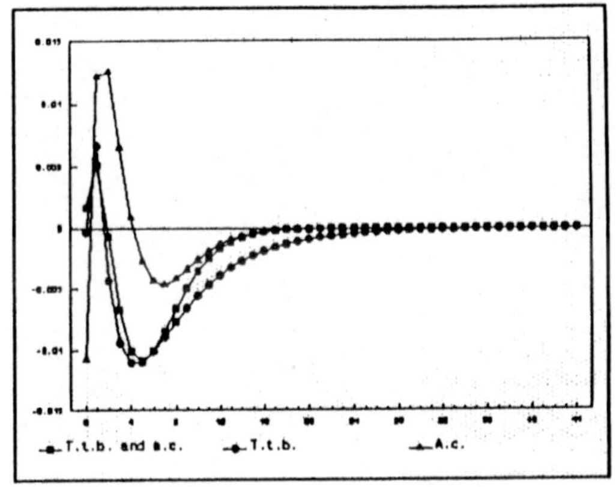

Fig. 3. Impulse from ε^p_{2t} to N

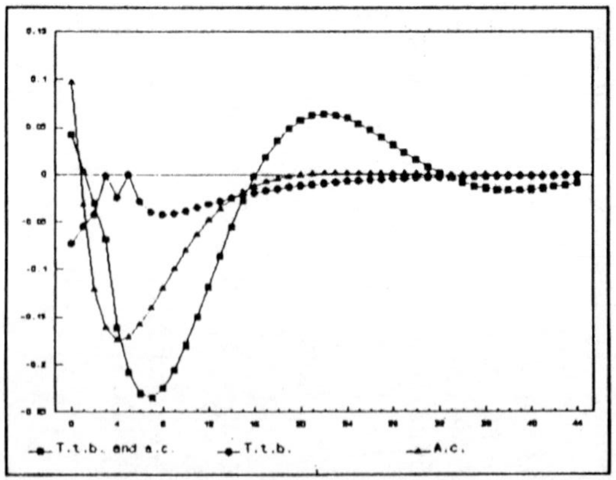

Fig. 4. Impulse from ε^p_{3t} to I^s

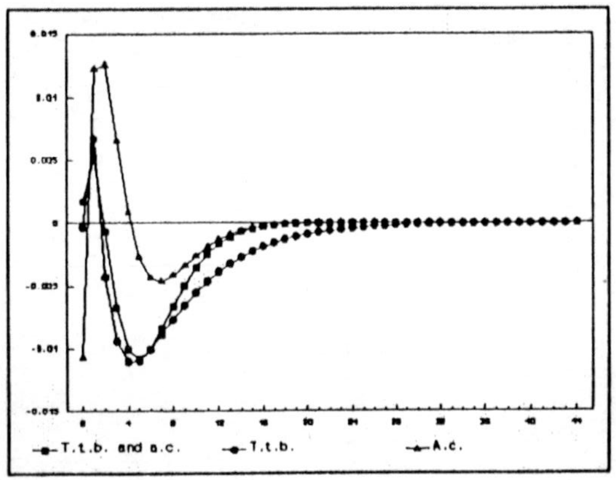

Fig. 5. Impulse from ε^p_{3t} to I^e

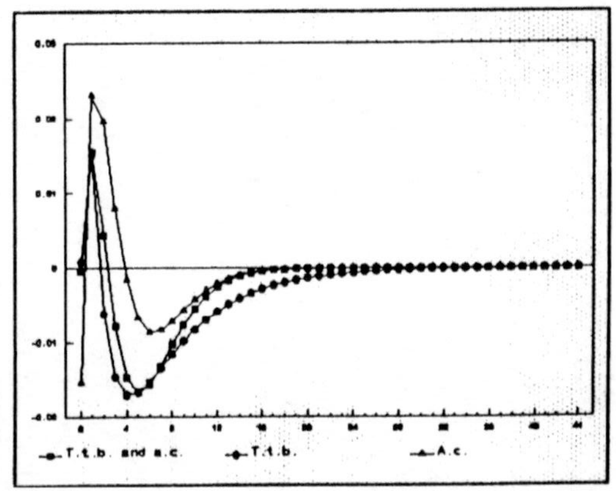

Fig. 6. Impulse from ε^p_{3t} to N

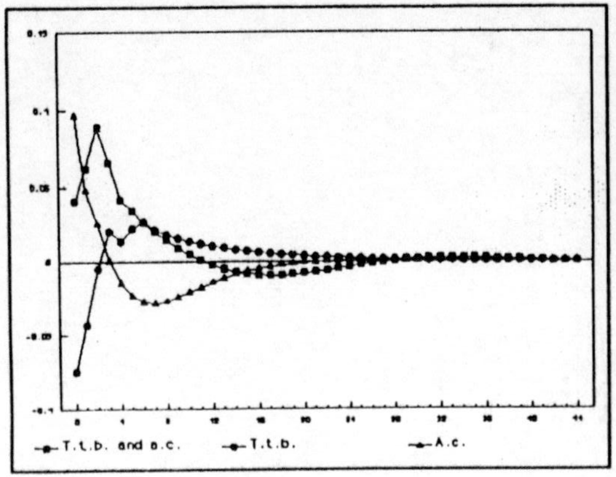

Fig. 7. Impulse from ε_{1t}^{p} to I^{s}

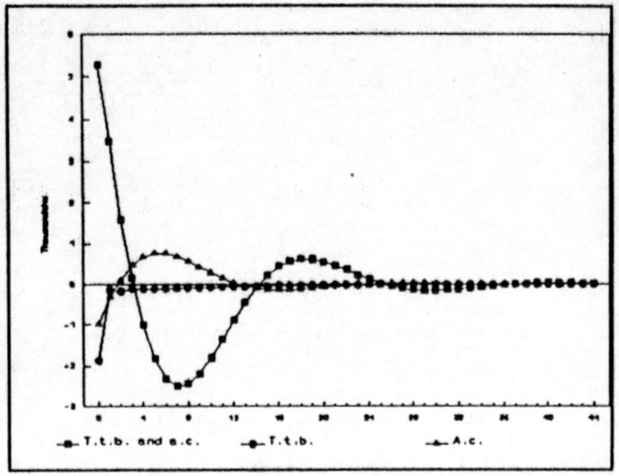

Fig. 8. Impulse from ε_{1t}^{p} to I^{e}

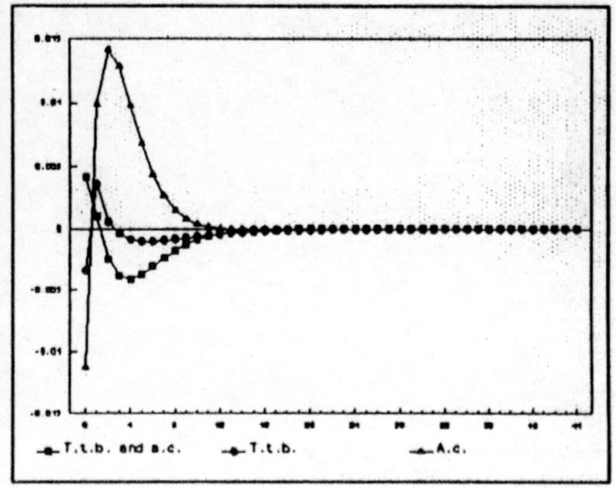

Fig. 9. Impulse from ε_{1t}^{p} to N

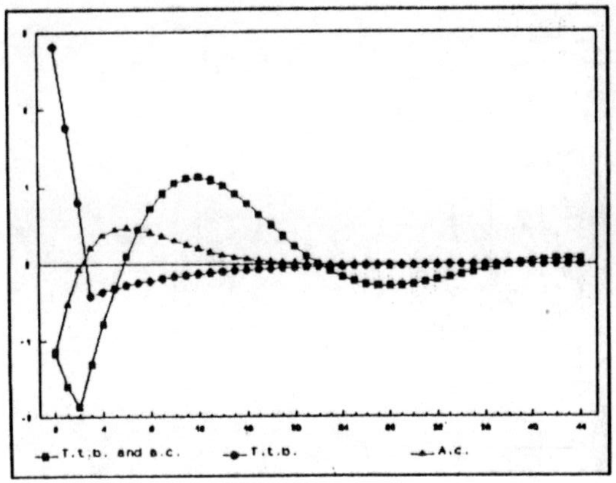

Fig. 10. Impulse from $\varepsilon_{2t}^{\lambda}$ to I^{s}

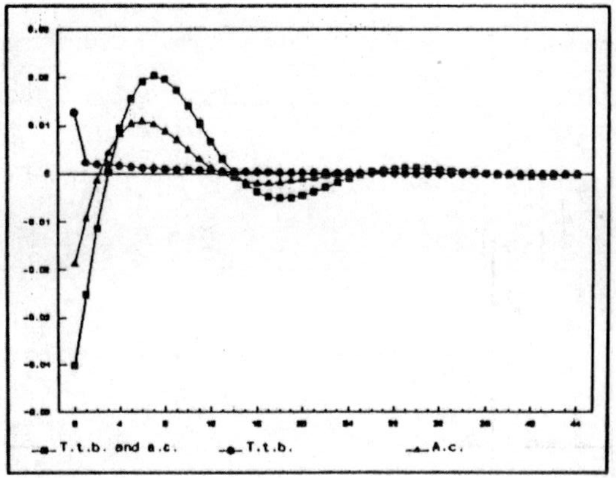

Fig. 11. Impulse from $\varepsilon_{2t}^{\lambda}$ to I^{e}

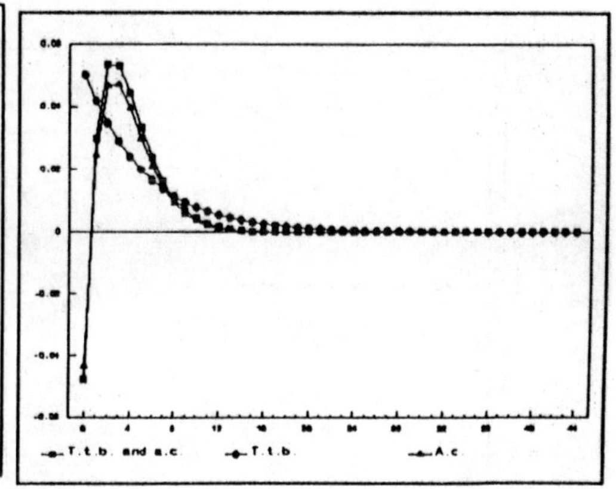

Fig. 12. Impulse from $\varepsilon_{2t}^{\lambda}$ to N

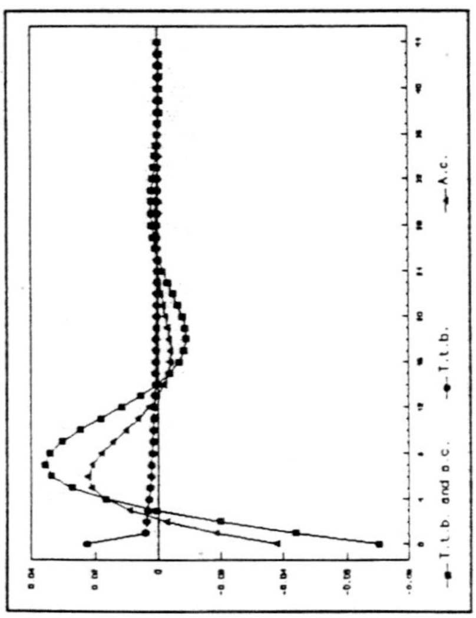

Fig. 13. Impulse from $\varepsilon_{3t}^{\lambda}$ to I^e

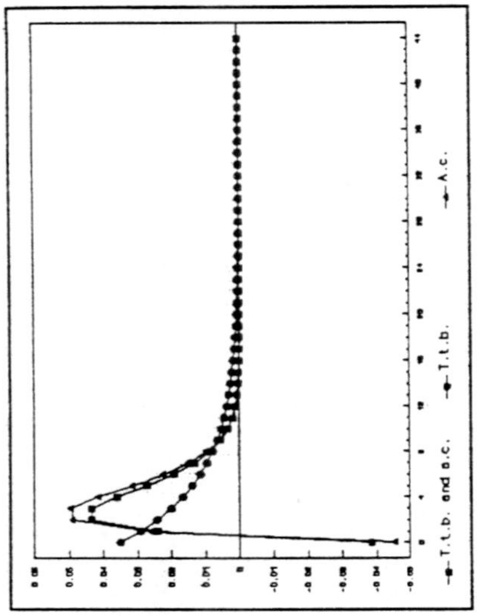

Fig. 14. Impulse from $\varepsilon_{3t}^{\lambda}$ to N

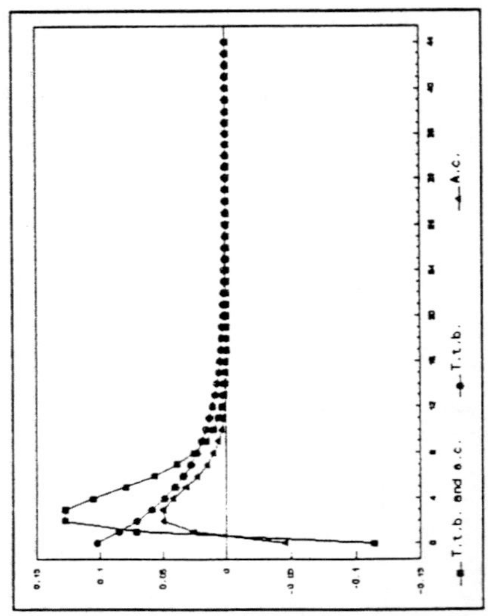

Fig. 15. Impulse from $\varepsilon_{1t}^{\lambda}$ to N

on uni-directional Granger causality from production factors to factor prices do not reject the assumptions made in the theoretical model.

Taking up these remarks the consequences of assuming interrelation of production factors within both the production function and the adjustment cost function are important. More information can be gathered with respect to the degree of complementarity or substitutability among labor, structures and equipment. The difficulty in analyzing these features in a model with time-to-build arises from the differences in lead times between production factors.

Most importantly, it was found that given all simplifying assumptions made, time-to-build considerations are found to be at least as important as adjustment costs in our model. The impulse response function associated with the model with time-to-build dynamics only has a much smoother shape than the response function of thc models based on adjustment costs. Comparisons of the results presented in this paper with the stylized facts from the real business cycle (RBC) literature, however, should be made with great caution. This paper investigates a partial equilibrium model of factor inputs, whereas RBC models describe economies instead of just demand or supply functions.

Appendix I Solving the Euler Equations for the Rational Expectations

We define $X_t^d = [N_t, K_{t+J}^s, K_{t+1}^e]'$, normalize the system (2.10a)–(2.10c) in the expectations variables and extend it by adding identities to yield in matrix form

$$\begin{bmatrix} X_t^d \\ E_t X_{t+1}^d \end{bmatrix} = \begin{bmatrix} 0 & I_3 \\ -\beta^{-1} I_3 & B_{22} \end{bmatrix} \begin{bmatrix} X_{t-1}^d \\ X_t^d \end{bmatrix} + \begin{bmatrix} 0 \\ D \end{bmatrix} Z_t \; , \tag{A.1}$$

where B_{22} is a 3×3 diagonal matrix with typical diagonal element $b_i = a_{ii}(\beta\gamma_{ii})^{-1} + \beta^{-1} + 1$, and D and Z_t given by

$$D = (\boldsymbol{\beta}\boldsymbol{\Gamma})^{-1} \begin{bmatrix} -\alpha_1 & -1 & 0 & 0 & 1 & 0 & 0 & 0 & 0 & 0 & \cdots & 0 \\ -\alpha_2 & 0 & -1 & 0 & 0 & \phi_J \beta^{-J} & 0 & \phi_{J-1}\beta^{-J+1} & 0 & \phi_{J-2}\beta^{-J+2} & \cdots & \phi_0 \\ -\alpha_3 & 0 & 0 & -1 & 0 & 0 & \beta^{-1} & 0 & (\kappa^e - 1) & 0 & \cdots & 0 \end{bmatrix}$$

$$Z_t' = [1 \;\; \lambda_{1t} \;\; E_t\lambda_{2,t+J} \;\; E_t\lambda_{3,t+1} \;\; W_t \;\; C_t^s \;\; C_t^e \;\; E_tC_{t+1}^s \;\; E_tC_{t+1}^e \;\; E_tC_{t+2}^s \;\; \cdots \;\; E_tC_{t+J}^s] \tag{A.2}$$

Define

$$B = \begin{bmatrix} 0 & I_3 \\ -\boldsymbol{\beta}^{-1} I_3 & B_{22} \end{bmatrix}.$$

If we can decompose B as

$$B = G^{-1}FG \tag{A.3}$$

and partition F and G in blocks of 3×3 matrices as

$$G = \begin{bmatrix} G_{11} & G_{12} \\ G_{21} & G_{22} \end{bmatrix}, \quad F = \begin{bmatrix} F_1 & 0 \\ 0 & F_2 \end{bmatrix} \quad \text{with} \quad F_1 = \begin{bmatrix} f_1 & 0 & 0 \\ 0 & f_2 & 0 \\ 0 & 0 & f_3 \end{bmatrix},$$

$$F_2 = \begin{bmatrix} f_4 & 0 & 0 \\ 0 & f_5 & 0 \\ 0 & 0 & f_6 \end{bmatrix},$$

the application of Blanchard and Kahn (1980) expresses factor demand X_t^d as

$$X_t^d = -G_{22}^{-1}G_{21}X_{t-1}^d - G_{22}^{-1}\sum_{i=0}^{\infty} F_2^{-i-1}G_{22}DE_t(Z_{t+i}) \tag{A.4}$$

From (A.3) it follows that

$$GB = FG \quad \Leftrightarrow \quad \begin{bmatrix} -\beta^{-1}G_{12} & G_{11} + G_{12}B_{22} \\ -\beta^{-1}G_{22} & G_{21} + G_{22}B_{22} \end{bmatrix} = \begin{bmatrix} F_1G_{11} & F_1G_{12} \\ F_2G_{21} & F_2G_{22} \end{bmatrix}$$

such that under the condition that the submatrices are invertible, the equality of the (2, 1) blocks gives

$$-\beta^{-1}G_{22} = F_2G_{21} \quad \Leftrightarrow \quad -G_{22}^{-1}G_{21} = G_{21}^{-1}(\beta F_2)^{-1}G_{21}. \tag{A.5}$$

Because F_2 is diagonal, the autoregressive part in the solution (A.4) is diagonal if G_{21} is diagonal. The characteristic polynomial of the matrix B can be written as (see also Palm and Pfann (1990))

$$(-f^2 + b_1 f - \beta^{-1})(-f^2 + b_2 f - \beta^{-1})(-f^2 + b_3 f - \beta^{-1}),$$

where b_1, b_2, b_3 are the eigenvalues of B_{22}. From this follows that the six eigenvalues f_i $(i = 1, 2, \ldots, 6)$ of B satisfy

$$f_1 f_4 = f_2 f_5 = f_3 f_6 = \beta^{-1} \tag{A.6a}$$

and

$$f_1 + f_4 = b_1, \qquad f_2 + f_5 = b_2, \qquad f_3 + f_6 = b_3, \tag{A.6b}$$

where it is assumed that

$$|f_i| \leq 1, \quad i = 1, 2, 3 \quad \text{and} \quad |f_i| > 1, i = 4, 5, 6.$$

The equality

$$-G_{22}^{-1}G_{21} = G_{21}^{-1}(\beta F_2)^{-1}G_{21} = G_{21}^{-1}F_1G_{21} \tag{A.7}$$

(see (A.5) and (A.6a)) then also holds.

Because B_{22} is diagonal, the decomposition (A.3) is easy to obtain

$$G^{-1} = \begin{bmatrix} 1 & 0 & 0 & 1 & 0 & 0 \\ 0 & 1 & 0 & 0 & 1 & 0 \\ 0 & 0 & 1 & 0 & 0 & 1 \\ f_1 & 0 & 0 & f_4 & 0 & 0 \\ 0 & f_2 & 0 & 0 & f_5 & 0 \\ 0 & 0 & f_3 & 0 & 0 & f_6 \end{bmatrix}, \quad \begin{aligned} f_i &= \tfrac{1}{2}b_i - \tfrac{1}{2}[b_i^2 - 4\beta^{-1}]^{1/2} , & i &= 1, 2, 3 , \\ f_i &= \tfrac{1}{2}b_{i-3} + \tfrac{1}{2}[b_{i-3}^2 - 4\beta^{-1}]^{1/2} & i &= 4, 5, 6 . \end{aligned}$$

Thanks to (A.7) and the diagonality of F_1 and G_{22}, formula (A.4) reduces to

$$X_t^d = F_1 X_{t-1}^d - \sum_{i=0}^{\infty} (\beta F_1)^{i+1} D E_t(Z_{t+i}) . \tag{A.8}$$

Notice that the necessary condition $|f_i| \leq 1$, $i = 1, 2, 3$ and $|f_i| > 1$, $i = 4, 5, 6$ follows from the assumptions $0 < \beta < 1$, $\gamma_{ii} > 0$ $(i = 1, 2, 3)$ and $a_{ii} > 0$ $(i = 1, 2, 3)$.

The rewriting of (A.8) in terms of Y_t gives (2.14). Separating the components of Z_t into a constant term, a technology component and a price component, we then rewrite (2.14) as

$$\begin{aligned} Y_t = C^* + F_1 Y_{t-1} &- F_1 \Gamma^{-1} \sum_{j=0}^{J} D_j \sum_{i=0}^{\infty} (\beta F_1)^i E_{t-j} [\lambda_{1,t+i-j}, \lambda_{2,t+i+J-j}, \lambda_{3,t+i+1-j}]' \\ &- F_1 \Gamma^{-1} \sum_{k=0}^{J} D_k^* \sum_{j=0}^{J} D_j \sum_{i=0}^{\infty} (\beta F_1)^i E_{t-j} P_{t+i+k-j} , \end{aligned} \tag{A.9}$$

where (see also (2.12))

$$C^* = -\sum_{j=0}^{J} D_j \sum_{i=0}^{\infty} (\beta F_1)^{i+1} \begin{bmatrix} \alpha_1 (\beta \gamma_{11})^{-1} \\ \alpha_2 (\beta \gamma_{22})^{-1} \\ \alpha_3 (\beta \gamma_{33})^{-1} \end{bmatrix} = \begin{bmatrix} \alpha_1 f_1 (\gamma_{11}(1 - \beta f_1))^{-1} \\ \kappa^s \alpha_2 f_2 (\gamma_{22}(1 - \beta f_2))^{-1} \\ \kappa^e \alpha_3 f_3 (\gamma_{33}(1 - \beta f_3))^{-1} \end{bmatrix}$$

and (see (2.14))

$$D_k^* = \begin{bmatrix} 1 & 0 & 0 \\ 0 & \beta^{-J+k} & 0 \\ 0 & 0 & \beta^{-1+k} \end{bmatrix} D_k , \qquad k = 0, 1, \ldots, J .$$

Using the assumption that λ_t is generated by a first order VAR (2.15), the part in (A.9) which is explained by technology shocks can be expressed as

$$\begin{aligned} & F_1 \Gamma^{-1} \sum_{j=0}^{J} D_j \sum_{i=0}^{\infty} (\beta F_1)^i E_{t-j} \begin{bmatrix} \lambda_{1,t+i-j} \\ \lambda_{2,t+i+J-j} \\ \lambda_{3,t+i+1-j} \end{bmatrix} \\ &= F_1 \Gamma^{-1} \sum_{j=0}^{J} D_j \sum_{i=0}^{\infty} (\beta F_1)^i \begin{bmatrix} \rho_1^i & 0 & 0 \\ 0 & \rho_2^{i+J} & 0 \\ 0 & 0 & \rho_3^{i+1} \end{bmatrix} \lambda_{t-j} = R^* \sum_{j=0}^{J} D_j \lambda_{t-j} , \end{aligned} \tag{A.10}$$

where

$$R^* = F_1 \Gamma^{-1}(I - \beta F_1 R)^{-1} \begin{bmatrix} 1 & 0 & 0 \\ 0 & \boldsymbol{\rho}_2^J & 0 \\ 0 & 0 & \boldsymbol{\rho}_3 \end{bmatrix} .$$

Similarly but in a far less obvious way, from the assumption of a first order VAR for ΔP_t (2.16), it follows that

$$\sum_{i=0}^{\infty} (\beta F_1)^i E_{t-j}(P_{t+i+k-j}) = V_k P_{t-j} - \left(\sum_{i=1}^{k} \overline{M}^i + \beta F_1 V_k \overline{M} \right) P_{t-1-j} ,$$

with

$$V_k - \beta F_1 V_k (I + \overline{M}) + (\beta F_1)^2 V_k \overline{M} = (I - \beta F_1) \sum_{i=1}^{k} \overline{M}^i + I_3 \qquad k \geq 0 . \tag{A.11}$$

such that

$$-F_1 \Gamma^{-1} \sum_{k=0}^{J} D_k^* \sum_{j=0}^{J} D_j \sum_{i=0}^{\infty} (\beta F)^i E_{t-j}(P_{t+i+k-j}) = \sum_{i=0}^{J+1} M_i^* P_{t-i} , \tag{A.12}$$

where

$$M_0^* = -F_1 \Gamma^{-1} \sum_{k=0}^{J} D_k^* D_0 V_k$$

$$M_i^* = -F_1 \Gamma^{-1} \sum_{k=0}^{J} D_k^* \left[D_i V_k - D_{i-1} \left(\sum_{j=1}^{k} \overline{M}^j + \beta F_1 V_k \overline{M} \right) \right] \qquad i = 1, 2, \ldots, J$$

$$M_{J+1}^* = F_1 \Gamma^{-1} \sum_{k=0}^{J} D_k^* D_J \left(\sum_{j=1}^{k} \overline{M}^j + \beta F_1 V_k \overline{M} \right) .$$

Only the matrices M_0^* and M_1^* have no zero elements. M_2^* has zero elements on the first row whereas M_k^* ($k = 3, 4, \ldots, J + 1$) has zero elements on the first and third row.

After substituting (A.10) and (A.12) into (A.9) and applying a Koyck transformation to eliminate the unobservable technology components λ_t, we obtain the model

$$Y_t = C + (R + F_1) Y_{t-1} - R F_1 Y_{t-2} + \sum_{j=0}^{J+2} M_j P_{t-j} + \varepsilon_t^y \tag{A.13}$$

with

$$\begin{aligned} C &= (I - R) C^* \\ M_0 &= M_0^* \\ M_i &= M_i^* - R M_{i-1}^* , \qquad i = 1, 2, \ldots, J + 1 \\ M_{J+2} &= -R M_{J+2}^* \end{aligned}$$

$$\varepsilon_t^y = -R^* \sum_{j=0}^{J} D_j \varepsilon_{t-j}^{\lambda} = R^* \begin{bmatrix} \boldsymbol{\varepsilon}_{1,t}^{\lambda} \\ \sum_{j=0}^{J} \boldsymbol{\phi}_{J-j} \boldsymbol{\varepsilon}_{2,t-j}^{\lambda} \\ \boldsymbol{\varepsilon}_{3,t}^{\lambda} + (\boldsymbol{\kappa}^e - 1)\boldsymbol{\varepsilon}_{3,t-1}^{\lambda} \end{bmatrix}.$$

Appendix II Quarterly Data for the Manufacturing Industry, 1960–1988

The variables are:

N	Average weekly hours, that is $L * H$ where: L = number of all employees H = weekly hours of work.
I^s, I^e	Gross fixed capital formation, structures and equipment respectively, in constant prices.
W	Real hourly earnings, that is hourly earnings deflated by the producer price index of industrial goods P_y.
C^s, C^e	Real costs of gross investments, structures and equipment respectively, that is $(C_c^i/I^i)/P_y$ $(i = s, e)$ where C_c^i = gross fixed capital formation of i in current prices, and I^i = gross fixed capital formation of i in constant prices.

Sources:

MEI	Main Economic Indicators, Organisation for Economic Cooperation and Development (OECD), various issues.
FS	Flows and Stocks of Fixed Capital, OECD, various issues.
QNA	Databank of Quarterly National Accounts, OECD.

The time series I^s, I^e, C_c^s, C_c^e, are taken from FS. All other time series are taken from MEI and are quarterly.

The annual (end of the year) series I^s, I^e, C_c^s, C_c^e are interpolated using the Ginsburgh method. National (non-residential) investment series from QNA for structures and equipment in both current and constant prices are used to describe quarterly fluctuations.

All series are seasonally unadjusted and are indexed at 1985.II. The graphs of the time series N, W, I^s, C^s, I^e, C^e are given in the next figures.

United States Manufacturing Industry 1960.I–1988.IV

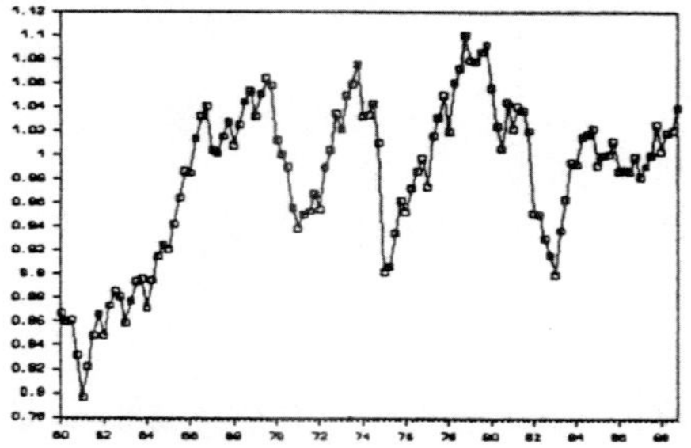

Labor (N)

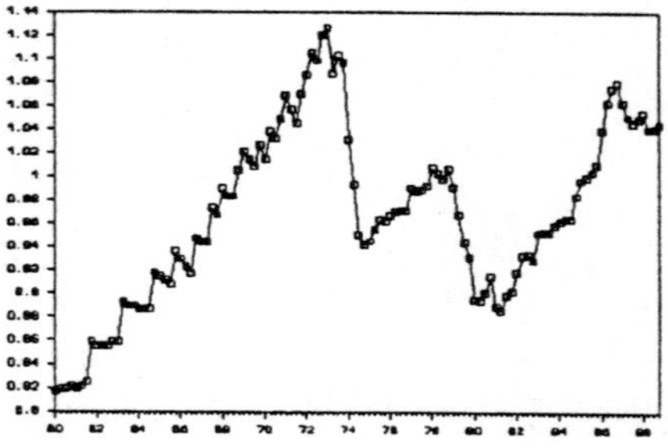

Wages (W)

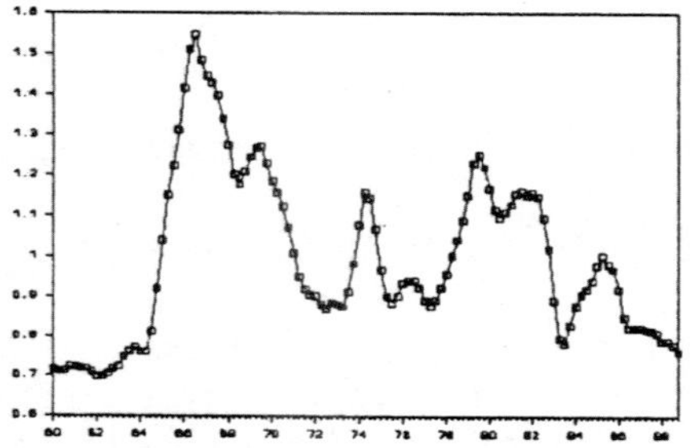

Structures Investment (I^s)

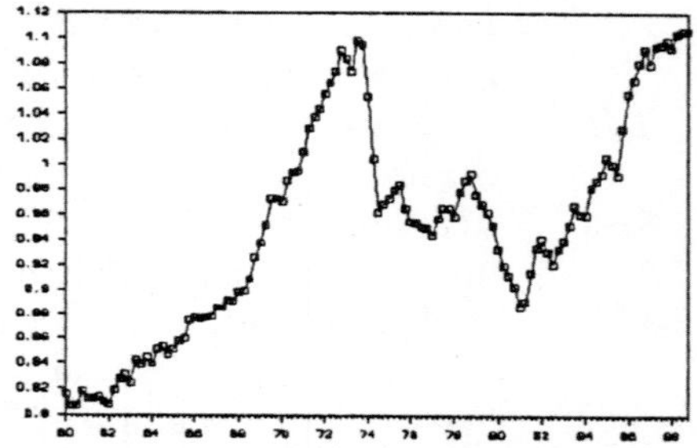

Price Structures Investment (C^s)

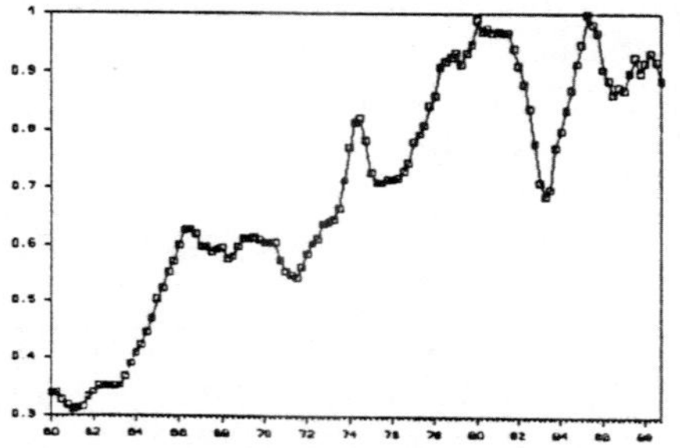

Equipment Investment (I^e)

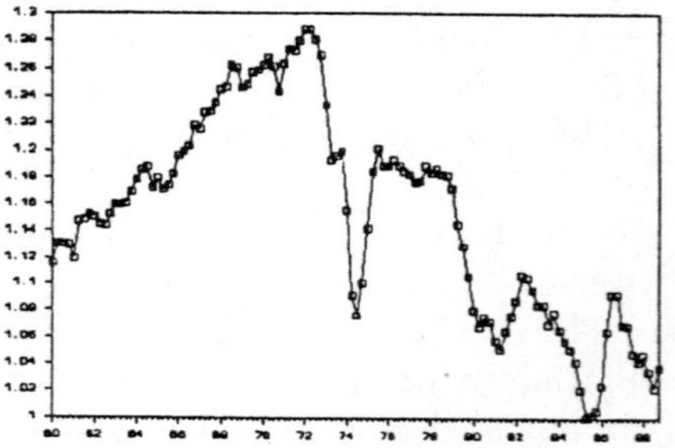

Price Equipment Investment (C^e)

References

Blanchard OJ, Kahn CM (1980) The solution of linear difference models under rational expectations. Econometrica 48:1305–11

Boudjellaba H, Dufour J-M, Roy R (1992) Testing causality between two vectors in multivariate ARMA models. Journal of the American Statistical Association 87:1082–1090

Engle RF, Hendry DF, J-F Richard (1983) Exogeneity. Econometrica 51:277–304

Hosking JRM (1980) The multivariate portmanteau statistic. Journal of the American Statistical Association 75:602–608

Jarque CM, Bera AK (1980) Efficient tests for normality, homoscedasticity and serial independence of regression residuals. Economics Letters 6:255–259

Johansen S (1991) The role of the constant term in cointegration analysis of nonstationary variables. Mimeo, Copenhagen

Johansen S, Juselius K (1990) Maximum likelihood estimation and inference on cointegration – with applications to the demand for money. Oxford Bulletin of Economics and Statistics 52:169–210

Kodde DA, Palm FC, Pfann GA (1990) Asymptotic least-squares estimation – efficiency considerations and applications. Journal of Applied Econometrics 5:229–243

Kydland FE, Prescott EC (1982) Time to build and aggregate fluctuations. Econometrica 50:1345–70

Lippi M, Reichlin L (1990) Diffusion of technical change and the identification of the trend component in real GNP. Observatoire Français des Conjonctures Economiques, Paris, Document de travail no. 90–94

Liu LM, Hudak GB, Box GEP, Muller ME, Tiao GC (1986) The SCA Statistical System – Reference Manual for Forecasting and Time Series Analysis. Illinois: SCA-Press

Lucas RE (1967) Adjustment costs and the theory of supply. Journal of Political Economy 75:321–34

Mayer Th (1960) Plant and equipment lead times. The Journal of Business 33:127–132

Nickell SJ (1985) Error correction, partial adjustment and all that: an expository note. Oxford Bulletin of Economics and Statistics 47:119–129.

Palm FC, Pfann GA (1990) Interrelated demand rational expectations models for two types of labour. Oxford Bulletin of Economics and Statistics 52:45–68

Palm FC, Pfann GA (1991) Interrelation, structural changes, and cointegration in a model for manufacturing factor demand in the Netherlands. Recherches Economiques de Louvain 51:221–243

Park JA (1984) Gestation lags with variable plans: An empirical study of aggregate investment. Ph.D. dissertation, Carnegie-Mellon University

Pfann GA (1990) Stochastic Adjustment Models of Labour Demand, Berlin Springer-Verlag

Pötscher BM (1989) Model selection under nonstationarity; autoregressive models and stochastic linear regressions models. The Annals of Statistics 17:1257–1274

Rossi PE (1988) Comparison of dynamic factor demand models. In: Barnett WA, Berndt ER, White H (eds) Dynamic econometric modeling, proceedings of the third international symposium in economic theory & econometrics, Cambridge, Cambridge University Press 357–376

Rouwenhorst KG (1991) Time to build and aggregate fluctuations. Journal of Monetary Economics 27:241–254

Schwarz G (1978) Estimating the dimension of a model. Annals of Statistics 6:461–464

Toda HY, Phillips PCB (1991) Vector autoregression and causality: A theoretical overview and simulation study. Cowles Foundation Discussion Paper no 1001, Yale University

Structural Change Analysis

Parameter Constancy in Cointegrating Regressions[1]

CARMELA E. QUINTOS

Department of Economics, Yale University, P.O. Box 2125 Yale Station, New Haven, Connecticut 06520-2125, USA

PETER C. B. PHILLIPS

Cowles Foundation for Research in Economics, Yale University, P.O. Box 2125 Yale Station, New Haven, Connecticut 06520-2125, USA

Abstract: This paper proposes an approach to testing for coefficient stability in cointegrating regressions in time series models. The test statistic considered is the one-sided version of the Lagrange Multiplier (LM) test. Its limit distribution is non-standard but is nuisance parameter free and can be represented in terms of a stochastic bridge process which is tied down like a Brownian bridge but relies on a random rather than a deterministic fraction to do so. The approach provides a test of the null hypothesis of cointegration against specific directions of departure from the null; subset coefficient stability tests are also available. A small simulation studies the size and power properties of these tests and an empirical illustration to Australian data on consumption, disposable income, inflation and money is provided.

JEL Classification System-Numbers: C22, C32

1 Introduction

A considerable number of statistical procedures that test for the presence of cointegration are available in the literature. The most commonly used methods in empirical research are the residual-based approaches, such as the augmented Dickey-Fuller test of Dickey-Fuller (1979, 1981) and the semiparametric Z-tests developed by Phillips (1987), and Johansen's (1988) likelihood ratio test for cointegration in vector autoregressions. The asymptotic properties of these tests are now well known, and the reader is referred to Phillips and Ouliaris (1990) for a detailed study of the various residual-based tests. All of these tests work from a null hypothesis of no cointegration. This approach has been criticized (see, for example, Engle and Yoo (1991)) because it is usually the alternative (i.e., cointegration) that is of primary interest in applications and the mechanism by which classical hypothesis testing is carried out ensures that the null hypothesis (here no cointegration) is accepted unless there is strong evidence against it.

In this paper we propose an approach to testing for parameter constancy and, hence, cointegration in regressions with nonstationary regressors. Our tests are extensions of the Lagrange Multiplier (LM) and locally best invariant (LBI) tests that are presently used in the literature to test for parameter constancy

[1] Our thanks go to Bruce Hansen for sending us a copy of his related work (1992a) and for the use of his GAUSS procedure for computing the fully modified least squares estimator.

in regressions with stationary regressors – see King-Hillier (1985), Leybourne-McCabe (1989) and Nabeya-Tanaka (1988). In our case, the parameter that is the focus of attention is a cointegrating coefficient, or as the case may be, a cointegrating submatrix in multivariate regressions. The approach allows for random evolution of the parameter(s) under the alternative hypothesis. The subset tests are especially useful because they provide a means of isolating the source of cointegration failure that is not available in residual-based tests.

The limit theory of our tests is developed and is characterized by a stochastic bridge process that resembles a Brownian bridge. However, the limiting bridge process in this case is tied down at its upper end by a random (as opposed to a deterministic) fraction of the interval [0, 1]. The random fraction is itself a stochastic process whose features depend on the stochastic properties and the number of cointegrating regressors.

The present paper is related to recent work by Tanaka (1993) and Hansen (1992a) that came to our attention when our work was nearly completed. Tanaka applies the LBI test to the coefficient of the nonstationary regressor that causes the failure of cointegration under the alternative, whereas we take the coefficient to be random and apply an LM test to the variance of the error process that governs the random parameter. In this sense, our approach accords more with the formulation of parameter constancy tests in the literature. Hansen (1992a) develops a limit theory for the LM test that corresponds with our own approach. His test of constancy applies to the full matrix of cointegrating coefficients and his test for cointegration is based on the constancy of the intercept in the regression. Our LM tests of coefficient constancy are developed and applied to submatrices of the cointegrating matrix as well as the full cointegrating matrix. The advantage of this formulation is that in empirical work, tests of the constancy of individual coefficients can be conducted, thereby isolating the variables that are responsible for failure in the null hypothesis.

The plan of the paper is as follows. Section 2 outlines the models under consideration and the assumptions required for the construction of our tests. The formulation of the test and its limiting distribution are given in Section 3. Section 4 presents multivariate extensions, specializations to cases where the regressors contain trends and subset tests. Some Monto Carlo experiments including size calculations and power comparisons are given in Section 5. Section 6 reports a brief empirical illustration of our methods and Section 7 gives some concluding remarks.

2 Models and Assumptions

Let $\{x_t, y_t\}$ be $I(1)$ processes and consider the following varying coefficient regression

$$y_t = \beta_t x_t + \varepsilon_{0t} \tag{1}$$

$$\Delta x_t = \varepsilon_{1t} \tag{2}$$

$$\beta_t = \beta_{t-1} + \eta_t\ , \qquad \eta_t \equiv \text{iid } N(0, \Sigma_\eta) \tag{3}$$

where we have assumed that the parameter variation follows a Gaussian random walk process, allowing the model to accommodate fundamental changes in structure over time. For reasons that will be made clear later we require that the initial condition β_0 be nonzero. The initial conditions for $\{x_t, y_t\}$ do not affect the subsequent theory so we allow (x_0, y_0) to be any random variable.

Throughout the paper, we assume the sequence $\{\varepsilon_t\} = (\varepsilon_{0t}, \varepsilon'_{1t})'$ has mean zero and satisfies an invariance principle. More precisely, it is assumed that for $r \in [0, 1]$

$$S_{[nr]} = n^{-1/2} \sum_{t=1}^{[nr]} \varepsilon_t \xrightarrow{d} B(r) \equiv \begin{pmatrix} B_0(r) \\ B_1(r) \end{pmatrix} \tag{4}$$

where $B(r)$ is a scaled Brownian motion and B_0 and B_1 need not be independent. In (4) and elsewhere in the paper, $[m]$ denotes the largest integer that does not exceed m.

The invariance principle (4) holds under very general conditions and is valid for the sequence $\{\varepsilon_t\}$ driven by a large class of models with varying degrees of heterogeneity and memory restrictions. Explicit conditions under which (4) holds are discussed in detail in earlier work by Phillips-Durlauf (1986) and Phillips-Solo (1992). When $\{\varepsilon_t\}_1^\infty$ is weakly stationary as would be the case when (1) and (2) form a cointegrated system, the following mixing and moment conditions, for example, are sufficient

Assumption 1:

i) $E|\varepsilon_1|^\rho < \infty$ *for some* $2 \le \rho < \infty$
ii) *either* $\sum_{m=1}^\infty \phi_m^{1-1/\rho} < \infty$, *or* $\rho > 2$ *and* $\sum_{m=1}^\infty \alpha_m^{1-2/\rho} < \infty$, *where* ϕ_m *and* α_m *are the uniform mixing and* α*-mixing coefficients for* $\{\varepsilon_t\}$ *respectively.*

This ensures that

$$\Psi = \lim_{n\to\infty} E(n^{-1} S_n S_n') = E(\varepsilon_1 \varepsilon_1') + \Sigma_{k=2}^\infty \{E(\varepsilon_1 \varepsilon_k') + E(\varepsilon_k \varepsilon_1')\}$$

is finite. When we work with Assumption 1, we presume none of the common exogeneity conditions for x_t and we allow for contemporaneous correlation of the form $Ex_t\varepsilon_{0t} \neq 0$.

The long-run covariance matrix Ψ of the limit Brownian motion B in (4) is partitioned as

$$\begin{aligned} \Psi &= \begin{pmatrix} \psi_{00} & \Psi_{01} \\ \Psi_{10} & \Psi_1 \end{pmatrix} \\ &= \lim_{n\to\infty} n^{-1} E(\Sigma_1^n \varepsilon_t)(\Sigma_1^n \varepsilon_t)' \\ &= \Sigma + \Lambda + \Lambda' \end{aligned} \tag{5}$$

where

$$\Sigma = \lim_{n\to\infty} n^{-1}\Sigma_1^n E(\varepsilon_t\varepsilon_t') = \begin{pmatrix} \sigma_0^2 & \Sigma_{01} \\ \Sigma_{10} & \Sigma_{11} \end{pmatrix}$$

$$\Lambda = \lim_{n\to\infty} n^{-1} \sum_{t=2}^{n} \sum_{j=1}^{t-1} E(\varepsilon_j\varepsilon_t') = \begin{pmatrix} \lambda_{00} & \Lambda_{01} \\ \Lambda_{10} & \Lambda_{11} \end{pmatrix}$$

with the partitions made conformable to that of the long-run variance matrix Ψ. If we require $\{\varepsilon_t\}$ to have continuous spectral density matrix $f_{\varepsilon\varepsilon}(\lambda)$ then Ψ is simply $f_{\varepsilon\varepsilon}(\cdot)$ evaluated at the zero frequency, i.e. $\Psi = 2\pi f_{\varepsilon\varepsilon}(0)$, the long-run covariance matrix of ε_t. If (1) and (2) form a cointegrated system, then Ψ is singular although we require Ψ_1 to be invertible. The model for which Ψ_1 is singular presents additional complications (see Phillips (1991b)) and will be considered in later work. For later discussion we define

$$\Upsilon = \Sigma + \Lambda = \begin{pmatrix} \Upsilon_{00} & \Upsilon_{01} \\ \Upsilon_{10} & \Upsilon_{11} \end{pmatrix} = \begin{bmatrix} \Upsilon_0 \\ \Upsilon_1 \end{bmatrix}. \tag{6}$$

If $\{\varepsilon_t\}$ is iid then of course $\Psi = \Sigma = \Upsilon$.

As a direct extension of (1) we also consider time series $\{y_t\}$ that are generated by

$$y_t = \beta_t x_t + \Gamma h_t + \varepsilon_{0t} \tag{1$'$}$$

where h_t is a deterministic function of time of order p. For example, h_t may consist of a constant ($p = 0$) or a time trend ($p = 1$).

The assumptions that allow h_t suitably standarized by a power of $n^{-1/2}$ to converge to a limit function $h(r)$ are discussed in Phillips and Hansen (1990) and Hansen (1990). Here we simply assume the existence of a diagonal matrix of weights γ_n such that $\gamma_n h_{[nr]} \to h(r)$ uniformly in r. For example if h_t consists of a simple time trend (t), $\gamma_n = \mathrm{n}^{-1}$ and $h(r) = r$.

In order to understand the LM approach to testing parameter constancy we first derive the test and its limit distribution under a set of simplifying assumptions. Specifically, we strengthen Assumption 1 to:

Assumption 2:

i) $\{\varepsilon_t\} \equiv$ iid
ii) $\{x_t\}$ *is strictly exogenous.*

As we shall see, extending the results to models that allow for stationary errors requires (possibly semiparametric) corrections to remove the bias introduced by the serial correlation and endogeneity of $\{\varepsilon_t\}$ and $\{x_t\}$.

3 The LM Test Statistics and their Limiting Distributions

We are interested in testing for the constancy of the coefficient β_0 in (1) and (1)'. In order to understand the behavior of the LM test, we begin with a single $I(1)$ regressor x_t and denote by ψ its long-run covariance matrix given in (5). The multivariate extension for x_t of dimension k will be dealt with later in the paper in which case we will retain the matrix notation Ψ for the long-run covariance matrix. By backward substitution of (3) we write model (1) as

$$\begin{aligned} y_t &= \beta_0 x_t + (\Sigma_1^t \eta_s) x_t + \varepsilon_{0t}, \qquad \eta_S \equiv \text{iid } N(0, \sigma_\eta^2) \\ &= \beta_0 x_t + w_t \end{aligned} \tag{7}$$

and (1)' as

$$y_t = \beta_0 x_t + \Gamma h_t + w_t \tag{7'}$$

then a test for constancy reduces to a zero restriction on the variance of the innovations that drive the random parameter, σ_η^2. We write this as

$$Ho\colon \sigma_\eta^2 = 0 \tag{8}$$

which we test against the alternative $Ha\colon \sigma_\eta^2 > 0$. Throughout the paper we assume that $\{\varepsilon_t\}$ satisfies Assumptions 1 or 2 so that under Ho, (7) is a constant coefficient cointegrating regression and (7)' is a constant coefficient cointegrating regression around a trend. Under Ha, (7) and (7)' are not cointegrated systems since w_t is non-stationary. Thus a test for constancy of the long-run coefficient can be interpreted as testing the null of cointegration.

Before we derive the LM test statistic we summarize some limit theory for the least squares estimators in (7) ($\hat{\beta}_0$) and (7)' ($\dot{\beta}_0$, $\dot{\Gamma}$). All integrals, such as $\int B^2$, are taken with the limits [0, 1] in what follows to simplify notation.

Lemma 1: (Park and Phillips (1988)). *For the model* (7) *under Ho*

(i) $n(\hat{\beta}_0 - \beta) \xrightarrow{d} (\int B_1^2)^{-1}(\int B_1\, dB_0 + \tau_{10})$

where $\tau_{10} = \Upsilon_{10}$, *as defined in* (6) *and* $B_1(r) = (\sigma_1^2)^{1/2} V_1$, $B_0 = (\sigma_0^2)^{1/2} W_0$ *where* V_1 *and* W_0 *are independent standard Brownian motions.* □

Lemma 2: (Phillips and Hansen (1990)). *For the model* (7)'

i) $n(\dot{\beta}_0 - \beta) \xrightarrow{d} (\int B_{1h}^2)^{-1}(\int B_{1h}\, dB_0 + \tau_{10})$

where $B_{1h} = B_1(r) - \int B_1 h'(\int hh')^{-1} h(r)$ *is a detrended Brownian motion.*

ii) $n^{1/2}(\dot{\Gamma} - \Gamma)\gamma_n^{-1} \xrightarrow{d} (\int h_1 h_1')^{-1}(\int h_1\, dB_0 + \tau_{10}^h)$

where $h_1 = h(r) - (\int hB_1)(\int B_1^2)^{-1} B_1(r)$ *and* $\tau_{10}^h = -\int hB_1(r)(\int B_1^2)^{-1}\tau_{10}$. □

To derive the LM test we define $y = (y_1, \ldots, y_n)'$, $x = (x_1, \ldots, x_n)'$, and $w = (w_1, \ldots, w_n)'$. The residual vector is $w = y - \beta_0 x$ and under Assumption 2 the likelihood conditional on x is

$$\mathscr{L} = -\frac{1}{2}\ln 2\pi - \frac{1}{2}\ln|\Omega| - \frac{1}{2}w'\Omega^{-1}w \tag{9}$$

where $\Omega = \mathrm{var}(w) = \sigma_0^2 I_n + \sigma_\eta^2 D_x LL'D_x'$, $D_x = \mathrm{diag}(x_1, \ldots, x_n)$,

$$L = \begin{bmatrix} 1 & 0 & & 0 \\ \vdots & & \ddots & \\ & & & 0 \\ 1 & 1 & 1 & 1 \end{bmatrix}$$

and LL' is the Choleski decomposition of $V = \{\min(i,j)\}_{n\times n}$. The score vector with respect to σ_η^2 is

$$s_c = -\frac{1}{2}\mathrm{tr}(\Omega^{-1}A) + \frac{1}{2}w'\Omega^{-1}A\Omega^{-1}w \tag{10}$$

where we have set $A = D_x LL'D_x'$. For testing purposes we concentrate on the stochastic part of the score $s_c^* = w'\Omega^{-1}A\Omega^{-1}w$ and observe that under H_0, $s_c^* = (\sigma_0^2)^{-2}w'Aw$ and $\mathrm{var}(s_c^*) = (\sigma_0^2)^{-2}\,\mathrm{tr}(A^2)$. Excluding the scale factor $\mathrm{tr}(A^2)$ the LM test is given by

$$LM = s_c^*/[\mathrm{var}(s_c^*)]^{1/2} = \tilde{w}'D_x LL'D_x'\tilde{w}/\tilde{\sigma}_0^2 \tag{11}$$

where $\tilde{w} = y - \tilde{\beta}_0 x$ and "$\sim$" denotes the restricted ML estimator. Observe that the test has the same form as the locally best invariant test of Nabeya and Tanaka (1988) and of Leybourne and McCabe (1989). This is so because we are working with the conditional likelihood so the variance of the error structure, Ω, is of the same form in either case. However, the asymptotics of the test are quite different as we now show.

The asymptotic distribution of the LM test is derived by noticing that pre-multiplying a vector by L' has the effect of forming a backwards cumulative sum. Tests based on either the forward or backward sums are equal in distribution and we can write

$$\tilde{w}'D_x LL'D_x'\tilde{w} = \sum_{k=1}^{n}[\Sigma_1^n x_s\tilde{w}_s - \Sigma_1^k x_s\tilde{w}_s]^2$$

$$= \sum_{k=1}^{n}[\Sigma_1^{k-1}x_s\tilde{w}_s]^2 \tag{12}$$

since $\Sigma_1^n x_s\tilde{w}_s = 0$ by the OLS normal equations. Set $[nr] = k - 1$ and using Lemma 1 we have

$$\zeta_n(r) = n^{-1}\sum_1^{[nr]} x_s\tilde{w}_s = n^{-1}\sum_1^{[nr]} x_s(y_s - \tilde{\beta}_0 x_s)$$

$$= n^{-1}\sum_1^{[nr]} x_s w_s - n(\tilde{\beta}_0 - \beta_0)n^{-2}\sum_1^{[nr]} x_s^2$$

$$\xrightarrow{d} \int_0^r B_1\,dB_0 - \frac{\int_0^r B_1^2}{\int_0^1 B_1^2}\int_0^1 B_1\,dB_0$$

$$= (\sigma_1^2\sigma_0^2)^{1/2}\left(\int_0^r V_1\,dW_0 - \frac{\int_0^r V_1^2}{\int_0^1 V_1^2}\int_0^1 V_1\,dW_0\right) \quad (13)$$

where V_1 and W_0 are independent standard Brownian motion. Squaring $\zeta_n(r)$ and dividing by consistent estimates of σ_1^2 and σ_0^2 yields an LM statistic with a limiting distribution that is free of nuisance parameters. The results are summarized in the following theorem.

Theorem 3.1: The LM statisic for parameter constancy that tests a null of cointegration in model (7) *satisfies*

$$LM_1 = n^{-3}\tilde{w}'D_xLL'D_x'\tilde{w}/\tilde{\sigma}_1^2\tilde{\sigma}_0^2 \xrightarrow{d} \int_0^1 W_{V_1}(r)^2\,dr,$$

where

$$W_{V_1}(r) = \int_0^r V_1\,dW_0 - \frac{\int_0^r V_1^2}{\int_0^1 V_1^2}\int_0^1 V_1\,dW_0,$$

$$\tilde{\sigma}_0^2 = n^{-1}\tilde{w}'\tilde{w} \xrightarrow[p]{} \sigma_0^2, \text{ and}$$

$$\tilde{\sigma}_1^2 = n^{-1}\sum_1^n \Delta x_t^2 \xrightarrow[p]{} \sigma_1^2. \qquad \square$$

This is a simple 'cointegrated system' extension of results in Nabeya-Tanaka (1988), Leybourne-McCabe (1989) and Kwiatkowski-Phillips-Schmidt-Shin (1992), where the limit distribution of the LM test is shown to be a functional of a Brownian bridge. The nature of the above extension is that, in a cointegrated system, the behavior of the test asymptotically has the form of a generalized Brownian bridge that is tied down at the fraction $r = 1$ but is scaled by a random fraction. Note that if $V_1 = 1$ we would have $W_1(r) = \int_0^r dW_0 - r\int_0^1 dW_0 = W_0(r) - rW_0(1)$, a Brownian bridge with deterministic fraction r. We call $W_{V_1}(r)$ a *V-based Brownian bridge* which, like a Brownian bridge, is tied down at $r = 1$ to zero (i.e. $W_{V_1}(1) = 0$) but has a random fraction $J(r) = \int_0^r V_1^2/\int_0^1 V_1^2$.

The effect of the additional random walk component V_1 and random fraction $J(r)$ on the LM test is reflected in the critical values obtained from the distributions constructed from either functionals. This is illustrated in Table 1 where it is shown that the LM test behaves very differently when it is constructed from a V-based and a standard Brownian bridge. The critical values given there are the

Table 1. Upper critical values of LM_1 test

	Size α		
	.01	.05	.10
v-based	.4898	.2086	.1299
standard	.7868	.4619	.3479

Notes: Data generated with iid $N(0, 1)$ errors.
Replication times = 10,000 and sample size = 250.

upper tail percentage points of the asymptotic density, computed by Monte Carlo simulations using $n = 250$.

Now suppose we are interested in testing for cointegration in a model with an included trend. When using residual-based tests in testing the null of no cointegration (see Phillips and Ouliaris (1990) and Hansen (1992b) for a study of these tests) this is of course equivalent to estimating the trend coefficient and then using it to form the residuals. In our case we write the residuals as $\tilde{w}_s^* = y_s - \dot{\tilde{\beta}}_0 x_s - \dot{\tilde{\Gamma}} h_s$ and using Lemma 2 we get

$$\zeta_n^*(r) = n^{-1} \sum_1^{[nr]} x_s w_s - n(\dot{\tilde{\beta}}_0 - \beta_0) n^{-2} \sum_1^{[nr]} x_s^2 - n^{1/2}(\dot{\tilde{\Gamma}} - \Gamma)\gamma_n^{-1} n^{-3/2} \sum_1^{[nr]} x_s h_s' \gamma_n'$$

$$\xrightarrow{d} \int_0^r B_1\, dB_0 - \left(\int_0^r B_1 Q\right)\left(\int_0^1 QQ'\right)^{-1} \int_0^1 Q\, dB_0 = B_Q(r), \qquad (13)'$$

where $Q(r) = (B_1(r), h(r)')$. Note that

$$B_Q(1) = \int_0^1 B_1\, dB_0 - \left(\int_0^1 B_1 Q\right)\left(\int_0^1 QQ'\right)^{-1} \int_0^1 Q\, dB_0 = \int_0^1 \underline{B}_1\, dB_0 = 0,$$

since $\underline{B}_1(r) = B_1(r) - \int_0^1 B_1 Q(\int_0^1 QQ')^{-1} Q(r) = 0$ is the L_2 projection residual of B_1 on the space orthogonal to $Q(r)$ (which of course, contains $B_1(r)$ in its span) – see Phillips (1988a) and Park-Phillips (1988) for a discussion of L_2 Hilbert projections in this context. Thus $B_Q(r)$ is a tied-down process.

The asymptotic behavior of parameter constancy tests in a model with integrated and trend regressors is summarized in the following Theorem.

Theorem 3.2: The LM statistic for parameter constancy that tests the null of cointegration with trend behaves in the limit as

$$LM_2^* = n^{-3} \tilde{w}^{*\prime} D_x L L' D_x' \tilde{w}^* / \tilde{\sigma}_1^2 \tilde{\sigma}_0^2 \xrightarrow{d} \int_0^1 W_Q(r)^2\, dr.$$

Consistent estimators $\tilde{\sigma}_1^2$ and $\tilde{\sigma}_0^2$ are constructed as in Theorem 3.1. □

The results in Theorems 3.1 and 3.2 hold even with the addition of a stationary, zero mean exogenous regressor. This is because the coefficient of the $I(1)$

regressor, β_0 (under Ho) is estimated consistently at rate $Op(n^{-1})$ as opposed to the coefficient of the stationary component which is estimated consistently at rate $Op(n^{-1/2})$. To see this consider the model

$$y_t = \beta_t x_t + \pi z_t + \varepsilon_{0t} \tag{1)''$$

$$\Delta x_t = \varepsilon_{1t}, \qquad z_t = \varepsilon_{2t}$$

where we assume $\{\varepsilon_t\} = (\varepsilon_{0t}, \varepsilon_{1t}, \varepsilon_{2t})'$ is iid and z_t and x_t are strictly exogenous. Under Ho, the asymptotic behavior of the LS estimator $\breve{\pi}$ is

$$n^{1/2}(\breve{\pi} - \pi) \xrightarrow{d} N(0, \sigma_0^2/\sigma_{22\cdot 1}^2), \qquad \sigma_{22\cdot 1}^2 = \sigma_2^2 - \sigma_{21}\sigma_1^{-2}\sigma_{12}. \tag{14}$$

The regression residual is $\breve{w}_s = w_s - (\breve{\beta}_0 - \beta_0)x_s - (\breve{\pi} - \pi)z_s$ and since the last term is $O_p(n^{-1/2})$ we have

$$\breve{\zeta}_n(r) \xrightarrow{d} \int_0^r B_1\, dB_0 - \frac{\int_0^r B_1^2}{\int_0^1 B_1^2} \int_0^1 B_1\, dB_0 \tag{15}$$

as for ζ_n in model (1), Theorem 3.1. This result is in contrast to that of Leybourne–McCabe (1989) who consider the case with stationary regressors, in which case the distribution of the test depends on the dimensions of the exogenous regressors as well. By similar calculations, $\breve{\zeta}_n$ converges weakly to the same limits as those of ζ_n^* used in Theorem 3.2.

3 Time Series Extensions

Extensions to the time series case with the error process $\{\varepsilon_t\}$ satisfying Assumption 1 is straightforward. It requires the use of an optimal estimator such as the fully modified least squares estimator developed by Phillips and Hansen (1990). Define

$$\hat{y}+ = y - \hat{\psi}_{01}\hat{\psi}_1^{-1}\Delta x$$

$$w_{0\cdot 1} = w - \hat{\psi}_{01}\hat{\psi}_1^{-1}\varepsilon_1\,.$$

The fully modified OLS estimator in the single equation (7) (under Ho) is given by

$$\hat{\beta}_0^+ = (x'x)^{-1}(x'\hat{y}^+ - n\hat{\delta}^+) \tag{16}$$

where $\hat{\delta}^+ = \hat{\Upsilon}_1 \begin{bmatrix} 1 \\ -\hat{\psi}_1^{-1}\hat{\psi}_{10} \end{bmatrix}$. From Phillips and Hansen the corrected estimator (16) has a compound normal limit distribution free of nuisance parameters

$$n(\hat{\beta}_0^+ - \beta_0) \xrightarrow{d} (\textstyle\int B_1^2)^{-1}(\int B_1\, dB_{0\cdot 1}) \tag{17}$$

where $B_{0\cdot 1} = B_0 - \psi_{01}\psi_1^{-1}B_1$ and the limit process B_1 and $B_{0\cdot 1}$ are independent of each other.

The limit theory for the LM test is derived following the arguments of the previous section using the optimal estimator (16). Write the corrected residual $\tilde{w}_s$ as

$$\tilde{w}_s^+ = \hat{y}_s^+ - \tilde{\beta}_0^+ x_s = w_s - (\tilde{\beta}_0^+ - \beta_0)x_s - \hat{\psi}_{01}\hat{\psi}_1^{-1}\Delta x_s \tag{18}$$

and using (17),

$$\begin{aligned}
\zeta_n^+(r) &= n^{-1}\sum_1^{[nr]} x_s\tilde{w}_s^+ \\
&= n^{-1}\sum_1^{[nr]} x_s w_s - n(\tilde{\beta}_0^+ - \beta_0)n^{-2}\sum_1^{[nr]} x_s^2 - \hat{\psi}_{01}\hat{\psi}_1^{-1}n^{-1}\sum_1^{[nr]}(x_s\Delta x_s) \\
&\xrightarrow{d} \int_0^r B_1\, dB_{0\cdot 1} - \frac{\int_0^r B_1^2}{\int_0^1 B_1^2}\int_0^1 B_1\, dB_{0\cdot 1} + r\delta^+ \\
&= (\psi_{0\cdot 1}\psi_1)^{1/2}W_{V_1+}(r) + r\delta^+
\end{aligned}$$

where $B_1(r) = \psi_1^{1/2}V_1(r)$. Observe that the limit of ζ_n^+ contains a nuisance parameter δ^+. This leads us to suggest the following modifications to the cumulative sum ζ_n^+. Let

$$\zeta_n^{++}(r) = n^{-1}\sum_1^{[nr]} x_s\tilde{w}_s^{++} = \zeta_n^+(r) - r\hat{\delta}^+ \tag{19}$$

then we have a nuisance parameter free distribution,

$$\zeta_n^{++}(r) \xrightarrow{d} (\psi_{0\cdot 1}\psi_1)^{1/2}W_{V_1+}(r) = \int_0^r V_1\, dW_{0\cdot 1} - \frac{\int_0^r B_1^2}{\int_0^1 B_1^2}\int_0^1 V_1\, dW_{0\cdot 1} \tag{20}$$

This gives us an extension of Theorem 3.1 to more general models.

Corollary 3.1: The limiting distribution of the LM statistic that tests the null of cointegration is

$$LM_1^+ = n^{-3}\tilde{w}^{++\prime}D_x LL'D_x'\tilde{w}^{++}/\hat{\psi}_{0\cdot 1}\hat{\psi}_1 \xrightarrow{d} \int_0^1 W_{V_1+}(r)^2\, dr$$

where $D_x'\tilde{w}^{++}$ *and* $W_{V_1+}(r)$ *are given in* (19) *and* (20) *respectively and* $\hat{\psi}_{0\cdot 1}$ *and* $\hat{\psi}_1$ *are consistent semiparametric estimators for* $\psi_{0\cdot 1}$ *and* ψ_1 *(see* Phillips (1987), Newey-West (1987) *and* Andrews (1991) *for a discussion of possible estimators).*

□

The result of Theorem 3.2 can also be extended to time series models by similar arguments. We will not go through the derivations but give the extensions in the results below. We use the fully modified LS estimators of the parameters in (7)′. These are:

$$\dot{\beta}_0^+ = \left(\sum_{t=1}^n x_{h_t}^2\right)^{-1}\left(\sum_{t=1}^n x_{h_t}\hat{y}_t^+ - n\hat{\delta}^+\right) \qquad \text{and}$$

$$\dot{\Gamma}^+ = \left(\sum_{t=1}^n h_{x_t}h_{x_t}'\right)^{-1}\left(\sum_{t=1}^n h_{x_t}\hat{y}_t^+ - n\hat{\delta}^h\right) \tag{21}$$

where $x_{h_t} = x_t - \sum_{t=1}^n x_t h_t'\left(\sum_{t=1}^n h_t h_t'\right)^{-1} h_t$, $h_{x_t} = h_t - \sum_{t=1}^n h_t x_t\left(\sum_{t=1}^n x_t^2\right)^{-1} x_t$ and $\hat{\delta}^h = \hat{\tau}_{10}^h - \hat{\psi}_{01}\hat{\psi}_1^{-1}\hat{\tau}_{11}^h$.

Corollary 3.2: Let $\tilde{w}_s^{*+} = \hat{y}_s^+ - \dot{\tilde{\beta}}_0^+ x_s - \dot{\tilde{\Gamma}}^+ h_s$ *and set*

$$\zeta_n^{*++}(r) = n^{-1}\sum_1^{[nr]} x_s\tilde{w}_s^{*++} = n^{-1}\sum_1^{[nr]} x_s\tilde{w}_s^{*+} - r\hat{\delta}^+ .$$

Then we have

$$LM_2^{*+} = n^{-3}\tilde{w}^{*++\prime}D_x LL'D_x'\tilde{w}^{*++}/\hat{\psi}_{0\cdot 1}\hat{\psi}_1 \xrightarrow{d} \int_0^1 W_Q^+(r)^2\, dr$$

where $W_Q^+(r) = \int_0^r V_1\, dW_{0\cdot 1} - (\int_0^r V_1 Q)(\int_0^1 QQ')^{-1}\int_0^1 Q\, dW_{0\cdot 1}$. □

Observe that the extension to the time series case consists of correcting for both serial correlation and endogeneity in $\tilde{\beta}_0$ and $D_x\tilde{w}$, and by replacing $\tilde{\sigma}_0^2$ and $\tilde{\sigma}_1^2$ by the long-run conditional variance $\hat{\psi}_{0\cdot 1}$ and long-run variance $\hat{\psi}_1$ respectively.

4 Multivariate Extensions

We now extend the results of the previous section to the case where the regressor $\{x_t\}$ is a column vector of order k, $\{x_t\} = (x_{1t}, \ldots, x_{kt})'$. Consider first the case where the innovations are iid. We have

$$y_t = \beta_t' x_t + \varepsilon_{0t} \tag{1)'''}$$

$$\Delta x_t = \varepsilon_{1t}, \qquad \varepsilon_{1t} \equiv \text{iid } N(0, \Sigma_{11}) \tag{2)''}$$

$$\beta_t = \beta_{t-1} + \eta_t, \qquad \eta_t \equiv \text{iid } N(0, \Sigma_\eta) \tag{3)''}$$

which we write as

$$y_t = \beta_0' x_t + w_t \tag{7)''}$$

with $\beta_0 = (\beta_{01}, \ldots, \beta_{0k})'$ and

$$w_t = \left(\sum_1^t \eta_s\right)' x_t + \varepsilon_{0t} = x_t'(I_k, I_k, I_k, \ldots, \underset{\substack{\uparrow \\ t\text{'th position}}}{I_k}, 0, \ldots, 0)\eta + \varepsilon_{0t}$$

$$= \underset{\sim}{D}_x \underset{\sim}{L}\eta + \varepsilon_{0t} \tag{22}$$

where $\eta = (\eta_1, \ldots, \eta_k)'$, $\underset{\sim}{D}_x = \mathrm{diag}(x_1', x_2', \ldots, x_n')$ and $\underset{\sim}{L} = \begin{bmatrix} I_k & 0 & \cdots & 0 \\ I_k & I_k & \cdots & 0 \\ \vdots & & \ddots & \vdots \\ I_k & I_k & & I_k \end{bmatrix}$. The likelihood is the same as before but now $\Omega = \mathrm{var}(w) = \sigma_0^2 I_n + \underset{\sim}{D}_x \underset{\sim}{L}(I_n \otimes \Sigma_\eta)\underset{\sim}{L}'\underset{\sim}{D}_x'$. The differential of the likelihood is

$$d\mathscr{L} = -(1/2)\,\mathrm{tr}(\Omega^{-1}\, d\Omega) + (1/2)w'\Omega^{-1}\, d\Omega\Omega^{-1}w - \mathrm{tr}(L\, d\Sigma_\eta) \tag{23}$$

with

$$d\Omega = \underset{\sim}{D}_x \underset{\sim}{L}(I_n \otimes d\Sigma_\eta)\underset{\sim}{L}'\underset{\sim}{D}_x' \tag{24}$$

and L is the matrix of Lagrange multipliers. Evaluating at the restricted elements and noting that $\tilde{\Omega} = \tilde{\sigma}_0^2 I$ we have

$$\begin{aligned} d\mathscr{L} = &-(1/2\tilde{\sigma}_0^2)\,\mathrm{tr}(\underset{\sim}{D}_x \underset{\sim}{L}(I_n \otimes d\Sigma_\eta)\underset{\sim}{L}'\underset{\sim}{D}_x') \\ &+ (1/2\tilde{\sigma}_0^4)\tilde{w}'\underset{\sim}{D}_x \underset{\sim}{L}(I_n \otimes d\Sigma_\eta)\underset{\sim}{L}'\underset{\sim}{D}_x'\tilde{w} - \mathrm{tr}(L\, d\Sigma_\eta) = 0. \end{aligned} \tag{25}$$

Writing $\underset{\sim}{L}$ in block partition form,

$$\underset{\sim}{L} = [\underset{\sim}{L}_{[1]}, \underset{\sim}{L}_{[2]}, \ldots, \underset{\sim}{L}_{[n]}] \tag{26}$$

we can show that

$$L = -(1/2\tilde{\sigma}_0^2)\sum_{i=1}^n \underset{\sim}{L}_{[i]}'\underset{\sim}{D}_x'\underset{\sim}{D}_x\underset{\sim}{L}_{[i]} + (1/2\tilde{\sigma}_0^4)\sum_{i=1}^n \underset{\sim}{L}_{[i]}'\underset{\sim}{D}'\tilde{w}\tilde{w}'\underset{\sim}{D}_x\underset{\sim}{L}_{[i]} \tag{27}$$

and thus concentrating on the stochastic part and excluding constants we have

$$\mathrm{tr}\, L = (1/\tilde{\sigma}_0^4)\tilde{w}'\underset{\sim}{D}_x\underset{\sim}{L}\underset{\sim}{L}'\underset{\sim}{D}_x'\tilde{w}. \tag{28}$$

Observe that (28) is equivalent in form to the LM statistic based on the score s_c^* given in (11). The limit theory follows through except that here premultiplying by $\underset{\sim}{L}'$ picks up the k'th block whereas postmultiplying by $\underset{\sim}{L}$ picks up the t'th element. Since the distribution is the same in either case we have

$$\begin{aligned} n^{-3}\tilde{w}'\underset{\sim}{D}_x\underset{\sim}{L}\underset{\sim}{L}'\underset{\sim}{D}_x'\tilde{w} &= \sum_{j=1}^n [\Sigma_1^{j-1}\tilde{w}_s x_s'][\Sigma_1^{j-1}x_s\tilde{w}_s] \\ &\xrightarrow{d} \sigma_0^2\,\mathrm{tr}\left\{\Sigma_{11}\int_0^1 \underset{\sim}{W}_{V_1}(r)\underset{\sim}{W}_{V_1}(r)'\, dr\right\} \end{aligned}$$

where $\underset{\sim}{W}_{V_1}(r) = \int_0^r V_1\, dW_0 - \int_0^r V_1 V_1'(\int_0^1 V_1 V_1')^{-1}\int_0^1 V_1\, dW_0$. To obtain a nuisance parameter free limit theory we set up

$$LM_3 = n^{-3}\tilde{w}'\underset{\sim}{D}_x\underset{\sim}{L}(I_n \otimes \hat{\Sigma}_{11}^{-1})\underset{\sim}{L}'\underset{\sim}{D}_x'\tilde{w}/\tilde{\sigma}_0^2$$

$$\xrightarrow{d} \operatorname{tr}\left\{\int_0^1 \underset{\sim}{W}_{V_1}(r)\underset{\sim}{W}_{V_1}(r)'\,dr\right\}$$

where $\tilde{\sigma}_0^2 = n^{-1}\tilde{w}'\tilde{w} \underset{p}{\rightarrow} \sigma_0^2$ and $\hat{\Sigma}_{11} = n^{-1}\sum_1^n(\Delta x_t\Delta x_t') \underset{p}{\rightarrow} \Sigma_{11}$. The limit distribution depends only on the rank of V_1.

Extending the results to the general time series case and to models with deterministic trends proceeds as before. The notation follows that of Section 3.2 except that the correction now takes the form $n^{-1}\sum_1^{[nr]} x_s\tilde{w}_s^{++} = n^{-1}\sum_1^{[nr]} x_s\tilde{w}_s^{+} - r\hat{\underset{\sim}{\delta}}^{+}$ where $\hat{\underset{\sim}{\delta}}^{+} = \hat{\Upsilon}_1\begin{bmatrix} 1 \\ -\hat{\Psi}_1^{-1}\hat{\Psi}_{10}\end{bmatrix}$. The multivariate extensions for Corollaries 3.1 and 3.2 are as follows

Theorem 4.1: The LM k-parameter constancy test for the null of cointegration in a model without trend is

$$LM_1^+ = n^{-3}\tilde{w}^{++\prime}\underset{\sim}{D}_x\underset{\sim}{L}(I_n \otimes \hat{\Psi}_1^{-1})\underset{\sim}{L}'\underset{\sim}{D}_x'\tilde{w}^{++}/\hat{\psi}_{0\cdot 1} \xrightarrow{d} \operatorname{tr}\left\{\int_0^1 \underset{\sim}{W}_{V_1+}(r)\underset{\sim}{W}_{V_1+}(r)'\,dr\right\}$$

where $\underset{\sim}{W}_{V_1+}(r) = \int_0^r V_1\,dW_{0\cdot 1} - \int_0^r V_1V_1'(\int_0^1 V_1V_1')^{-1}\int_0^1 V_1\,dW_{0\cdot 1}$. □

Theorem 4.2: The LM k-parameter constancy test for the null of cointegration in a model with trend is

$$LM_2^* = n^{-3}\tilde{w}^{*++\prime}\underset{\sim}{D}_x\underset{\sim}{L}(I_n \otimes \hat{\Psi}_1^{-1})\underset{\sim}{L}'\underset{\sim}{D}_x'\tilde{w}^{*++}/\hat{\psi}_{0\cdot 1}$$

$$\xrightarrow{d} \operatorname{tr}\left\{\int_0^1 \underset{\sim}{W}_Q^+(r)\underset{\sim}{W}_Q^+(r)'\,dr\right\}$$

where $\underset{\sim}{W}_Q^+(r) = \int_0^r V_1\,dW_{0\cdot 1} - (\int_0^r V_1Q)(\int_0^1 QQ')^{-1}\int_0^1 Q\,dW_{0\cdot 1}$. □

Observe that the limit distributions are nuisance parameter free and depend only on the number of regressors. The latter test, LM_2^*, also depends on the order (p) of the trend regressors. In fact, for many applications of parameter constancy tests as tests for cointegration, the limit distribution of the LM statistic will depend only on these regressor counts. If the regressors are not cointegrated, then the rank of V_1 corresponds to the number of the regressors $\{x_t\}$. If we allow cointegration among regressors, then Ψ_1 is singular and the situation is a little more complex. It may be handled by the methods recently developed in Phillips (1991).

4.1 Testing when Regressors Contain Trends

The test can also be applied to models where regressors are allowed to contain both deterministic and stochastic trends. For example, consider the regression equation (1)‴ with the regressors $\{x_t\}$ generated by

$$x_t = Ah_{1t} + x_t^o, \qquad x_t^o = \sum_{s=1}^{t} \varepsilon_{1s} + x_0. \tag{2'''}$$

Here x_t^o is a k dimensional vector of stochastic trends, h_{1t} is a p dimensional vector of deterministic trends and A is a $k \times p$ matrix of parameters. As in the previous section, convergence of the deterministic trends $h_{1[nr]}$ to the limit vector $h_1(r)$ will be given by a diagonal matrix of weights γ_{1n} such that $\gamma_{1n}h_{1[nr]} \to h_1(r)$ uniformly in r.

To separate the trends driving $\{x_t\}$, we define an orthogonal matrix $J = [J_1, J_2]$ where $J_1 = A(A'A)^{-1/2}$, $J_2 = A_\perp$ so that $J'J = I_k$. Furthermore, we denote by Z_t the variables transformed by J,

$$Z_t = J'x_t = \begin{pmatrix} (A'A)^{1/2}h_{1t} + J_1'x_t^o \\ J_2'x_t^o \end{pmatrix} = \begin{pmatrix} Z_{1t} \\ Z_{2t} \end{pmatrix},$$

where Z_{1t} and Z_{2t} are of dimension p and $k - p$ respectively. Then we can rewrite (7)″ as

$$\begin{aligned} y_t &= \beta_0'(JJ')x_t + w_t \\ &= C_1'Z_{1t} + C_2'Z_{2t} + w_t = Z_t'C + w_t \end{aligned} \tag{7'''}$$

where $C = \begin{pmatrix} C_1 \\ C_2 \end{pmatrix} = \begin{pmatrix} J_1'\beta_0 \\ J_2'\beta_0 \end{pmatrix}$. The variables Z_{1t} and Z_{2t} contain the deterministic and stochastic trends respectively since, given the weight matrix

$$\Gamma_n = \begin{pmatrix} \Gamma_{1n} \\ \Gamma_{2n} \end{pmatrix} = \begin{pmatrix} \gamma_{1n}(A'A)^{-1/2} & 0 \\ 0 & 1/\sqrt{n} \end{pmatrix},$$

we have

$$\Gamma_n Z_{[nr]} = \begin{pmatrix} \gamma_{1n}(A'A)^{-1/2}Z_{1[nr]} \\ 1/\sqrt{n}Z_{2[nr]} \end{pmatrix} \xrightarrow{d} \begin{pmatrix} h_1(r) \\ \bar{B}_1(r) \end{pmatrix} = \bar{Q}(r) \tag{30}$$

where $\bar{B}_1(r) = J_2'B_1(r)$. Using (30), we find that the coefficients in the regression (7)‴ are distributed as follows.

Lemma 3:

i) $n^{1/2}\Gamma_{1n}^{-1}(\tilde{C}_1 - C_1) \xrightarrow{d} (\int h_1^+ h_1^{+\prime})^{-1}(\int h_1^+ \, dB_0 + \Upsilon_{10}^h)$

where $h_1^+ = h_1(r) - \int h_1 \bar{B}_1'(\int \bar{B}_1 \bar{B}_1')^{-1}\bar{B}_1(r)$ *and* $\Upsilon_{10}^h = -\int h_1 \bar{B}_1'(\int \bar{B}_1 \bar{B}_1')^{-1}J_2'\Upsilon_{10}$.

ii) $n^{1/2}\Gamma_{2n}^{-1}(\tilde{C}_2 - C_2) \xrightarrow{d} (\int \bar{B}_1^+ \bar{B}_1^{+\prime})^{-1}(\int \bar{B}_1^+ \, dB_0 + J_2' \Upsilon_{10})$

where $\bar{B}_1^+ = \bar{B}_1(r) - \int \bar{B}_1 h_1' (\int h_1 h_1')^{-1} h_1(r)$.

The limit theory for the LM test is derived following the arguments of the previous section using the asymptotics of Lemma 3. Write the correct residual from (7)‴ as $\tilde{w}_s^+ = w_s - Z_s'(\tilde{C} - C) - \Delta x_s' \hat{\Psi}_1^{-1} \hat{\Psi}_{10}$ and our score is now

$$\begin{aligned} n^{-1/2}\Gamma_n \sum_1^{[nr]} Z_s \tilde{w}_s^+ &= n^{-1/2} \sum_1^{[nr]} \Gamma_n Z_s w_s - n^{-1} \sum_1^{[nr]} \Gamma_n Z_s Z_s' \Gamma_n' n^{1/2} \Gamma_n^{-1}(\tilde{C} - C) \\ &\quad - n^{-1/2} \sum_1^{[nr]} \Gamma_n Z_s \Delta x_s' \hat{\Psi}_1^{-1} \hat{\Psi}_{10} \\ &\xrightarrow{d} \int_0^r \bar{Q} \, dB_{0\cdot 1} - \int_0^r \bar{Q}\bar{Q}' \left(\int_0^1 \bar{Q}\bar{Q}' \right)^{-1} \int_0^1 \bar{Q} \, dB_{0\cdot 1} + r \begin{pmatrix} 0 \\ J_2' \underset{\sim}{\delta}^+ \end{pmatrix} \\ &= B_{\bar{Q}}(r) + r \begin{pmatrix} 0 \\ J_2' \underset{\sim}{\delta}^+ \end{pmatrix}. \end{aligned}$$

To eliminate the nuisance parameter $J_2' \underset{\sim}{\delta}^+$ at the limit we set $\bar{Z}_s = \Gamma_n Z_s$ and write $\sum_1^{[nr]} \bar{Z}_s \tilde{w}_s^{++} = \sum_1^{[nr]} \bar{Z}_s \tilde{w}_s^+ - r \begin{pmatrix} 0 \\ J_2' \hat{\underset{\sim}{\delta}}^+ \end{pmatrix}$ as before. Then the LM test is

$$\begin{aligned} LM_{\underset{\sim}{3}} &= n^{-2} \tilde{w}^{++\prime} \underset{\sim}{D}_{\bar{Z}} \underset{\sim}{L} (I_n \otimes \hat{\Psi}_1^{-1}) \underset{\sim}{L}' \underset{\sim}{D}_{\bar{Z}}' \tilde{w}^{++} / \hat{\psi}_{0\cdot 1} \\ &\xrightarrow{d} \operatorname{tr} \left\{ \int_0^1 W_{\bar{Q}}(r) W_{\bar{Q}}(r)' \, dr \right\} \end{aligned}$$

where $\hat{\Psi}_1$ and $\hat{\psi}_{0\cdot 1}$ are semiparametric estimators of the long-run variances for $\{x_t\}$ generated by (2)‴ and are constructed after first detrending the series $\{x_t\}$. Methods of estimating these long-run variances are now well-known and are discussed in detail, for example, in Andrews (1991). The limit distribution in this case depends only on the p and $k - p$ deterministic and stochastic trends contained in $\bar{Q}(r)$.

4.2 *Subset Testing*

Suppose that instead of testing for the constancy of the k-parameter vector β, we test for the constancy of a subset k_1 of the coefficients where $1 \le k_1 < k$. This is useful in empirical cases where cointegration among three or more variables fails and one is interested in which coefficient "caused" the failure. Consider for example the following system

$$y_t = \beta_{at}' x_{at} + \beta_b' x_{bt} + \varepsilon_{0t} \tag{31}$$

$$\Delta x_t = \varepsilon_{1t}, \qquad \varepsilon'_{1t} = (\varepsilon'_{at}, \varepsilon'_{bt}) \tag{32}$$

$$\beta_{at} = \beta_{at-1} + \eta_{at} \tag{33}$$

which we can write as

$$y_t = \beta'_{a0} x_{at} + \beta'_b x_{bt} + w_{at}, \qquad w_{at} = (\Sigma_1^t \eta'_{as}) x_{at} + \varepsilon_{0t}. \tag{31$'$}$$

The multivariate invariance principle is $n^{-1/2} \Sigma_1^{[nr]} \varepsilon_{1t} \xrightarrow{d} B_1(r) = (B'_a(r), B'_b(r))'$ where the partition is conformable with that of $\{x_t\}$. Because $\{\varepsilon_{0t}\}$ is stationary we have the cointegrating vector $(1, -\beta_{a0}, -\beta_b)$ under the null of constant coefficients. With the alternative $\Sigma_\eta > 0$, rejection of the null indicates that the failure of cointegration is caused by the instability of the k_1 parameters β_a.

The LM test as before is

$$LM_a = n^{-3} \tilde{w}_a^{++\prime} \underset{\sim}{D}_{x_a} \underset{\sim}{L} (I_n \otimes \hat{\Psi}_a^{-1}) \underset{\sim}{L}' \underset{\sim}{D}'_{x_a} \tilde{w}_a^{++} / \hat{\psi}_{0\cdot 1} \tag{34}$$

with $n^{-1} \Sigma_1^{[nr]} x_{as} \tilde{w}_{as}^{++} = n^{-1} \Sigma_1^{[nr]} x_{as} (w_s - x'_s(\tilde{\beta}_0 - \beta_0) - \Delta x'_s \hat{\Psi}_1^{-1} \hat{\Psi}_{10}) - r \hat{\delta}_a^+$ and $\hat{\delta}_a^+ = \hat{\Upsilon}_{a0} - \hat{\Upsilon}_{a1} \hat{\Psi}_1^{-1} \hat{\Psi}_{10}$. The limit theory is easy to deduce along the lines of our earlier analysis and is given by

$$LM_a \xrightarrow{d} \operatorname{tr}\left\{ \int_0^1 \underset{\sim}{W}_{V_a}^+(r) \underset{\sim}{W}_{V_a}^+(r)' \, dr \right\}, \tag{35}$$

where $\underset{\sim}{W}_{V_a}^+(r) = \int_0^r V_a \, dW_{0\cdot 1} - (\int_0^r V_a V'_1)(\int_0^1 V_1 V'_1)^{-1}(\int_0^1 V_1 \, dW_{0\cdot 1})$. Here the limit theory depends only on the rank of the $I(1)$ regressors (k) and the rank of the subset of the regressors being tested (k_1). Observe that at $r = 1$ we have $\underset{\sim}{W}_{V_a}^+(r) = \int_0^1 V_a \, dW_{0\cdot 1} - (\int_0^1 V_a V'_1)(\int_0^1 V_1 V'_1)^{-1}(\int_0^1 V_1 \, dW_{0\cdot 1}) = \int_0^1 \underline{V}_a \, dW_{0\cdot 1} = 0$, since $\underline{V}_a(r) = V_a(r) - (\int_0^1 V_a V'_1)(\int_0^1 V_1 V'_1)^{-1} V_1(r) = 0$, being the L_2 projection residual of $V_a(r)$ on the space orthogonal to $V_1(r)' = (V_a(r), V_b(r))$. Thus, $\underset{\sim}{W}_{V_a}^+(r)$ is a tied-down process.

In summary, we have considered models with and without trend for the case of univariate and multivariate regressors. In both cases, the null that is of interest is cointegration or the stability of the coefficients of the $I(1)$ regressors. When the model contains deterministic trends, the version of the LM test that is to be used depends on the treatment of the trends. If interest is in a test of a null of stochastic cointegration, the appropriate test is Corollary 3.2 or Theorem 4.2 for the univariate and multivariate cases, respectively. If the null of interest is deterministic cointegration, then the version of the test given in Section 4.1 is appropriate.

5 Limit Theory Under Local Alternatives and Some Simulation Results

It is important to know if the empirical LM tests will have good power properties under general alternative hypotheses. One important criterion is test consistency. Clearly the LM tests considered above diverge when $\sigma_\eta^2 > 0$ (or $\Sigma_\eta > 0$) so the tests are consistent. The behavior of the tests under local alternatives can also be considered. Let the sequence of local alternatives for the regression coefficient be given by

$$Ha\colon \beta_t = \beta_0 + \gamma_t/n \tag{36}$$

where γ_t can be any constant or a random variable that is $Op(1)$. The specification (36) can be interpreted as a condition of *near cointegration* as discussed in Phillips (1988b) and Tanaka (1993). Because the parameter of interest in our case is the variance term σ_η^2, it is convenient to let

$$\gamma_t = n^{-1/2}\Sigma_1^t \eta_s . \tag{37}$$

With this specification for γ_t, (36) is in fact a triangular array (i.e., $\gamma_t = \gamma_{tn}$, $\beta_t = \beta_{tn}$), but we will not overburden the notation to accommodate this fact but instead continue to work with single indexed functions like β_t. The model under the alternative is

$$\begin{aligned} y_t &= \beta_t x_t + \varepsilon_{0t} \\ &= \beta_0 x_t + \frac{1}{n}(n^{-1/2}\Sigma_1^t \eta_s)x_t + \varepsilon_{0t} \\ &= \beta_0 x_t + n^{-1/2}(n^{-1}\Sigma_1^t \eta_s x_t') + \varepsilon_{0t} . \end{aligned} \tag{38}$$

Now $n^{-1/2}\Sigma_1^{[nr]}\eta_s \xrightarrow{d} B_3(r)$ and $n^{-1}\Sigma_1^{[nr]}\eta_s x_{[nr]} \xrightarrow{d} B_3(r)B_1(r) \equiv G_{31}^B(r)$, say. Now write $G_{13}^B(r) = (\sigma_1^2\sigma_\eta^2)^{1/2}W_1(r)W_3(r) = \sigma_1\sigma_\eta G_{13}^W(r)$. It follows that $\tilde\beta$ is still consistent since (taking the innovations to be iid)

$$\begin{aligned} n(\tilde\beta - \beta_0) &= \left(\frac{1}{n^2}\Sigma_1^n x_t^2\right)^{-1}\frac{1}{n}\Sigma_1^n x_t\left(\frac{1}{\sqrt{n}}\Sigma_1^t \frac{\eta_s x_t}{n} + \varepsilon_{0t}\right) \\ &= \left(\frac{1}{n^2}\Sigma_1^n x_t^2\right)^{-1}\left(\frac{1}{n}\Sigma_1^n\left(\frac{x_t}{\sqrt{n}}\right)^2\left(\frac{1}{\sqrt{n}}\Sigma_1^t \eta_s\right) + \frac{1}{n}\Sigma_1^n x_t\varepsilon_{0t}\right) \\ &\xrightarrow{d} \left(\textstyle\int B_1^2\right)^{-1}\left(\textstyle\int B_1 G_{13}^B + \int B_1\, dB_0\right). \end{aligned} \tag{39}$$

But our LM test is now a functional of

$$\begin{aligned} \frac{1}{n}\sum_1^{[nr]} x_s w_s &= n^{-1}\sum_1^{[nr]}\frac{x_s}{\sqrt{n}}\Sigma_1^s\frac{\eta_j x_s}{n} + \frac{1}{n}\sum_1^{[nr]} x_s\varepsilon_{0s} - n(\tilde\beta_0 - \beta_0)n^{-2}\sum_1^{[nr]} x_s^2 \\ &\xrightarrow{d} \int_0^r B_1 G_{13}^B - \frac{\int_0^r B_1^2}{\int_0^1 B_1^2}\int_0^1 B_1 G_{13}^B + (\sigma_1^2\sigma_0^2)^{1/2}W_{0W_1}(r) \\ &= \sigma_1^2(\sigma_\eta^2)^{1/2}G_{13W_1}^W + (\sigma_1^2\sigma_0^2)^{1/2}W_{0W_1}(r) \end{aligned} \tag{40}$$

which is well defined and distinct from the null distribution provided $\sigma_\eta^2 \neq 0$. When $\sigma_\eta^2 = 0$ the statistic converges to the distribution of the score under the

Table 2. Empirical size of LM_1 test

	Size α		
	.01	.05	.10
$n = 100$	.0086	.0480	.1040
$n = 150$	.0086	.0476	.1022
$n = 200$	.0114	.0536	.1084

Notes: Number of iterations = 5000, α = nominal "asymptotic" size, n = sample size.

Table 3. Power of LM_1 test

	Size α		
σ_η^2	.01	.05	.10
.5	.1370	.2490	.3244
1	.1999	.3246	.4070
2	.2863	.4240	.5075
4	.3825	.5315	.6073
6	.4474	.5998	.6766
8	.4780	.6219	.6972
10	.5239	.6645	.7359
12	.5523	.6838	.7559
16	.5989	.7281	.7921
20	.6317	.7646	.8241

Notes: Number of iterations = 10,000, $n = 250$, α = nominal "asymptotic" size.

null. In the last line of (40), $G_{13W_1}^W$ and $W_{0W_1}(r)$ are bridge processes constructed from $G_{13}^W(r)$ and $W_0(r)$ using the Brownian motion $W_1(r)$.

In order to examine the performance of the LM test in finite samples we performed some small-scale simulations for the simplest case of iid errors. The first experiment checked the performance of the LM test under the null of no parameter variation. From Table 2 we see that the LM test has only minor size distortion in samples of size $n = 100, 150, 200$.

The second experiment checked the empirical power of the LM test. The sample size used was 250 and critical values based on Table 1 were employed. Table 3 shows the frequency of rejection of the null using the upper 1%, 5% and 10% asymptotic critical values. It is clear that it takes a relatively large variance (σ_η^2) for the test to attain high power, although it has at least 50% power at the 10% and 5% levels with $\sigma_\eta^2 = 2$ and $\sigma_\eta^2 = 4$, respectively. This evidence suggests that the upper 5% and 10% tails of the density may be better suited for use in empirical testing.

Tables 4.A (a)–(d) give the 1%, 5%, 10% and 20% asymptotic critical values of the test for the model

$$y_t = \mu + \beta_t x_t + \varepsilon_t \tag{41}$$

Table 4.A.

(a) Critical values at the 1% level

Total regressors	Number of subset regressors $k = 1$	$k = 2$	$k = 3$	$k = 4$	$k = 5$
$k = 1$	.2422	—	—	—	—
$k = 2$	.2362	.3652	—	—	—
$k = 3$	.2107	.3339	.4320	—	—
$k = 4$	.1900	.3225	.4243	.5344	—
$k = 5$	.1942	.2946	.4041	.5086	.6109

(b) Critical values at the 5% level

Total regressors	Number of subset regressors $k = 1$	$k - 2$	$k = 3$	$k = 4$	$k = 5$
$k = 1$	.1052	—	—	—	—
$k = 2$	.0989	.1747	—	—	—
$k = 3$	.0891	.1596	.2266	—	—
$k = 4$	.0834	.1503	.2138	.2784	—
$k = 5$	.0819	.1433	.2038	.2652	.3252

(c) Critical values at the 10% level

Total regressors	Number of subset regressors $k = 1$	$k = 2$	$k = 3$	$k = 4$	$k = 5$
$k = 1$	.0661	—	—	—	—
$k = 2$	.0625	.1172	—	—	—
$k = 3$	.0568	.1074	.1548	—	—
$k = 4$	.0519	.1013	.1474	.1939	—
$k = 5$	.0501	.0952	.1400	.1843	.2271

(d) Critical values at the 20% level

Total regressors	Number of subset regressors $k = 1$	$k = 2$	$k = 3$	$k = 4$	$k = 5$
$k = 1$	.0380	—	—	—	—
$k = 2$	.0351	.0730	—	—	—
$k = 3$	.0320	.0663	.1000	—	—
$k = 4$	.0291	.0623	.0948	.1271	—
$k = 5$	.0373	.0582	.0882	.1178	.1481

Notes: Number of iterations = 20,000, $n = 500$.

where μ is the intercept and the dimension of x is k ($k = 1, 2, 3, 4, 5$). When the $\{x_t\}$ (for $k < 1$) are allowed to contain both deterministic and stochastic trends, the critical values of the test differ and are given in Table 4.B. Table 4.C contains the critical values for $\{x_t\}$ being $I(1)$ without drift but with the regression model (41) containing a trend. The sample size used was 500 and the number of iterations = 20,000.

Table 4.B. Upper critical values with trends in regressors

(a) Critical values at the 1% level

Total regressors	Number of subset regressors $k = 1$	$k = 2$	$k = 3$	$k = 4$	$k = 5$
$k = 2$	.2356	.2888	—	—	—
$k = 3$	.2166	.3484	.4034	—	—
$k = 4$	.1940	.3197	.4357	.4987	—
$k = 5$	.1836	.3019	.4071	.5096	.5655

(b) Critical values at the 5% level

Total regressors	Number of subset regressors $k = 1$	$k = 2$	$k = 3$	$k = 4$	$k = 5$
$k = 2$	.0982	.1463	—	—	—
$k = 3$	.0923	.1661	.2019	—	—
$k = 4$	.0832	.1511	.2168	.2528	—
$k = 5$	.0789	.1440	.2078	.2669	.3023

(c) Critical values at the 10% level

Total regressors	Number of subset regressors $k = 1$	$k = 2$	$k = 3$	$k = 4$	$k = 5$
$k = 2$	.0606	.0918	—	—	—
$k = 3$	.0561	.1091	.1377	—	—
$k = 4$	.0513	.1000	.1475	.1759	—
$k = 5$	.0485	.0960	.1415	.1861	.2143

(d) Critical values at the 20% level

Total regressors	Number of subset regressors $k = 1$	$k = 2$	$k = 3$	$k = 4$	$k = 5$
$k = 2$	.0342	.0571	—	—	—
$k = 3$	.0311	.0654	.0856	—	—
$k = 4$	.0285	.0605	.0924	.1109	—
$k = 5$	.0267	.0570	.0878	.1169	.1358

Notes: Number of iterations = 20,000, $n = 500$.

Table 4.C. Upper critical values with trend in regression

(a) Critical values at the 1% level

Total regressors	Number of subset regressors $k = 1$	$k = 2$	$k = 3$	$k = 4$	$k = 5$
$k = 1$	.4412	—	—	—	—
$k = 2$	.3455	.5511	—	—	—
$k = 3$	.2643	.4304	.5689	—	—
$k = 4$	.2077	.3257	.4443	.5597	—
$k = 5$	.1818	.2803	.3739	.4722	.5685

(b) Critical values at the 5% level

Total regressors	Number of subset regressors $k = 1$	$k = 2$	$k = 3$	$k = 4$	$k = 5$
$k = 1$	.1980	—	—	—	—
$k = 2$	.1544	.2704	—	—	—
$k = 3$	.1233	.2158	.3040	—	—
$k = 4$	.1002	.1747	.2453	.3141	—
$k = 5$	.0850	.1493	.2106	.2665	.3228

(c) Critical values at the 10% level

Total regressors	Number of subset regressors $k = 1$	$k = 2$	$k = 3$	$k = 4$	$k = 5$
$k = 1$	.1252	—	—	—	—
$k = 2$	.0996	.1872	—	—	—
$k = 3$	.0809	.1535	.2187	—	—
$k = 4$	.0673	.1245	.1792	.2327	—
$k = 5$	.0571	.1069	.1537	.2008	.2451

(d) Critical values at the 20% level

Total regressors	Number of subset regressors $k = 1$	$k = 2$	$k = 3$	$k = 4$	$k = 5$
$k = 1$	.0723	—	—	—	—
$k = 2$	.0581	.1205	—	—	—
$k = 3$	.0485	.0994	.1476	—	—
$k = 4$	.0413	.0828	.1226	.1624	—
$k = 5$	.0353	.0713	.1069	.1402	.1744

Notes: Number of iterations = 20,000, $n = 500$.

6 Empirical Application

In this section we apply our testing method to Australian aggregate macroeconomic data and study the long-run form of the aggregate Australian consumption function following Phillips (1992). Our LM statistic is presented, together with other classical statistical procedures, to test for the long-run relationships between private consumption expenditure, household disposable income and real wealth.[2] Comparison between outcomes of these tests facilitates a study of the sensitivity of our LM procedure in detecting departures from the null.

6.1 *Description and Characteristics of the Data*

The data set we use covers the period 1965(1)–1988(4) and consists of nominal private cosumption expenditure (C), household disposable income (YD), the consumer price deflator (P) and real liquid assets ($M3/P$). Real variables are constructed from the data and are denoted by lower case letters: $c = C/P$ = real consumption expenditure; $yd = YD/P$ = real household disposable income; and $m3 = M3/P$ = real money stock. All variables are seasonally adjusted and the constant price series are at average 1984/1985 prices.

Figures 1(i)–(ii) graph these series (in log levels) to illustrate their relationship with each other over time. Clearly, consumption and income move closely together, although the nominal series appear to move closer than the real series. The real money stock, $m3$, in Figure 1(ii) exhibits divergent behavior midway through and towards the end of the sample.

Tests were conducted to determine the presence of stochastic trends in the data. Table 5 reports the results for the Augmented Dickey-Fuller (ADF) test and Phillips (1987) Z_a and Z_t tests for both the nominal and real series with a constant and trend in the regression equations (i.e. trend degree = 1). The null that is tested is that of a unit root and in all cases, for the consumption, income and wealth series at lags = 2, 5, the null cannot be rejected at the 5% level. These results corroborate Phillips' finding of a unit root in sample data on consumption and income over the longer period 1959(3)–1988(4).

---

[2] Phillips conducted a similar analysis and compared classical statistical procedures to the Phillips–Ploberger (1991) Bayesian posterior odds test.

(i) Nominal *YD* & *C*

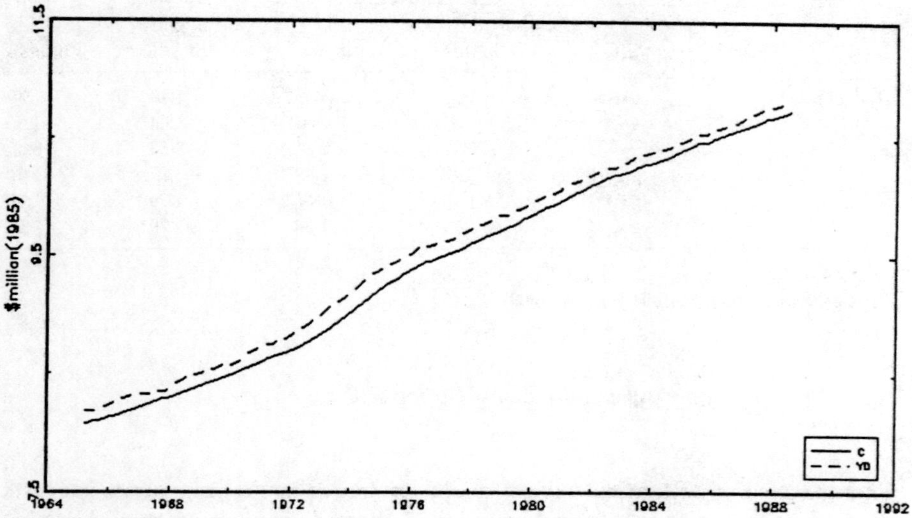

(ii) Real: *yd*, *c*, & *m*3

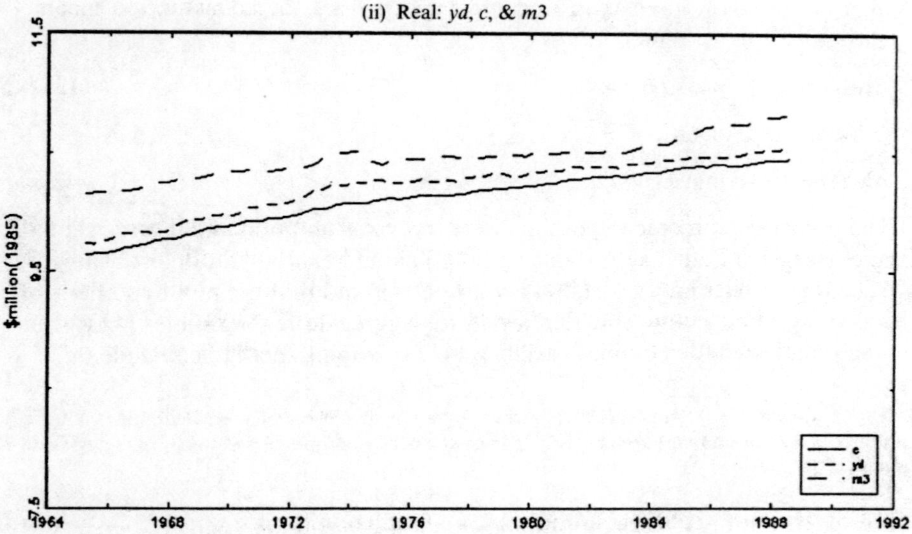

Fig. 1.

Table 5. Unit root tests

Test	lag	Nominal ln(C)	ln(YD)	ln(c)	Real ln(yd)	ln($m3$)
ADF	2	−1.51	−1.22	−1.95	−1.89	−1.59
	5	−2.21	−1.63	−2.31	−1.64	−1.55
Z_a	2	−3.03	−2.74	−2.86	−3.67	−6.69
	5	−3.76	−3.49	−2.49	−3.77	−6.46
Z_t	2	−1.31	−1.16	−1.56	−1.78	−1.69
	5	−1.44	−1.31	−1.54	−1.79	−1.66

5% Critical values: $Z_a = -20.84$; ADF, $Z_t = -3.46$.
(Critical values from Phillips-Perron (1988)).

6.2 *The Aggregate Australian Consumption Function*

The presence of deterministic and stochastic trends in the time series suggests that the long-run form of the Australian consumption function should exhibit co-movement between the determinants of consumption behavior and consumption expenditure. The simplest specification of the long-run consumption function under the permanent income hypothesis is the consumption-income relation

$$\ln(C) = \alpha + \beta \ln(YD) + u_t \tag{42.N}$$

or its real equivalent

$$\ln(c) = \alpha + \beta \ln(yd) + u_t . \tag{42.R}$$

If the permanent income hypothesis were true, consumption and income should be cointegrated and the residuals u_t in (42) should exhibit stationary behavior. In fact, an earlier study by Hall-Trevor (1991) found that the null hypothesis of no cointegration could not be rejected for aggregate real variables (42.R) but could be rejected for nominal variables (42.N), leading them to conclude that

"... for *real* consumer expenditure an aggregate equation should not be estimated.... In contrast, results for the *nominal* variables suggest that it would be appropriate to estimate the aggregate model."[3]

However, Phillips (1991a) found somewhat different results. Using Bayesian and classical procedures, his conclusion was that both nominal and real variables do not exhibit long-run cointegrating relationships. Following earlier work on alternative forms of the consumption function that incorporate the effects of

---

[3] V. B. Hall and R. G. Trevor (1991), "Long-run equilibrium estimation and inference: A nonparametric approach," to appear in P.C.B. Phillips (ed.), *Models, Methods and Applications of Econometrics: Essays in Honour of Rex Bergstrom*, p. 13.

inflation (notably Hendry-von Ungern-Sternberg (1981) and Anstie-Gray-Pagan (1983)), Phillips used the equation

$$\ln(C) = \alpha + \beta \ln(YD^*) + u_t . \tag{43}$$

Here, the variable YD^* is the "perceived income" or disposable income adjusted for the loss in liquid wealth due to inflation (π):

$$YD^* = YD\{1 - \phi(\hat{\pi} * M3/YD)\} = YD\{1 - \text{loss}\}, \tag{44}$$

and the parameter ϕ is introduced to allow for scale effects resulting from an inappropriate choice of an inflation measure $\hat{\pi}$ (= average inflation rate over the past four quarters) or for choosing $M3$ as a measure of liquid assets. Taking the logarithm of (44) the approximation to (43) is given by

$$\ln(C) = \alpha + \beta \ln(YD) + \gamma \text{ loss} + u_t \tag{45.N}$$

$$\ln(c) = \alpha + \beta \ln(yd) + \gamma \text{ loss} + u_t \tag{45.R}$$

which correspond to equations (33) and (34) in Phillips (1992). For both equations, using classical and Bayesian procedures, Phillips found that these augmented regression equations for consumption are cointegrating. Table 6 reports the long-run parameter estimates of the regression equations using fully modified least squares. We see that the loss measure is significant in explaining consumption in both equations (t-ratio = -6.34 and -3.13 for the real and

Table 6. Long-run parameter estimates

	Nominal	
	Parameter	t-Ratio
(42.N)	$\hat{\alpha} = -.224$	-7.52
	$\hat{\beta} = 1.012$	324.86
(45.N)	$\hat{\alpha} = -.229$	-5.78
	$\hat{\beta} = 1.024$	171.68
	$\hat{\gamma} = -1.8e - 06$	-3.13

	Real	
	Parameter	t-Ratio
(42.R)	$\hat{\alpha} = -.271$	-0.47
	$\hat{\beta} = 1.016$	18.07
(45.R)	$\hat{\alpha} = -1.087$	-3.91
	$\hat{\beta} = 1.104$	39.4
	$\hat{\gamma} = -4.69e - 06$	-6.34
(46.R)	$\hat{\alpha} = -1.34$	-3.63
	$\hat{\beta} = .9895$	15.18
	$\hat{\gamma} = -3.69e - 06$	-4.96
	$\hat{\delta} = .134$	1.65

(i) Nominal consumption and perceived income

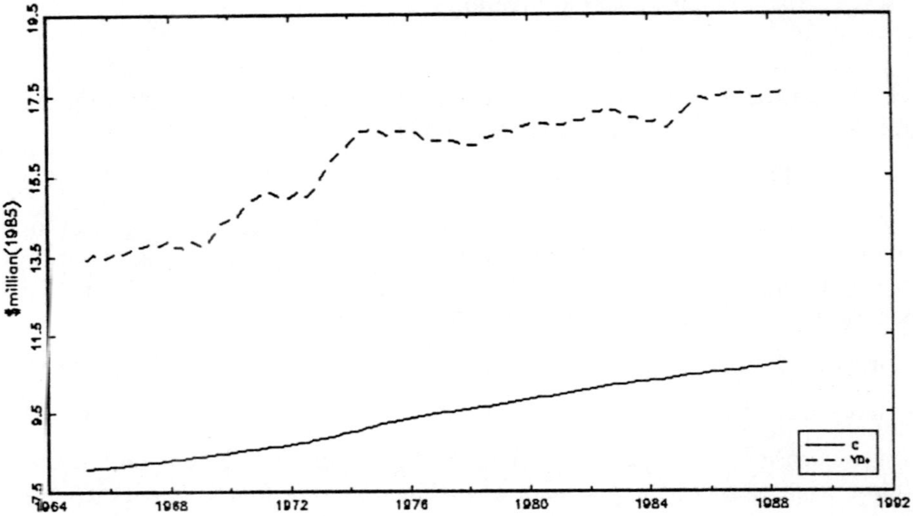

(ii) Real consumption and perceived income

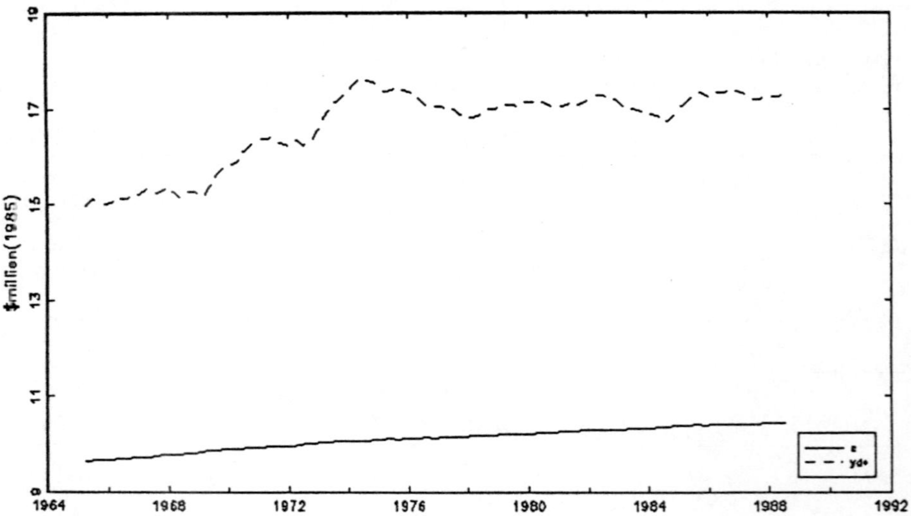

Fig. 2.

nominal equations respectively). Furthermore, although the marginal propensity to consume out of disposable income is not significantly different from unity in (42), the propensity to consume is more sensitive to shocks in inflation – adjusted income as the marginal propensity to consume out of income is greater in (45). The behavior of perceived income YD^* is graphed together with consumption in Figure 2(i)–(ii) in log levels. Clearly inflationary effects introduce more sample variability into income and support the conclusion that inflation plays a useful role in relating consumption behavior to income expenditure in the long-run.

In order to determine the sensitivity of our tests to departures from the null of cointegration, we report the results of our LM_3 test applied to equations (42) and (45) in the upper panel of Table 7. Hansen's (1992a) parameter constancy test on the intercept term is denoted by LM_i and is also reported in the table. The lower panel presents the results of the other classical procedures that test the null of no cointegration, and the estimated autoregressive coefficients in the residuals are denoted by $\hat{\rho}_N$ and $\hat{\rho}_R$ for the nominal and real regressions, respectively. For the first consumption equation (42), the ADF, Z_a and Z_t tests do not reject the null of no cointegration for both the nominal and real variables corroborating Phillips' finding. The LM tests for the null of cointegration present conflicting results. Our LM_3 test confirms cointegration in the nominal case but rejects cointegration in the real case (this corroborates the Hall-Trevor result). The LM_i test supports the presence of cointegration in both cases. Thus the empirical evidence is mixed. One possible explanation for these mixed findings

Table 7. Tests for cointegration

				Ho: Cointegration				
Test	42.N	42.R	5% cv	45.N	45.R	5% cv	46.R	5% cv
LM_3	0.03	0.18*	0.06	0.02	0.14	0.15	0.14	0.20
LM_i	0.32	0.29	0.62	0.06	0.25	0.78	0.21	0.90

				Ho: No cointegration				
Test-lag	42.N	42.R	5% cv	45.N	45.R	5% cv	46.R	5% cv
$ADF - 2$	−2.07	−1.98	−3.40	−4.05*	−3.8**	−3.84	−3.46	−4.22
5	−1.45	−1.39	−3.40	−3.56**	−3.01	−3.84	−2.79	−4.22
$Z_a - 2$	−9.33	−8.39	−19.19	−32.33*	−26.82*	−24.52	−23.74	−29.39
5	−10.19	−9.19	−19.19	−37.89*	−31.78*	−24.52	−28.50**	−29.39
$Z_t - 2$	−2.33	−2.17	−3.40	−4.39*	−4.01*	−3.84	−3.69	−4.22
5	−2.42	−2.26	−3.40	−4.69*	−4.29*	−3.84	−4.00**	−4.22
$\hat{\rho}$	0.86	0.88		0.62	0.67		0.70	

* – reject null at 5% level
** – reject null at 10% level

is that the statistics test different null hypotheses. The classical tests supports the null of no cointegration unless there is strong evidence to the contrary, whereas the *LM* tests support the null of cointegration unless there is strong evidence against parameter constancy. Note that the LM_3 coefficient test shows more discriminatory capability than the LM_i intercept test, since it supports a deviation from the null of parameter constancy in the real regression equation.[4]

The suggestion that perhaps it is perceived income rather than disposable income that is more relevant to consumption decisions leads us to test for a cointegrating relation in equation (45). From Table 7 we see that the *LM* and classical tests for both nominal and real variables agree with Phillips' earlier result that consumption in the long-run is affected by perceived income. These findings suggest that equation (45) better describes a long-run relationship for both nominal and real variables between consumption and income rather than the relation (42). Figures 3(i)–(ii) plot the residuals from the two regressions. The behavior of the residuals for the nominal and real case are similar over the sample period in Figure 3(ii) but differ substantially in Figure 3(i). Thus, the cointegration found for the nominal case (45.N) should also hold in the real case (45.R), and the outcome from Table 7 seems to support this visual evidence.

A final empirical formulation is to alter the steady-state solution by the addition of the wealth effect in the regression equation

$$\ln(c) = \alpha + \beta \ln(yd) + \gamma \text{ loss} + \delta \ln(m3) + u_t . \tag{46.R}$$

An interesting outcome of Phillips' analysis is that although (46.R) is cointegrating, Bayesian posteriors support the specification of (45.R) to (46.R) and show an appreciable probability of misspecification in equation (46.R) (i.e. no cointegration among the four variables). Our test results support this analysis and are reported in the last panel of Table 7. Both the *LM* tests cannot reject the null of cointegration, while the other tests cannot reject the null of no cointegration at the 5% level, reflecting, in part, the problem with classical hypothesis – testing ($\hat{\rho}_R = .702$). We perform a subset test on the parameter δ to find out whether the conflicting results presented above can be explained by the instability in the real money stock. The value of our LM_3 test equals .02, and with critical value = .0923 at the 5% level (see Table 4.B(b)) we cannot confirm any instability of the real money stock coefficient. Still, the inclusion of an additional, insignificant (t-ratio = 1.65) variable in a cointegrating equation carries some cost, especially in small samples where the additional variable in the regression introduces additional uncertainty in the regression residuals. This is, in fact, illustrated in Figure 3(iii), where the behavior of the residuals from (46.R) exhibit more variance over the sample period and differ substantially from the residuals of (45.R)

[4] When the test was applied to the full sample data, the *LM* test could not reject the hypothesis of cointegration for the real variables. One possible explanation is that the noise in the series is toward the middle of the sample, and extending the data to accommodate the periods with less noise gives the test lesser power to detect deviations from the null of stability.

(i) between C & YD

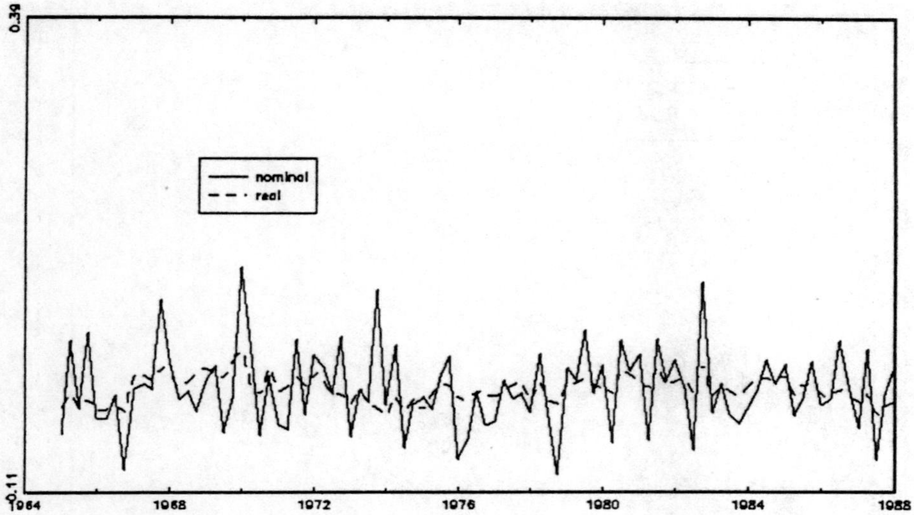

(ii) between C, $YD*$

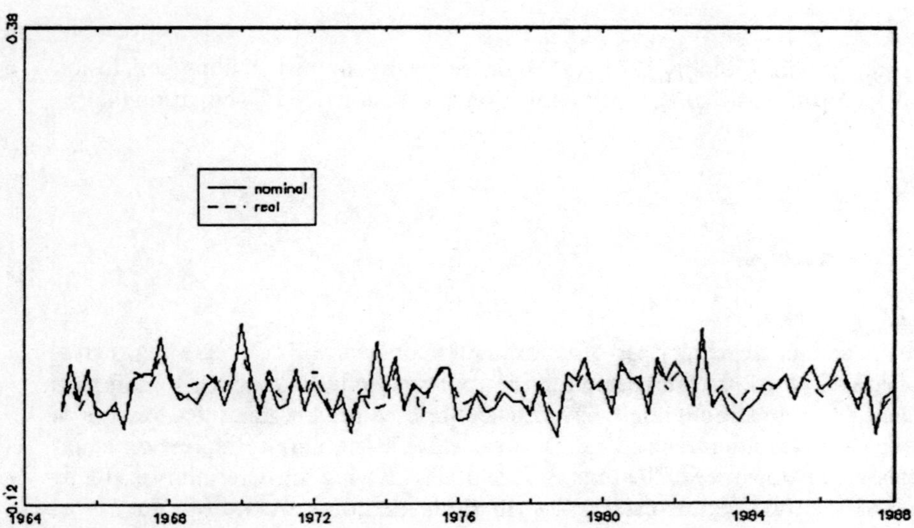

Fig. 3. Cointegrating regression residuals

(iii) between (45.R) and (46.R)

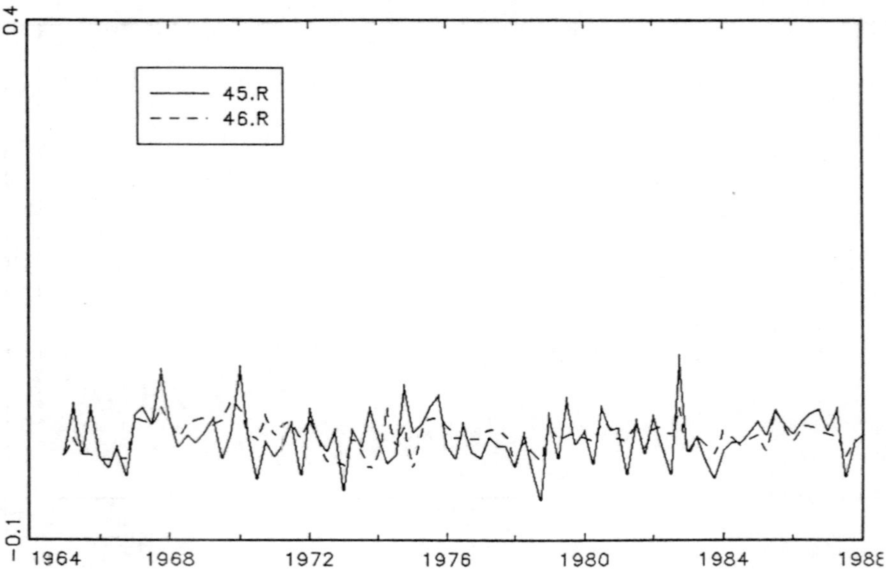

Fig. 3. (*cont'd*)

in some periods (notably 1974–1976). These results support Phillips' conclusion that the form of the consumption function is best described by equation (45).[5]

7 Conclusion

This paper has developed tests for parameter constancy in cointegrating regressions. These tests provide an alternative approach to testing for cointegration in time series regression models. The tests considered are the one-sided version of the *LM* test commonly used to test for coefficient stability in regression equations. A limit theory for the tests is developed allowing for deterministic trends and multivariate regressors. The distributions are non-standard but are free of nuisance parameters and in the multivariate case, depend only on the rank of certain regressors. A small Monte Carlo study suggests that the *LM* test is

[5] We have also considered an alternative formulation where a trend term is included in regressions (42), (45) and (46.R) so that we test for cointegration between the stochastic components only. But the coefficients of income ($\hat{\beta}$) in the regressions with the real variables ranged from .60 to .70. We prefer the economically more plausible coefficients that are closer to 1.

adequate for use in empirical testing with sample sizes greater than 100 and asymptotic sizes chosen at the 5% or 10% levels. The tests are easy to use and have optimal asymptotic properties, being in fact extensions of the locally best invariant tests for parameter constancy used in models with fixed regressors.

The tests are constructed so that the null under test is the hypothesis of cointegration. This formulation is useful in many applications because it is the hypothesis of coinegration rather than that of no cointegration that is often of primary interest. Such a formulation accords satisfactorily with classical hypothesis testing, since the hypothesis of cointegration is sharp in our formulation, whereas the hypothesis of no cointegration is composite, including a vast class of integrated processes. Formal statistical tests of the form suggested in this paper are helpful because they enable researchers to detect the presence of cointegration and help to determine the sources of cointegration failure when the tests reject.

The theory presented in this paper deals with the case where the stochastic regressors are not themselves cointegrated. Extension of the theory to the case where the regressors are cointegrated is more complex. Buth they have been worked out and will be presented in later work.

References

Andrews DWK (1991) Heteroskedasticity and autocorrelation consistent covariance matrix estimation Econometrica 59:817–858

Anstie RK, Gray MR, Pagan AR (1983) Inflation and the consumption ratio. In Pagan AR, Trivedi PK (eds). The effects of inflation: Theoretical investigations and australian evidence. Canberra: Centre for Economic Policy Research ANU

Bhargava A (1986) On the theory of testing for unit roots in observed time series. Review of Economic Studies 3: 174: 369–384

Chu CS James, White H (1990) Testing for structural change in some simple time series models. Manuscript, University of California, San Diego

Davies RB (1987) Hypothesis testing when a nuisance parameter is present only under the alternative. Biometrika 74:33–43

Dickey D, Fuller WA (1979) Distribution of the estimators for autoregressive time series with a unit root. Journal of American Statistical Association 74:427–431

Dickey D, Fuller WA (1981) The likelihood ratio statistics for autoregressive time series with a unit root. Econometrica 49:1057–1072

Engle RF, Yoo BS (1991) Cointegrated time series: A survey with new results. In: Granger and Engel (ed) Long-run Economic Relationships. London: Oxford University Press 237–266

Hall VB, Trevor RG (1991) Long-run equilibrium estimation and inference: A non-parametric approach. To appear in: Phillips PCB (ed) Essays in the theory and measurement of consumer behaviour in honour of rex bergstrom. Oxford: Basil Blackwell (forthcoming)

Hansen BE (1990) Testing for structural change of unknown form in models with non-stationary regressors. Manuscript, University of Rochester

Hansen BE (1992a) Tests for parameter instability in regressions with $I(1)$ processes. Journal of Business and Economic Statistics, 10:321–335

Hansen BE (1992b) Efficient estimation and testing of cointegrating vectors in the presence of deterministic trends. Journal of Econometrics, forthcoming

Hendry DF, von Ungern-Sternberg T (1981) Liquidity and inflation effects on consumers' expenditure. In: Deaton A (ed) Essays in the theory and measurement of consumer behaviour in honour of Sir Richard Stone. Cambridge: Cambridge University Press 237–260

Johansen S (1988) Statistical analysis of cointegration vectors. Journal of Economics Dynamics and Control 12:231–254

King ML, Hillier GH (1985) Locally best invariant tests of the error covariance matrix of the linear regression model. Journal of the Royal Statistical Society B 47 1:98–102

Kwiatkowski D, Phillips PCB, Schmidt P, Shin Y (1992) Testing the null hypothesis of stationarity against the alternative of a unit root: How sure are we that economics time series have a unit root?. Journal of Econometrics 54:154–178

Leybourne SJ, McCabe BPM (1989) On the distribution of some test statistics for coefficient constancy. Biometrika 76:169–177

McCabe BPM, Leybourne SJ (1988) Testing for variation in multivariate random coefficient regression models. Manuscript, University of Sydney

Nabeya S, Tanaka K (1988) Asymptotic theory of a test for the constancy of regression coefficients against the random walk alternative. Annals of Statistics 16:218–235

Newey WK, West KD (1987) A simple positive semi-definite heteroskedasticity and autocorrelation consistent covariance matrix. Econometrica 55:703–708

Park J, Phillips PCB (1988) Statistical inference in regressions with integrated processes: Part I. Econometric Theory 4:468–497

Park J, Phillips PCB (1989) Statistical inference in regression with integrated processes: Part II. Econometric Theory 5:95–131

Phillips PCB (1987) Time series regression with unit roots. Econometrica 55:277–301

Phillips PCB (1988a) Multiple regression with integrated regressors. Statistical Inference from Stochastic Processes, Contemporary Mathematics 80:79–106

Phillips PCB (1988b) Regression theory for near integrated time series. Econometrica 56:1021–1044

Phillips PCB (1989) Partially identified econometric models. Econometric Theory 5:181–240

Phillips PCB (1991) Time series regression with cointegrated regressors. Mimeograph, Yale University

Phillips PCB (1992) The long-run austrialian consumption function reexamined: An empirical exercise in bayesian inferences. 11:287–322. In: Hargreaves C (ed) Long Run Equilibrium and Macroeconomic Modelling. Cheltenham: Edward Elgar

Phillips PCB, Durlauf SN (1986) Multiple time series regression with integrated processes. Review of Economic Studies 53:473–496

Phillips PCB, Hansen B (1990) Statistical inference in instrumental variables regression with $I(1)$ processes. Review of Economic Studies 57:99–125

Phillips PCB, Ouliaris S (1990) Asymptotic properties of residual based tests for cointegration. Econometrica 58:165–194

Phillips PCB, Perron P (1988) Testing for a unit root in time series regression. Biometrika 75, 2:335–346

Phillips PCB, Ploberger W (1991) Time series modelling with a bayesian frame of reference. I. Concepts and illustrations. Cowles Foundation Discussion Paper No 980

Phillips PCB, Solo V (1992) Asymptotics of linear processes. Annals of Statistics, forthcoming

Stock JH, Watson MW (1988) Testing for common trends. Journal of the American Statistical Association 83:1097–1107

Tanaka K (1993) An alternative approach to the asymptotic theory of spurious regression, cointegration and near cointegration. Econometric Theory 9:36–61

The HUMP-Shaped Behavior of Macroeconomic Fluctuations

PIERRE PERRON[1]

Département de Sciences Economiques et C.R.D.E. Université de Montréal C.P. 6128, Succ. A Montréal, Québec, Canada, H3C-3J7

Abstract: We analyze the nature of persistence in macroeconomic fluctuations. The current view is that shocks to macroeconomic variables (in particular real *GNP*) have effects that endure over an indefinite horizon. This conclusion is drawn from the presence of a unit root in the univariate time series representation. Following Perron (1989), we challenge this assessment arguing that most macroeconomic variables are better construed as stationary fluctuations around a breaking trend function. The trend function is linear in time except for a sudden change in its intercept in 1929 (The Great Crash) and a change in slope after 1973 (following the oil price shock). Using a measure of persistence suggested by Cochrane (1988) we find that shocks have small permanent effects, if any. To analyze the effects of shocks at finite horizon, we select a member of the $ARMA(p, q)$ class applied to the appropriately detrended series. For the majority of the variables analyzed the implied weights of the moving-average representation have the once familiar humped shape.

Key Words: Measures of persistence, unit root, trend-stationarity, *ARMA* models, non-stationarity, structural change.

JEL Classification System-Numbers: C22, E32

1 Introduction

The most widely used modeling device in empirical economics characterizes a time series variable by some dynamic structure subject to shocks that are uncorrelated over time. There are many ways to incorporate this approach in a particular analysis. The approach popularized by Box and Jenkins (1970) analyzes the behavior of a univariate series by an autoregressive moving-average representation. Here, the dynamics of the system, or the propagation mechanism, is represented by the effect of past values of the variable and of the underlying shocks on the present value of the variable. Movements of a given variable are essentially driven by the present and past realizations of the shocks.

The nature of these shocks is generally left unspecified and can encompass various factors such as monetary policy surprises, technological shocks, changes

[1] I wish to thank Christian Dea and Serena Ng for research assistance as well as Charles Nelson and John Campbell who kindly provided some of the data used in this study. Research support from the Social Sciences and Humanities Research Council of Canada and the Fonds pour la Formation de Chercheurs et l'Aide à la Recherche du Québec is acknowledged.

in foreign conditions, exogenous governmental policy variations, etc. In general, the shocks may be viewed as a composite of factors.

A problem that has received considerable attention in the literature concerns the effects of a shock on future values of the level of the variable. As an example of such concern, consider the opening of Blanchard's article (1981, p. 150):

> One of the few undisputed facts in macroeconomics is that output is humped shaped, or more precisely that the distribution of weights of the moving average representation of the deviation of quarterly output from an exponential trend has a hump shape.

Of course, this so-called 'undisputed fact' has been seriously challenged recently, to the extent that it is now perceived as counterfactual. A composite shock is now thought to have a lasting effect on the level of output and most other macroeconomic variables. The latter view contrasts sharply with the 'hump-shaped' description, which defines a case where the effects of a shock are negligible after some period of time.

The contrasting assessments result essentially from different methods of making a series stationary, i.e., different detrending procedures. According to the earlier wisdom used by Blanchard to obtain the hump-shaped result, the trend exhibited by many macroeconomic variables is essentially deterministic. The trend can be succinctly represented by a linear first-order polynomial in time applied (usually) to the logarithm of the series. This view has been challenged, most notably by Nelson and Plosser (1982), who argue that the trend is primarily stochastic due to the presence of a unit root (with drift) in the univariate representation of the series. The unit-root characterization implies that shocks have a permanent effect on the level of the series.

Various studies have attempted to calculate the long-term percentage change in the level of a variable following a one percent innovation. These include Campbell and Mankiw (1987a, b, 1989), Cochrane (1988), Evans (1989), Clark (1987), Watson (1986) and Blanchard and Quah (1989). While the authors may disagree as to the precise long-term effect, and particularly whether it is greater or less than one percent, the consensus appears to be that it most likely is greater than zero. For example, Campbell and Mankiw (1987b, p. 111) argue that "Much disagreement remains over exactly how persistent are shocks to output. Nonetheless, among investigators using postwar quarterly data, there is almost unanimity that there is a substantial permanent effect."

The purpose of the present study is to try to refloat the hypothesis that the effects of shocks on most macroeconomic variables are short-lived and are, in fact, hump-shaped. We extend a previous analysis (Perron (1989)), where we argued that the statistical non-rejection of the unit-root hypothesis for macroeconomic data was essentially due to the presence of the 1929 Great Crash and the post-1973 (post-oil-price shock) slowdown in growth. These extraordinary events correspond to a shift in the intercept of the trend function in 1929 and a sudden change in its slope in 1973. Regardless of whether these two events are seen as large outliers or as exogenous (i.e., not realizations of the underlying probability structure of the shocks), the results in Perron (1989) suggest that the non-rejection of a unit root is due in large part to the occurrence of these two events. A way to isolate the events, i.e., to take them out of the noise function characterizing the variables, is to allow for non-linear trends. More specifically, if a sudden change in the intercept of the trend function in 1929 and a change in its slope in 1973 are permitted, the evidence for a unit-root hypothesis is considerably weakened. Here, shocks have no permanent effects except those associated with the 1929 crash and the slowdown in growth after 1973.

The present paper deals with two issues. The first is a reassessment of the findings described above, using the method following Cochrane (1988) and Campbell and Mankiw (1987a), which calculates the long-term effect of shocks by estimating the spectral density of the first-differences of the series at the zero frequency. This approach is particularly useful since this measure of persistence will be shown to be (asymptotically) unaffected by the presence of a 'crash' (i.e., a sudden change in the intercept of the trend function). We investigate various series for real *GNP*, including a long span of annual data and a post-war quarterly series. We also analyze the series used in Nelson and Plosser (1982). Our findings tend to confirm our earlier results. The effects of shocks vanish over a long horizon. It must be noted, however, that the present analysis is not intended to provide a formal statistical test to discriminate between the classes of trend-stationary (possibly with breaks) and differenced-stationary processes. Rather, our intention is to provide qualitative results that support our earlier claim as well as offering a possible explanation of differing results found by Cochrane and Campbell and Mankiw.

The second aim of the paper is to characterize the stochastic structure of the 'detrended' series using the non-linear trend described above. To this effect, we use the Akaike and Schwartz criteria to select members within the class of *ARMA* models. With very few exceptions, the appropriate stochastic structure is an $AR(2)$ or $ARMA(1, 1)$ with very similar dynamic properties. In most cases, the weights in the moving-average representation have a hump-shape.

The paper is organized as follows. Section 2 introduces the models considered and discusses the non-parametric statistic used to measure the persistence effects. Section 3 analyses the behavior of this statistic under the hypothesis that the trend function contains a single break. Section 4 presents an empirical analysis of the Nelson-Plosser data set, and Section 5 considers various real *GNP* series. In each case, the impulse-response function corresponding to the selected stochastic models are described. Finally, Section 6 presents some concluding comments and a discussion of the implications of our results for macroeconomic modeling, forecasting and the issue of detrending to achieve stationarity.

2 The Models and the Statistics

The 'extraordinary' nature of the 1929 crash and the 1973 oil-price shock when compared to the modern historical experience motivates the present analysis. The 1929 crash witnessed a sudden and dramatic decline in aggregate economic activity, while the 1973 oil-price shock is associated with the beginning of the slowdown in growth experienced by most western industrialized countries.

There are several possible statistical modeling strategies to incorporate these major events. On the one hand, one can view the 1929 crash as a realization of a shock issued from the same probability distribution as any other shock. This would imply a fat-tailed distribution, possibly one with infinite variance. The problem with this approach is that most statistical techniques are valid for finite variance distributions, and there is a clear possibility that such a single major event biases the statistics in favor of the unit-root hypothesis. This was shown formally in Perron (1989). Since the issue here is whether or not "regular" shocks have permanent effects, one may wish to remove the influence of a big outlier and see what the rest of the noise can tell us about the properties of the system. On the other hand, one can view such a large event, not as a realization issued from the same probability distribution as the other shocks, but as a quite separate random event. The idea is that the economy is regularly subjected to some shocks (call them "regular shocks," say) but that once in a while it is disrupted by a major event. This modeling strategy would allow two types of shocks issued from quite different probability distribution functions. For instance, one may wish to model the major events as realizations from a Poisson process. To be more precise, consider the following specification for a given variable y_t:

$$y_t = \eta_t + Z_t \; ; \qquad \eta_t = \mu_t + \beta_t t \tag{1}$$

where $A(L)Z_t = B(L)e_t$; $e_t \sim$ i.i.d.$(0, \sigma^2)$; $\mu_t = \mu_{t-1} + V(L)v_t$ and $\beta_t = \beta_{t-1} + W(L)w_t$. Here, the Z_t's are (not necessarily stationary) deviations from the trend function η_t. The intercept and the slope of the trend functions, μ_t and β_t, are themselves random variables modeled as integrated processes with $W(L)$, $V(L)$ stationary and invertible polynomials. However, the important distinction is that the timing of the occurrence of the shocks v_t and w_t are rare relative to the sequence of innovations $\{e_t\}$; for example, Poisson processes with arrival rates specified such that their occurrences are rare relative to the frequency of the realizations in the sequence $\{e_t\}$. The intuitive idea behind this type of modeling is that the coefficients of the trend function are determined by long-term economic fundamentals (e.g., the structure of the economic organization, population growth, etc.) and that these fundamentals are rarely changed. In our examples, v_t is non-zero in 1929 (the great depression) and w_t is non-zero in 1973 (the oil-price shock).

In any event, since we are interested in the effects of "regular" shocks (the e_t in the notation of (1)) through time on various aggregate variables, a useful way to approach the problem is to view these major events as part of the deterministic trend function. This follows the spirit of the Box-Tiao (1975) intervention analysis where we take "outlier" or "aberrant" events out of the noise function and analyze what the remaining noise can tell us about the properties of interest. This is the route we follow.

Following Nelson and Plosser (1982), Campbell and Mankiw (1987a), Cochrane (1988) and others, we parameterize a model which possibly exhibits permanent effects of shocks by the imposition of an autoregressive unit root with a possibly non-zero drift. However, the approach is generalized to allow a one-time change in the structure occurring at a time T_B ($1 < T_B < T$, where T is the sample size). Three different models are considered under this hypothesis: one that permits an exogenous change in the level of the series (a "crash"), one that permits an exogenous change in the rate of growth and one that allows both changes. The models are, under the null hypothesis of a unit root:

Model (A): $y_t = \mu + \gamma D(TB)_t + y_{t-1} + e_t$,

Model (B): $y_t = \mu + \theta DU_t + y_{t-1} + e_t$,

Model (C): $y_t = \mu + \gamma D(TB)_t + \theta DU_t + y_{t-1} + e_t$,

where $D(TB)_t = 1$ if $t = T_B + 1$, 0 otherwise, $DU_t = 1$ if $t > T_B$, 0 otherwise, and $A(L)e_t = B(L)v_t$, $v_t \sim$ i.i.d.$(0, \sigma^2)$ with $A(L)$ and $B(L)$, p^{th} and q^{th} order polynomials, respectively, in the lag operator L. More general conditions on the errors $\{e_t\}$ are possible but to ease the presentation we shall only consider these simpler ones.[2]

The cases where the shocks have no permanent effect on the level of the series $\{y_t\}$ are represented by trend-stationary models parameterized as follows:

Model (A): $y_t = \mu + \gamma DU_t + \beta t + w_t$,

Model (B): $y_t = (\mu - \theta T_B) + \beta t + \theta DT_t + w_t$,

Model (C): $y_t = (\mu - \theta T_B) + \gamma DU_t + \beta t + \theta DT_t + w_t$,

where $DT_t = t$, if $t > T_B$, 0 otherwise, and $F(L)w_t = D(L)v_t$; $v_t \sim$ i.i.d.$(0, \sigma^2)$, with $F(L)$ and $D(L)$ again finite order polynomials in L. Model (A) describes what we refer to as the crash model. The parameter γ represents the magnitude of the change in the intercept of the trend function occurring at time T_B. Model (B) is referred to as the "changing growth" model and θ represents the magnitude of the change in the slope of the trend function. Model (C) allows for both effects to take place simultaneously, i.e., a sudden change in the level of the series followed by a different growth path.

---

2 Note also that we describe the models in terms of the "additive outlier version" as opposed to the "innovational outlier version," a distinction which is discussed in Perron (1989). This does not affect any of the results that follow.

In our earlier study, we considered testing the null hypothesis of a unit root in a variety of macroeconomic time series allowing for such changes in the trend function. The statistics derived were in the spirit of the Dickey-Fuller (1979) procedure and required the tabulation of a new set of critical values. An alternative is to consider the procedure suggested by Cochrane (1988) and Campbell and Mankiw (1987a) to provide a measure of the persistence effect of shocks. It is based on the properties of the noise function of the first-differences of the data. Unit-root and trend-stationary models can be nested as:

$$\text{Model (A): } \Delta y_t = \kappa + \gamma D(TB)_t + u_t \ , \tag{2}$$

$$\text{Model (B): } \Delta y_t = \kappa + \theta DU_t + u_t \ , \tag{3}$$

$$\text{Model (C): } \Delta y_t = \kappa + \gamma D(TB)_t + \theta DU_t + u_t \ . \tag{4}$$

Under the unit-root hypothesis, $\kappa = \mu$ (the drift) and $u_t = e_t = A(L)^{-1}B(L)v_t$. Under the hypothesis that the series is trend-stationary, $\kappa = \beta$ (the initial slope of the deterministic trend function) and $u_t = (1 - L)w_t = (1 - L)F(L)^{-1}D(L)v_t$. Hence, when the models are parameterized in first-differences, the only difference between each hypothesis is with respect to the nature of the errors $\{u_t\}$. When the model is trend-stationary, there is a unit root in the moving-average representation of the errors, denoted $u_t = \psi(L)v_t$. The long-horizon effect of a unit shock in v_t on the level of y_t is given by $\psi(1) = \lim_{i\to\infty} \sum_{j=0}^{i} \psi_j$, where ψ_j are the coefficients in the polynomial $\psi(L)$. If the model is trend-stationary, $\psi(1) = 0$ since $\psi(L) = (1 - L)F(L)^{-1}D(L)v_t$. On the other hand, if the model contains an autoregressive unit root $\psi(1) > 0$.

Cochrane (1988) has proposed an alternative measure of persistence that can be estimated non-parametrically. The measure is based on the autocovariance function of the differenced process, which can be related to the moving average polynomial $\psi(z)$ as $C(z) = \psi(z)\psi(z^{-1})\sigma_v^2$ where $C(z) = \sum_{j=-\infty}^{\infty} C_j z^j$, C_j is the jth autocovariance of the first-differenced process, and σ_v^2 is the variance of the innovations $\{v_t\}$. Denoting the variance of the first-differenced process as σ^2 $(= C_0)$, the measure of persistence is given by $V = C(1)/\sigma^2$, and is related to $\psi(1)$ by $V = (\sigma_v^2/\sigma^2)[\psi(1)]^2$. The measure V is simply 2π times the normalized spectral density of the process $\{u_t\}$ evaluated at frequency zero. V and $\psi(1)$ are not equivalent except in some special cases, in particular when $\psi(1) = 0$ when there is no persistence. For us, this is the interesting case, and we shall work directly with the measure V and show that for most series its estimate turns out to be close to zero.

Let $\overline{\Delta y}_t = y_t - y_{t-1} - \hat{\mu}$ where $\hat{\mu} = T^{-1}\sum_1^T (y_t - y_{t-1}) = T^{-1}(y_T - y_0)$ is the estimate of the slope of the trend function. A general class of estimators of the spectral density at the origin is given by:

$$\hat{V}^k = 1 + 2 \sum_{j=1}^{k} w(k, j)\hat{\rho}_j \ , \tag{5}$$

where

$$\hat{\rho}_j = (T/(T-j)) \sum_{t=j+1}^{T} (\overline{\Delta y}_t \overline{\Delta y}_{t-j}) \Big/ \sum_{t=1}^{T} (\overline{\Delta y}_t)^2 \ , \tag{6}$$

with k a truncation lag parameter and $w(k, j)$ a lag window.[3] Many possible choices of lag windows are available, and for ease of comparison of our results with the previous literature, we choose the Bartlett triangular window defined by $w(k, j) = 1 - j/(k+1)$. $\hat{V}^k$ is a consistent estimate of V if $k \to \infty$ and $k/T \to 0$ as $T \to \infty$. Its asymptotic standard error is given by (see, e.g., Priestley (1981, p. 463)):

$$\text{s.e.}\,[\hat{V}^k] = \hat{V}^k/[(3/4)(T/(k+1))]^{1/2} \ . \tag{7}$$

As a measure of persistence, $\hat{V}^k$ has several advantages due mainly to the fact that it is non-parametric. However, a problem in finite samples concerns the appropriate choice of the truncation lag parameter k. Campbell and Mankiw (1987b) conducted a small Monte Carlo experiment with 130 observations with a random walk and a stationary $AR(2)$ model. They found that a value k of at least 30, and preferably 40 or 50 (i.e., more than 1/3 of the total sample size) is needed to be able to distinguish the above-mentioned models. Perron and Ng (1992) found that the exact mean-squared error of $\hat{V}^k$ is minimized using a large value of k if V is small, and a small value of k if V is large (e.g., in the vicinity of 1). Given our earlier results (Perron (1989)) that most macroeconomic time series appear to be best construed as "trend-stationary" if allowance is made for a shift in the trend function, more weight should be given to estimates of $\hat{V}^k$ with k quite large, say between 1/3 and 1/2 of total sample size. This approach is taken in the empirical sections, though we present estimates $\hat{V}^k$ for a wide range of values for k.[4]

It is by now understood that statistics such as the variance ratio or any estimate of the spectral density at the origin have poor properties as formal tests to distinguish trend-stationary versus difference-stationary processes (see, in particular, Cecchetti and Lam (1991)). The basic problem is that the finite sample confidence intervals are very wide if the process has a unit root. We verified

---

[3] $\hat{V}^k$ as defined by (5) and (6) does not necessarily lead to a non-negative estimate of V. It would do so if the biased estimates of ρ_j were used, i.e., without the correction factor $(T/(T-j))$. We report results using $\hat{V}^k$, as defined in (5) and (6), to permit a comparison with previous studies, namely those of Cochrane (1988) and Campbell and Mankiw (1987a). Estimates of V using a variety of windows and truncation lags were also computed and are available upon request. The results are not very sensitive to other choices of windows and lead to the same conclusions.

[4] The use of data-dependent methods to select the truncation lag parameter k, as in Andrews (1991) for example, is problematic in the present context. Such methods usually start with a preliminary estimation of a simple time series model, such as an $AR(1)$. The optimal truncation lag is then a function of the estimated value of this autoregressive parameter. The problem with applying such a procedure is that, as shown in Perron (1989), the presence of a break in the trend function will bias the estimated first-order autocorrelation coefficient towards 1. In this context, the chosen truncation lag parameter may be inappropriate. We therefore prefer the presentation of a range of values to assess the robustness of the results.

this by doing the following experiment. We first assumed no break in the data and estimated, for each series, an AR process with a unit root. We then simulated the statistic $\hat{V}^k$ for various values of k. Except in some rare cases, the confidence intervals were so wide that no discrimination was possible.

With this caveat in mind we nevertheless applied the following modification of an asymptotic test suggested by Phillips and Ouliaris (1988). The test is based on the fact that $\hat{V}^k$ is asymptotically normal with mean V and variance given by the square of (7). Their procedure is a bounds test based on the asymptotic distribution. Let H be the hypothesis that the process is trend-stationary. Also let z_α be the α-percentage point of the normal distribution. We say that we accept H if $\hat{V}^k + z_\alpha\{\text{s.e.}(\hat{V}^k)\} < c^*$, for some bound c^*; correspondingly we say that we reject H if $\hat{V}^k - z_\alpha\{\text{s.e.}(\hat{V}^k)\} > c^*$. If none of the inequalities are satisfied the test is viewed as inconclusive. Of course, the procedure is quite arbitrary in the sense that a choice of c^* must be made. Moreover, for any such choice of c^* the test will likely have some size distortions in finite sample for particular classes of data-generating processes. In any event, it nevertheless provides an asymptotically valid procedure and permits us to infer, in some sense, the most likely hypothesis (see the discussion in Phillips and Ouliaris (1988)). The particular choice of c^* is discussed in the empirical sections.[5]

3 Properties of $\hat{V}^k$ with a Breaking Trend Function

To understand the empirical results described in the next sections, it is instructive to analyze the asymptotic behavior of the usual sample autocorrelations (with only a constant mean subtracted) when the trend function contains a break. We wish to derive the limit of $\hat{\rho}_j$ when in fact the true process is either given by equation (2) (a change in the intercept of the trend function) or equation (3) (a change in the slope of the trend function). As will be apparent from the results below, the behavior of $\hat{\rho}_j$ when the true model is equation (4) (both changes allowed) is equivalent to that under equation (3).

To perform the asymptotic analysis, we require T_B to increase at the same rate as T. For simplicity, we let $T_B/T = \lambda$ for all values of T. We denote by ρ_j the true autocorrelation coefficient at lag j of the process $\{u_t\}$ and $C(j)$ the true autocovariance at lag j of the same process. We collect our results in the following Theorem, whose proof can be obtained by slight modifications of the proof of Theorem 1 in Perron (1990).

[5] We view the bounds test of Phillips and Ouliaris (1988) not as a formal test per se but rather as providing indirect evidence. We discuss in more detail, in the empirical sections, the strategy used to select the bound and how such a choice can help us draw some inference of interest.

Theorem 1: Let $\hat{\rho}_j$ be defined by (6). *Then as $T \to \infty$ with $T_B/T = \lambda$ for all T, we have: a) if Δy_t is generated according to* (2): $\hat{\rho}_j \to \rho_j$; *b) if Δy_t is generated according to either* (3) *or* (4), $\hat{\rho}_j \to [\lambda(1-\lambda)\theta^2 + C(j)]/[\lambda(1-\lambda)\theta^2 + C(0)]$.

This Theorem shows that the standard sample autocorrelations are consistent estimates of their population values only for Model (A) where a break is present in the intercept of the trend function. This result is intuitively clear, since the mean of the first-differenced series is constant except for a single period. The effect of neglecting this change vanishes asymptotically. There may, however, remain a bias in finite sample.

Things are different when there is a break in the slope of the trend function. Here, thc sample autocorrelations are inconsistent estimates of the population autocorrelation coefficient. An interesting feature is that the limit is greater than the population value at any lag. The asymptotic bias is positive for all autocorrelations. The bias is greater the larger the relative magnitude of $\lambda(1-\lambda)\theta^2$ compared to $C(j)$ and $C(0)$. In particular, the larger the break the greater is the bias. For a given value of θ, the bias is maximized when $\lambda = 1/2$, with a break at mid-sample. A consequence of this result is that one can expect $\hat{V}^k$ to be an inconsistent estimate of V if a break in the slope of the trend function is not taken into account. More importantly, $\hat{V}^k$ (using the standard autocorrelations $\hat{\rho}_j$) will tend to overestimate V, thereby suggesting a much greater degree of persistence than exists. In particular, $\hat{V}^k$ will suggest some persistence even if the shocks have no long-term effects.

To obtain consistent estimators in the presence of a change in the slope of the trend function we need alternative estimates of the autocorrelation function of $\{u_t\}$. To this effect, first denote by $\Delta\tilde{y}_t$ the "demeaned" series Δy_t where allowance is made for a possible change in mean at time T_B. More specifically $\Delta\tilde{y}_t$ is defined as the residuals in the following regression estimated by ordinary least-squares:

$$\Delta y_t = \tilde{\kappa} + \tilde{\theta} DU_t + \Delta\tilde{y}_t \tag{8}$$

with $DU_t = 1$ if $t \geq T_B$ (0 otherwise). $\hat{V}^k$ is computed using (5–6) with $\Delta\tilde{y}_t$ instead of $\overline{\Delta y}_t$.

4 Analysis of the Nelson-Plosser Series

We analyze the series considered by Nelson and Plosser (1982) for several reasons. First, it is a rich data set with a wide range of annual series covering a long historical period. More importantly, it allows us to make some interesting comparisons between the results in the original Nelson-Plosser study and Perron

(1989). An interesting feature is that all series end in 1970 and cover the period of the 1929 crash. Hence, for each series only one break is likely to be present. For reasons discussed in Perron (1989), we consider model (A) (only a change in the intercept in 1929) for the series Real *GNP*, Nominal *GNP*, Real Per Capita *GNP*, Industrial Production, Employment, *GNP* Deflator, Consumer Prices, Nominal Wages, Money Stock, Velocity and Interest Rate. We consider model (C) (a change in both the intercept and the slope in 1929) for Real Wages and Common Stock Prices. We do not consider any change in the trend function for the unemployment series since there is agreement that it is stationary for the period under consideration.[6]

For most of the series considered there is only a change in the intercept of the trend function. On the basis of Theorem 1, $\hat{V}^k$ is not influenced, asymptotically, by the presence of such a change. However, as discussed in Perron (1989), standard Dickey-Fuller tests for a unit root are biased toward non-rejection of the unit-root hypothesis even asymptotically. Hence, it can be viewed as an alternative to standard tests for a unit root which is robust to a sudden change in the intercept of the trend function and should, in principle, yield results similar to those obtained in our earlier study.

The estimated measures of persistence (without any corrections for changes in the trend function) are presented in Table 1. We tabulate results for the following values of the truncation lag parameter k: 8, 16, 20, 30, 40 and 50. The results are quite striking. The estimates show very little evidence of persistence for all series, with the exception of Consumer Prices, Velocity and Interest Rate, precisely those series for which the unit root could not be rejected in Perron (1989). The results are sometimes quite extreme. For example, consider the Industrial Production index, where $\hat{V}^k$ is 0.07 with $k = 50$ (less than half of total sample size). This result is quite contrary to the unit-root hypothesis found in Nelson-Plosser but is in accord with our earlier results. The results are not so dramatic for all series but are indeed suggestive that most of them exhibit little persistence, if at all. Apart from the above-mentioned three exceptions, all series show an estimate less than 0.33 at $k = 40$ (except *GNP* Deflator with 0.50 and Common Stock Prices with 0.49).

We also present in Table 1.a estimates for the Real Wages and Common Stock Price series when allowance is made for a change in slope in 1929. Following the results of Zivot and Andrews (1992) and Perron (1991) we also present the estimates with a change in slope in 1939 for Real Wages and 1936 for Common Stock Prices. These dates were selected as the outcome of tests for unit roots allowing the break point to be unknown. As expected from the theoretical result of Section 3, the estimates are noticeably smaller when allowance is made for a change in slope. For the Common Stock Prices series the choice of 1936 as opposed to 1929 as the break date has a more significant impact.

[6] Related results, using the Nelson-Plosser data set can be found in Zivot and Andrews (1992) and Raj (1993). Evidence of rejections of the unit root with historical data from many countries can be found in Raj (1992).

Table 1. Non-parametric estimates of persistence ($\hat{V}^k$); Nelson-Plosser data

Series	T	$k = 8$	$k = 16$	$k = 20$	$k = 30$	$k = 40$	$k = 50$
Real *GNP*	62	1.01	.41	.16[a]	.37	.21	.11[a]
		(.45)	(.25)	(.11)	(.30)	(.20)	(.12)
Nominal *GNP*	62	1.59[rr]	1.01	.69	.35	.23	.06[a]
		(.71)	(.62)	(.47)	(.29)	(.22)	(.06)
Real Per Capita *GNP*	62	1.03	.43	.45	.34	.20	.12[a]
		(.46)	(.26)	(.30)	(.28)	(.19)	(.13)
Industrial Production	111	.45	.17[a]	.21[aa]	.19[aa]	.15[a]	.07[a]
		(.15)	(.08)	(.11)	(.12)	(.11)	(.06)
Employment	81	1.07[rr]	.55	.49	.29	.11[a]	.17
		(.41)	(.29)	(.30)	(.21)	(.09)	(.16)
Unemployment Rate	81	.56	.20[aa]	.16[a]	.12[a]	.01[a]	.06[a]
		(.22)	(.11)	(.09)	(.09)	(.01)	(.06)
GNP Deflator	82	2.16[r]	1.81	1.38	.45	.50	.68
		(.83)	(.96)	(.81)	(.32)	(.41)	(.62)
Consumer Prices	111	2.39[r]	2.23[rr]	2.00	1.65	1.49	1.18
		(.79)	(1.01)	(1.01)	(1.01)	(1.05)	(.93)
Nominal Wages	71	1.91[rr]	1.15	.68	.32	.33	.17
		(.79)	(.65)	(.43)	(.25)	(.29)	(.17)
Real Wages	71	.82	.49	.49	.48	.31	.19
		(.34)	(.28)	(.31)	(.37)	(.27)	(.19)
Money Stock	82	2.63[r]	1.35	.76	.40	.19	.28
		(1.01)	(.71)	(.45)	(.29)	(.16)	(.26)
Velocity	102	.76	.72	.81	.86	.86	.92
		(.26)	(.34)	(.42)	(.55)	(.63)	(.75)
Interest Rate	71	2.06[r]	2.95	3.03	2.82	1.73	.76
		(.85)	(1.68)	(1.91)	(2.17)	(1.53)	(.75)
Common Stock Prices	100	.74	.67	.63	.57	.49	.46
		(.26)	(.32)	(.34)	(.37)	(.36)	(.38)

Table 1.a: Non-parametric estimates of persistence ($\hat{V}^k$) with break in trends at time T_b

Series	T_b	$k = 8$	$k = 16$	$k = 20$	$k = 30$	$k = 40$	$k = 50$
Real Wages	1929	.65	.27	.24	.19	.09[a]	.05[a]
		(.27)	(.15)	(.15)	(.15)	(.08)	(.05)
	1939	.71	.30	.29	.27	.14[a]	.08[a]
		(.29)	(.17)	(.18)	(.21)	(.12)	(.08)
Common Stock Prices	1929	.70	.58	.52	.46	.44	.41
		(.24)	(.28)	(.28)	(.30)	(.33)	(.34)
	1936	.59	.40	.31	.19[a]	.12[a]	.09[a]
		(.20)	(.19)	(.16)	(.08)	(.09)	(.07)

Notes: i) Asymptotic standard errors computed according to (7) are in parentheses. ii) [rr] and [r] denote a rejection of the trend-stationarity hypothesis, at the 10% and 5% level respectively, using the bounds test described in Section 2 with $c^* = 0.40$. Similarly, [aa] and [a] denote acceptance of this hypothesis at the 10% and 5% level, respectively.

Tables 1 and 1.a also present the outcome of Phillips and Ouliaris' (1988) bounds test. As noted in Section 2, this test depends on the arbitrary choice of the bound c^*. We selected .40 as the value to be used in the test. The reason for such a choice is that it allows accepting the trend-stationarity hypothesis for the Unemployment series at the 5% level for values of k greater than or equal to 20 and at the 10% level for all values of k greater than or equal to 16. Since it is generally agreed that over this sample period the Unemployment Rate series is stationary, one would like the outcome of the test to reflect this feature, and this particular choice achieves this goal. Nevertheless, the tests presented should be viewed as rather suggestive and subject to the caveats discussed in Section 2.

In many instances the tests yield an inconclusive outcome. For values of k other than 8, only one series, the Consumer Price index, shows a test that suggests rejection of the trend-stationarity hypothesis (for $k = 16$ only). The tests suggest accepting the trend-stationarity hypothesis with large values of k for Real *GNP*, Nominal *GNP*, Real per Capita *GNP*, Industrial Production, Employment as well as for Real Wages and Common Stock Price, when allowance is made for a change in slope in the latter two series.

These results are, in an important sense, complementary to those obtained in Perron (1989). The issue is as follows. The measures presented in Table 1 suggest the absence of long-term persistence effects of shocks. However, standard unit-root testing procedures fail to reject the unit root hypothesis. Furthermore, as argued by Nelson and Plosser (1982), univariate *ARMA* models of these series suggest a process close to an $IMA(1, 1)$ whose first-differences are positively correlated. The latter would suggest a high degree of persistence. Hence, the two approaches yield quite different implications. One way to reconcile these results is by viewing the 1929 crash as a change in the intercept of the trend function. As argued in Section 3, the presence of such a change will have no effect (in large samples) on the non-parametric measure of persistence. However, as argued in Perron (1989), it will bias the unit-root tests towards non-rejection of the unit-root hypothesis suggesting that standard univariate *ARMA* modeling will show a higher degree of persistence than is present. Given our earlier results of the many rejections of the unit root when allowance is made for a change in the intercept of the trend function in 1929, we incorporate such a change prior to estimating the *ARMA* models for the noise function.

To analyze the effects of shocks at finite horizons we therefore adopt the following strategy. We detrend the data by allowing a change in the intercept between 1929 and 1930. The residuals, considered estimates of the noise of the series, are analyzed within the class of $ARMA(p, q)$ models. We estimated all models with p and q less than or equal to 5. The optimal parameterization was chosen using either the Schwartz (1978) or the Akaike (1974, 1976) criteria. The Akaike criterion minimizes $2 \ln L + 2m$ where L is the likelihood and $m = p + q$ is the number of parameters. The Schwartz criterion minimizes $2 \ln L + m \ln T$ where T is the total number of observations. For the sample sizes considered here, the Schwartz criterion penalizes extra parameters more heavily. We carried

Table 2. Model impulse responses; Nelson-Plosser series (horizon in years)

Series	Detrending Procedure	Model	1	2	3	4	6	8	10	15	20	30
Real *GNP*	*A*	(2, 0)	1.049	.716	.348	.090	−.076	−.038	−.002	.001	.000	.000
	A	(1, 1)	1.041	.628	.378	.228	.083	.030	.011	.001	.000	.000
Nominal *GNP*	*A*	(2, 0)	.870	.478	.173	.017	−.034	−.008	.001	.000	.000	.000
	A	(1, 1)	.872	.438	.220	.111	.028	.007	.004	.000	.000	.000
Real P.C. *GNP*	*A*	(2, 0)	1.114	.857	.526	.256	−.006	−.041	−.018	.001	.000	.000
	A	(1, 1)	1.106	.750	.509	.346	.159	.073	.338	.005	.001	.000
Ind. Production	*A*	(0, 4)	.855	.561	.498	.273	—	—	—	—	—	—
Employment	*A*	(2, 0)	1.084	.865	.602	.384	.130	.035	.007	.000	.000	.000
	A	(1, 1)	1.044	.798	.610	.466	.272	.159	.093	.024	.006	.000
	A	(3, 2)	1.066	.758	.472	.301	.166	.107	.065	.018	.005	.000
Unemp. Rate	none	(1, 1)	1.124	.683	.415	.253	.093	.035	.013	.001	.000	.000
GNP Deflator	*A*	(2, 0)	1.000	.798	.595	.434	.226	.117	.060	.016	.002	.000
	A	(1, 1)	.985	.757	.581	.447	.263	.155	.092	.025	.009	.000
	A	(1, 0)	.824	.678	.559	.460	.312	.212	.144	.054	.021	.003
Wages	*A*	(2, 0)	.940	.626	.345	.163	.018	−.004	−.003	.000	.000	.000
	A	(1, 1)	.945	.579	.355	.218	.082	.031	.012	.001	.000	.000
Real Wages	*C*1	(2, 1)	.483	.045	−.288	−.508	−.642	−.494	−.239	−.147	−.057	−.104
	*C*3	(1, 0)	.622	.387	.241	.150	.058	.022	.009	.001	.000	.000
Money Stock	*A*	(2, 0)	1.149	1.013	.811	.620	.341	.182	.096	.019	.004	.000
	A	(1, 1)	1.137	.926	.754	.614	.407	.331	.220	.079	.023	.003
Stock Prices	*C*1	(1, 1)	1.177	.722	.443	.271	.102	.038	.014	.001	.000	.000
	*C*2	(3, 1)	.788	.328	−.089	−.389	−.647	−.598	−.417	−.024	.055	−.003

Notes: i) For the detrending model (A) means that a dummy variable which is 1 after 1929 and 0 prior is included; and ($C1$, $C2$, $C3$) means that a dummy that is t after 1929, 1936 and 1939, respectively, and 0 prior is also included in addition. The entries under the column 'model' indicate the order of the estimated $ARMA(p, q)$ models.

out this procedure for all Series except Consumer Prices, Velocity and Interest Rate, given that for these series the unit-root hypothesis is not rejected.

For the majority of the series, the first and second choices, according to both criteria, are $AR(2)$ and $ARMA(1, 1)$. One notable exception is the Industrial Production series, where the chosen model is $ARMA(0, 4)$. Table 2 presents the implied weights of the moving-average representation for each model selected. Not only are the impulse responses similar across models for a given series, they are also quite similar across series. The typical pattern is that of a hump-shape with most of the effects vanishing within 4 to 8 years.

The evidence presented in this section appears inconsistent with the notion that shocks have permanent effects on a wide variety of macroeconomic variables. The fluctuations around the trend function are transitory, and the weights in the moving-average representation have the once-familiar humped-shape. Given that more attention is given to results pertaining to real *GNP* in the literature, the next section presents a more detailed analysis focusing on a number of available indices of Real *GNP*.

5 An Empirical Analysis of Real *GNP*

We analyze three *GNP* series that are commonly used in the literature. The first one is Post-war Quarterly Real *GNP* 1947:1–1985:4 (seasonally adjusted) from the National Income and Product Accounts. This is the same series analyzed in Campbell and Mankiw (1987a) except for some minor data revisions. In this case, we allow for a change in the slope of the trend function after 1973:1 (designated as detrending method B). The second series is Annual Real *GNP* 1869–1983 taken from Balke and Gordon (1986). Here, we allow two breaks: a change in the intercept after 1929 and a change in the slope after 1973 (detrending method D). The third series is Annual Real Per Capita *GNP* 1869–1975 taken from Friedman and Schwartz (1982). This series was analyzed by Perron and Phillips (1987) and Stock and Watson (1986). Here, we allow only for a change in the intercept after 1929 (detrending method A) since the bias due to the change in the slope of the trend function is likely to be small with only two data points after the change in slope in 1973.

The estimated measures of persistence are presented in Table 3. Consider first the Post-war Quarterly Real *GNP* series. Row (1) reproduces the results of Campbell and Mankiw (1987a). Row (2) gives the estimates allowing for a shift in the slope of the trend function (Model B) after 1973:1. It uses the residuals from regression (8) with T_B set at 1973:1. The results clearly show much weaker evidence for persistence. For instance, at $k = 50$ (1/3 of total sample size), the estimate is reduced from 0.68 to 0.13, allowing for the break; at $k = 100$, it is reduced from 0.57 to 0.05. Furthermore, the outcome of Phillips and Ouliaris'

Table 3. Non-parametric estimates of persistence $\hat{V}^k$; real GNP series

Row	Series	Sample Size	Detrending Correction	$k = 10$	$k = 20$	$k = 30$	$k = 40$	$k = 50$	$k = 60$	$k = 70$	$k = 80$	$k = 100$
Post-war Quarterly Real *GNP*												
(1)	47:1–85:4	156	none	1.70[r]	1.32	1.13	.88	.68	.72	.76	.71	.57
				(.52)	(.56)	(.58)	(.52)	(.45)	(.52)	(.59)	(.59)	(.53)
(2)	47:1–85:4	156	(8)	1.58[r]	1.06	.72	.37	.13[a]	.18[aa]	.23	.19	.05[a]
				(.49)	(.45)	(.37)	(.22)	(.09)	(.13)	(.18)	(.16)	(.05)
(3)	73:2–85:4	51	none	1.72	.38	−.06[aa]	.35	—	—	—	—	—
				(.93)	(.28)	(—)	(.37)	(—)	(—)	(—)	(—)	(—)
(4)	47:1–73:1	105	none	1.64[r]	1.30	.80	.31	.03[a]	—	—	—	—
				(.62)	(.67)	(.50)	(.22)	(.02)	(—)	(—)	(—)	(—)
Annual Real *GNP*												
(5)	1869–1983	115	none	.73	.46	.40	.31	.25	.13[a]	.12[a]	.12[a]	.10[a]
				(.26)	(.23)	(.24)	(.21)	(.19)	(.11)	(.11)	(.12)	(.11)
(6)	1869–1983	115	(8)	.71	.46	.40	.32	.29	.15[a]	.09[a]	.05[a]	.001[a]
				(.25)	(.23)	(.24)	(.22)	(.22)	(.13)	(.08)	(.05)	(.001)
(7)	1869–1929	61	none	.42	.23	.22	.23	—	—	—	—	—
				(.21)	(.16)	(.18)	(.22)	(—)	(—)	(—)	(—)	(—)
(8)	1930–1983	54	none	.89	.27	.22	.12[a]	—	—	—	—	—
				(.47)	(.19)	(.19)	(.12)	(—)	(—)	(—)	(—)	(—)
(9)	1930–1983	54	(8)	.82	.21	.17	.10[a]	—	—	—	—	—
				(.43)	(.15)	(.15)	(.10)	(—)	(—)	(—)	(—)	(—)
(10)	1930–1972	43	none	.83	.17[aa]	.13[a]	.04[a]	—	—	—	—	—
				(.49)	(.14)	(.13)	(.04)	(—)	(—)	(—)	(—)	(—)

Table 3. (continued)

Row Series	Sample Size	Detrending Correction	$k = 10$	$k = 20$	$k = 30$	$k = 40$	$k = 50$	$k = 60$	$k = 70$	$k = 80$	$k = 100$
Annual Real Per Capita *GNP*											
(11) 1869–1975	107	none	.56	.21^{aa}	.18^{a}	.09^{a}	.10^{a}	.02^{a}	.02^{a}	.01^{a}	—
			(.21)	(.11)	(.11)	(.06)	(.08)	(.02)	(.02)	(.01)	(—)
(12) 1869–1929	61	none	.26	.06^{a}	.07^{a}	.05^{a}	−.02^{a}	—	—	—	—
			(.13)	(.04)	(.06)	(.05)	(—)	(—)	(—)	(—)	(—)
(13) 1930–1975	46	none	.78	.20	.14^{a}	−.04^{a}	—	—	—	—	—
			(.44)	(.16)	(.13)	(—)	(—)	(—)	(—)	(—)	(—)
(14) 1909–1975	67	none	.68	.27	.21	.11^{a}	.06^{a}	—	—	—	—
			(.32)	(.18)	(.17)	(.10)	(.06)	(—)	(—)	(—)	(—)

Notes: i) Asymptotic standard errors computed according to (7) are in parentheses. ii) The entries under the "detrending correction" column indicate the procedure used in constructing the sample autocorrelations. An entry "none" indicates that the estimated sample mean without any correction is subtracted from the first-differences of the data as in (5). An entry (8) indicates that the autocorrelations are constructed using the residuals from equation (8) where allowance is made for a possibly different mean in the pre- and post-1973 samples; i.e., we set T_b at 1973:1 with quarterly data and 1973 with annual data. iii) ^{rr} and ^{r} denotes a rejection of the trend-stationarity hypothesis, at the 10% and 5% level, respectively, using the bounds test described in Section 2 with $c^* = 0.40$. Similarly, ^{aa} and ^{a} denote acceptance of this hypothesis at the 10% and 5% level, respectively.

bounds test, with $c^* = .40$ again, suggests accepting the trend-stationarity hypothesis when allowance is made for this change in slope in 1973. Rows (3) and (4) present results using split-sample estimates with no correction for break, i.e., pre- and post-1973:1. At $k = 30$, the post-1973 sample yields an estimate of -0.06 while at $k = 50$, the pre-1973 sample estimate is 0.03.[7] Hence, these results are consistent with the fact that the high value of the measure of persistence using the full sample with no break correction is simply due to a change in the slope of the trend function after 1973:1.

Rows (5) through (10) present results using annual real *GNP* from 1869 to 1983. Rows (5) and (6) show the estimates without and with corrections for shifts in the trend function respectively (the corrected estimates are constructed with the residuals from (8) setting $T_B = 1973$). Again, the estimates are lower with corrections, though here, the differences are smaller. For both cases thc outcome of the bounds test suggests accepting the trend-stationarity hypothesis for large values of k.

The result, that the differences in the estimates with and without corrections for breaks are small, is because the proportion of the total sample where the change in the slope of the trend function occurs is much smaller with the sample of annual data ($\lambda = 105/115$) than with the sample of quarterly data ($\lambda = 105/156$). From Theorem 1 we can expect the bias to be smaller with the former set of data if no correction is made.

Campbell and Mankiw (1987a) argued that the small measure of persistence obtained by Cochrane (1988) was due partially to the presence of the pre-1929 data in the annual sample (compare rows (7) and (8)). However, if a correction is made for the shift in the trend function in the post-1929 sample (again allowing for a shift in the slope of the trend function in 1973), $\hat{V}^k$ is smaller for the post-1929 than for the pre-1929 period for any value of k greater than 10 (compare row (7) and row (9)). This conclusion is supported from results for the period 1930–1972 without any corrections; for k greater than 10, the measure of persistence is indeed small. Hence, the differences between Cochrane's and Campbell and Mankiw's results appear not to be due to the inclusion or not of the pre-1929 sample but to the importance of the post-1973 period relative to the total sample.

Rows (11) through (14) present the results for Friedman and Schwartz's Annual Real Per Capita *GNP* series. Here no correction is made in constructing the estimates $\hat{V}^k$. Using either the full sample or any sub-samples, the estimates suggest that the shocks have little permanent effects. For example, for 1869–1975, $\hat{V}^k = 0.02$ at $k = 60$, for 1869–1929 it is 0.07 at $k = 30$, for 1930–1975 it is

---

[7] As noted in footnote 2, $\hat{V}^k$ does not yield a non-negative estimate by construction. When a negative value is obtained, the asymptotic standard errors given by (7) are non-sensible, hence we do not report them. We interpret negative values of $\hat{V}^k$ as suggestive of a true value close to zero. This interpretation is supported by other estimates of V (not reported) which use alternative lag windows that yield non-negative estimates by construction.

Table 4. Model impulse responses; real *GNP* series

a) Quarterly real *GNP* (47:1–85:4)

Detrending Procedure	Model	Horizon (Quarters)											
		1	2	3	4	5	6	8	10	12	16	24	32
B	(2, 0)	1.318	1.334	1.225	1.076	.923	.782	.551	.461	.267	.129	.030	.007
B	(3, 0)	1.235	1.393	1.351	1.230	1.054	.861	.498	.228	.062	−.040	−.011	.002
B	(1, 3)	1.234	1.463	1.434	1.163	.943	.765	.503	.331	.218	.094	.018	.003

b) Annual real *GNP* (1889–1983)

Detrending Procedure	Model	Horizon (Years)									
		1	2	3	4	6	8	10	15	20	30
D	(2, 0)	1.013	0.739	.458	.251	.053	.003	−.003	.000	.000	.000
D	(1, 1)	.984	.676	.465	.320	.151	.071	.034	.005	.001	.000
D	(1, 2)	1.022	.761	.430	.243	.077	.025	.008	.000	.000	.000

Note: The entry under the "detrending method" column indicates that a linear time trend and a constant (estimated by *OLS*) were substracted from the original data along with: 1) *B*: a dummy variable taking value $t - T_b$ after 1973:1 and 0 otherwise, where T_b is the value of t in 1973:1; 2) *D*: the same variable as in (*B*) (with 1973 instead of 1973:1 given annual data) plus a dummy variable taking value 1 after 1929 and 0 otherwise. The entries under the column 'model' indicate the order of the estimated $ARMA(p, q)$ models.

0.20 at $k = 20$ and for 1909–1975 it is 0.21 at $k = 30$. In all cases, the bounds test suggests accepting the trend-stationarity hypothesis.

To analyze the effects of shocks at finite horizons we adopted the following strategy. Since the estimates $\hat{V}^k$, when appropriately corrected for the 1973 shift in the slope of the trend function, show little evidence of persistence, we detrended the data by allowing a change in the intercept after 1929 and a change in the slope of the linear time trend after 1973. The residuals are then considered as the noise of the series and are analyzed within the class of $ARMA(p, q)$ models. We estimated all models with p and q less than or equal to 5 and the models were selected using either the Schwartz or Akaike criteria.

For the Post-war Quarterly Real *GNP* series, the Akaike criterion selects the $ARMA(1, 3)$ model, while the Schwartz criterion favors an $AR(3)$ model. However, the $AR(2)$ model is a close contender according to both criteria. Table 4 presents the estimated impulse response function for each model; i.e., the weights in the moving-average representation. The results are very similar across the three models and clearly show a hump-shaped pattern with a peak after 2 quarters. Almost all the effects vanish after 16 quarters.

The results for the Annual Real *GNP* series are similar. According to both criteria the chosen model is an $AR(2)$ with the $ARMA(1, 1)$ a close second and $ARMA(1, 2)$ a close third. The estimated impulse-response functions in Table 4 show again the hump-shaped pattern with a peak in the first year consistent with the evidence from the quarterly data. Most of the effects of the shocks vanish sometime between the 4th and 6th years.

The evidence presented in this section is inconsistent with the notion that shocks have a permanent effect on real *GNP*. As with the Nelson-Plosser data, the fluctuations around the trend function are transitory and the weights in the moving-average representation have the once popular humped-shape.

6 Conclusions

The present study has several implications for empirical macroeconomics. First, it suggests an alternative procedure for detrending to achieve stationarity. Some authors, using post-war quarterly data on economic aggregates, have detrended using a break in trend following the 1973 oil-price shock (e.g., Blinder (1981, 1986) and Blinder and Holtz-Eakin (1986)). Our results provide a formal justification for such a procedure.

More interestingly, our results present an alternative picture of economic fluctuations somewhere in-between the current view that fluctuations have permanent effects and the view that fluctuations are stationary around a deterministic (strictly) linear time trend. This alternative view suggests that, most of the time, fluctuations have transitory effects and that the economy tends to revert to a stable-trend growth path. However, occasionally the economy is disrupted by a major event which has a lasting effect. The view suggested here is that such permanent shocks have been quite rare but are very important in magnitude. The non-rejection of tests of the unit root, when only a time invariant linear trend function is allowed, can be explained within the present context by noting that, even though the shocks which have permanent effects are rare, they are of such magnitude as to account for a substantial portion of the total variability of the series. Hence, it is not too surprising to find such wide evidence for unit roots. However, this evidence tells us only that something significant and permanent occurred. We cannot infer that most shocks have permanent effects.

A third interesting issue concerns confidence intervals for long-range forecasts. The view of stationary fluctuations around a strictly linear time trend implies an accurate long-horizon forecast. This is thought to be quite implausible, thereby making the unit-root characterization more plausible, since it implies forecasts with ever-increasing confidence intervals. The view suggested here implies that forecasts constructed using the estimated trend-stationary model are adequate for short-term forecasting, i.e., conditional on no major break in the trend function occurring in the near future. For long-horizon forecasting, it becomes implausible to suggest that no shift in the trend function will occur. Hence, one would expect to have confidence intervals for a long-horizon forecast that eventually increase. However, to make this statement precise, we must transform the short-term conditional forecast into unconditional forecasts. This means that the breaks in the trend function must be modeled statistically to produce forecasts of the occurrence and nature of the future breaks. This is indeed an interesting subject for future research.

References

Andrews DWK (1991) Heteroskedasticity and autocorrelation consistent covariance matrix estimation. Econometrica 59:817–858

Akaike H (1974) A new look at statistical model identification. IEEE Transactions on Automatic Control AC-19:716–23

Akaike H (1976) Canonical correlation analysis in time series and the use of an information criterion. In: System identification: Advances and case studies Mehra RK, Lainiotis DG (eds) New York: Academic Press 52–107

Balke NS, Gordon RJ (1986) Historical data appendix. In: The American business cycle: Continuity and change, Gordon RJ (ed) Chicago: The University of Chicago Press 781–850

Blanchard OJ (1981) What is left of the multiplier accelerator?. American Economic Review, Papers and Proceedings 71:150–154

Blanchard OJ, Quah D (1989) The dynamic effects of aggregate demand and supply disturbances. American Economic Review 79:655–673

Blinder AS (1981) Retail inventory behavior and business fluctuations. Brookings Paper on Economic Activity 2:443–505

Blinder AS (1986) Can the production smoothing model of inventory behavior be saved?. Quarterly Journal of Economics 101:431–453

Blinder AS, Holtz-Eakin D (1986) Inventory fluctuations in the United States since 1929. In: The American Business Cycle: Continuity and Change, Gordon RJ (ed) Chicago: The University of Chicago Press 183–236

Box GEP, Jenkins GM (1970) Time series analysis: Forecasting and Control, Holden Day, San Francisco

Box GEP, Tiao GC (1975) Intervention analysis with applications to economic and environmental problems. Journal of the American Statistical Association 70:70–79

Campbell JY, Mankiw NG (1987a) Are output fluctuations transitory?. Quarterly Journal of Economics 102:857–880

Campbell JY, Mankiw NG (1987b) Permanent and transitory components in macroeconomic fluctuations. American Economic Review, Papers and Proceedings 77:111–117

Campbell JY, Mankiw NG (1989) International evidence on the persistence of economic fluctuations. Journal of Monetary Economics 23:319–333

Cecchetti SG, Lam P-S (1991) What do we learn from variance ratio statistics? A study of stationary and nonstationary models with breaking trends. Mimeo

Clark PK (1987) The cyclical component of US economic activity. Quarterly Journal of Economics 102:798–814

Cochrane JH (1988) How big is the random walk in *GNP*. Journal of Political Economy 96:893–920

Dickey DA, Fuller WA (1979) Distribution of the estimators for autoregressive time series with a unit root. Journal of the American Statistical Association 74:427–431

Evans GW (1989) Output and unemployment dynamics in the United States: 1950–1985. Journal of Applied Econometrics 4:213–238

Friedman M, Schwartz AJ (1982) Monetary trends in the United States and the United Kingdom: Their relation to income, prices and interest rates 1867–1975 Chicago: University of Chicago Press

Nelson CR, Plosser CI (1982) Trends and random walks in macroeconomic time series. Journal of Monetary Economics 10:139–162

Perron P (1989) The great crash, the oil price shock and the unit root hypothesis. Econometrica 57:1361–1401

Perron P (1990) Testing for a unit root in a time series with a changing mean. Journal of Business and Economic Statistics 8:153–162

Perron P (1991) Further evidence of breaking trend functions in macroeconomic variables. Mimeo, Princeton University

Perron P, Ng S (1992) The exact error in estimating the spectral density at the origin. Mimeo, Princeton University

Perron P, Phillips PCB (1987) Does *GNP* have a unit root? A reevaluation. Economics Letters 23:139–145

Phillips PCB, Ouliaris S (1988) Testing for cointegration using principal components methods. Journal of Economic Dynamics and Control 12:205–230

Priestly MB (1981) Spectral analysis and time series. Academic Press: New York

Raj B (1992) International evidence on persistence in output in the presence of an episodic change. Journal of Applied Econometrics 7:281–293

Raj B (1993) The size of the random walk in macroeconomic time series. Journal of Macroeconomics 15:139–151

Schwartz G (1978) Estimating the dimension of a model. Annals of Statistics 6:461–464

Stock JH, Watson MW (1986) Does *GNP* have a unit root?. Economics Letters 22:147–151

Watson MW (1986) Univariate detrending methods with stochastic trends. Journal of Monetary Economics 18:1–27

Zivot E, Andrews DWK (1992) Further evidence on the great crash, the oil price shock and the unit root hypothesis. Journal of Business and Economic Statistics 10:251–270

The Sources of the U.S. Money Demand Instability

HELMUT LÜTKEPOHL[1]

Institut für Statistik und Ökonometrie, Humboldt-Universität zu Berlin,
Spandauer Str. 1, 10178 Berlin, Germany

Abstract: The structural stability of money demand relations has been the issue of a substantial number of empirical studies. In most studies for the U.S. structural breaks were found in the 1970s and the 1980s. In the present study a money demand function is specified in error-correction-form which involves real *M* 1, real *GNP*, the deflator and a short-term interest rate. Using flexible least squares it is shown for the U.S. that the long-run coefficients of *M* 1, *GNP* and the interest rate are relatively stable over a period of more than 30 years while the deflator does not enter the relation. The instability of the relation is mainly due to changes in the short-term dynamics.

JEL Classification System-Numbers: C22, C51, C52

1 Introduction

Where does the apparent instability of U.S. money demand functions in the 1970s and 1980s come from? This question has been discussed extensively in the recent literature (see Judd & Scadding (1982) and Leventakis & Brissimis (1991) for surveys). Many studies focus on standard money demand functions of the type

$$M = f(Y, P, r) \ , \tag{1.1}$$

where M is a money variable, Y is the transactions volume, P is the price level and r is an interest rate. Usually a log-linear dynamic relation is postulated and analyzed. In many studies it was found that changes in the parameters of money demand functions of this type occur in the middle of the 1970s and again at the end of the 70s and the beginning of the 80s. The former period is often called the "episode of missing money" while the second period is known as the "episode of the great velocity decline". An explanation for the money demand instability in the middle of the 70s that has been put forward by a number of researchers is the advent of financial innovations that enabled the public to restructure their demand for transactions balances. For the period of the great velocity decline different sources for the money demand instability have been identified in a

---

[1] The author thanks Martin Moryson for outstanding research assistance. The computations were performed with a GAUSS program written by the late Wolfgang Schneider.

number of empirical studies. Some researchers find that the relation between money and income has changed while others attribute the functional instability to changes in the relation between money and interest rates (see Leventakis & Brissimis (1991)).

In the present study some new light will be shed on these explanations. In contrast to many other studies the money demand function is specified in error-correction (*EC*) form. Such a specification has the advantage that it distinguishes between a long-run relation and the short-run dynamics or transitory effects. The purpose of this study is to investigate the intertemporal stability of the individual parameters of such a specification in order to determine which of the coefficients are the sources of the instabilities found in previous studies. It turns out that all long-run coefficients are relatively stable over a period from 1954–1987. The least stable long-run coefficient is that of the interest rate while the coefficient of the transactions volume is very stable over the whole period. However, the short-run coefficients are seen to be clearly more volatile than the long-run coefficients over the period in question.

The flexible least squares (*FLS*) method of Kalaba & Tesfatsion (1989, 1990) is used to investigate the stability properties of the U.S. money demand function. It is based on minimizing the sum of two terms. The first term is the usual sum of squared regression errors of a regression equation with varying parameters and the second term involves the squared parameter variations. The relative weight assigned to these two terms essentially determines the parameter variation over time. Changing the weights exhibits the relative variation of the coefficients and illuminates which coefficients are the most and least stable ones. An *FLS* analysis of a U.S. money demand relation was performed earlier by Tesfatsion & Veitch (1990). These authors do not use an *EC* model, though, and they interpret their findings in a different manner.

It is perhaps worth emphasizing that the *FLS* method was designed as a purely descriptive tool which has the advantage that possibly dubious stochastic assumptions are not required at an early stage of the analysis. This requires that some thought be given to the types of quantities that can be interpreted in a meaningful way. Also, without a complete set of stochastic assumptions (that is, without a complete specification of the model) it is difficult to argue that a model represents an adequate or a poor description of the data generation process. It is still possible, however, to analyze certain features of the data by descriptive tools. For instance, the relative variability of the coefficients may be compared. Thus, the objective of this study is much more moderate than that of other studies such as Baba, Hendry & Starr (1992) who work in a stochastic framework and strive for a final model which is an adequate representation of the true data generation process and which is superior to other models with a similar objective. Specifically they aim at finding a constant coefficient money demand function which is not the objective of the present study.

The structure of this paper is as follows. In the next section the basic model and the data are described. In Section 3 the *FLS* method is presented and in Section 4 the empirical analysis is carried out. Conclusions follow in Section 5.

2 The Money Demand Function

The money demand function in (1.1) is the basic relation to be analyzed in the following. Thus, it remains to specify the functional form and the precise variables used. Various different definitions of the money variable are available. However, many money demand studies have focused on $M1$ (money deposits plus currency held by the public) (e.g., Judd & Scadding (1982)). This definition of money is in line with the transactions theory, where money is thought of as a means of payment. Therefore we will use this measure in the following analysis. This choice permits a comparison of our results with other researchers' findings.

In many previous studies real GNP has been used as a proxi for the transactions volume. Although there have been arguments in favor of including permanent income or wealth in the money demand function, GNP will be used in the following. This choice suggests using the GNP deflator as a measure of the price level P. As a consequence, real money is obtained by deflating $M1$ with the GNP deflator.

A range of different interest rate variables have been used in previous money demand investigations. For example, Goldfeld (1973) in his influencial article used a short-term market rate and the interest rate on savings deposits while Hamburger (1977) used returns on savings deposits and on government bonds as well as the dividend-price ratio on equities. A survey of a number of other earlier articles can be found in Judd & Scadding (1982). I will use a short-term rate, namely the discount rate on 91-day Treasury bills, in the basic model because short-term securities are close alternatives to holding money and therefore are a better measure for the opportunity cost of holding money than a long-term yield.

As noted in the introduction, a log-linear relation is often assumed and so do I. Thus, the basic relation is

$$m_t = \alpha_1 gnp_t + \alpha_2 r_t^s + \alpha_3 p_t \ , \tag{2.1}$$

where $m_t = \ln(M1_t/P_t)$, $gnp_t = \ln$ real GNP_t, $p_t = \ln P_t$ and r_t^s denotes logarithms of 1 plus the short-term interest rate specified earlier. Equation (2.1) should be regarded as a long-run equilibrium relation which holds if no further changes occur in the system. Thus, it is not what is actually observed because there is always some movement in the system. Therefore the adjustment mechanism has to be specified which is in operation when the system is not in equilibrium. In early work by Goldberger (1973) and others the short-term dynamics are often simply accounted for by including lags of one or more of the variables involved. In contrast to most previous work on the subject the model is set up in EC form in the present study (see e.g. Hendry & Richard (1983)):

$$\begin{aligned}\Delta m_t = {} & v_0 + v_1(m_{t-1} - \alpha_1 gnp_{t-1} - \alpha_2 r_{t-1}^s - \alpha_3 p_{t-1}) \\ & + \gamma_1 \Delta gnp_t + \gamma_2 \Delta r_t^s + \gamma_3 \Delta p_t + u_t \ ,\end{aligned} \tag{2.2}$$

where u_t represents a random error term and Δ is the usual difference operator (e.g., $\Delta m_t = m_t - m_{t-1}$). The virtue of this specification is that it directly includes the hypothesized long-run relation (2.1). Obviously, if all variables settle down so that all Δ variables and u_t are zero, (2.2) reduces to (2.1).

The model (2.2) is similar to one analyzed by Rose (1985) who also considers an *EC* form. His model breaks down in the late 1970s and thus there is some potential for finding a structural break if the sample period is extended to the 1980s. It is also of interest to locate the specific coefficients responsible for the structural breakdown. I will return to Rose's study at a later stage.

In Section 4 the stability of the money demand function (2.2) is investigated using quarterly data for the years 1954–1987. The *M*1 and *GNP* data are seasonally adjusted and the deflator is obtained as the ratio of nominal and real adjusted *GNP*. In the next section the *FLS* method is briefly described.

3 The Method of Analysis

In analyzing the stability of the relation (2.2) we allow the coefficients to vary over time. Thus, the v_i, α_i and γ_i in (2.2) are replaced by v_{it}, α_{it} and γ_{it} respectively. The flexible least squares (*FLS*) method of Kalaba & Tesfatsion (1989, 1990) will be used to determine the time paths of the coefficients. Given a regression model with time varying coefficients,

$$y_t = x_t\beta_t + u_t \ , \qquad t = 1, \dots, T \ , \tag{3.1}$$

where $x_t = (x_{t1}, \dots, x_{tK})$ and the β_t are $(K \times 1)$ vectors, the *FLS* method provides the time paths $\beta_1, \dots, \beta_T$ of the coefficient vectors which minimize the loss function

$$\sum_{t=1}^{T} (y_t - x_t\beta_t)^2 + \lambda \sum_{t=1}^{T-1} (\beta_{t+1} - \beta_t)'D(\beta_{t+1} - \beta_t) \ , \tag{3.2}$$

where λ is a prespecified positive constant and D is a fixed $(K \times K)$ matrix. D may be chosen to compensate for different scalings of the regressors. I follow Tesfatsion & Veitch (1990) and choose a diagonal matrix D with diagonal elements $d_{ii} = \sum_{t=1}^{T} x_{ti}^2/T$. This choice guarantees that multiplication of a regressor by a constant leaves the shape of the time path of the corresponding coefficient unchanged. It just changes the size of the coefficient. More precisely, when a regressor is multiplied by a constant c the new time path of its coefficient is obtained by dividing the previous time path by c.

Obviously, the choice of λ to some extent determines the coefficient variation. A large λ heavily penalizes coefficient variation. In fact, for $\lambda \to \infty$ the β_t become constant and approach the constant parameter *LS* solution. On the other hand, if λ approaches zero, coefficient variation is not penalized very much and therefore the coefficients tend to become more volatile with decreasing λ. Of course, for $\lambda = 0$ the coefficients can be chosen so that $y_t = x_t\beta_t$ is exactly satisfied. Evaluating the time paths of the β_t for various values of λ provides information about the relative stability of individual coefficients. This approach will be used in the following to demonstrate that the coefficients of the long-run money demand function (2.1) are much more stable than the γ_i coefficients which represent the short-term dynamics in (2.2). Note that no stochastic assumptions have been made so far. Thus, the approach is purely descriptive and consequently the analysis differs from a classical econometric analysis where usually stochastic assumptions are made.

To offer some more insight into the method it may still be useful to indicate potential stochastic frameworks for the method. One possibility is to consider a state space model with measurement equation (3.1) and transition equation

$$\beta_{t+1} = \beta_t + w_t , \qquad t = 1, \ldots, T-1 . \tag{3.3}$$

The conditional density of the β_t is

$$\begin{aligned} g(\beta_1, \ldots, \beta_T | y_1, \ldots, y_T) & \\ \propto f(y_1, \ldots, y_T | \beta_1, \ldots, \beta_T) g(\beta_1, \ldots, \beta_T) & \\ = f(y_1 | \beta_1, \ldots, \beta_T) f(y_2 | y_1; \beta_1, \ldots, \beta_T) \cdots f(y_T | y_1, \ldots, y_{T-1}; \beta_1, \ldots, \beta_T) & \\ \cdot g(\beta_1) g(\beta_2 | \beta_1) \cdots g(\beta_T | \beta_1, \ldots, \beta_{T-1}) . & \end{aligned} \tag{3.4}$$

Assuming that u_t and w_t are independent white noise processes with $u_t \sim N(0, \sigma_u^2)$ and $w_t \sim N\left(0, \frac{\sigma_u^2}{\lambda} D^{-1}\right)$, -1 times the logarithm of the resulting density function becomes

$$\begin{aligned} -\ln g(\beta_1, \ldots, \beta_T | y_1, \ldots, y_T) = {} & const. + \frac{T}{2} \ln \sigma_u^2 + \frac{1}{2\sigma_u^2} \sum_{t=1}^{T} (y_t - x_t\beta_t)^2 \\ & + \frac{T-1}{2} \ln\left(\frac{\sigma_u^2}{\lambda}\right) + \frac{T-1}{2} \ln|D^{-1}| \\ & + \frac{\lambda}{2\sigma_u^2} \sum_{t=1}^{T-1} (\beta_{t+1} - \beta_t)' D (\beta_{t+1} - \beta_t) - \ln g(\beta_1) . \end{aligned} \tag{3.5}$$

Consequently, if $g(\beta_1)$ is constant (the initial state is diffuse), the *FLS* algorithm computes those coefficient values which maximize the conditional density. In other words, it computes the conditional expectations $E(\beta_t | y_1, \ldots, y_T)$. Hence, it may be regarded as a special Kalman smoother.

Alternatively, if (3.4) is interpreted as a-posteriori-density obtained from a prior $g(\beta_1, \ldots, \beta_T)$ and a sample density $f(y_1, \ldots, y_T | \beta_1, \ldots, \beta_T)$, the *FLS* solution is seen to be the mode of the a-posteriori-density and thus a Bayesian solution. Although these interpretations are technically possible, Kalaba & Tesfatsion (1990) emphasize that the philosophical background is quite different because a stochastic framework is explicitly excluded for the *FLS* method.

4 Empirical Analysis

In order to investigate the model (2.2) by the *FLS* method we use $y_t = \Delta m_t$,

$$x_t = (1, m_{t-1}, gnp_{t-1}, r^s_{t-1}, p_{t-1}, \Delta gnp_t, \Delta r^s_t, \Delta p_t)$$

and

$$\beta_t = (v_{0t}, v_{1t}, -v_{1t}\alpha_{1t}, -v_{1t}\alpha_{2t}, -v_{1t}\alpha_{3t}, \gamma_{1t}, \gamma_{2t}, \gamma_{3t})' \ .$$

From the time paths of β_t we get the time paths of the α_{it} as $\hat{\alpha}_{it} = \widehat{v_{1t}\alpha_{it}}/\hat{v}_{1t}$.

The time paths of the coefficients of interest obtained with $\lambda = .001$ are shown in Figure 1 and the corresponding means, standard deviations and coefficients of variation (standard deviation divided by the mean) are given in Table 1. As mentioned earlier, the shapes of the coefficient time paths do not change when the right-hand side variables are multiplied by a constant. Therefore I have divided each coefficient by its mean prior to plotting the time paths. Thus, the empirical distributions of all the plotted coefficients have the same mean of 1 and their standard deviation is just the absolute value of the coefficient of variation of the original coefficient. The advantage of such a transformation is that the variations of different coefficients are more easily comparable. Otherwise the size of a coefficient and its variance might be an artifact of the scale of its regressor variable. In Figure 1 for each coefficient except γ_{3t} the same scale is used so that the relative variability of the different coefficients can be seen easily. The exception for γ_{3t} is made because it varies much more than all the other coefficients. Therefore using the scale of its plot in all the other panels would have prevented a comparison of the other coefficients.

It is quite obvious in the figure that v_{0t}, v_{1t}, α_{1t}, α_{2t} and α_{3t} exhibit very little time variation even for λ as small as .001. Practically all the coefficient variation is in the γ_{it}'s and hence in the short-term dynamics. Although the volatile short-term coefficients become more stable with increasing λ they still move much more than v_{0t}, v_{1t}, α_{1t} and α_{2t} even for $\lambda = 1000$ (see Table 1). On the other hand, the coefficient of variation of α_{3t} increases with growing λ.

It is conceivable that a coefficient shows substantial variability just because its variable does not belong into the model. In that case the coefficient of variation may be large and the path of the coefficient may be erratic just because the estimated mean is close to zero and hence even small variations are magnified by dividing by the mean. In Table 1, for $\lambda = .001$, the mean of γ_{3t} is indeed seen to be very small which may indicate a problem of the aforementioned type. The same is true for α_{3t} when $\lambda = 1000$. Since I have not made any stochastic assumptions formal statistical significance tests for these coefficients are not possible under the present conditions. Instead I have also performed *FLS* analyses of the reduced models

$$\Delta m_t = v_{0t} + v_{1t}(m_{t-1} - \alpha_{1t}gnp_{t-1} - \alpha_{2t}r^s_{t-1} - \alpha_{3t}p_{t-1}) + \gamma_{1t}\Delta gnp_t + \gamma_{2t}\Delta r^s_t + u_t \qquad (4.1)$$

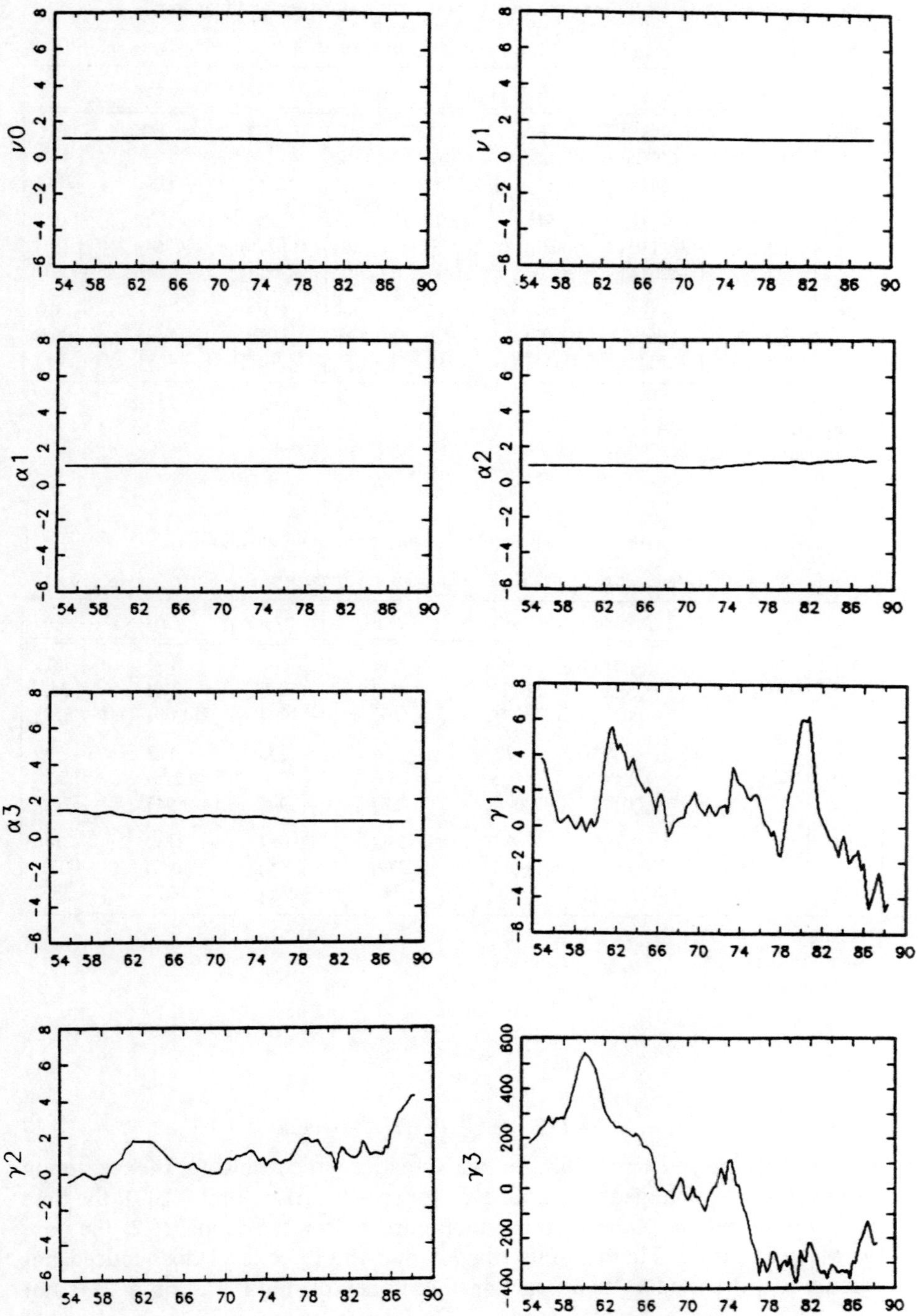

Fig. 1. Time paths of the coefficients of the money demand function (2.2) for $\lambda = .001$.

Table 1. Summary statistics for the coefficients of the basic money demand function

$\Delta m_t = \nu_{0t} + \nu_{1t}(m_{t-1} - \alpha_{1t} gnp_{t-1} - \alpha_{2t} r^s_{t-1} - \alpha_{3t} p_{t-1}) + \gamma_{1t} \Delta gnp_t + \gamma_{2t} \Delta r^s_t + \gamma_{3t} \Delta p_t + u_t$

λ	ν_{0t}	ν_{1t}	α_{1t}	α_{2t}	α_{3t}	γ_{1t}	γ_{2t}	γ_{3t}
.001	.394[a]	−.354	.669	−2.77	−.087	.100	−.392	.0016
	(.0031)[b]	(.0005)	(.0021)	(.370)	(.017)	(.226)	(.359)	(.411)
	[.0078][c]	[−.0014]	[.0031]	[−.133]	[−.196]	[2.27]	[−.918]	[261]
1	.351	−.331	.676	−2.93	−.082	.089	−.373	.022
	(.0028)	(.0005)	(.0020)	(.373)	(.017)	(.229)	(.314)	(.387)
	[.0079]	[−.0014]	[.0030]	[−.128]	[−.206]	[2.58]	[−.841]	[18.0]
1000	.157	−.108	.655	−5.13	−.0072	.100	−.133	−.310
	(.0003)	(.0001)	(.0007)	(.050)	(.0056)	(.090)	(.061)	(.093)
	[.0022]	[−.0005]	[.0011]	[−.010]	[−.787]	[.907]	[−.463]	[−.301]

[a] mean;
[b] standard deviation;
[c] coefficient of variation.

Table 2. Summary statistics for the coefficients of the money demand function

$\Delta m_t = \nu_{0t} + \nu_{1t}(m_{t-1} - \alpha_{1t} gnp_{t-1} - \alpha_{2t} r^s_{t-1} - \alpha_{3t} p_{t-1}) + \gamma_{1t} \Delta gnp_t + \gamma_{2t} \Delta r^s_t + u_t$

λ	ν_{0t}	ν_{1t}	α_{1t}	α_{2t}	α_{3t}	γ_{1t}	γ_{2t}
.001	.329[a]	−.373	.695	−2.56	−.107	.132	−.415
	(.0039)[b]	(.0006)	(.0025)	(.461)	(.019)	(.219)	(.352)
	[.012][c]	[−.0017]	[.0037]	[−.180]	[−.174]	[1.66]	[−.850]
1	.281	−.341	.704	−2.76	−.100	.117	−.399
	(.0036)	(.0006)	(.0025)	(.465)	(.019)	(.226)	(.304)
	[.013]	[−.0017]	[.0036]	[−.168]	[−.194]	[−1.94]	[−.761]
1000	.193	−.106	.608	−5.67	.034	.122	−.186
	(.0005)	(.0001)	(.0011)	(.077)	(.009)	(.082)	(.071)
	[.0026]	[−.0008]	[.0018]	[−.014]	[.261]	[.677]	[−.380]

[a] mean;
[b] standard deviation;
[c] coefficient of variation.

and

$$\Delta m_t = \nu_{0t} + \nu_{1t}(m_{t-1} - \alpha_{1t} gnp_{t-1} - \alpha_{2t} r^s_{t-1}) + \gamma_{1t} \Delta gnp_t + \gamma_{2t} \Delta r^s_t + u_t \,. \qquad (4.2)$$

Some results are given in Tables 2 and 3. Obviously the results for the remaining coefficients have changed very little even for small λ. Also, for $\lambda = .001$, the time paths are about the same as those in Figure 1. For the model (4.2) they are shown in Figure 2. These results suggest that the price level does indeed not belong into the model. Its absence in the money demand relation (4.2) is not implausible given that real money and *GNP* variables are used. Note also that all long-run coefficients in (4.2) have the expected signs. Using the means from

Table 3. Summary statistics for the coefficients of the money demand function

$$\Delta m_t = v_{0t} + v_{1t}(m_{t-1} - \alpha_{1t}gnp_{t-1} - \alpha_{2t}r^s_{t-1}) + \gamma_{1t}\Delta gnp_t + \gamma_{2t}\Delta r^s_t + u_t$$

λ	v_{0t}	v_{1t}	α_{1t}	α_{2t}	γ_{1t}	γ_{2t}
.001	.585[a]	−.349	.604	−2.69	.103	−.395
	(.0063)[b]	(.0010)	(.0041)	(.521)	(.230)	(.395)
	[.011][c]	[−.0029]	[.0067]	[−.194]	[2.23]	[−1.00]
1	.511	−.315	.613	−2.92	.092	−.377
	(.0053)	(.0009)	(.0038)	(.536)	(.233)	(.339)
	[.010]	[−.0027]	[.0062]	[−.184]	[2.52]	[−.899]
1000	.168	−.107	.638	−5.60	.125	−.191
	(.0005)	(.0001)	(.0012)	(.084)	(.080)	(.073)
	[.0032]	[−.0008]	[.0018]	[−.015]	[.638]	[−.380]

[a] mean;
[b] standard deviation;
[c] coefficient of variation.

Table 3 for $\lambda = 1$ we get a long-run relation

$$m_t = .61 gnp_t - 2.92 r^s_t$$

meaning that, ceteris paribus, a higher transactions volume leads to a higher money demand while a larger interest rate implies a lower long-run money stock. Moreover, the sign of v_{1t} is negative and thus, if m_t is lower than its equilibrium value, there is a tendency for money demand to increase in the next period, as expected.

One could of course argue that the means of all short-term coefficients γ_{it} are small and hence, using the same arguments as for α_{3t} and γ_{3t}, they may in fact be zero. To check this possibility I have performed an *FLS* analysis of the model

$$\Delta m_t = v_{0t} + v_{1t}(m_{t-1} - \alpha_{1t}gnp_{t-1} - \alpha_{2t}r^s_{t-1}) + u_t \tag{4.3}$$

and give some summary results in Table 4. The results are surprisingly similar to those for model (4.2) (see Table 3). However, it is not clear that they are similar enough to justify an elimination of the short-term dynamics altogether. In any case, the long-run money demand relation is relatively stable over a period of more than 30 years from 1954–1987. This result is nice because the concept of a long-run relation would be dubious if that relation were changing every once in a while.

Despite this relative stability it may be of interest to take a closer look at the long-run coefficients. From Table 3 it is apparent that among the α_{it} the interest rate coefficient is the most volatile one. To get a better impression of its movement we have plotted the time paths of the coefficients v_{0t}, v_{1t}, α_{1t} and α_{2t} in Figure 3 on a scale which is different from that used in Figure 2. Now it can be seen that the interest rate varies somewhat. However, it is relatively stable until 1974. The movement after 1974 is in accord with other researchers' findings. It

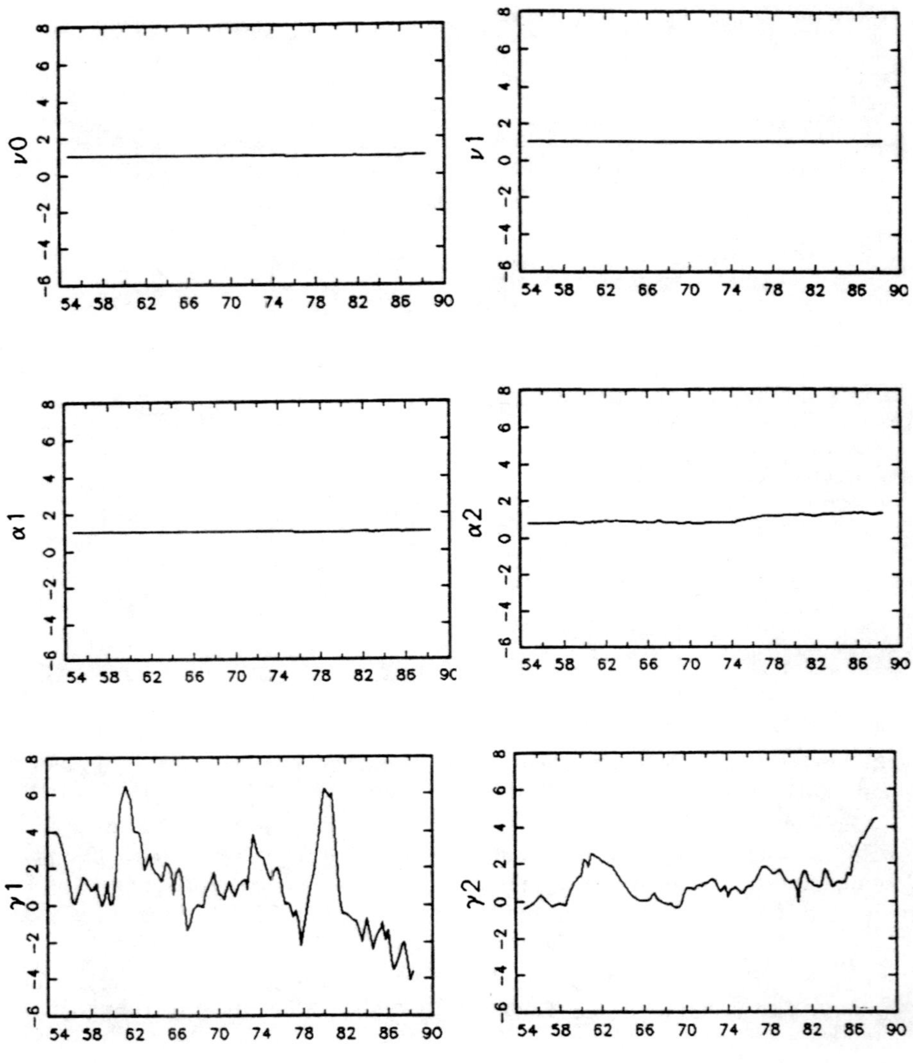

Fig. 2. Time paths of the coefficients of the money demand function (4.2) for $\lambda = .001$.

may for instance reflect the adjustment of the money demand to financial innovations as argued by some authors. As mentioned in the introduction, the great velocity decline at the beginning of the 80s has been attributed to a change in the relation between *GNP* and *M*1. Since the income coefficient is very stable over the complete period the present results indicate that such a change is not likely.

The instability of the short-run dynamics may have various sources. For instance, it is possible that important variables are missing in the model. It is

Table 4. Summary statistics for the coefficients of the money demand function

$$\Delta m_t = v_{0t} + v_{1t}(m_{t-1} - \alpha_{1t}gnp_{t-1} - \alpha_{2t}r^s_{t-1}) + u_t$$

λ	v_{0t}	v_{1t}	α_{1t}	α_{2t}
.001	1.75[a]	−.464	.325	−1.53
	(.0053)[b]	(.0009)	(.0021)	(.369)
	[.0030][c]	[−.0019]	[.0065]	[−.241]
1	1.28	−.386	.389	−1.94
	(.0042)	(.0007)	(.0022)	(.368)
	[.0033]	[−.0018]	[.0056]	[−.189]
1000	.203	−.111	.605	−5.46
	(.0006)	(.0001)	(.0012)	(.095)
	[.0029]	[−.0008]	[.0020]	[−.017]

[a] mean;
[b] standard deviation;
[c] coefficient of variation.

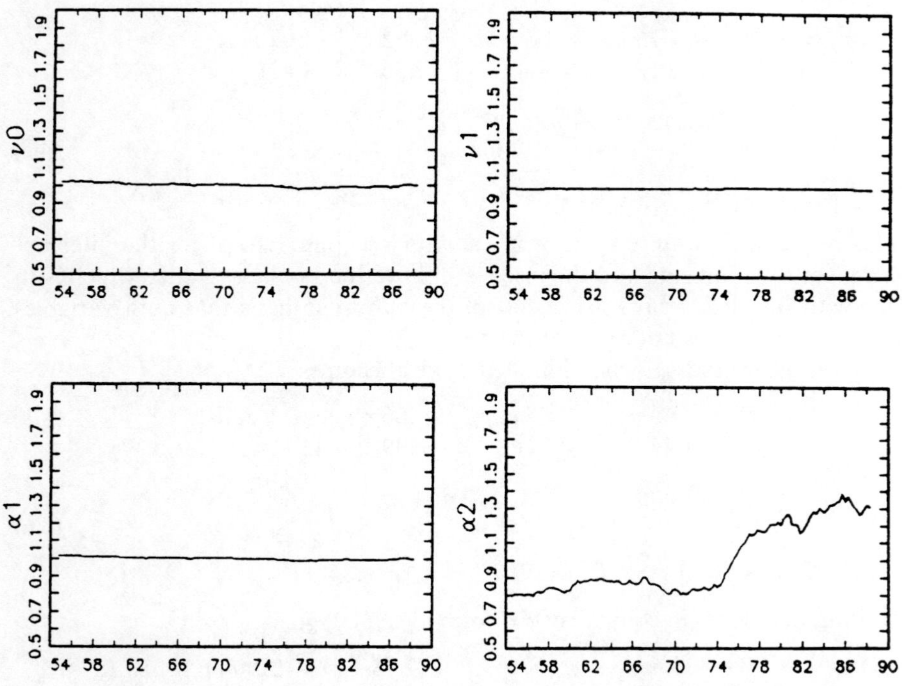

Fig. 3. Rescaled time paths of the stable coefficients of the money demand function (4.2) for $\lambda = .001$.

also conceivable that the dynamics allowed for in the model are insufficient. Given the results of other studies both types of misspecification may be responsible for the present findings. Before I discuss some of these other studies it may be instructive to compare the *FLS* results to constant coefficient regression models of the same type. For instance, for model (2.2) we get

$$\begin{aligned}\Delta m_t = \underset{(1.19)}{.10} - \underset{(-3.77)}{.08}\, m_{t-1} + \underset{(3.62)}{.06}\, gnp_{t-1} - \underset{(-6.21)}{.46}\, r^s_{t-1} + \underset{(.12)}{.001}\, p_{t-1}\\ + \underset{(1.42)}{.13}\, \Delta gnp_t - \underset{(-1.53)}{.17}\, \Delta r^s_t - \underset{(-3.50)}{.55}\, \Delta p_t + \hat{u}_t \end{aligned} \quad (4.4)$$

$$\hat{\sigma}^2_u = 8.36 \times 10^{-5}, \qquad R^2 = .49, \qquad R^2_{adj} = .465$$

Here t-ratios are given in parentheses underneath the coefficient estimates. Of course, these quantities may not be very meaningful if there is indeed coefficient variation over the sample period.

Since the relation may have been more stable before 1974 a constant coefficient model was also estimated with *OLS* for a sample period 1954–1973. The result is

$$\begin{aligned}\Delta m_t = \underset{(-.87)}{-.15} - \underset{(-1.91)}{.07}\, m_{t-1} + \underset{(4.87)}{.08}\, gnp_{t-1} - \underset{(-7.36)}{.62}\, r^s_{t-1} - \underset{(-1.83)}{.02}\, p_{t-1}\\ + \underset{(3.04)}{.21}\, \Delta gnp_t - \underset{(-2.14)}{.27}\, \Delta r^s_t - \underset{(1.66)}{.30}\, \Delta p_t + \hat{u}_t \end{aligned} \quad (4.5)$$

$$\hat{\sigma}^2_u = 2.58 \times 10^{-5}, \qquad R^2 = .60, \qquad R^2_{adj} = .56$$

This model differs quite a bit from the previous one. Except for the intercept term, the inflation rate and the price level have the smallest t-ratios which is in line with the *FLS* results. An F-test of the null hypothesis that both variables can be deleted does not reject at the 5% level.

Deleting Δp_t and p_{t-1} the estimated model becomes

$$\begin{aligned}\Delta m_t = \underset{(-.73)}{-.09} - \underset{(-1.44)}{.04}\, m_{t-1} + \underset{(4.71)}{.05}\, gnp_{t-1} - \underset{(-6.99)}{.56}\, r^s_{t-1} + \underset{(3.11)}{.22}\, \Delta gnp_t\\ - \underset{(-1.84)}{.23}\, \Delta r^s_t + \hat{u}_t \end{aligned} \quad (4.6)$$

$$\hat{\sigma}^2_u = 2.68 \times 10^{-5}, \qquad R^2 = .57, \qquad R^2_{adj} = .54$$

Writing the model in equivalent *EC* form as in (4.2) gives

$$\Delta m_t = -.09 - .04(m_{t-1} - 1.16 gnp_{t-1} + 12.78 r^s_{t-1}) + .22 \Delta gnp_t - .23 \Delta r^s_t + \hat{u}_t \, .$$

The coefficient values are quite different from the mean values of the *FLS* time paths given in Table 3 even for $\lambda = 1000$ which may be interpreted as evidence for coefficient variation over the longer time period used in the *FLS* analysis. The model (4.6) does not pass a Chow test for structural change over the next 32 quarters at any reasonable level of significance. The test value is 5.37 while the null distribution is $F(32, 73)$. Obviously such a test is not very informative about the specific reasons for model failure, that is, which coefficients change and where they change. Such a more detailed information can be obtained from an *FLS* analysis.

Of course, all the model diagnostics discussed in the foregoing are problematic if the model for the period 1954–1973 is unstable even in this time span. Another advantage of the *FLS* analysis is that it does not require such a stability assumption. Also it does not require prior knowledge of a break point. In the following I will compare the *FLS* results of the present study to some previous analyses. For a discussion of other studies see Baba, Hendry & Starr (1992).

Tesfatsion & Veitch (1990) perform an *FLS* analysis of the model

$$m_t = \beta_{0t} + \beta_{1t} m_{t-1} + \beta_{2t} gnp_t + \beta_{3t} r_t^s + \beta_{4t} \Delta p_t + u_t \ . \tag{4.7}$$

Due to their particular scaling all their coefficients look relatively volatile in their Figure 3. However, from their Table 2 it is apparent that in terms of the coefficient of variation β_{4t} is the most volatile coefficient while β_{0t}, β_{1t}, β_{2t} and β_{3t} are relatively stable. Taking into account the different parameterization of my models this result is well in line with mine. Thus, although the interpretation of Tesfatsion & Veitch is different their results are in accordance with those of the present analysis.

My results are also roughly in line with Rose (1985) and Baba, Hendry & Starr (1992). Rose's preferred model has an error-correction term involving real money and income only and no interest rate (see his Equation (7)). Otherwise he has a few more lags in his equation than in my models (4.1) and (4.2). Interestingly he finds that his model breaks down at the end of the 70s. From his results it is not clear whether this is due to a change in the short-run dynamics or the *EC* term. My present *FLS* analysis suggests that the model failure may come from changes in the short-run dynamics, at least if an interest rate is included in the *EC* term.

At this time the Baba, Hendry & Starr (1992) study is too fresh to be rejected by new data. They also use an *EC* type set-up. In addition to my standard variables they have more interest rate variables in the model including the *NOW* and Super*NOW* rates which represent financial innovations. Furthermore they include a variable measuring the risk of holding a long-term debt. The rather elaborate dynamic structure of their model is chosen by a healthy amount of data mining. A similar model is also discussed by Hendry & Ericsson (1991). Given the interesting dynamics of these models I predict that they will not survive very long when more data become available. When they break down, *FLS* can be a useful tool for pinning down the relative variability of the individual coefficients. Hendry & Ericsson (1991) use recursive *LS* for that purpose. An advantage of *FLS* over the latter method is that it uses the full data set in computing the time paths while recursive *LS* only uses past and present data in each time point. In addition, estimates are always computed under the constancy assumption with recursive *LS* while *FLS* explicitly allows for coefficient variation.

5 Conclusions

In the foregoing it is shown that a money demand relation with relatively stable long-run coefficients exists for the U.S. Setting up the money demand function in *EC* form it is possible to separate the long-run relation from the short-run dynamics. In a basic money demand relation involving *GNP* and a short-term interest rate the long-run coefficients turn out to be relatively stable over a period of more than 30 years from 1954–1987. The most variable long-run coefficient is that of the interest rate while the *GNP* coefficient is very stable for the whole period. These findings are in line with the financial innovations explanation of the money demand instability and they also demonstrate that during the period of the great velocity decline the possible instability is more likely to be due to the interest rate coefficient than to the income coefficient. The analysis also shows that the *FLS* method is a useful tool for analyzing the relative stability of regression coefficients. It is a descriptive method which does not require stochastic assumptions for the underlying model. Therefore it has a wider applicability than many tests and other model diagnostics. Also, in contrast to the common stability tests *FLS* provides detailed information on the variability of individual coefficients.

Data Sources

In this study quarterly data from the Business Conditions Digest, U.S. Department of Commerce, Bureau of Economic Analysis, are used. The *GNP* deflator is obtained as the ratio of nominal and real *GNP* in prices of 1982.I. *GNP*, *M*1 and the *GNP* deflator are seasonally adjusted. The *GNP*, *M*1 and interest rate data are also listed in Table E.3 of Lütkepohl (1991, Appendix E).

References

Baba Y, Hendry DF, Starr RM (1992) The demand for *M*1 in the USA, 1960–1988. Review of Economic Studies 59:25–61

Goldfeld SM (1973) The demand for money revisited. Brookings Papers on Economic Activity 3:577–638

Hamburger MJ (1977) Behavior of the money stock: Is there a puzzle? Journal of Monetary Economics 3:265–288

Hendry DF, Ericsson NR (1991) Modeling the demand for narrow money in the United Kingdom and the United States. European Economic Review 35:833–886

Hendry DF, Richard JF (1983) The econometric analysis of economic time series. International Statistical Review 51:111–148

Judd JP, Scadding JL (1982) The search for a stable money demand function: A survey of the post-1973 Literature. Journal of Economic Literature 20:993–1023
Kalaba R, Tesfatsion L (1989) Time-varying linear regression via flexible least squares. Computers and Mathematics with Applications 17:1215–1245
Kalaba R, Tesfatsion L (1990) Flexible least squares for approximately linear systems. IEEE Transactions on Systems, Man, and Cybernetics SMC-20:978–989
Leventakis JA, Brissimis SN (1991) Instability of the US money demand function. Journal of Economic Surveys 5:131–161
Lütkepohl H (1991) Introduction to multiple time series analysis, Berlin: Springer-Verlag
Rose AK (1985) An alternative approach to the American demand for money. Journal of Money, Credit and Banking 17:439–455
Tesfatsion L, Veitch J (1990) US money demand instability: A flexible least squares approach. Journal of Economic Dynamics and Control 14:151–173

Seasonality, Cointegration and Fractional Integration

On the (Mis)Specification of Seasonality and its Consequences: An Empirical Investigation with US Data[1]

ERIC GHYSELS

C.R.D.E. and Département de Sciences Economiques Université de Montréal Montréal, P.Q., H3C 3J7, Canada

HAHN S. LEE

Department of Economics Tulane University New Orleans, LA 70118-5698, USA

PIERRE L. SIKLOS

Department of Economics Wilfrid Laurier University Waterloo, Ontario, N2L 3C5, Canada

Abstract: It is well known that mis-specification of a trend leads to spurious cycles in detrended data (see, e.g., Nelson and Kang (1981)). Seasonal-adjustment procedures make assumptions, either implicitly or explicitly, about roots on the unit circle both at the zero and seasonal frequencies. Consequently, seasonal-adjustment procedures may produce spurious seasonal variation and other statistically undesirable effects. In this paper we document for a large class of widely used US quarterly macroeconomic series the effects of competing seasonal-adjustment procedures on the univariate time-series properties of the adjusted series. We also investigate which procedures are most appropriate given the properties of the data. Overall, we find very significant differences and evidence that several U.S. macroeconomic time series contain a mixture of deterministic and stochastic seasonal components.

JEL Classification System-Numbers: C22, C52

1 Introduction

Mis-specification of a trend leads to spurious cycles in detrended data, as for instance, Nelson and Kang (1981) emphasized. What is perhaps less obvious is the fact that seasonal-adjustment procedures may produce similar effects. This paper takes up the question of whether spurious seasonal fluctuation occurs

[1] The first author would like to acknowledge the financial support of the SSHRC and NSERC as well as the Fonds FCAR of Quebec. Part of this paper was done while the first author was on sabbatical leave at the Cowles Foundation, Yale University. Its financial support and hospitality is also gratefully acknowledged. The third author is grateful for the hospitality of the University of California, San Diego, where he was a visiting scholar during the Spring of 1991, to Wilfrid Laurier University for financial support through a short-term research grant, a Course Remission Grant, and the Academic Development Fund. Comments by anonymous referees on earlier drafts helped improve the paper considerably. A companion C.R.D.E. (Université de Montréal) working paper with a more detailed account of the empirical results is available on request.

when seasonals are removed via an adjustment procedure based on a misspecified model of seasonality.

There exists a vast literature on the ideal properties of seasonal-adjustment procedures, including the fact that they should leave the time-series properties of the series unaffected except at the seasonal frequencies (see, e.g., Nerlove et al. (1979), Bell and Hillmer (1984) and Hylleberg (1986) for surveys and detailed discussion). As is now well known, many time series are nonstationary and are widely believed to contain a unit root at the zero frequency (see Campbell and Perron 1991 for a recent survey). Similarly, usual seasonal-adjustment procedures make either implicit or explicit assumptions about roots on the unit circle both at the zero as well as at the seasonal frequency and its harmonics. Occasionally, in applied research, adjustment for seasonality assumes that seasonality is deterministic and can be removed via seasonal dummies, thus ignoring the possibility of the stochastic and nonstationary nature of seasonality (e.g., Barsky and Miron 1989). More often, the monthly Census X-11 program, for instance, is applied, which implies data transformations which is approximated by the $(1 + L + L^2 + \cdots + L^{11})$ filter, where L^i is the lag operator for i periods), resulting in a "removal" of unit roots at the monthly seasonal frequency and its harmonics.[2]

Data transformations that go along with the removal of seasonals may or may not be appropriate, just as trend removal can be inadequately done. In this paper we document for several quarterly U.S. post-World War II time series how data transformations typically associated with seasonal adjustment affect the univariate time-series properties of interest to economists, such as the autocorrelation and partial autocorrelation functions of the transformed data. Using tests proposed by Hylleberg, Engle, Granger and Yoo (1990; henceforth HEGY) we also discuss which data transformation appears to be most appropriate. That is, based on the univariate time-series properties of the raw data, we determine which seasonal filter transforms the raw data into a series that is well represented by a stationary *ARMA* process.

With one exception, all the data transformations we consider imply the same treatment with regard to zero frequency detrending. Namely, all transformations assume the data have a unit root at the zero frequency, except for the case where a first difference is combined with a seasonal difference. In the latter case we obtain two unit roots at the zero frequency. All seasonal-adjustment data transformations differ, however, with regard to the treatment of deterministic and stochastic seasonality and the presence of unit root at seasonal frequencies in the stochastic case. In general, it is found that summary statistics of the data are quite sensitive to the way seasonal adjustment is applied. Very different conclusions can be found for the univariate characterization of the data, depending on the way seasonals are eliminated, and even with the detrending being kept constant across different adjustment procedures.

---

[2] For a discussion of the X-11 filter and its linear approximation see, e.g., Wallis (1974), and Ghysels and Perron (1993).

A by-product of our paper is a theoretical extension of the *HEGY* procedure. As the procedure involves an *AR* polynomial expansion similar to Dickey-Fuller tests for unit roots at the zero frequency, one has to select a lag length to calculate the test statistics. Recently, Hall (1990) derived the limiting distribution of the augmented Dickey-Fuller test when the *AR* polynomial expansion is chosen using data-based methods, as is most often done in practice. We extend Hall's zero-frequency results to *HEGY* tests for unit roots at the zero and seasonal frequencies.

It may be worth emphasizing a few limitations of our paper. We will only discuss the effect of filtering on the univariate characterization of data and not the consequences of filtering on estimation and testing. Hence, we will not elaborate on the issue of filtering and estimation and testing, in part because this subject is documented in detail in, for instance, Sims (1974), Wallis (1974), Sims (1985), Ghysels and Perron (1993), Hansen and Sargent (1993), Sims (1993), among others.

The paper is organized as follows. In Section 2 we discuss the autocorrelation and partial autocorrelation functions of a representative set of U.S. quarterly time series which have been adjusted with a set of four commonly used filters for removal of seasonal fluctuations. Next, we present a summary of the *HEGY* procedure and extend it to allow for data-based augmentation-lag selection. Empirical results of the *HEGY* procedure are reported in Section 3. Conclusions appear in Section 4.

2 Univariate Time-Series Properties of U.S. Quarterly Data

Quarterly data on a variety of U.S. macroeconomic series were considered, similar to Barsky and Miron (1989; hereafter *BM*), whose sample usually begins in 1946 and ends in 1985 (see their Table 1). Not all of the series used by *BM* were considered in this paper. We omitted the components of fixed-investment expenditures, the money multiplier, state and local govemment spending, and final sales. However, we added per capita versions of *GNP* and consumption expenditures and their components as well as a measure of real balances.[3] We also, however, updated the data used by BM up to the fourth quarter of 1989. In the results reported below, we report only the test results for the extended sample for a subset of the available data set.[4]

---

[3] Since there were no differences between the real and real per capita measures of *GNP* and consumption, the results for the latter series are not reported.

[4] Conclusions are generally unaffected by the addition of the 16 most recent quarterly observations. See, however, Section 4 below. These, and the data, are available from the third author upon request. Some test results for the sample used by *BM* are reported in the Appendix of the working-paper version.

Table 1. Autocorrelations of some key macroeconomic variables with different seasonal-adjustment filters

		Autocorrelations							
		Lag							
Series	Transform	1	2	3	4	5	6	7	8
GNP	Level	.98	.96	.94	.92	.90	.89	.87	.85
	Δ	−.60	.34	−.61	.90	−.63	.32	−.60	.66
	Δ_4	.83	.54	.22	−.06	−.18	−.16	−.07	.04
	Δ_{SA}	.37	.25	.00	−.10	−.12	−.06	−.02	−.08
	Δ-SD	−.02	−.003	−.15	.38	−.28	−.13	−.15	.31
	$\Delta\Delta_4$	.32	.12	−.12	−.46	−.36	−.21	−.07	−.00
Cons.	Level	.98	.97	.95	.93	.92	.90	.88	.86
	Δ	−.68	.41	−.67	.94	−.65	.39	−.65	.91
	Δ_4	.78	.65	.50	.32	.33	.30	.35	.38
	Δ_{SA}	.05	.22	.04	−.03	−.06	−.12	.05	−.18
	Δ-SD	−.41	.30	−.38	.61	−.30	.19	−.32	.54
	$\Delta\Delta_4$	−.22	.13	.03	−.43	.11	−.21	.08	−.02
*M*1	Level	.98	.96	.94	.91	.89	.87	.84	.82
	Δ	.10	−.15	.01	.72	.02	−.16	−.05	.66
	Δ^4	.92	.80	.67	.56	.50	.46	.41	.37
	Δ_{SA}	.57	.40	.30	.17	.29	.26	.09	.06
	Δ-SD	.36	.16	.21	.50	.21	.10	.08	.41
	$\Delta\Delta_4$	.31	.05	−.04	−.40	−.02	.05	−.14	−.06

* All series are seasonally unadjusted except for the Δ_{SA} filter, which relies on seasonally adjusted data at the source. All series are in logarithms of the levels.

Table 1 displays the sample autocorrelations (henceforth denoted *AC*) for three of the key macroeconomic time series considered in this paper which are "seasonally adjusted" using a selection of filters. The aim is to illustrate divergent patterns in the autocorrelation and partial autocorrelation functions subjected to different filters. The data transformations considered are those typically associated with adjustment for seasonality. The most prominent, of course, is the official X-11 adjustment procedure used by the U.S. Bureau of the Census. The entry Δ_{SA} corresponds to the first differenced seasonally adjusted series by the Census. The transformation associated with Δ_{SA} assumes a unit root at the zero frequency as well as the seasonal frequency and its harmonics.[5] A transformation making the same assumptions is to take the annual. i.e., fourth order

[5] The technical details of this argument are omitted here. They can be summarized as follows: it is assumed that the X-11 procedure is applied to the monthly data first, which is then aggregated to quarterly series. The monthly X-11 filter can be approximated by the sub-filter $(1 + L + \cdots + L^{11})$, as discussed in Bell (1992) removing unit roots at the monthly seasonal frequency and its harmonics. Temporal aggregation to quarterly series will make this equivalent to $(1 + L + L^2 + L^3)$. See Granger and Siklos (1992), and Hylleberg, Jorgenson and Sorensen (1992) for further discussion of temporal aggregation and seasonal unit roots.

difference, which is denoted by Δ_4. It should be noted, though, that Δ_{SA} and Δ_4, while making the same assumptions about roots in the unit circle, entail quite different data transformations. The fourth difference is a fairly transparent transformation, while Δ_{SA} corresponds to several transformations, including judgemental corrections, aggregation across industries, time, etc.

Other transformations considered in Table 1 include a first difference with seasonal dummies, denoted Δ-SD, and a multiplicative $\Delta\Delta_4$ adjustment advanced by Box and Jenkins (1976). The former assumes a deterministic seasonal pattem, while the latter takes two unit roots at the zero frequency.[6]

For the purposes of comparison, we also listed the AC function for the level of the series as well as the first difference where seasonals are ignored. Let us first discuss in detail the first series listed in Table 1, namely, U.S. GNP. The autocorrelation at lag 1 ranges from .98 to −.60, depending on which transformation (or lack of it) is considered. The .98 value comes, of course, from the level series but, even with Δ_4, the removal of the annual seasonal still leaves a very high autocorrelation at the first lag, equal to .83. The differences between the Census adjusted result of .37 and the common transformation Δ-SD (yielding −.02) reaffirms the well-known results that transformations can have important effects on some of the time-series properties of the data.

The differences in the patterns displayed in Table 1 for GNP are fairly representative for the other cases as well. Consumption and $M1$ are just two of the examples appearing in Table 1 (additional details are also contained in the discussion-paper version).

What is clearly to be concluded, as a first impression from the results in Table 1, is that modelling seasonality, and the adjustment of data on the basis of such a model, seems to greatly affect whatever is left in univariate time-series behavior at lags other than the seasonal ones. The question which needs to be raised, then, is which data transformation appears most appropriate. For that, we turn to the issue of testing for unit roots at the seasonal frequency, as each of the data transformations considered treat this key feature differently.

3 The *HEGY* Procedure with Pretest Data-Based Model Selection

In order to ascertain the presence of unit roots at the seasonal frequencies, as well as at the zero frequency, we follow the procedures outlined by *HEGY*, and applied by Beaulieu and Miron (1993), Engle, Granger, Hylleberg and Lee

6 The transformation which consists in eliminating the pair of roots $(1 - L^2)$ or $(1 - L)(1 + L)$ corresponding to the biannual frequency apparently common in many macroeconomic time series (e.g., Lee and Siklos (1991a, 1991b, 1991c)) was also considered. The results are contained in the Appendix of the companion discussion paper.

(1993; henceforth *EGHL*), Franses (1991), Lee and Siklos (1991a), Otto and Wirjanto (1991), among others. Moreover, Ghysels. Lee and Noh (1991) found the *HEGY* procedure compares favorably with altemative procedures such as the Dickey, Hasza and Fuller (1984) tests, in terms of finite sample size and power properties. In this section we introduce the *HEGY* procedure. Since it has been widely documented elsewhere our discussion will be brief. Our main focus will instead be directed towards extending the *HEGY* procedure to take account of the fact that one usually determines the order of the *AR* polynomial expansion used in the test on the basis of the data. The fact that the lag-length selection is data based, something usually ignored in theory but quite relevant and important in practice, results in some nontrivial distributional issues regarding the test statistics. Recently Hall (1990) considered data-based model selection in tests for unit roots at the zero frequency. We extend Hall's results to the *HEGY* procedure.

The *HEGY* approach consists in estimating the following regression:

$$\Delta_4 x_t = \pi_1 y_{1,t-1} + \pi_2 y_{2,t-1} + \pi_3 y_{3,t-2} + \pi_4 y_{3,t-1} + \mu + \beta' D_t + \delta t + a_1 \Delta_4 x_{t-1} + a_2 \Delta_4 x_{t-2} + \cdots + a_p \Delta_4 x_{t-p} + \varepsilon_t \tag{3.1}$$

where μ is a constant, δ is the slope coefficient of the linear trend, D_t is a vector containing three deterministic seasonal dummies with coefficient vector β, $(a_1, \ldots, a_p)$ are the *AR* lag augmentations, and the y_{kt}'s ($k = 1, 2, 3$) are series adjusted for unit roots at other frequencies such that

$$y_{1t} = (1 + L + L^2 + L^3)x_t$$

$$y_{2t} = -(1 - L + L^2 - L^3)x_t$$

$$y_{3t} = -(1 - L^2)x_t \ .$$

Thus, y_{1t} is the series x_t, after all seasonal unit roots have been removed, leaving only a unit root at the zero frequency. By contrast y_{2t} leaves a unit root at the biannual frequency for quarterly data so that $(1 + L)y_{2t}$ is stationary; and y_{3t} then possesses a pair of complex roots of the annual frequency so that $(1 + L^2)y_{3t}$ is stationary.

The test for the presence of unit roots is based on the t-statistic for π_1, for the zero frequency, and π_2 for the biannual frequency. For the annual frequency we require a joint test on π_3 and π_4, namely, an F-test of the null hypothesis that $\pi_3 = \pi_4 = 0$. Alternatively, the t-statistic on π_3, when $\pi_4 = 0$, may be used. Critical values for the tests were tabulated by *HEGY* (1990), and the asymptotic distribution theory is discussed in *EGHL* (1993).

A key assumption typically made both in the application of augmented Dickey-Fuller tests (henceforth denoted *ADF*) as well as the *HEGY* procedure is that the *AR* lag augmentation p is known a priori. Yet in many applications this assumption is not appropriate, as researchers usually decide on the value of p on the basis of the available data. As noted by Hall (1990), it is clear that if p is chosen using a data-based model-selection procedure, like testing which AR coefficients are significant, etc., then the ADF test, or the $HEGY$ procedure, are actually based on a pre-test estimator. Whether or not the asymptotic distribution of the ADF test changes, and for which model-selection rules it doesn't, has also been studied by Hall. Drawing on his analysis and the results in Ghysels, Lee and Noh (1991) showing the correspondence between the ADF and $HEGY$ tests will enable us to extend Hall's analysis to the $HEGY$ procedure.

Consider first the data-generating process the $HEGY$ procedure is designed to test:

$$x_t = \mu_0 + \alpha x_{t-4} + \mu_t \qquad t = 1, \ldots, T \tag{3.2}$$

where the error process has an $AR(p_0)$ representation, namely

$$\mu_t = \sum_{j=1}^{p_0} \theta_j \mu_{t-j} + e_t \tag{3.3}$$

The set-up in equations (3.2) and (3.3) portrays the data-generating processes that go along with null and altemative hypotheses of $HEGY$ procedure.[7] For simplicity, though not without loss of generality, we stripped away the time trend and seasonal dummies. Hence, with $\alpha = 1$ in (3.2), we obtain a unit root at all four frequencies of interest. In addition, the seasonal differenced process $\Delta_4 x_t$ follows an $AR(p_0)$ process, which is the raison d'être for discussing AR augmentation. In particular, let:

Assumption 3.1

1) The initial vector $(x_0, x_{-1}, \ldots, x_{-p_0-3})$ has a fixed distribution independent of $\{e_t\}$.
2) The roots of the characteristic equation of the $AR(p_0)$ polynomial in (3.3) lie outside the unit circle.
3) The sequence of innovations $\{e_t\}$ are i.i.d. zero mean and constant variance $\sigma^2 > 0$.

The order p of the AR expansion in the $HEGY$ equation (3.1) is selected by using a model-selection procedure applied to the data. Namely, assume that $p = \hat{p}_T$ is selected as the estimated value of p_0. The estimated AR expansion has a well-defined probability distribution for any sample size T, and $\Pi(\hat{p}_T = j)$ represents the probability of obtaining an expansion of order j, where $j = 0, 1, \ldots, J < \infty$.

7 Note that the model in (3.2) and (3.3) is not identified unless $\alpha = 1$. For example, an AR process with $\alpha = .7$ and $\theta_4 = 0$ can also be represented by $\alpha = 0$ and $\theta_4 = .7$. This identification problem, however, does not affect the discussion below concerning the distribution of the statistics t_{ij} in theorem 3.1.

Moreover, for any $\hat{p}_T = j$ we define the t-statistics t_{ij} where $i = 1, \ldots, 4$ corresponding to the *OLS* estimates of π_1 through π_4 in the *HEGY* equation (3.1). The following assumption will be key to the main result.

Assumption 3.2

The model-selection procedure satisfies the following conditions:

1) as $T \to \infty$, $\hat{p}_T - p_0 \xrightarrow{p} 0$ where p_0 has a well-defined probability distribution;
2) the distribution of $\hat{p}_T$ is asymptotically independent of the distribution of the statistics t_{ij} $(i = 1, \ldots, 4)$ for $j > p_0$.
3) $\Pi(\hat{p}_T < p_0) = 0$, i.e. the probability of underestimating p_0 is zero as $T \to \infty$.

The latter of the three conditions is important as it guarantees the convergence of the t-statistics of the *HEGY* procedure to their distribution as characterized in Engle, Granger, Hylleberg and Lee (1993). Hence, under assumption 3.2 the model-selection rule leaves the test statistics unaffected. This is summarized in the following theorem.

Theorem 3.1

Letting assumptions 3.1 and 3.2 hold, and using $\hat{p}_T$ to determine the *AR* lag expansion in the *OLS* equation (3.1) yields the asymptotic distributions:

$$t_{1j} \Rightarrow \{w_1(1)^2 - 1\}/2\left[\int_0^1 w_1(r)^2\,dr\right]^{1/2}$$

$$t_{2j} \Rightarrow \{w_2(1)^2 - 1\}/2\left[\int_0^1 w_2(r)^2\,dr\right]^{1/2}$$

$$t_{3j} \Rightarrow \int_0^1 (w_3 dw_3 + w_4 dw_4)\Big/\left[\int_0^1 (w_3(r)^2 + w_4(r)^2)\,dr\right]^{1/2}$$

$$t_{4j} \Rightarrow \int_0^1 (w_3 dw_4 - w_4 dw_3)\Big/\left[\int_0^1 (w_3(r)^2 + (w_4(r)^2)\,dr\right]^{1/2}$$

where $\Rightarrow$ denotes weak convergence in distribution, $j = \hat{p}_T$ and $w_i(r)$, $(i = 1, 2, 3, 4)$ are mutually independent standard Brownian motions on the unit intervals $[0, 1]$.

The proof of the theorem appears in the Appendix. We should note that several model-selection criteria satisfy the assumption 3.2. Hall (1990) discusses several of them and analyzes their relative merits via a Monte Carlo investigation. While several of the criteria yield more or less similar results, Hall's simulations showed a slight advantage to using what is known as a general-to-specific model-selection rule, starting with some upper bound on the length of the *AR* expansion. In the final analysis, the length of the *AR* expansion is determined by the longest statistically significant lag, where statistically significant means at a conventional significance level such as 5% or 10%. The application of this selection procedure outperformed the resort to other selection criteria, in particular the Hannan and Quinn criterion. Since there were few differences in the empirical results with the different criteria, and since the simulation evidence in Hall tended to favor the general-to-specific rule, we will only report the empirical evidence with the latter in the following section.

4 Testing for Seasonal Unit Roots

We now report test results to determine whether there is evidence of seasonal unit roots. Table 2 contains empirical evidence based on the *HEGY* procedure described in section 3. Such tests will allow us to shed some light on which transformation is the most appropriate for generating the stationary component of a particular time series. Table 2 indicates whether the hypothesis of a unit root at the seasonal and zero frequencies can be rejected. If not, Table 2 labels such a result by a 1, an indication that the time-series in question is integrated of order one or $I(1)$. Otherwise, Table 2 labels a result with a zero because the series is $I(0)$ at the frequency in question. All inferences are based on a 5% significance level. Moreover, Table 2 only shows test results for the case where equation (3.1) includes a constant, a trend, and deterministic seasonal dummies. The volume of results precludes a complete description of test outcomes for all the combinations of equation (3.1) which could have been considered.

The sensitivity of unit-root findings may be influenced by the choice of lag-length selection criteria for the autoregressive correction factor in equation (3.1). Akaike's information criterion (*AIC*) and Schwartz's information (*SC*) are well known and commonly employed criteria. *EGHL* (1993) rely on the "augmentation" approach which consists, first, in estimating equation (3.1) for some lag length (seven quarters in the present case). One then establishes which of the lags are statistically significant at, say, the 5% level. Finally, one re-estimates equation (3.1) by including only the statistically significant autoregressive correction terms. The net result is to leave gaps or "holes" in the lag distribution of the *AR* terms in equation (3.1). The rationale for this approach is "to whiten the residuals at the cost of the minimum number of parameters. Too many parameters will decrease the power of the tests while too few will render the size far greater than the level of significance" (*EGHL* 1993). Based on Hall (1990), however, the preferred approach consists in estimating the number of *AR* terms in equation (3.1) according to the longest lag with a statistically significant coefficient, beginning with a maximum lag length of 7 quarters. Below we report

Table 2. Seasonal unit-root test results: *HEGY* method[1]

	Lag Selection		Coefficients in (3.1)				
Series	Criterion	[lags]	π_1	π_2	π_3	π_4	$\pi_3 \cap \pi_4$
GNP	Longest sig. lag	[1]	1	0	1	0	0
Consumption		[5]	1	1	1	0	1
Consumption Non-Durables		[5]	1	1	1	1	1
Consumption Durables		[0]*	1	0	0	0	0
Consumption Services		[5]	1	1	0	1	0
Fixed Investment		[1]	0	0	0	0	0
Government Exp.		[1]*	0	0	0	0	0
Government Exp. Federal		[0]	1	0	1	0	0
Government Exp. Defense		[0]*	1	0	0	0	0
Exports		[1]	1	0	0	0	0
Imports		[0]	1	0	0	0	0
Change in Bus. Inventories		[5]	0	1	0	0	0
Employment		[1]	1	0	1	0	0
Unemployment		[1]	0	0	1	0	0
Average Hours		[0]	1	0	1	0	0
Labor Force		[1]	1	0	0	0	0
Cons. Price Index		[0]	1	0	0	0	0
Interest Rate		[4]	1	0	0	0	0
Ex post real interest rate		[0]	0	0	0	0	0
Average Wage		[2]	1	0	1	0	0
Average Real Wage		[7]	1	0	1	1	1
Monetary Base		[0]*	1	0	0	0	0
Money Supply – *M*1		[1]	1	0	1	0	0
Real Balances		[5]	1	0	0	0	0

[1] Based on a version of equation (3.1) which includes a constant, trend, and deterministic seasonal dummies. Sample ends in 1989.4.

* Signifies that the test result for the π, coefficient differed as between the seasonally adjusted and unadjusted series.

results using such a test procedure, again at the 5% level of significance. To conserve space we only present test results in Table 2 based on the general-to-specific selection path. It should be noted, however, that the finding of an $I(1)$ or $I(0)$ was not generally sensitive, especially at the zero frequency, to the lag-selection technique.[8]

Turning to the results, it is apparent, especially from the last column of Table 2, that very few series possess a unit root at the annual frequency. The only exceptions are total consumption spending, consumption of non-durables, and the average real wage. These results reinforce the comparative difficulty of finding seasonal unit roots at the annual frequency found by other researchers using macroeconomic data from other countries such as Canada and Japan (e.g., Lee and Siklos 1991a, and *EGHL* 1993, respectively). This also means that the $\Delta\Delta_4$ filter advocated by Box and Jenkins is generally unwarranted. The implication, then, is that, as in Osborn (1990), Box and Jenkins type adjustments which ignore deterministic seasonality can be mis-specified.[9] Moreover, since there are differences in the stochastic behavior of consumption and income at the seasonal frequencies, these results may also have implications for the estimation and interpretation of consumption functions (see Lee and Siklos 1991a).

There is, however, more evidence of roots on the unit circle at the biannual frequency such as for consumption of non-durables, consumption of services, and the change in business inventories. If we restrict the analysis to the sample chosen by Barsky and Miron (1989) there is still more evidence of a seasonal unit root at the biannual frequency, since for the labor force and wages series, one cannot reject the null that $\pi_2 = 0$, nor for the series found to have a biannual seasonal unit root for the extended sample. However, the foregoing exceptions to the finding of no seasonal unit roots at the biannual frequency are interesting. For example, in the case of the inventory series, the omission of stochastic seasonality may have implications for models which purport to show a link between inventory fluctuations and business cycles (e.g., see Ramey 1989, and references therein). The finding of a seasonal unit root for the services component of total consumption reveals the possible importance of aggregation in estimating economic relationships such as the consumption function. Thus, the seasonal unit-root tests potentially reveal a considerable amount of mis-specification of seasonality when only deterministic seasonality is assumed to exist.

These tests with officially adjusted and raw unadjusted data confirm not only the outcome of most unit-root tests at the zero frequency, applied to a wide

---

[8] The unemployment rate and fixed investment may be possible exceptions. Lee and Siklos (1991b) also reached the same conclusion in their Canadian sample. This result is interesting because some economists have formulated explanations of business-cycle fluctuations based on the assumption that unemployment rate and *GNP* possess different univariate time series properties (e.g., Blanchard and Quah, 1989).

[9] As noted previously, we conducted all our tests with and without deterministic seasonals, and omission of the latter feature of the data influences the conclusions reached in Table 2.

variety of U.S. seasonally adjusted macroeconomic data by several researchers (see Campbell and Perron 1991a for a recent survey), but also reaffirm the neutrality of the X-11 seasonal-adjustment procedure with respect to its impact on the existence of a unit root (see Lee and Siklos 1991a for Canadian evidence). One must therefore conclude that while deterministic seasonal dummies capture much of the seasonal variation in the data, there is sufficient evidence of the existence of seasonal unit roots to warrant the statement that the "no-seasonal-unit-root" approach leads to mis-specification of univariate time series behavior. This "in-between" result is probably best explained by arguments along the lines of structural instability in seasonal patterns. Indeed, when seasonality changes due to structural breaks it will not be captured by deterministic seasonal patterns and will lead to spurious findings of roots at seasonal frequencies.

5 Conclusions

This paper has investigated the properties of various filters applied for the purposes of seasonal adjustment. Examination of autocorrelation and partial autocorrelation functions for widely used US quarterly macroeconomic time series suggests considerable differences across the various data transformations considered. We also extended Hall's work on the issue of lag-length selection in unit-root tests to the unit-root test introduced by *HEGY*.

The empirical results suggest that, while seasonal dummies capture a great deal of seasonal patterns, they do not seem to adequately describe all attributes. Indeed, unit roots at some seasonal frequencies are regularly found. Moreover, none of the standard transformations typically used to remove seasonals match the findings emerging from *HEGY* data-based model-selection rules. One possible explanation for our findings is that seasonal patterns change, though only occasionally, as noted in Ghysels (1991) and Canova and Ghysels (1992). As such, none of the standard transformations suit this framework. Moreover, whatever transformation is applied seems to have a great impact on what is left as non-seasonal variation.

Appendix

Proof of Theorem 3.1

We concentrate our proof on the case of t_{1j} as the arguments for t_{2j} through t_{4j} are similar. Ghysels, Lee and Noh (1991), henceforth denoted *GLN*, show there is a finite sample as well as an asymptotic equivalence between the *HEGY* t_{1j} statistic, for fixed and finite *j*, and the *ADF* *t*-statistic with a $(j + 3)$ *AR* polynomial expansion. To discuss the equivalence we shall first make abstraction of the fact that a trend and seasonal dummies appear in equation (3.1). Consider, first, the *DGP* as described by (3.2) and (3.3). Then *GLN* show that the regression equation

$$\Delta x_t = \phi_1 x_{t-1} + \phi_2 \Delta x_{t-1} + \phi_3 \Delta x_{t-2} + \phi_4 \Delta x_{t-3} + \mu_t$$

where $\phi_1 = \alpha - 1$, while $\phi_i = -\alpha$ for $i = 2, \ldots, 4$, yields a *t* statistic for ϕ_1 whose finite sample and asymptotic distribution is the same as that of the *HEGY* t_{10} test. Naturally, this equation corresponds to that of an *ADF* regression with an $AR(3)$ expansion. This equivalence can be extended to *HEGY* procedures with j *AR* lags for $j = 1, \ldots, J < \infty$, and also to *HEGY* procedures which include a trend and/or seasonal dummies. In the latter case, as Dickey, Bell and Miller (1986) show, one consults the *DF* distribution for a test statistic with a constant in the *ADF* regression equation. With this correspondence between *HEGY* t_{ij} and *ADF* with a $(j + 3)$ expansion being established we can rely on the theoretical results in Hall (1990). In particular, assumption 3.2 still holds with the transformation showing the equivalence between *HEGY* and *ADF*, namely (1) $(\hat{p}_T + 3) - (p_0 + 3) \xrightarrow{P} 0$; (2) the distribution of $\hat{p}_T + 3$ is still independent of the *t* statistic; and (3) $\Pi(\hat{p}_T + 3 < p_0 + 3) = 0$ also holds. Then applying theorem 2.1 and corollary 2.1 in Hall (1990) yields the result for the t_{1j} statistic. Similar arguments also apply to the test statistics t_{2j} through t_{4j} (see *GLN* (1991) for further discussion).

References

Barsky RB, Miron JA (1989) The seasonal cycle and the business cycle. Journal of Political Economy 97:503–34

Beaulieu JJ, Miron JA (1993) Seasonal unit roots in aggregate US data. Journal of Econometrics 55:305–28

Bell WR (1992) On some properties of linear approximations to the X-11 program. Statistical Research Division, US Bureau of the Census (mimeo)

Bell WR, Hillmer SC (1984) Issues involved with seasonal adjustment of economic time series. Journal of Business and Economic Statistics 2:526–534

Blanchard OJ, Quah D (1989) The dynamic effects of aggregate demand and aggregate supply disturbances. American Economic Review 79:655–73

Box GEP, Jenkins GM (1976) Time series analysis: Forecasting and control, Revised Edition (San Francisco: Holden-Day)

Campbell JY, Perron P (1991) Pitfalls and opportunities: What macroeconomists should know about unit roots. NBER Macroeconomic Annual (MIT Press, Cambridge) 141–200

Canova F, Ghysels E (1992) Changes in seasonal patterns: Are they cyclical? Journal of Economic Dynamics and Control (forthcoming).

Dickey DA, Bell WR, Miller RB (1986) Unit roots in time series models: Tests and implications. The American Statistician 40:12–26
Dickey DA, Hasza DP, Fuller WA (1984) Testing for unit roots in seasonal time series. Journal of the American Statistical Association 79:355–367
Engle RF, Granger CWJ, Hylleberg S, Lee HS (1993) Seasonal cointegration: The Japanese consumption function. Journal of Econometrics 55:275–98
Franses PH (1991) A multivariate approach to modeling univariate seasonal time series. Econometric Institute Report No 910/A
Ghysels E (1991) On seasonal asymmetries and their implications for stochastic and deterministic models of seasonality. Manuscript, Université de Montréal
Ghysels E, Lee HS, Noh J (1991) Testing for unit roots in seasonal time series – some theoretical extensions and a Monte Carlo investigation. Journal of Econometrics (forthcoming)
Ghysels E, Perron P (1993) The effect of seasonal adjustment filters on tests for a unit root. Journal of Econometrics 55:57–98
Granger CWJ, Siklos PL (1992) Temporal aggregation, seasonal adjustment, and cointegration: Theory and Evidence. Manuscript, Wilfrid Laurier University
Hall A (1990) Testing for a unit root in time series with pretest data based model selection. Discussion Paper, Dept. of Economics NCSU
Hansen LP, Sargent TJ (1993) Seasonality and approximation errors in rational expectations models. Journal of Econometrics 55:21–56
Hylleberg S (1986) Seasonality in Regression (Academic Press, New York)
Hylleberg S, Engle RF, Granger CWJ, Yoo BS (1990) Seasonal integration and cointegration. Journal of Econometrics 44:215–38
Hylleberg S, Jorgensen C, Sorensen NK (1992) Aggregation and seasonal unit roots: A note. Institute of Economics, University of Aarhus (mimeo)
Lee HS, Siklos PL (1991a) Unit roots and seasonal unit roots in macroeconomic time series: Canadian evidence. Economics Letters 35:273–77
Lee HS, Siklos PL (1991b) The influence of seasonal adjustment on unit roots and cointegration: Canadian Consumption Function 1947–91. Canadian Journal of Economics (forthcoming)
Lee HS, Siklos PL (1991c) Seasonality in econometric time series: Money-income correlations in US data revisited. Manuscript, Wilfrid Laurier University
Nelson C, Kang H (1981) Spurious periodicity in inappropriately detrended time series. Econometrica 49:741–57
Nerlove M et al (1979) Analysis of Economic Time Series – A Synthesis (Academic Press, New York)
Osborn DR (1990) A survey of seasonality in UK macroeconomic variables. International Journal of Forecasting 6:227–36
Otto D, Wirjanto T (1991) Dynamic adjustment of the demand for money for Canada. Working paper no 9114, University of Waterloo
Ramey VA (1989) Inventories as factors of production and economic fluctuations. American Economic Review 79:338–54
Sims CA (1974) Seasonality in regression. Journal of the American Statistical Association 69:618–26
Sims CA (1985) Comment on 'issues involved with the seasonal adjustment of economic time series' by Bell WR, Hillmer SC. Journal of Business and Economic Statistics 3:92–4
Sims CA (1993) Rational expectations modeling with seasonally adjusted data. Journal of Econometrics 55:9–20
Wallis KF (1974) Seasonal adjustment and relations between variables. Journal of the American Statistical Association 69:18–32

Seasonal Cointegration, Common Seasonals, and Forecasting Seasonal Series[1]

ROBERT M. KUNST

Institute for Advanced Studies, Department of Economics, Stumpengasse 56, 1060 Vienna, Austria

Abstract: Seasonal cointegration generalizes the idea of cointegration to processes with unit roots at frequencies different from 0. Here, "common seasonals," also a dual notion of common trends, is adopted for the seasonal case. The features are demonstrated in exemplary models for German and U.K. data. An evaluation of the predictive value of accounting for seasonal cointegration shows that seasonal cointegration may be difficult to exploit to improve predictive accuracy even in cases where seasonal non-cointegration is clearly rejected on statistical grounds. The findings from the real-world examples are corroborated by Monte Carlo simulation.

JEL Classification System-Numbers: C32, C15, E17

1 Introduction

The notion of seasonal cointegration (SC) was introduced in two core articles by Engle et al. (1989) and Hylleberg et al. (1990, HEGY). Compared to the tremendous impact of trend cointegration on empirical econometrics incited by the seminal work of Engle and Granger (1987), SC has not yet caught on in a similar magnitude.

Three main reasons for this disregard can be identified. Firstly, in contrast to the widespread acceptance of the unit-root model for trending economic series, many investigators cling to the view that seasonal phenomena are well modeled by dummy-style deterministic cycles. Without seasonal unit roots (seasonal integration), however, SC does not make sense. Secondly, interest in seasonal phenomena as such is limited in economics. Many economists view seasonality as a sort of nuisance to be gotten rid of by adjustment methods. Thirdly, the usefulness of findings of SC for empirical tasks, such as forecasting or business cycle analysis, has yet to be established.

Responding to such critiques, it can now be stated safely that, though seasonal patterns are changing more slowly than growth trends and timing of annually recurrent events is pronounced, repetitive seasonal-dummy patterns are unable to capture seasonality exhaustively. Findings on seasonal unit roots

---

[1] Part of this paper was written while the author was visiting professor at the University of California San Diego.

have been reported, e.g., by Ghysels (1990), Osborn (1990b), Lee and Siklos (1991), and Kunst (1993). Even if interest in seasonal phenomena per se is low, good models of seasonal patterns can be crucial for analyzing sub-annual series. The accuracy of short-run leading indicators or forecasts – commonly constructed from adjusted series – should benefit from the use of refined seasonal models on raw series.

Here, two strategies are used to gauge the effects of modeling SC on prediction. Firstly, two exemplary systems of macroeconomic series on German and U.K. data are studied. Secondly, a small artificial data simulation is conducted. Both methods lead to the same tentative conclusion, viz., that gains achieved by modeling SC with respect to forecasting are typically small. This conclusion is, of course, subject to the collection of further evidence. Such evidence may be obtained from analyzing other model systems or from more refined Monte Carlo simulations.

The organization of this paper is as follows. Section 2 summarizes the main results on SC from the literature and introduces the seasonal counterpart of common trends, "seasonal common factors," which notion is demonstrated on the two exemplary data sets. Section 3 studies the relative forecasting performance of different seasonal models for this data. Section 4 reports a simulation experiment to gauge the effects of SC on prediction. Section 5 concludes.

2 Seasonal Cointegration and Common Seasonals

The concept of SC is now fairly well known and has been extensively described in the literature. For all details, compare HEGY and Lee (1992) in particular. The definition adopted here starts by assuming there is a vector process X of N interdependent seasonally integrated time series of quarterly observations. A variable is said to be *seasonally integrated* if seasonal differencing is required to obtain stationarity. Such series are also said to "have unit roots at ± 1 and $\pm i$", i.e., the zeros of the seasonal differencing operator $\Delta_4 = 1 - B^4$.[2] The unit roots $+1$, -1, $\pm i$ imply spectral poles at the respective frequencies 0, π, $\pi/2$. Hence, the variable is also said to be integrated at these frequencies. Given this framework, the N series are said to be *seasonally cointegrated* at frequency ω if there is a linear combination of the variables which is not integrated at ω.

SC can perhaps be analyzed best in a vector autoregressive framework, an idea taken up by Lee (1992), who extended Johansen's (1988, 1991) maximum likelihood strategy for joint estimation and testing in cointegrated systems to the seasonal case. Any vector autoregression of order p can be written as (see

[2] B denotes the backshift or lag operator.

HEGY)

$$\Phi(B)\Delta_4 X_t = \mu + D_1 Y_{1t-1} + D_2 Y_{2t-1} + D_3 Y_{3t-1} + D_4 Y_{3t-2} + \varepsilon_t \quad (1)$$

$\Phi(B)$ is a polynomial matrix of order $p - 4$ with all zeros of its determinant outside the unit circle. The ranks r_1 and r_2 of D_1 and D_2 give the number of linearly independent cointegrating relations at frequencies 0 and π. Both matrices can be decomposed into $N \times r_i$-factors as $D_i = \alpha_i \beta_i'$ with β_i containing the cointegrating vectors. Variables Y_i are transforms of observed variables:

$$Y_{1t} = (1 + B + B^2 + B^3)X_t$$
$$Y_{2t} = (1 - B + B^2 - B^3)X_t \quad (2)$$
$$Y_{3t} = (1 - B^2)X_t$$

Y_1 is trending but non-seasonal, while Y_2 and Y_3 are non-trending and display seasonal cycles at π and $\pi/2$, respectively.

Lee (1992) shows that maximum likelihood estimation of (1) under rank restrictions can be conducted via solving the generalized eigenvalue or "canonical correlation" problem

$$|\lambda S_{pp} - S_{p0} S_{00}^{-1} S_{0p}| = 0 \quad (3)$$

S_{00} and S_{pp} are empirical partial second moments matrices of $\Delta_4 X_t$ and Y_{1t-1}, conditioned on Y_{2t-1}, Y_{3t-1}, Y_{3t-2} and on the short-run influences $\Delta_4 X_{t-1}$, $\Delta_4 X_{t-2}, \ldots, \Delta_4 X_{t-p+4}$. S_{0p} and S_{p0} are similarly defined cross-moment matrices. The eigenvectors corresponding to the r_1 largest eigenvalues of (3) form the columns of an estimate for β_1. Clearly, if there is no SC, and $D_2 = D_3 = D_4 = 0$, then the original Johansen cointegration form is recovered for the transformed process Y_{1t}.

Solving an analogous canonical problem between $\Delta_4 X_t$ and Y_{2t-1}, conditioning on short-run influences and on Y_{1t-1}, Y_{3t-1}, Y_{3t-2}, and selecting the eigenvectors to the r_2 largest roots yields an estimate for β_2. Thus, β_1 and β_2 contain those vectors that maximize correlation between $\beta_1' Y_{1t-1}$ and $\beta_2' Y_{2t-1}$ versus $\Delta_4 X_t$. One looks for linear combinations of the de-seasonalized but trending Y_1 and of the trend-free but only partially de-seasonalized Y_2 which correlate well with stationary $\Delta_4 X_t$. As a by-product, the canonical problems yield the loading matrices α_1 and α_2 and a sequence of test statistics to determine r_1 and r_2.

If $D_3 = 0$ then β_4 is obtained from the canonical problem of $\Delta_4 X_t$ versus X_{3t-2} conditioning on the short run and on Y_{1t-1}, Y_{2t-1}. Similarly, β_3 could be estimated after restricting $D_4 = 0$, but synchronous annual fluctuations are generally preferred to asynchronous ones. Empirical evidence tends to support this preference, and freely estimated D_3 is often close to 0. If D_3 and D_4 are estimated without restrictions, so called polynomial cointegrating vectors complicate the analysis.

Apart from Lee's canonical analysis, two alternative approaches for testing and estimating SC have been presented in the literature. Following the treatment of trend cointegration outlined by Engle and Granger (1987), HEGY suggest reducing multivariate SC problems to univariate testing on residuals. This approach is technically simple and appealing but theoretically inefficient and faces problems if more than one cointegrating vector is present. A genuinely multivariate alternative is the frequency-domain test proposed by Joyeux (1992).

The common seasonals to be introduced here complete the picture evoked by the notion of SC. Common seasonals are "dual" to SC; hence seasonal behavior of a multivariate process expresses itself equally through its r_i SC structures and through its $N - r_i$ common seasonals or distinct sources of seasonal fluctuations.

Suppose that the data-generating process (1) has some cointegrating structures reflected by rank-deficient $D_i = \alpha_i \beta_i'$. Multiplication of $\alpha_1^{\perp\prime}$ into (1) from the left cancels the first term which is responsible for trend integration. $\alpha_1^{\perp\prime} X$ describes an $(N - r_1)$-dimensional process whose seasonal differences do not depend on $\beta_1' Y_{1t-1}$. Consequently, first differences of the seasonally averaged $\alpha_1^{\perp\prime} Y_1$ do not depend on any frequency-zero error correction variables. $\alpha_1^{\perp\prime} Y_1$ corresponds to the definition of common trends in non-seasonal systems used by Johansen (1992) and Gonzalo and Granger (1991).[3]

Now let equation (1) be premultiplied with $\alpha_2^{\perp\prime}$. The second term cancels out; thus $\alpha_2^{\perp\prime} X$ is an $(N - r_2)$-dimensional process whose seasonal differences do not depend on $\beta_2' Y_{2t-1}$. Sums (or averages) of successive observations from $\alpha_2^{\perp\prime} X$, cleaned from the irrelevant unit roots by filtering through $(1 - B)(1 + B^2)$, do not depend on lagged error correction factors at frequency π. Thus $\alpha_2^{\perp\prime} Y_2$ approaches an $(N - r_2)$-dimensional random jump process

$$Z_t + Z_{t-1} = \varepsilon_t \tag{4}$$

$\alpha_2^{\perp\prime} Y_2 = (1 - B + B^2 - B^3)\alpha_2^{\perp\prime} X$ will be called the vector of "*common biannual seasonals*" of the system. Similarly, assuming $D_3 = 0$, $\alpha_4^{\perp\prime} Y_3 = (1 - B^2)\alpha_4^{\perp\prime} X$ can be called the "*common annual seasonals*" of X.

In a vector autoregression with only unit roots at $+1$ permitted, Johansen (1992) demonstrated that $\alpha_1^{\perp\prime}$ is formed from the eigenvectors corresponding to the smallest (theoretically zero) eigenvalues of the canonical problem dual to his version of (3)

$$|\lambda S_{00} - S_{0p} S_{pp}^{-1} S_{p0}| = 0 \tag{5}$$

This result naturally carries over to the four-roots case. After additional conditioning on Y_{2t-1}, Y_{3t-1}, Y_{3t-2}, the eigenvectors corresponding to the $N - r_1$ smallest eigenvalues constitute $\alpha_1^{\perp\prime}$. Analogously, the conditional canonical problem between $\Delta_4 X_t$ and Y_{2t-1} yields $N - r_2$ eigenvectors $\alpha_2^{\perp\prime}$ of the zero (or "insignificant") roots. Assuming $D_3 = 0$, a similar problem can be solved for $\Delta_4 X_t$ and Y_{3t-2}. The resulting matrices of stacked eigenvectors describe the system's common seasonals. Hence, a common seasonal can be viewed as a

[3] Divergent definitions of "common trends" were given by Kasa (1992) and Stock and Watson (1988).

variable whose respective deseasonalizing averages such as $1 + B$ or $1 + B^2$ have as little correlation as possible with past system variables, approximating the behavior of "pure" processes such as (4), where such transformations are unpredictable white noise.

Two real-world examples may serve to highlight these features. Most reported applications of SC technology concern systems of two variables but, particularly with respect to common trend and common seasonals, slightly larger systems are more telling. Here, macroeconomic core systems with matching quarterly observations from two European countries are analyzed. The systems were adopted from Kunst (1993), with the real interest rate dropped. Constructed real rates are differences of almost non-seasonal interest rates and seasonal price deflators, which often display absurd behavior and may not correspond to economically relevant real interest. Such rates could be constructed accounting for *annual* instead of quarter-to-quarter inflation, but then they stand little chance of being seasonal as, in a way, they have already been "filtered" by Δ_4. Thus, systems contain five variables: gross domestic product; private consumption; gross fixed investment; goods exports; and a wage rate. Variables are in logarithms of constant prices.

Countries investigated are the Federal Republic of Germany (historical data from 1960 through 1988) and the United Kingdom (data starting 1963). Kunst (1993) reports that these countries exhibit opposite extremes of seasonal behavior: seasonal structures are mainly deterministic in the U.K. and pronouncedly stochastic in Germany.

Univariate seasonal unit-root tests ("HEGY" tests) reject unit roots in the exports series. After incorporating seasonal dummies alternatives into the test, unit roots are also rejected in other British series but not in the German ones. Hence, exports literally do not obey one of the basic assumptions of the model. Nevertheless, any series which is not integrated at ω can be incorporated into the system, and formally defined to be cointegrating with itself at ω, with the cointegrating vector being the corresponding unit vector.

In solving canonical problems like (3) or (5), one conditioning lag of $\Delta_4 X_t$ was used for Germany and none for the U.K., in accordance with the lag orders suggested by Akaike's Information Criterion (AIC). Formal statistical tests on the number of non-zero eigenvalues identified one significant cointegrating vector at each frequency for Germany. For the U.K., three cointegrating vectors are supported at the seasonal frequencies, but again only one for frequency zero. Table 1 shows those canonical vectors that have been found significant by the testing procedure.

As in the six-variable models of Kunst (1993), the vectors are difficult to interpret. Additionally, vectors at frequencies π and $\pi/2$ bear little resemblance. Exports show comparatively little seasonality; thus most SC vectors have large coefficients on exports. The space spanned by British cointegrating vectors at π is "close" to one spanned by $(1, -1, -1, 0, 0)$, $(0, 0, 0, 1, 0)$, $(0, 0, 1, 0, 1)$. At least the first two vectors have straightforward interpretations: seasonal fluctuations in output are explained exclusively from aggregating seasonal fluctuations in the main demand components, and exports are non-seasonal, hence the fourth unit vector cointegrates.

The dual canonical problems (5) yield common trend and common seasonal factor vectors. The common seasonals corresponding to the smallest eigenvalues are depicted graphically as Figure 1 for the U.K. data. While German first common seasonals at both frequencies (not shown) evolve through time in a rather stable fashion, British seasonals change substantially in the early 1980s, with peaks and troughs switching between quarters. In both countries, first

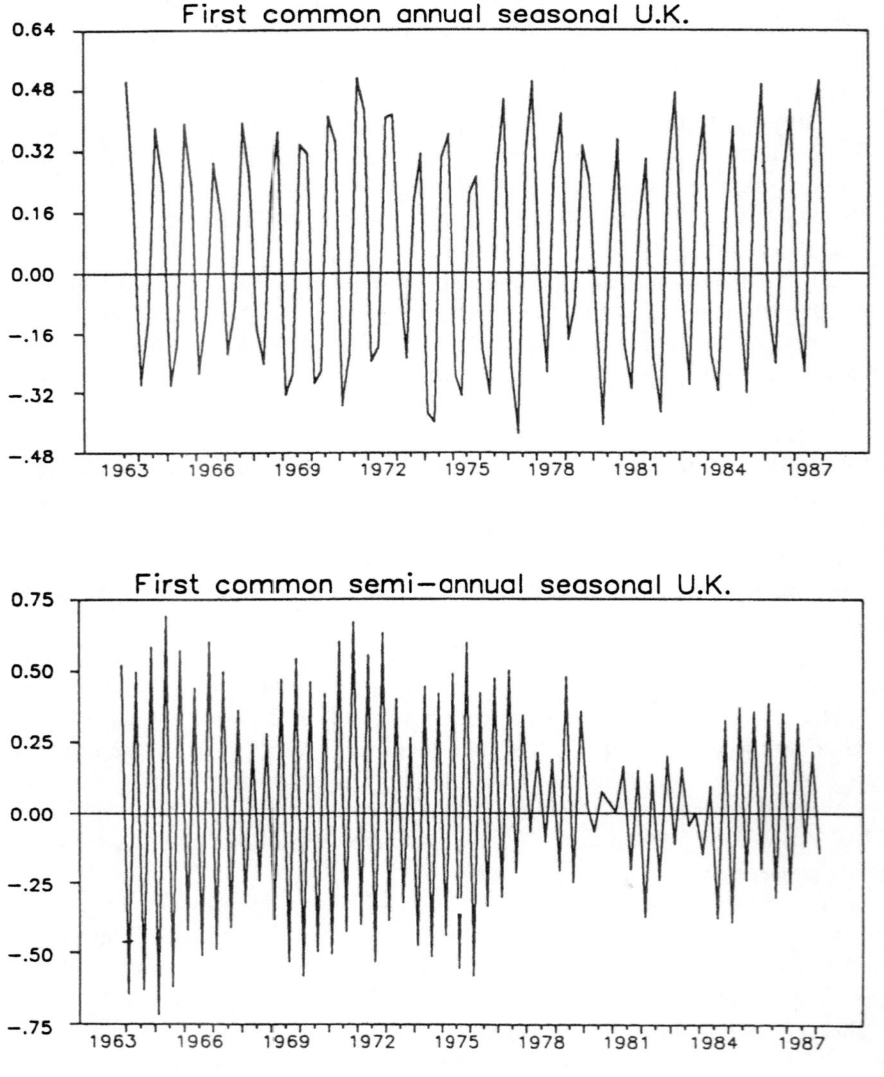

Fig. 1. Common seasonals in the U.K. macroeconomic system

common seasonals are driven primarily by consumption and wages at the bi-annual and by consumption alone at the annual frequency. Second common seasonals mainly pick up seasonal cycles in investment.

3 Forecasting Seasonal Systems

As pointed out in the introduction, forecasting of sub-annual series offers itself as a promising field of research in conjunction with seasonal models. Coverage of this problem in the recent literature is scarce, except for univariate prediction experiments (see Franses (1991), Plosser (1979), among others). First I will tum to some theoretical motivation.

Assuming that the true N-variate data-generating process features SC, it can be written as in (1) with rank-deficient matrices D_i. Ignoring SC is equivalent to restricting $D_2 = D_3 = D_4 = 0$. In practice, such misspecification typically occurs if individual series are seasonally averaged and trend cointegration analysis is applied to the resulting system. Such an approach, again, is similar to seasonally adjusting individual series, e.g., by Census X-11, as many seasonal adjustment procedures approximately contain the factor $1 + B + B^2 + B^3$ (see Wallis [1982]). In both cases-averaging or Census X-11 – misspecification can incur increased lag orders.

A common alternative to the seasonal unit-root model is the integrated model with deterministic seasonals:

$$\Phi(B)\Delta X_t = a_1 d_{1t} + a_2 d_{2t} + a_3 d_{3t} + a_4 d_{4t} + \varepsilon_t \tag{6}$$

d_{it} denotes a dummy variable being 1 in the i-th quarter and 0 otherwise. (6) can be extended to cover trend cointegration. Forecasts from its simplest variant with $\Phi(\cdot) \equiv 1$ are repetitious seasonal patterns. More general short-run structures replicate the main feature of prediction based on this class of models, viz., a tendency to return to an average seasonal pattern encountered in the sample. As pointed out by Bell (1987), (6) can be seen as a special case of the general vector moving-average model for $\Delta_4 X_t$ with seasonal unit roots in the moving-average polynomial. Equation (6), however, is not encompassed by the autoregressive representation (1). Hence, it makes sense to speak of misspecifying (1) as (6) or vice versa.

Forecasting properties under the assumption of stochastic seasonality due to seasonal unit roots are pronouncedly different. In the purest model

$$\Delta_4 X_t = \mu + \varepsilon_t \tag{7}$$

the last seasonal pattern is extrapolated into the future rather than the average one. While, again, short-run lag structures may blur this distinction, the basic

Table 1. Cointegrating vectors within the German and the British macroeconomic systems at frequencies 0, $\pi/2$, π.

a) Germany frequency	GDP	C	INV	EXP	WAGE
0	0.61	0.59	0.27	−0.38	−0.62
π	0.68	−1.64	−0.53	2.98	1.13
$\pi/2$	1.57	1.10	−0.55	−3.00	−0.02

b) United Kingdom frequency	GDP	C	INV	EXP	WAGE
0	0.15	0.04	0.40	0.12	−0.65
π	−3.09	2.90	2.40	−0.02	0.95
	0.28	1.09	−0.31	−1.79	0.57
	−3.23	2.30	0.21	0.33	−3.24
$\pi/2$	−3.49	1.69	0.79	2.07	2.27
	0.73	0.07	−0.21	−0.78	4.63
	5.68	−3.78	−0.77	0.25	−0.74

Note: Labels stand for the following macroeconomic series: gross domestic product, private consumption, gross fixed investment, exports, (real) wages.

fact remains that deterministic models favor the average pattern and stochastic models the most recent one.

Forecasting properties of stochastic models with SC are in between the extremes (6) and (7). Seasonality is allowed to change permanently, but changes in individual series move together so that a rather stable "backbone" – the common seasonals as shown in Table 1 – is retained.

Case studies are an important tool for gauging the relative benefits of different procedures (again compare Franses (1991) and Plosser (1979)). This paper evaluates forecasting performance in the two model systems based on the following specifications:

[a] A seasonally cointegrating vector autoregression.

[b] A cointegrating vector autoregression of seasonally averaged variables. This approach approximates traditional seasonal adjustment of individual series.

[c] A vector autoregression with seasonal dummies included and with eventual trend cointegration.

Model [a] encompasses [b], but with respect to [c] there is a non-nested situation. E.g., a basic lag order of 5 for vector autoregression in levels was taken as indicating one conditioning lag of $\Delta_4 X_t$ for [a] and [b] but four lags of ΔX_t for [c], thus allowing a more flexible short-run lag structure. In the SC model [a], $D_3 = 0$ was imposed, while r_1 was set at 1 in both systems, r_2 and r_4 at 1 for Germany and at 3 for the U.K. The resulting seasonal error correction models look

$$\Delta_4 X_t = \mu + \Gamma \Delta_4 X_{t-1} + \sum_{i=1}^{2} \alpha_i \beta_i' Y_{i,t-1} + \alpha_4 \beta_4' Y_{3,t-2} + \varepsilon_t \tag{8}$$

with $\Gamma = 0$ for the U.K. and α_i and β_i having dimension $5 \times r_i$.

Forecasts were generated in the following way. All parameters (i.e., Γ, α_i, β_i, but not r_i) were estimated from reduced samples such as $t = 1, \ldots, T-1$, and a one-step forecast for X_T was generated from these parameter estimates. Then, observations $X_1, \ldots, X_{T-2}$ were used to forecast X_{T-1}. Thus, 20 one-step forecasts for $X_T, \ldots, X_{T-19}$ were generated. Similarly, n-step forecasts for $n = 1, \ldots, 8$ were produced for the last 20 observations (i.e, 5 years) of the original samples.

Tables 2 and 3 summarize the results of the experiment by average squared errors. Squared errors are given for one-step to four-step and for eight-step forecasts. Each series has individual peculiarities to be taken into account in an evaluation: GDP contains seasonal cycles from all demand aggregates; investment is more volatile than consumption but both series are highly seasonal; and

Table 2. Average square errors over 20 out-of-sample forecasts for the German data set.

step	series	[a]	[b]	[c]	
1	GDP	.18	.20	.25	× 0.0001
	C	.09	.08	.14	× 0.0001
	INV	.12	.13	.22	× 0.001
	EXP	.72	1.1	.77	× 0.0001
	WAGE	.23	.25	.29	× 0.0001
2	GDP	.24	.23	.36	× 0.0001
	C	.17	.14	.23	× 0.0001
	INV	.14	.14	.25	× 0.001
	EXP	.11	.18	.15	× 0.001
	WAGE	.27	.25	.34	× 0.0001
3	GDP	.17	.14	.25	× 0.0001
	C	.16	.18	.22	× 0.0001
	INV	.16	.16	.24	× 0.001
	EXP	.15	.19	.23	× 0.001
	WAGE	.25	.18	.30	× 0.0001
4	GDP	.20	.17	.25	× 0.0001
	C	.17	.20	.26	× 0.0001
	INV	.16	.17	.20	× 0.001
	EXP	.26	.25	.40	× 0.001
	WAGE	.42	.26	.54	× 0.0001
8	GDP	.18	.14	.15	× 0.0001
	C	.20	.22	.22	× 0.0001
	INV	.13	.13	.12	× 0.001
	EXP	.25	.25	.30	× 0.001
	WAGE	.49	.41	.37	× 0.0001

Note: [a] denotes predictions from a seasonally cointegrated model; [b] denotes predictions if only trend cointegration is accounted for; [c] predictions are based on the specification of dummy-style deterministic seasonality with eventual trend cointegration.

Table 3. Average square errors over 20 out-of-sample forecasts for the U.K. data set.

step	series	[a]	[b]	[c]	
1	GDP	.26	.23	.38	× 0.0001
	C	.60	.60	.22	× 0.0001
	INV	.15	.19	.16	× 0.001
	EXP	.86	1.1	.90	× 0.0001
	WAGE	.16	.28	.11	× 0.0001
2	GDP	.27	.23	.40	× 0.0001
	C	.62	.60	.34	× 0.0001
	INV	.21	.19	.24	× 0.001
	EXP	1.1	.98	1.0	× 0.0001
	WAGE	.20	.29	.13	× 0.0001
3	GDP	.23	.24	.23	× 0.0001
	C	.58	.61	.44	× 0.0001
	INV	.20	.19	.21	× 0.001
	EXP	.87	.84	.78	× 0.0001
	WAGE	.26	.29	.16	× 0.0001
4	GDP	.24	.24	.18	× 0.0001
	C	.69	.61	.64	× 0.0001
	INV	.22	.19	.19	× 0.001
	EXP	.92	.83	.76	× 0.0001
	WAGE	.39	.29	.23	× 0.0001
8	GDP	.30	.24	.28	× 0.0001
	C	.65	.64	.68	× 0.0001
	INV	.23	.20	.24	× 0.001
	EXP	.92	1.1	1.1	× 0.0001
	WAGE	.34	.28	.34	× 0.0001

Note: See Table 2.

exports are more or less non-seasonal. Due to the highly seasonal nature of most series and the inevitable small-sample bias, eight-step forecasts are not necessarily much worse than one-step forecasts.

For the German data, SC apparently plays little role, but mean squared errors deteriorate if [c] imposes a purely repetitive seasonal pattern. Gains from accounting for SC relative to model [b] are substantial for exports only where SC mitigates the effects of the spuriously imposed seasonal unit roots. The dummy specification, inferior for one- or two-step forecasts with most series, gains ground if the forecast horizon is extended. This observation may arouse doubts concerning the seasonal unit-root model, but the pattern is not atypical for SC models, as the simulations in Section 4 will show.

For the U.K. data, where fixed seasonal cycles are indicated by some statistical tests (see Kunst [1993]), the dummy model fails to dominate as clearly as would have been expected. For small step sizes, [c] performs well for consumption and wages but fails for the GDP aggregate series. Differences among models are eroded for longer horizons. Purely deterministic seasonality would result formally in four SC vectors at both seasonal frequencies, with the one remaining common seasonal factor comprising all deterministic cycles. The finding of only three cointegrating vectors and the remarkable instabilities in seasonal patterns in Figure 1 shed doubt on this entirely deterministic view of U.K. seasonality.

Both model systems are susceptible to aberrations from the basic Gaussian VAR assumptions, which can be seen from performing statistical tests on residuals. When restricting attention exclusively to the class of vector autoregressions, however, all suggested variants [a], [b], [c] closely approximate the optimum structure identified by AIC. None of the three competitors can be "improved" without blurring the distinctions among them entirely. Consequently, though the two model systems are just two examples for real-world cases, they are quite typical, as one cannot reasonably assume that reality is being generated by Gaussian vector autoregressions. The documented experiment reflects the situation of a forecaster who, confronted with a selection of interrelated series, makes predictions based on an off-the-shelf time series procedure. The next section will show that the outcome might not be too different if his/her reality were actually generated from Gaussian VARs with seasonal unit roots.

4 A Monte Carlo Experiment

The real-world prediction experiments entail the question whether the observed features are typical for SC systems. This point should become clearer from Monte Carlo simulations based on the following data-generating process, which is known to be seasonally cointegrated.

$$\begin{bmatrix} \Delta_4 X_{1t} \\ \Delta_4 X_{2t} \\ \Delta_4 X_{3t} \end{bmatrix} = \begin{bmatrix} 0 \\ -0.2 \\ -0.1 \end{bmatrix} [Y^S_{1t-1} + Y^S_{2t-1} + Y^S_{3t-1}] + \begin{bmatrix} 0.2 \\ 0.3 \\ 0 \end{bmatrix} [X_{1t-2} - X_{1t-4} - 0.8X_{2t-2} + 0.8X_{2t-4}] + [\varepsilon_{1t}\varepsilon_{2t}\varepsilon_{3t}]' \quad (9)$$

with

$$Y^S_{it} = X_{it} + X_{it-1} + X_{it-2} + X_{it-3}$$

and $N(0, 1)$ serially and mutually uncorrelated errors. In the notation of (8), $\alpha_1 = (0\ -0.2\ -0.1)$, $\beta_1 = (1\ 1\ 1)$, $\alpha_4 = (0.2\ 0.3\ 0)$, $\beta_4 = (1\ -0.8\ 0)$ and all remaining α_i, β_i, Γ are 0. There is one trend cointegrating vector which influences X_2 strongly and X_3 more weakly. X_1 makes part of the vector but is not affected by error correction itself. The SC vector operates at $\pi/2$ and only concerns X_1 and X_2. Hence, seasonality in X_3 fluctuates freely, while long-run movements of X_1 are unbridled and X_2 is controlled in both aspects.

Departing from some zero starting values, 120 observations of the process (9) were generated. Then, predictions for the last 20 observations from estimates based on the first 100 observations were obtained using several variants of the models [a], [b], [c] used in Section 3. A graphical summary of the results is given in Figure 2. As in Tables 2 and 3, all reported squared errors correspond to fourth differences, not to level variables. If levels are evaluated, differences at longer forecast horizons become more pronounced due to pile-up effects.

Figure 2 reveals that benefits from accounting for SC are small and disappear entirely for longer forecast horizons. Beyond 8 steps, the seasonally cointegrated – i.e., the true(!) – model even falls markedly behind the misspecified model without SC.

This feature appears to be due to the fact that SC vectors have to be estimated and are not known. In more detail, one-step prediction errors calculated from the estimated model (8) are sums of the following terms: innovations ε_t; a time-constant estimation error in the constant μ, say $\mu^* - \mu$; errors from estimating the short-run lag structure, $(\Gamma^* - \Gamma)\Delta_4 X_{t-1}$; and, finally, objects like $(\alpha_i^* \beta_i^{*\prime} - \alpha_i \beta_i^{\prime}) Y_{it-1}$. The last term is the only one non-stationary unless $\beta_i^* = \beta_i$ or $\beta_i^* = 0$. Discarding the error correction imposes $\beta_i^* = 0$ and makes this last term stationary but increases the other ones. Such a trade-off may be advantageous to the forecaster, and this paper gives evidence on cases where it actually is.

The difference between the stationary seasonal error-correction factor and the estimated nonstationary variable piles up for longer horizons. Not surprisingly, relative gains from accounting for SC are most obvious for very short horizons in series 1 and 2, whereas they need 2 to 3 steps to feed through to the third series.

The dummy model performs considerably worse than the other models. The lag order, which was identified by AIC, remained largely unaffected by the misspecification; hence, longer lags were unable to make up for the loss of information due to ignoring seasonal unit roots.

Some concomitant experiments with regression estimates of SC structures as suggested in HEGY allow the conclusion that Lee's canonical algorithm dominates straightforward regression up to around 10 steps (as compared to 100 observations) but quickly deteriorates for longer horizons. The reason appears to be that, though canonical parameter estimates are more accurate,[4] the considerable bias toward zero encountered in regression estimates can even be helpful for long-term prediction, as it involuntarily reduces the pile-up effect outlined above.

---

[4] For the canonical Lee procedure, the average re-scaled coefficient of X_2 was 0.81 with a standard deviation of 0.15. For X_3, the average coefficient was 0.01 [0.11]. Corresponding values for HEGY's regression algorithm were 0.66 [0.12] and 0.00 [0.10]. True values are 0.8 and 0.0.

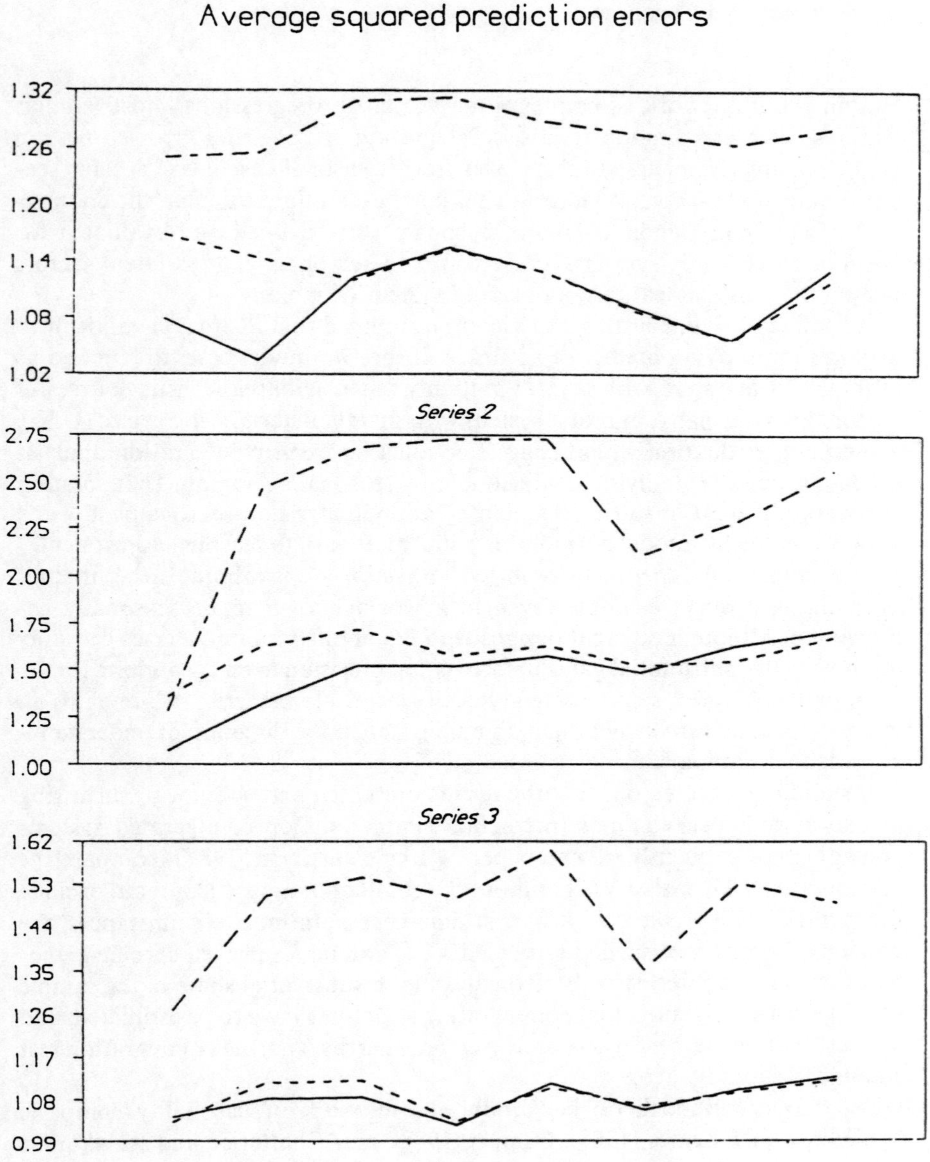

Fig. 2. Forecasting a seasonally cointegrated system: Averages of 1000 Monte Carlo simulations for 1- to 8-step out-of-sample predictions. Solid lines stand for predictions based on true SC model; short dashes denote predictions based on cointegrated VAR without SC; alternating dashes denote seasonal dummy model.

5 Summary and Conclusion

Within the framework of cointegrating vector autoregressions, most familiar features, such as common trends, cointegrating vectors, and error-correction factor loadings immediately carry over to the seasonal case if one accepts seasonal unit roots as a valid model for seasonal cycles. In particular, the counterpart of common trends, common seasonals, were defined and evaluated for two macroeconomic systems. These common seasonals express latent factors behind the seasonal features of observed system variables.

A rudimentary forecasting experiment insinuated that SC may be difficult to exploit in improving predictive accuracy. If the two model cases are viewed as examples of a system with several mutually independent stochastic sources of seasonality (Germany) and of a system with mainly deterministic cycles (U.K.), a summary evaluation would suggest conducting trend cointegration analysis on data series after individual adjustment by seasonal averaging. That solution is not too different in spirit from cointegration analysis on seasonally adjusted data, while the SC model harmonizes with "multivariate seasonal adjustment."

The simulation experiment reported in Section 4 corroborates the findings from the real-world examples even in a world known to be seasonally cointegrated. Although different designs with SC at different frequencies certainly modify results, substantial gains in forecasting precision from accounting for SC seem unlikely, unless samples are atypically large. Nevertheless, SC remains an interesting feature in its own right and a big step in the direction of understanding seasonal economic mechanisms.

It should be pointed out that the results presented here are not so surprising as they may appear, as most prediction simulations on cointegrated systems (including the frequently quoted paper by Engle and Yoo [1987]) compare the cointegrated VAR with a VAR without the cointegration restriction but exclude the formally misspecified VAR in first differences.[5] In most circumstances, the predictive accuracy of such misspecified VAR dominates its well-specified competitors once the forecasting horizon becomes a substantial share of the sample size. The reason, again, is that cointegrating structures have to be estimated, and their estimation error brings in an I(1) error, whereas ignoring cointegration just entails a stationary error.

Recently, economic theory has produced some work on seasonality (compare, e.g., Miron and Zeldes (1988), Osborn (1988), and Chatterjee and Ravikumar (1992)) and econometrics has developed the periodic cointegration model (see Osborn (1990a) and Franses and Kloek (1991)), which is an alternative to both the deterministic and the seasonal unit-roots model. More results in both areas are to be expected and will permit further insight into the true nature of seasonality.

[5] Simulations including the misspecified VAR in differences have been presented by, e.g., Brandner and Kunst (1990) and Reimers (1991, pp. 178–206).

Acknowledgment: The author wishes to thank Clive Granger, the anonymous referees and the editor for helpful comments and Pierre Siklos for a GAUSS routine which was used, partly in modified versions, to estimate seasonal cointegrating vectors and common seasonals.

References

Bell WR (1987) A note on overdifferencing and the equivalence of seasonal time series models with monthly means and models with $(0, 1, 1)_{12}$ seasonal parts when $\Phi = 1$. Journal of Business and Economic Statistics 5:383–387

Brandner P, Kunst RM (1990) Forecasting vector autoregressions – the influence of cointegration. Research Memorandum No 265, Institute for Advanced Studies, Vienna

Chatterjee S, Ravikumar B (1992) A neoclassical model of seasonal fluctuations. Journal of Econometrics 29:59–86

Engle RF, Granger CWJ (1987) Co-integration and error correction: representation, estimation and testing. Econometrica 55:251–276

Engle RF, Granger CWJ, Hallman JJ (1989) Merging short- and long-run forecasts: An application of seasonal cointegration to monthly electricity sales forecasting. Journal of Econometrics 40:45–62

Engle RF, Yoo BS (1987) Forecasting and testing in co-integrated systems. Journal of Econometrics 35:143–159

Franses PH (1991) Seasonality, non-stationarity and the forecasting of monthly time series. International Journal of Forecasting 7:199–208

Franses PH, Kloek T (1991) A periodic cointegration model of quarterly consumption in Austria and Japan. Paper presented at the ESEM, Cambridge

Ghysels E (1990) Unit-root tests and the statistical pitfalls of seasonal adjustment: The case of US postwar real gross national product. Journal of Business and Economic Statistic 8:145–152

Gonzalo J, Granger CWJ (1991) Estimation of common long-memory components in cointegrated systems. Discussion Paper 91-33, University of California, San Diego

Hylleberg S, Engle RF, Granger CWJ, Yoo BS (1990) Seasonal integration and cointegration. Journal of Econometrics 44:215–238

Johansen S (1988) Statistical analysis of cointegration vectors. Journal of Economic Dynamics and Control 12:231–254

Johansen S (1991) Estimation and hypothesis testing of cointegration vectors in Gaussian vector autoregressive models. Econometrica 59:1551–1580

Johansen S (1992) Estimating systems of trending variables. Mimeo, University of Copenhagen

Joyeux R (1992) Tests for seasonal cointegration using principal components. Journal of Time Series Analysis 13:109–118

Kasa K (1992) Common stochastic trends in international stock markets. Journal of Monetary Economics 29:95–154

Kunst RM (1993) Seasonal cointegration in macroeconomic systems: Case studies for small and large European economies. To appear in Review of Economics and Statistics

Lee HS (1992) Maximum likelihood inference on cointegration and seasonal cointegration. Journal of Econometrics 54:1–48

Lee HS, Siklos P (1991) Unit roots and seasonal unit roots in macroeconomic time series: Canadian Evidence. Economics Letters 35:273–277

Miron JA, Zeldes SP (1988) Seasonality, cost shocks and the production smoothing model of inventories. Econometrica 56:877–908

Osborn DR (1988) Seasonality and habit persistence in a life cycle model of consumption. Journal of Applied Econometrics 3:255–266

Osborn DR (1990a) The implications of periodically varying coefficients for seasonal time-series processes. Journal of Econometrics 48:373–384

Osborn DR (1990b) A survey of seasonality in UK macroeconomic variables. International Journal of Forecasting 6:327–336

Plosser CI (1979) Short-term forecasting and seasonal adjustment. Journal of the American Statistical Association 74:15–24

Reimers HE (1991) Analyse kointegrierter Variablen mittels vektorautoregressiver Modelle (Analysis of cointegrated variables by means of vector autoregressive models). Physica-Verlag, Heidelberg (in German)

Stock JH, Watson MW (1988) Testing for common trends. Journal of the American Statistical Association 83, 404:1097–1107

Wallis KF (1982) Seasonal adjustment and revision of current data: Linear filters for the X-11 method. Journal of the Royal Statistical Society A 145:74–85

A Note on Johansen's Cointegration Procedure when Trends are Present[1]

PIERRE PERRON

Département de Sciences Economiques, Université de Montréal, C.P. 6128, Succ. A, Montréal, Canada, H3C-3J7

JOHN Y. CAMPBELL

Woodrow Wilson School, Robertson Hall, Princeton University, Princeton, NJ, 08544, USA

Abstract: This note discusses some issues that arise when Johansen's (1991) framework is used to analyze cointegrating relationships among variables with deterministic linear time trends. We distinguish "stochastic" and "deterministic" cointegration, arguing that stochastic cointegration is sufficient for the existence of an error correction representation and that it is often the hypothesis of interest in empirical applications. We show that Johansen's (1991) method, which includes only a constant term in the estimated regression system, does not allow for stochastic cointegration. We propose to modify Johansen's method by including a vector of deterministic linear trends in the estimated model. We present tabulated critical values of the maximal eigenvalue and trace statistics appropriate for this case. We discuss the circumstances under which our modification may be useful.

Key Words: Cointegration, Vector Autoregressive Models, Hypothesis Testing, Unit Roots, Nonstationary Time Series.

JEL Classification System-Number: C32

1 Introduction

Following the seminal contribution of Engle and Granger (1987), cointegration has become popular both as a topic for theoretical investigation of statistical issues and as a framework within which many empirical propositions can be reevaluated[2]. A method of estimation and testing that has received particular attention is the maximum likelihood approach based on a finite VAR Gaussian system developed by Johansen (1991)[3]. In the majority of empirical applications, the regression system estimated is:

$$\Delta y_t = \mu + \Pi y_{t-1} + \Sigma_{j=1}^{k} \Gamma_j \Delta y_{t-j} + e_t \ , \tag{1}$$

1 Financial support from the National Science Foundation and the Fonds pour la Formation de Chercheurs et l'Aide à la Recherche du Québec (F.C.A.R.) is acknowledged. We wish to thank Sangjoon Kim for computational assistance, Serena Ng for comments and Hiro Y. Toda for pointing out an error in a previous draft.

2 The reader is referred to Campbell and Perron (1991) for a list of relevant references.

3 For a description of the procedure and detailed empirical applications, see Johansen (1989) and Johansen and Juselius (1990).

where y_t is an n-vector of variables, μ is an n-vector of constants, Π and Γ_j ($j = 1, \ldots, k$) are n by n matrices of parameters, and e_t is an n-vector of residuals normally distributed with mean 0 and contemporaneous covariance matrix $E(e_t e_t') = \Sigma$. (The vector e_t is assumed to be serially uncorrelated). Cointegration is present if the matrix Π has a rank greater than zero, say r, in which case $\Pi = \alpha\beta'$ for some n by r matrices α and β. This rank is the number of cointegrating relationships which are described by the cointegration matrix β whose columns are cointegration vectors. Johansen (1991) discussed two statistics, the "maximal eigenvalue" and "trace" tests, based on the maximum likelihood estimate of model (1), that can be used to determine this cointegration rank. Conditioning on the resulting estimate of the rank of Π and the estimate of the cointegrating matrix β, the short run behavior of the system can then be analyzed using the error-correction representation in terms of $z_t = \beta' y_t$, the equilibrium error of the system:

$$\Delta y_t = \mu + \alpha z_{t-1} + \Sigma_{j=1}^{k} \Gamma_j \Delta y_{t-j} + e_t \ . \tag{2}$$

A striking feature of the regression system (1) is the absence of a vector of linear time trends as regressors. Yet, this model has been routinely applied to systems of variables that are trending. Johansen (1991) discussed how trending data affect inference. However, there still remain two features of interest that a regression model without trends cannot permit: 1) the presence of trend-stationary variables with non-zero trends, and 2) the possibility of testing for "stochastic cointegration". These features are potentially of substantial practical importance and we discuss, in Section 3, several examples showing their relevance.

The aim of this note is not to argue that Johansen's method implemented using the regression system (1) is faulty or of little practical relevance. On the contrary, our goal is to show that care must be exercised when analyzing multivariate systems allowing nonstationary variables when the data are trending over time.

We first discuss in Section 2 the difference between "stochastic" and "deterministic" cointegration and argue that the former is, in a sense to be made precise, a more relevant concept of cointegration. Section 3 illustrates via examples some pitfalls that can occur if a regression model without trends, such as (1), is used as a basis for inference with trending data. Section 4 presents a table of critical values for the two tests for cointegration proposed by Johansen when trends are included as regressors. Section 5 offers concluding comments and some technical details are collected in an Appendix.

2 Stochastic and Deterministic Cointegration

We consider an n-vector of variables y_t that is described by the sum of a deterministic trend component (TD_t) and a stochastic component (W_t), namely:

$$y_t = TD_t + W_t \ , \tag{3}$$

$$TD_t = \kappa + \delta t \ , \tag{4}$$

$$A(L)W_t = e_t \ , \tag{5}$$

where κ and δ are n-vectors of parameters, $A(L) = I - A_1 L - \cdots - A_p L^p$ with the A_j's n by n matrices of parameters, and $e_t \sim$ i.i.d. $N(0, \Sigma)$.

It is important to note that the Data Generating Process (DGP) considered throughout this paper is the system given by equations (3) to (5). We believe that there are a number of advantages in specifying the DGP this way rather than directly from a reduced form representation such as (1). First, it makes clear what the assumptions about the nature of the trend are, namely at most a first-order polynomial in time. Second, it helps one understand how the parameters of the reduced form are related to the coefficients of primary interest (e.g. the slopes of the trends and the autoregressive coefficients of the matrix polynomial $A(L)$). Most importantly, perhaps, it allows a clear distinction between the DGP and the regression system used to construct the estimates.

Denote by $C_i(L)$ the implied univariate autoregressive lag polynomial associated with variable i. We assume that $C_i(L)$ contains at most one root on the unit circle and that all other roots are outside the unit circle. We say that a variable y_{it} is $I(0)$ if $C_i(L)$ does not contain a unit root, i.e. if W_{it} is a stationary autoregressive process. Such a variable is trend-stationary but is not necessarily stationary as the coefficient on the trend, δ_i, may be non-zero. We say that y_{it} is $I(1)$ if its autoregressive polynomial contains a unit root. Note that we do not rule out the presence of stationary noise components in the system (3) and we thereby allow the system to contain trend-stationary, $I(0)$, variables.

Definitions:

a) A vector of variables y_t is said to be "stochastically cointegrated" if there exists at least one non-zero n-element vector β_i such that $\beta_i' y_t$ is $I(0)$. β_i is then called a cointegrating vector. If there are r such linearly independent vectors, we say that y_t is cointegrated with cointegrating rank r. We define the cointegrating matrix $\beta = (\beta_1, \ldots, \beta_r)$.
b) A vector of variables y_t is said to be "deterministically cointegrated" if (a) holds and β satisfies the further restriction that $\beta'\delta = 0$.

If y_t is stochastically cointegrated with cointegrating rank r, there are r linearly independent combinations of the variables y_t that are $I(0)$. These combinations may have nonzero deterministic trends. If y_t is deterministically cointegrated with cointegrating rank r, the r combinations of the data that are $I(0)$ must be stationary with no deterministic trends. In other words, under deterministic cointegration the same cointegrating vectors that eliminate stochastic nonstationarity also eliminate deterministic nonstationarity.

Engle and Granger's (1987) definition of cointegration corresponds to what is termed "deterministic cointegration". This distinction between stochastic and deterministic cointegration was first introduced, to our knowledge, by Ogaki and Park (1992) and is discussed in more detail in Campbell and Perron (1991). At first, it may seem redundant to have these two separate definitions. Indeed, any stochastically cointegrated system can be made deterministically cointegrated by augmenting the system with a deterministic trend variable, i.e. $y_t^{*\prime} = (y_t', t)$ is deterministically cointegrated if y_t is stochastically cointegrated. However, we feel that the distinction is important enough to warrant separate definitions since stochastic cointegration is a useful concept as we now discuss.

One of the important properties of cointegrated systems is described by the so-called Granger representation theorem which states that any cointegrated system has an error correction representation. An interesting fact is that this property holds under stochastic cointegration, i.e. regardless of whether the cointegrating vectors eliminate the deterministic nonstationarity. This feature has, we believe, been overlooked in the literature. To see this, note that we can describe y_t as follows (using (3) to (5)):

$$\Delta y_t = \mu^* + \Pi(y_{t-1} - \delta(t-1) - \kappa) + \Sigma_{j=1}^{k} \Gamma_j \Delta y_{t-j} + e_t \ , \tag{6}$$

where $k = p - 1$, $\Pi = -A(1)$, $\Gamma_j = -\Sigma_{i=j+1}^{p} A_i$ $(j = 1, \ldots, k)$, and $\mu^* = (\Phi - \Pi)\delta$, with $\Phi = \Sigma_{i=1}^{p} i A_i$ being the mean lag matrix. We note from (3)–(4) that $y_{t-1} - \delta(t-1) - \kappa = W_{t-1}$, the noise component of the system. If cointegration is present we have the familiar decomposition of Π into $\alpha\beta'$ with α and β n by r matrices. Hence, we can write (6) as:

$$\Delta y_t = \mu^* + \alpha\beta' W_{t-1} + \Sigma_{j=1}^{k} \Gamma_j \Delta y_{t-j} + e_t \ , \tag{7}$$

or

$$\Delta W_t = \mu^{**} + \alpha\beta' W_{t-1} + \Sigma_{j=1}^{k} \Gamma_j \Delta W_{t-j} + e_t \ , \tag{7'}$$

for some constant μ^{**}. Equation (7′) is an error correction model provided $\beta' W_{t-1}$ is stationary. The last condition is equivalent to the requirement that the series be stochastically cointegrated. Thus an error correction representation will exist provided the system is stochastically cointegrated. It is not required that the system be deterministically cointegrated. In this sense, stochastic cointegration may be a more useful definition of cointegration given that Granger's representation theorem (see Engle and Granger (1987)) applies directly. That is, a multivariate system is stochastically cointegrated if and only if it has an error correction representation. Note, in particular, that a system may have an error correction representation of the form (7′) and not be deterministically cointegrated.

Of course, in practice W_t is unobservable and we must resort to an alternative regression model for estimation. The use of the regression system (1) implies a substitution of the actual series y_{t-1} for the noise W_{t-1}. Hence, the implicit assumption for such a regression system to be well specified is that the data be deterministically cointegrated. This can be seen by looking at (6) where the trend terms disappear (and are therefore not necessary regressors) provided $\Pi\delta = 0$ or $\beta'\delta = 0$.

It is also important to remark that the adoption of a regression model such as (1) implies that $I(0)$ variables with non-zero trends are not permitted, while stationary variables without trends are permitted. This can be seen by noting that if a trend-stationary variable is present the system is trivially stochastically cointegrated with a cointegrating vector consisting of zeros and a one for the variable of interest. Since the application of the regression system (1) only permits deterministic cointegration, a non-zero trend for this variable is precluded.

To summarize, regression (1) has the following restrictions: a) it imposes a priori that if cointegration is present it is of the deterministic variety; and b) it precludes the inclusion of $I(0)$ variables with non-zero trends. We now illustrate via examples why it can often be of interest to relax these restrictions and how their imposition can lead to biased inference.

3 Illustrative Examples

We consider a 3 variable system $y_t = (y_{1t}, y_{2t}, y_{3t})$. All variables are characterized by a linear trend function of the form $\kappa_i + \delta_i t$ $(i = 1, 2, 3)$. We assume that y_{2t} and y_{3t} are $I(1)$ variables with non-zero trend coefficients δ_2 and δ_3, respectively. Furthermore, y_{2t} and y_{3t} are stochastically cointegrated such that $y_{2t} - \theta y_{3t}$ is an $I(0)$ variable with non-zero trend coefficient $\delta_2 - \theta\delta_3$. On the other hand, y_{1t} is assumed to be an $I(0)$ process with non-zero trend δ_1. Hence, the system is stochastically cointegrated with two cointegrating vectors given by $\beta_1 = (\psi, 1, -\theta)$, with ψ any real number, and $\beta_2 = (1, 0, 0)$. For the cointegrating matrix to be identified we need r^2 restrictions. To see this, note that abstracting from short run components, the system can be described by the r equations:

$$\beta' y_t + \gamma t = v_t \ , \tag{8}$$

where v_t is a stationary process. Equation (8) can be viewed as a standard structural model with r equations. Hence, a necessary condition for identification is the usual order condition that r^2 restrictions is needed (a sufficient condition is given by the usual rank condition)[4]. With two cointegrating vectors we therefore need four restrictions to identify the model. The specifications discussed above implicitly imposes three restrictions (a normalization for each vectors β_1 and β_2 and the fact that the last two elements of β_2 are proportional to the last two elements of β_1). To obtain the fourth restriction, we set $\psi = 0$

[4] See Park (1990) and Phillips (1991) for details on identification issues.

so that the first cointegrating vector becomes $\beta_1 = (0, 1, -\theta)$. There is no loss of generality in doing so. Under the more restrictive definition of deterministic cointegration there will exist only one cointegrating vector, namely $\beta_1^* = (-a, 1, -\theta)$ where $a = (\delta_2 - \theta\delta_3)/\delta_1$.

To motivate this illustration, let us consider the example where y_{1t} is the logarithm of real income, y_{2t} is the logarithm of the money stock and y_{3t} is the logarithm of an aggregate price index. In this case, real income is trend-stationary while money and prices are $I(1)$ processes that are stochastically cointegrated[5]. Note that, in general, velocity will be an $I(1)$ process with a non-zero trend. It will be $I(0)$ if $\theta = 1$, i.e. if real money balances are $I(0)$ and will additionally be trendless if $(\delta_2 - \delta_3)/\delta_1 = 1$ which corresponds to the case of deterministic cointegration with cointegrating vector $\beta_1^* = (-1, 1, -1)$.

As an alternative example consider the system analyzed by Ogaki (1992) who studies expenditure shares on food using addilog utility. In his case y_{1t} is food consumption, y_{2t} is consumption on other goods and y_{3t} is the relative price of food (all variables are in logarithmic form). Ogaki argues that the food consumption series is $I(0)$ and that the series of consumption of other goods and the relative price of food are $I(1)$. All three series have a non zero trend and consumption on other goods and the relative price of food are stochastically but not deterministically cointegrated. He also argues that $y_{1t} - \alpha_1 y_{2t} - \alpha_2 y_{3t}$ is stationary where α_1 and α_2 are addilog utility parameters.

Consider now a simple specification of the short-run dynamics of the system in the velocity example. We assume that the noise function is a vector $AR(1)$ process $W_t = AW_{t-1} + e_t$ where $W_t = (w_{1t}, w_{2t}, w_{3t})$, $e_t = (e_{1t}, e_{2t}, e_{3t})$ are i.i.d. innovations that are contemporaneously uncorrelated; $A = [A_{ij}; i, j = 1, 2, 3]$ are fixed coefficients. Under the assumptions described above the model's error correction representation is given by:

$$\begin{bmatrix} \Delta y_{1t} \\ \Delta y_{2t} \\ \Delta y_{3t} \end{bmatrix} = \begin{bmatrix} \delta_1 \\ \delta_2 \\ \delta_3 \end{bmatrix} + \begin{bmatrix} \alpha_{11} & \alpha_{12} \\ \alpha_{21} & \alpha_{22} \\ \alpha_{31} & \alpha_{32} \end{bmatrix} \begin{bmatrix} 0 & 1 & -\theta \\ 1 & 0 & 0 \end{bmatrix} \begin{bmatrix} w_{1t-1} \\ w_{2t-1} \\ w_{3t-1} \end{bmatrix} + \begin{bmatrix} e_{1t} \\ e_{2t} \\ e_{3t} \end{bmatrix}$$
$$= \begin{bmatrix} \delta_1 \\ \delta_2 \\ \delta_3 \end{bmatrix} + \begin{bmatrix} \alpha_{11}(w_{2t-1} - \theta w_{3t-1}) + \alpha_{12} w_{1t-1} \\ \alpha_{21}(w_{2t-1} - \theta w_{3t-1}) + \alpha_{22} w_{1t-1} \\ \alpha_{31}(w_{2t-1} - \theta w_{3t-1}) + \alpha_{33} w_{1t-1} \end{bmatrix} + \begin{bmatrix} e_{1t} \\ e_{2t} \\ e_{3t} \end{bmatrix}. \quad (9)$$

Suppose, for the sake of illustration that y_{2t} is not Granger caused by y_{1t} in which case $\alpha_{22} = 0$ but is caused by innovations to y_{3t} ($\alpha_{21} \neq 0$) (in the first example, money is not caused by income but is caused by prices). Suppose also that y_{2t} does not cause y_{1t} ($\alpha_{11} = 0$) (i.e. money does not cause income in our

---

[5] This characterization is not exactly what the data appear to suggest. However, it can be argued that it is close to what is suggested by empirical tests based on historical U.S. data if allowance is made for breaks in the trend function in 1929 (the intercept) and 1973 (the slope). See Perron (1989, 1990), in particular. This generalization would, however, take us away from the intended purpose of this note.

example). We now ask what the application of regression (1), with trends not included in the regression, will tell us about the pattern of causality and the number of cointegrating vectors present.

Consider first the case where all three variables are incorporated in a regression model such as (1) without trends. As mentioned above, since only deterministic cointegration is permitted in this framework, the outcome of the test will be (for large enough samples) that there is only one cointegrating vector given by $\beta_1^* = (-a, 1, -\theta)$ where $a = (\delta_2 - \theta\delta_3)/\delta_1$. Hence, the implied error correction model is

$$\begin{bmatrix} \Delta y_{1t} \\ \Delta y_{2t} \\ \Delta y_{3t} \end{bmatrix} = \begin{bmatrix} \delta_1 \\ \delta_2 \\ \delta_3 \end{bmatrix} + \begin{bmatrix} \alpha_1^* \\ \alpha_2^* \\ \alpha_3^* \end{bmatrix} [-a \quad 1 \quad -\theta] \begin{bmatrix} w_{1t-1} \\ w_{2t-1} \\ w_{3t-1} \end{bmatrix} + \begin{bmatrix} e_{1t} \\ e_{2t} \\ e_{3t} \end{bmatrix}$$
$$= \begin{bmatrix} \delta_1 \\ \delta_2 \\ \delta_3 \end{bmatrix} + \begin{bmatrix} \alpha_1^*(w_{2t-1} - \theta w_{3t-1}) - \alpha_1^* a w_{1t-1} \\ \alpha_2^*(w_{2t-1} - \theta w_{3t-1}) - \alpha_2^* a w_{1t-1} \\ \alpha_3^*(w_{2t-1} - \theta w_{3t-1}) - \alpha_3^* a w_{1t-1} \end{bmatrix} + \begin{bmatrix} e_{1t} \\ e_{2t} \\ e_{3t} \end{bmatrix}. \tag{10}$$

This system does not correspond to the correct error correction model and also yields misleading inference with respect to the causality hypotheses. Consider first the fact that under the true model y_{2t} does not Granger cause y_{1t}. For this to hold in (10), where only the deterministic cointegrating vector is considered, we need $\alpha_1^* = 0$. But this cannot hold since it implies that $\Delta y_{1t} = \mu_1 + e_{1t}$ which is contrary to the stated assumption that y_{1t} is a process without a unit root component. Secondly, consider the hypothesis that y_{2t} is not caused by y_{1t} but is caused by y_{3t}. This cannot hold under (10) since if $\alpha_2^* = 0$, y_{2t} is exogenous, while if $\alpha_2^* \neq 0$, y_{2t} is caused by both y_{1t} and y_{3t}. Hence, not only does the imposition of deterministic cointegration yields misleading inference about the cointegrating relations, it also yields incorrect inference about simple causality relations.

Consider now applying a pre-test for a unit root to each series and applying the cointegration analysis only to the set of variables that are found to be $I(1)$. Again, for large enough samples, tests that allow for the presence of a trend will yield the correct inference that y_{1t} is $I(0)$ while y_{2t} and y_{3t} are $I(1)$. The cointegration tests are then applied to the set $y_t^* = (y_{2t}, y_{3t})$. If use is made of a regression framework such as (1) where no trends are included, the inference will be, in large samples, that no cointegration is present[6].

These problems of inference can be solved by incorporating time trends in the regression system (1), that is by considering a regression system of the form:

---

6 This result is similar to the result described in Perron (1988) concerning univariate unit root tests, which states that if a series is $I(0)$ with a non-zero trend and this trend is not taken into account, unit root tests will never reject the unit root asymptotically. The problem is exactly analogous here since in the model considered y_{2t} and y_{3t} are stochastically but not deterministically cointegrated.

$$\Delta y_t = \mu^* + \delta^* t + \Pi y_{t-1} + \Sigma_{j=1}^{k} \Gamma_j \Delta y_{t-j} + e_t \ . \tag{11}$$

In large samples this will be equivalent to a regression using detrended variables. Since the detrended version of y_t is W_t the regression system (11) looks like equation (7′) in which the noise component W_t enters, as it should, in the cointegrating relations. In that sense, the regression system (11) is well specified even in the cases where trend-stationary processes are present and/or deterministic cointegration does not hold.

Note that the need to use a regression system with trends is not restricted to models where a trend-stationary variable is present. Consider the case of Deaton and Muellbauer's (1980) Almost Ideal Demand System where the dependent variable for each equation is the expenditure share on a given good and the explanatory variables are the logarithm of total real expenditure, the logarithm of the price of the numeraire good and the relative prices (logarithms of the ratios) of all goods other than the numeraire. If consumer choice theory holds in the long run, in particular the implied homogeneity condition, this system is cointegrated. However, as Deaton and Muellbauer (1980) pointed out, time trends are necessary to remove much of the conflict between the data and the theory. Ng (1992) examined the model taking into account the nonstationarity of the variables and allowing tastes and demographics to shift as functions of time. In this extended formulation, the relationship based on aggregate data will involve time trends and stochastic cointegration is the appropriate criterion to judge the long run validity of the theory. Using quarterly US data over the period 1954–1990, Ng cannot reject the null hypothesis of no cointegration when time trends are excluded from the regression, but rejects it, for some equations, when time trends are included. In all cases, the evidence against homogeneity is weaker.

The next section discusses distribution results concerning the limiting distribution of Johansen's maximal eigenvalue and trace statistics when a Gaussian maximum likelihood procedure is applied to (11).

4 Tabulated Critical Values of a Cointegration Test with Trends

The estimation procedure for the regression system (11) is exactly analogous to that for the regression system (1) where no trends are present. For details the reader is referred to Johansen (1991). To summarize briefly, let R_{0t} and R_{1t} be the residuals from a least squares projection of Δy_t and y_{t-1}, respectively, on a vector of constants, a vector of trends and $\{\Delta y_{t-j}; j = 1, \ldots, k\}$. Define the residual product moment matrices by $S_{ij} = T^{-1}\Sigma_{t=1}^{T} R_{it} R'_{jt}$ $(i, j = 0, 1)$. Under the hypothesis of r cointegrating vectors (i.e. $\Pi = \alpha\beta'$, for α and β n by r matrices), the inference can be carried from the equations:

$$R_{0t} = \alpha\beta' R_{1t} + e_t \ . \tag{12}$$

The estimate of β is obtained by reduced rank regression and is found by solving the eigenvalue problem $|\lambda S_{11} - S_{10}S_{00}^{-1}S_{01}| = 0$. The MLE of β is then the matrix of the r eigenvectors, $\beta = (v_1, \ldots, v_r)$, associated with the r largest eigenvalues $\hat{\lambda}_1 > \cdots > \hat{\lambda}_r$. The so-called trace statistic is the likelihood ratio test for the null hypothesis of r cointegrating vectors versus the alternative hypothesis of n cointegrating vectors. It is based on the remaining smallest $n - r$ eigenvalues and is given by:

$$TR_T(n - r) = -T\Sigma_{i=r+1}^{n} ln(1 - \hat{\lambda}_i) \ . \tag{13}$$

Similarly the so-called maximal eigenvalue statistic is the likelihood ratio test for the null hypothesis of r cointegrating vector versus the alternative hypothesis of $r + 1$ cointegrating vectors and is given by:

$$ME_T(n - r) = -Tln(1 - \hat{\lambda}_{r+1}) \ . \tag{14}$$

The asymptotic distribution of these statistics is described in the Appendix. Selected critical values are presented in Table 1.

After completing the first draft of this paper, we became aware of two studies which considered similar testing procedures, namely Johansen (1992) and Osterwald-Lenum (1992). The test discussed by these authors is, however, different. Unlike us, they impose the condition that the trend coefficients of the nonstationary components are zero. To see the validity of these restrictions, note that the coefficients of the time trends in (11) satisfy $\delta^* = \Pi\delta = \alpha\beta'\delta$. Let $\alpha_\perp$ be the n x $(n - r)$ full rank matrix that is orthogonal to α, then we have $\alpha_\perp\delta^* = 0$. Hence, there are $(n - r)$ linear combinations of the coefficients of the vector δ^* that are 0. These zero linear combinations are those corresponding to the $(n - r)$ non-stationary components or common trends. To enforce these restrictions, Johansen (1992) and Osterwald-Lenum (1992) consider the follow-

Table 1. Distribution of the maximal eigenvalue and trace test statistics

Regression: $\Delta y_t = \mu^* + \delta^* t + \Pi y_{t-1} + \Sigma_{j=1}^{k} \Gamma_j \Delta y_{t-j} + e_t$.

$n - r$	50%	80%	90%	95%	97.5%	99%
Maximal Eigenvalue						
1	4.73	7.76	9.75	11.62	13.43	15.74
2	10.21	13.90	16.20	18.33	20.34	22.83
3	15.60	19.85	22.51	24.79	27.02	29.76
4	20.97	25.66	28.51	31.07	33.41	36.40
5	26.33	31.44	34.45	37.09	39.51	42.78
Trace						
1	4.73	7.76	9.75	11.62	13.43	15.74
2	13.80	18.44	21.22	23.65	26.03	28.83
3	26.87	32.98	36.52	39.67	42.55	46.06
4	43.75	51.22	55.57	59.44	62.81	67.06
5	64.52	73.38	78.40	82.68	86.68	91.39

ing regression framework:

$$\Delta y_t = \mu^* + \alpha(\beta', \beta_1)(y'_{t-1}, t)' + \Sigma_{j=1}^{k} \Gamma_j \Delta y_{t-j} + e_t \ , \tag{15}$$

where $\beta_1 = \beta'\delta$ is a r by n matrix of coefficients. Critical values for the trace and maximal eigenvalue statistics for cointegration from (15) are different than those provided here and can be found in Table 2* of Osterwald-Lenum (1992) and Table 4 of Johansen (1992). To better understand the difference between the testing procedure presented here and that of Johansen (1992) and Osterwald-Lenum (1992), we briefly discuss the analogous situation in the univariate case. Suppose that the data for a single series $\{y_t\}$ are generated by

$$y_t = \kappa + \delta t + z_t \ , \qquad z_t = \alpha z_{t-1} + e_t \ , \tag{16}$$

where $\{e_t\}$ is an i.i.d. $(0, \sigma^2)$ sequence. The DGP (16) can alternatively be represented by:

$$y_t = \mu + \beta t + \alpha y_{t-1} + e_t \ , \tag{17}$$

where $\mu = (1 - \alpha)\kappa + \alpha\delta$ and $\beta = (1 - \alpha)\delta$. Under the null hypothesis of a unit root, $\alpha = 1$. In that case $\mu = \delta$ and $\beta = 0$. The latter restriction is of particular relevance since it implies that, under the null hypothesis of a unit root, the coefficient on the trend in (17) is restricted to be zero. In the univariate context, unit root tests are available for both cases where the zero restriction on the coefficient of the trend is imposed or not under the null hypothesis. The most commonly applied unit root test is the $t_{\tilde{\alpha}}$ statistic of Dickey and Fuller (1979) which is based on the t-statistic for testing $\alpha = 1$ in (17) and which thereby does not impose the zero restriction on the coefficient of the trend. An alternative procedure is to use the $\Phi(3)$ statistic of Dickey and Fuller (1981) which jointly tests the null hypothesis that $\alpha = 1$ and $\beta = 0$ in (17).

The test statistic proposed by Johansen (1992) and Osterwald-Lenum (1992) can be seen as the multivariate equivalent of Dickey and Fuller's (1981) $\Phi(3)$ statistic in the univariate context (where the unit root is tested jointly with the zero restriction on the coefficient of the trend). On the other hand, the procedure presented here is equivalent to Dickey and Fuller's (1979) $t_{\tilde{\alpha}}$ statistic where the unit root is tested without imposing the zero restriction on the coefficient of the trend under the null hypothesis.

Simulation evidence in the univariate case tends to show that $t_{\tilde{\alpha}}$ is more powerful than $\Phi(3)$. The simulation results of Toda (1993) show a similar phenomenon in the multivariate context and documents that our procedure is indeed more powerful than that suggested by Johansen (1992) and Osterwald-Lenum (1992).

Note also that Johansen (1992) discusses an asymptotically chi-squared test to assess if the $I(0)$ components are trending or not, i.e. a test of $\delta^* = 0$ in (11). It is important to recognize, however, that the distributional properties of such a test are conditional upon a given cointegrating rank obtained from prior cointegration tests. Hence, even with the availability of this test, one cannot avoid one of the extended procedures discussed above.

5 Concluding Comments

Several points deserve emphasis. First, we are not suggesting that all empirical studies dealing with trending data should use a regression model with time trends included. Our intention is to highlight the fact that in some empirical applications of interest the presence or absence of the trend components in the estimated model can lead to quite different inferences. We have shown that in some realistic cases the inclusion of trends is necessary.

The advantages of incorporating a trend vector in a regression model for trending data are as follows: a) it permits the presence of $I(0)$ series with non-zero trends; b) it avoids the dependence of the limiting distribution of the statistics on the trend characteristics of the data; c) it allows one to test the hypothesis of stochastic cointegration, which we have argued may, in many cases, be the hypothesis of interest. Indeed, as we have shown, stochastic cointegration is the relevant condition for a cointegrated system to have an error correction representation. The disadvantages are: a) it tests stochastic cointegration instead of deterministic cointegration (which in many applications is the hypothesis of interest), b) by analogy with univariate unit root tests, it is likely to yield test statistics with lower power if indeed deterministic cointegration holds.

Technical Appendix

Theorem 1: Suppose that the data are generated by the model described by equations (3) through (5) and that the statistics $TR_T(n-r)$ and $ME_T(n-r)$ are given by (13) and (14) respectively with $\hat{\lambda}_i$ $(i = 1, \ldots, n)$ the eigenvalues resulting from the application of Gaussian MLE to the regression model (11). Denoting weak convergence in distribution by "⇒", we have:

$$a)\ TR_T(n-r) \Rightarrow tr\left\{\int_0^1 (dW)F'\left[\int_0^1 FF'dt\right]^{-1}\int_0^1 F(dW')\right\},$$

$$b)\ ME_T(n-r) \Rightarrow \lambda_{\max}\left\{\int_0^1 (dW)F'\left[\int_0^1 FF'dt\right]^{-1}\int_0^1 F(dW')\right\},$$

where $tr(\cdot)$ denotes the trace of the matrix, and $\lambda_{\max}(\cdot)$ its associated maximal eigenvalue. $W(t) = \{W_1(t), \ldots, W_{n-r}(t)\}$ is an $n-r$ dimensional Wiener process with identity covariance matrix, and $F(t) = \{F_1(t), \ldots, F_{n-r}(t)\}$ where $F_i(t)$ $(i = 1, \ldots, n-r)$ are defined as the residual processes from a projection of the Wiener processes $W_i(t)$ on the functions $\{1, t\}$.

The proof of Theorem 1 is entirely analogous to the proof presented by Johansen (1991) for the case where no trends are present and is therefore omitted. We simply mention the crucial feature that the asymptotic distribution of the statistics are invariant to the value of the coefficients δ associated with the trends. Therefore, unlike Johansen's (1991) regression system (1), there is no need to analyze separately the cases where the series are trending or not trending.

Percentages points of the limiting distributions stated in Theorem 1 were obtained in a manner analogous to that described in the appendix of Johansen and Juselius (1990) except for the following features: a) we approximate $\int FF'dt$ by $N^{-2}\Sigma_{j=1}^{N}(X_{j-1} - X_{-1}^{*})(X_{j-1} - X_{-1}^{*})'$ and $\int FdW'$ by $N^{-1}\Sigma_{j=1}^{N}(X_{j-1} - X_{-1}^{*})\varepsilon_j'$, where ε_j is an $n - r$ vector of i.i.d. $N(0, 1)$ random variables, $X_j = \Sigma_{s=1}^{j}\varepsilon_s$, and X_{-1}^{*} is the projection of $X_{-1} = \{X_0, \ldots, X_{N-1}\}(X_0 = 0)$ on a constant and a trend; b) we use $N = 1000$ steps in the calculations; and c) we use 50,000 replications.

References

Campbell JY, Perron P (1991) Pitfalls and opportunities: What macroeconomists should know about unit roots. In: NBER Macroeconomics Annual Blanchard OJ, Fischer S (eds) Cambridge MIT Press 141–201

Deaton A, Muellbauer J (1980) An almost ideal demand system. American Economic Review 70: 312–326

Dickey DA, Fuller WA (1979) Distribution of the estimators for autoregressive time series with a unit root. Journal of the American Statistical Association 74:427–431

Dickey DA, Fuller WA (1981) Likelihood ratio statistics for autoregressive time series with a unit root. Econometrica 49:1057–1072

Engle RF, Granger CWJ (1987) Co-integration and error correction: representation, estimation and testing. Econometrica 55:251–276

Johansen S (1989) Likelihood based inference on cointegration theory and applications. Centro Interuniversitario di Econometria, Bologna

Johansen S (1991) Estimation and hypothesis testing of cointegration vectors in Gaussian vector autoregressive models. Econometrica 59:1551–1580

Johansen S (1992) The role of the constant term in cointegration analysis of nonstationary variables. Forthcoming in Econometric Reviews

Johansen S, Juselius K (1990) Maximum likelihood estimation and inference on cointegration—with applications to the demand for money. Oxford Bulletin of Economics and Statistics 52:169–210

Ng S (1992) Testing for homogeneity in demand systems with non-stationary regressors. Mimeo, Princeton University

Ogaki M (1992) Engel's law and cointegration. Journal of Political Economy 100:1027–1046

Ogaki M, Park JY (1992) A cointegration approach to estimating preference parameters. Mimeo, University of Rochester

Osterwald-Lenum M (1992) A note with quantiles of the asymptotic distribution of the maximum likelihood cointegration rank test statistics. Oxford Bulletin of Economics and Statistics 54:461–471

Park JY (1990) Maximum likelihood estimation of simultaneous cointegrated models. Memo 1990-18, Institute of Economics, University of Aarhus

Perron P (1988) Trends and random walks in macroeconomic time series: Further evidence from a new approach. Journal of Economic Dynamics and Control 12:297–332

Perron P (1989) The great crash, the oil price shock and the unit root hypothesis. Econometrica 57:1361–1401

Perron P (1990) Further evidence on breaking trend functions in macroeconomic variables. Econometric Research Program Memorandum 350 Princeton University

Phillips PCB (1991) Unidentified components in reduced rank regression estimation of ECM's. Cowles Foundation Discussion Paper 1003 Yale University

Toda HY (1993) Finite sample properties of likelihood ratio tests for cointegrating ranks when linear trends are present. Manuscript, University of Tsukuba

Small Sample Bias in Conditional Sum-of-Squares Estimators of Fractionally Integrated ARMA Models[1]

CHING-FAN CHUNG AND RICHARD T. BAILLIE

Department of Economics, Michigan State University, 101 Marshall Hall, East Lansing, Michigan 48824-1038, USA

Abstract: This paper considers estimation of the parameters for the fractionally integrated class of processes known as ARFIMA. We consider the small sample properties of a conditional sum-of-squares estimator that is asymptotically equivalent to MLE. This estimator has the advantage of being relatively simple and can estimate all the parameters, including the mean, simultaneously. The simulation evidence we present indicates that estimation of the mean can make a considerable difference to the small sample bias and MSE of the other parameter estimates.

JEL Classification System-Number: C22

1 Introduction

This paper is concerned with the estimation of fractionally integrated $I(d)$ time-series processes, which were originally introduced by Granger (1980), Granger and Joyeux (1980), and Hosking (1981). An $I(d)$ process exhibits long memory and generates very slow, but eventual, decay in its impulse-response weights, or moving-average representation. Hence, one attraction of $I(d)$ processes is that they avoid knife-edge choices between unit-root $I(1)$ processes, which generate complete persistence, and the alternative of stationary and invertible ARMA models, which imply relatively rapid exponential decay in their impulse-response weights. There has recently been considerable interest in the possibility that many macroeconomic and financial time series possess long-memory properties consistent with $I(d)$ behavior. Studies by Shea (1989, 1991), Diebold and Rudebusch (1989, 1991), Sowell (1992b), Baillie, Chung, and Tieslau (1992) and others have applied $I(d)$ processes to a variety of economic problems.

Section 2 of this paper provides a brief survey of some characteristics of the fractional white noise process and the ARFIMA(p, d, q) model where the $I(d)$ behavior is appended with ARMA behavior. Section 3 then discusses different estimation procedures that have been suggested for the ARFIMA process. The most attractive estimator currently available is a full maximum likelihood estimator (MLE) proposed by Sowell (1992a). A recent study by Cheung and Die-

[1] We gratefully acknowledge helpful comments from the editor, Baldev Raj, and three anonymous referees.

bold (1993) has provided further simulation evidence on the performance of Sowell's full MLE in estimating the fractional white noise, or ARFIMA(0, d, 0) model, compared to an approximate MLE of Fox and Taqqu (1986). When the mean of the process is known, Cheung and Diebold not surprisingly find Sowell's estimator to be quite satisfactory. However, when the mean of the process is unknown, the approximate MLE of Fox and Taqqu yields similar biases and mean squared errors of the parameter estimates.

The main contribution of this paper is to provide a further study about the small sample performance of the estimation of the ARFIMA model based on the conditional sum-of-squares (CSS) estimator. With the initial observations fixed, the CSS estimator is asymptotically equivalent to full MLE (a brief proof of this is provided in the appendix). The CSS estimator has been widely used for ARMA models, transfer function models, ARCH and GARCH models, and has been suggested for $I(d)$ processes by Hosking (1984) and Li and McLeod (1986). In section 3 of this paper we discuss some of the advantages of the CSS estimator. In particular, the CSS estimator can deal with quite complicated ARFIMA models with non-normal disturbances and innovations that exhibit time-dependent heteroskedasticity of the ARCH form.

The results of a detailed simulation study are reported in section 4. Unlike previous work in this area, this paper considers the estimation of ARFIMA(p, d, q) processes with p and q equal to 1 or 2, as opposed to the pure fractional white-noise case. Since the CSS estimator is asymptotically equivalent to MLE, our interest is in determining its performance in small samples. In particular, we find that when the unknown mean is estimated jointly with the fractional differencing parameter d and the ARMA parameters, substantial bias may result in small sample. Interestingly, when we evaluate three different estimators of the mean, we find that in some cases the sample median may perform better than the more usual sample mean or the MLE of the mean.

2 Fractional Integrated Processes

Following Granger (1980, 1981), Granger and Joyeux (1980), and Hosking (1981), a discretely observed time-series process y_t, with mean μ is said to be integrated of order d, i.e., $I(d)$, if

$$(1 - L)^d(y_t - \mu) = u_t \ , \tag{1}$$

where u_t is a weakly stationary $I(0)$ process and $-0.5 < d < 0.5$. For $0 < d < 0.5$, the process y_t exhibits long memory in the sense that its autocorrelations will have a hyperbolic rate of convergence. For $-0.5 < d < 0$, the process y_t is said to have intermediate memory. If u_t is a stationary and invertible ARMA process, then y_t is generated by the Autoregressive Fractionally Integrated

Moving Average, or ARFIMA(p, d, q) process:

$$\phi(L)(1-L)^d(y_t-\mu)=\theta(L)\varepsilon_t\ , \tag{2}$$

where $\phi(L)=1-\sum_{j=1}^{p}\phi_j L^j$ and $\theta(L)=1+\sum_{j=1}^{q}\theta_j L^j$ are polynomials in the lag operator of order p and q respectively and have all their roots lying outside the unit circle, and ε_t is a white-noise sequence with a variance σ^2. Granger (1981) and Hosking (1981) show that the infinite autoregressive weights, the infinite moving-average representation weights and the autocorrelation functions all decline at a hyperbolic rate, as opposed to the conventional exponential rate associated with the stationary and invertible class of ARMA processes. For example, for the fractionally integrated white-noise process

$$(1-L)^d(y_t-\mu)=\varepsilon_t\ , \tag{3}$$

provided $d<0.5$, the process will be stationary and will possess the infinite moving-average representation,

$$y_t=\sum_{j=0}^{\infty}\psi_j\varepsilon_{t-j}\ , \tag{4}$$

where $\psi_j=\Gamma(j+d)/[\Gamma(d)\Gamma(j+1)]$. Also, provided $d>-0.5$ the process will be invertible and can be expressed as an infinite autoregressive representation,

$$y_t=-\sum_{j=1}^{\infty}\pi_j y_{t-j}+\varepsilon_t\ , \tag{5}$$

where $\pi_j=\Gamma(j-d)/[\Gamma(-d)\Gamma(j+1)]$. The autocorrelation coefficients ρ_j for the fractional white-noise ARFIMA(0, d, 0) process are given by:

$$\rho_j=\frac{\Gamma(j+d)\Gamma(1-d)}{\Gamma(j-d+1)\Gamma(d)}\ .$$

Parametric expressions for the autocorrelations of the general ARFIMA (p, d, q) process are given by Sowell (1992a). They are complicated functions of the hypergeometric function. However, for large lags, hyperbolic decay takes place in the autoregressive representation weights, the moving-average representation weights and the autocorrelations of the ARFIMA(p, d, q) process. In particular, Granger (1980) and Hosking (1981) show that

$$\pi_j\sim j^{-(1+d)}\ ,\qquad \psi_j\sim j^{d-1}\qquad \text{and}\qquad \rho_j\sim j^{(2d-1)}\ .$$

3 Estimation of Fractionally Integrated Processes

We now consider estimation of the $p+q+3$ dimensional vector of parameters $\lambda=(d,\mu,\phi_1,\ldots\phi_p,\theta_1,\ldots\theta_q,\sigma^2)$. Several different approaches have been suggested for parameter estimation. First, Geweke and Porter-Hudak (1983) suggested a two-step estimator that allowed d to be estimated from a regression of ordinates of the periodogram of y_t on a trigonometric function. Although the estimator is straightforward to apply and is potentially robust to non-Gaussian disturbances, Agiakoglou, Newbold and Wohar (1992) have recently shown this estimator to be severely biased in the presence of strong autocorrelation in the u_t process. There is the additional disadvantage that it is a two-step estimator, and the ARMA parameters would have to be estimated from a series with the $I(d)$ component removed by filtering.

An approximate maximum likelihood procedure in the frequency domain has been suggested by Fox and Taqqu (1986). The estimator assumes unconditional normality and numerically minimizes the quantity

$$\frac{\sigma^2}{2\pi}\int_{-\pi}^{\pi}\frac{1}{f(\omega)}\left|\sum_{t=0}^{T-1} y_t e^{it\omega}\right|^2 d\omega \ ,$$

where $f(\omega) = \dfrac{\sigma^2}{2\pi}\dfrac{\theta(e^{i\omega})\theta(e^{-i\omega})}{\phi(e^{i\omega})\phi(e^{-i\omega})}\dfrac{1}{|1-e^{-i\omega}|^{2d}}$ is the spectral density evaluated at frequency ω.

In a seminal paper, Sowell (1992a) was able to derive the full maximum likelihood estimator (MLE) for the ARFIMA(p, d, q) process with normally distributed innovations. Following Sowell (1992a), and under normality, the logarithm of the likelihood can be expressed in the time domain as

$$L(\lambda) = -\frac{T}{2}\log 2\pi - \frac{1}{2}\log|\Sigma| - \frac{1}{2}(y-\mu)'\Sigma^{-1}(y-\mu) \ ,$$

where y is the T dimensional vector of y_t and Σ is the corresponding $T \times T$ autocovariance matrix, where each element is a non-linear function of hypergeometric functions. Sowell (1992b) has also provided a detailed example of the application of his estimator to US real GNP data.

In this paper we consider the properties of an alternative conditional sum-of-squares (CSS) estimator which minimizes

$$\begin{aligned} S(\lambda) &= \frac{1}{2}\log\sigma^2 + \frac{1}{2\sigma^2}\sum_{t=1}^{T}\varepsilon_t^2 \\ &= \frac{1}{2}\log\sigma^2 + \frac{1}{2\sigma^2}\sum_{t=1}^{T}[\phi(L)\theta(L)^{-1}(1-L)^d(y_t-\mu)]^2 \ . \end{aligned}$$

If the initial observations $y_0, y_{-1}, y_{-2}, \ldots$ are assumed fixed, then minimizing the conditional sum-of-squares function will be asymptotically equivalent to MLE. The minimum CSS procedure in the context of ARFIMA processes was originally suggested by Hosking (1984). It is worth noting that similar estimation methods have been implemented in the stationary and invertible class of ARMA models. Box and Jenkins (1976) used the minimum CSS estimator, while Newbold (1974) considered the full MLE with the initial observations treated as stochastic. For an infinite number of observations the CSS estimator will be equivalent to MLE. In the appendix we show that the effect of initial observations is negligible asymptotically. Similar results for ARMA processes are provided by Pierce (1971).

There are several reasons for considering the CSS estimator of potential interest for practical applications. First, it is readily extendable to situations where the innovations possess time-dependent heteroskedasticity of the ARCH form. It is well known that even for relatively simple non-linear dynamic models, e.g., Engel's (1982) ARCH process, full MLE is intractable and a type of CSS estimator has to be used. Indeed, in a study on the variability of inflation, Baillie, Chung and Tieslau (1992) use the CSS approach to estimate the parameters of an ARFIMA(0, d, 1)-GARCH(1, 1) process with a conditional density of student t. While it is beyond the range of the present study to examine the properties of the CSS estimator in such a complex setting, it is desirable to look at the CSS estimator for at least some simple ARFIMA models.

Secondly, although Sowell's (1992a) work provides an elegant approach for computing the full MLEs of the "vanilla" ARFIMA model with unconditional normality and no ARCH effects, it is nevertheless computationally demanding, with every iteration of the likelihood requiring inversion of a T-dimensional covariance matrix and having each element a non-linear function of hypergeometric functions.

A third reason for being interested in the CSS estimator is that it does share many features with the the approximate MLE[2] of Fox and Taqqu (1986) when the basic vanilla ARFIMA model is being estimated; and in many cases the Fox-Taqqu estimator has at least as desirable characteristics as the full MLE of Sowell. Some simulation evidence on the relative performance of Sowell's full MLE and the approximate MLE of Fox and Taqqu (1986) has been provided by Cheung and Diebold (1993). In the case of the mean μ being known, Cheung and Diebold document the excellent performance of Sowell's (1992a) full MLE. However, when μ is unknown and has to be estimated, they found the Fox-Taqqu estimator to perform as well as the full MLE. The simulation study of Cheung and Diebold is confined to the ARFIMA(0, d, 0), case. It is of interest to see whether the CSS estimator shares similar properties with the Fox-Taqqu estimator. By extending the range of our investigation to include ARFIMA (p, d, q) models instead of just the fractional white-noise ARFIMA(0, d, 0) model, we hope to gain further insight into this problem. It is possible that the inclusion of ARMA parameters will exacerbate the bias problems caused by estimation of the unknown mean estimator. One of the purposes of our simulation study is to assess this issue on both the parameter estimates and their standard errors.

---

2 While it is not the purpose of this study to compare the CSS estimator with the full MLE of Sowell (1992a), it should be noted that we have some preliminary work on this issue and which is available from us on request. Initial work with a relatively small number of replications suggests the CSS estimator performs about the same as the full MLE in sample sizes of $T = 100$.

Li and McLeod (1986) have shown that with μ equal to zero, the estimates of the remaining parameters are $T^{1/2}$ consistent and have conjectured that they are also asymptotically normal. Taqqu (1975) has considered the sample mean of fractional white noise, while Yajima (1988) has considered the properties of OLS and GLS estimates in the regression model with $I(d)$ disturbances. A corollary of these results is that the sample mean is convergent at a rate of $T^{1/2-d}$ to its limiting distribution. Due to the unusually slow (when d is greater than 0) convergence rate of the estimator of μ, an important issue concerns the performance of the estimation with μ being jointly estimated. As previously described, the study by Cheung and Diebold (1993) noted the unexpected performance of Sowell's full MLE of the fractional-differencing parameter d when μ is unknown in an ARFIMA(0, d, 0) model. Our simulation study goes one step further to examine the effect of the estimation of μ on all parameters in an ARFIMA(p, d, q) model.

4 Simulation Results

In this section we report the results of the simulation of the small sample properties of the CSS estimator with all the parameters estimated simultaneously. We consider different values of p and q as 0, 1 or 2. Hence our study is the first to consider the estimation of the $I(d)$ process in the presence of ARMA parameters and an unknown mean.

Unless stated to the contrary all the simulations were based on 500 replications of a sample size of 100. For each replication 100 values were generated from the standard normal random variable and assigned into a column vector denoted by e. We then computed the analytic autocovariance matrix Σ together with its Cholesky decomposition matrix[3] denoted by C, i.e., $\Sigma = CC'$. As mentioned earlier, the autocovariance matrix Σ was first derived by Sowell (1992a) who presented complete formulas that involve combinations of hypergeometric functions. The vector y of 100 realized values is then constructed as:

$$y = \mu + Ce ,$$

where μ is the mean of the process.[4] The Monte Carlo results are independent of the mean and variance and for convenience both μ and σ^2 were set as one

[3] All our computations are conducted using the personal computer programming language GAUSS, including Cholesky decomposition, which is also available in many other software packages.

[4] It has been suggested in the literature that, in order for the long-memory ARFIMA series y not to be affected by "the initial values," it is advisable to simulate longer series and drop the first subset of values. We find that such a practice is unnecessary if y is simulated using our method.

throughout the study. For each configuration of parameter values the CSS estimator is computed for each realization. Apart from the CSS estimator of μ we also report the median, since this may be more robust to "outliers" caused by the persistence of the autocovariances of an ARFIMA process.

As usual, the estimator of the asymptotic covariance matrix of the parameter estimates is based on the numerically computed Hessian. Part of the interest in our simulation study is to assess the accuracy of the estimated standard errors with the theoretical standard errors.

The simulation results[5] are summarized in Tables 1A through 1C. In each block on the extreme left, the true parameter values used in the data-generating process are given. For the ARFIMA(1, d, 0) process, values of ϕ corresponding to 0.7, 0.2, -0.3 and -0.8 are used. For the ARFIMA(0, d, 1) process values of θ corresponding to 0.9, 0.5, -0.3 and -0.8 are used. For ARFIMA(1, d, 1) processes the assigned values for the ARMA parameters are the four different combinations of ± 0.2 and ± 0.5. For each data-generating process, the next three blocks in Tables 1A–1C, under the headings CSS, Mean, Median, contain the estimation biases, as well as the square roots of the mean square errors (SRMSE) in the parentheses, based on 500 replications. For each replication μ is estimated by the CSS, the sample mean, and the sample median, respectively. The CSS method estimates all the parameters simultaneously while the other methods estimate μ by the sample mean or median before estimating the other parameters. The simulation results for the estimates of σ^2 are omitted to save space. Since we are especially interested in the estimates of the fractional difference parameter d, the least bias in estimating d among the three estimation procedures is underlined in each row.

The main conclusion resulting from these tables is that, with a sample size of 100, the bias in estimating the ARFIMA model by CSS can be quite substantial when the mean μ is also estimated. A closer examination of the Monte Carlo results shows the following patterns: (a) when the true values of d, ϕ, and θ are all positive, the CSS estimator contains relatively small biases; (b) when the true values of d, ϕ, and θ are all negative, estimation based on the sample mean produces the least bias; (c) for all other cases, estimation based on sample medians generally produces the least bias, which may be due to the median being robust to outliers.

One interesting aspect of the study concerns the degree to which the parameter estimation bias is due to the intercept μ being estimated. Before examining this issue, we first note that Table 1C for the model ARFIMA(1, 0.3, 1) contains some of the most substantial biases. When the values of the ARMA parameters ϕ and θ are both positive, the best estimator (based on the MLE of μ) of d gives a downward bias that is greater than 0.2. Moderate bias is also observed when the ARMA parameters have negative values. These typical results based on the

---

5 Simulations based on ARFIMA(2, d, 0) and ARFIMA(0, d, 2) processes have also been conducted. The results are similar to those reported in this paper.

Table 1A. Simulation of the ARFIMA (1, d, 0) model

True		CSS			Mean			Median		
d	ϕ	d	ϕ	μ	d	ϕ	μ	d	ϕ	μ
0.3	0.7	0.010	−0.042	0.121	−0.086	0.023	0.140	−0.099	0.034	0.020
		(0.233)	(0.201)	(2.142)	(0.185)	(0.149)	(1.469)	(0.169)	(0.136)	(1.398)
0.3	0.2	−0.240	0.192	0.031	−0.270	0.222	0.010	−0.221	0.182	−0.030
		(0.335)	(0.318)	(0.587)	(0.321)	(0.312)	(0.533)	(0.285)	(0.286)	(0.512)
0.3	−0.3	−0.106	0.081	0.004	−0.098	0.072	−0.001	−0.069	0.053	0.001
		(0.217)	(0.222)	(0.334)	(0.159)	(0.166)	(0.331)	(0.150)	(0.163)	(0.325)
0.3	−0.8	−0.054	0.031	−0.004	−0.057	0.032	−0.004	−0.035	0.023	−0.002
		(0.107)	(0.079)	(0.236)	(0.103)	(0.074)	(0.233)	(0.095)	(0.075)	(0.256)
0.	0.7	−0.063	0.007	0.012	−0.106	0.038	0.017	−0.090	0.033	0.023
		(0.217)	(0.173)	(0.499)	(0.170)	(0.126)	(0.308)	(0.166)	(0.130)	(0.339)
0.	0.2	−0.270	0.220	−0.001	−0.248	0.199	−0.005	−0.151	0.124	0.002
		(0.319)	(0.308)	(0.136)	(0.285)	(0.288)	(0.123)	(0.252)	(0.265)	(0.150)
0.	−0.3	−0.093	0.070	0.004	−0.092	0.068	0.004	−0.036	0.031	0.005
		(0.153)	(0.171)	(0.082)	(0.142)	(0.162)	(0.076)	(0.128)	(0.145)	(0.115)
0.	−0.8	−0.059	0.030	−0.001	−0.052	0.027	−0.000	0.023	0.010	−0.011
		(0.100)	(0.073)	(0.059)	(0.096)	(0.069)	(0.058)	(0.093)	(0.067)	(0.116)
−0.3	0.7	−0.100	0.037	0.007	−0.094	0.037	0.002	−0.011	−0.023	0.002
		(0.158)	(0.124)	(0.106)	(0.161)	(0.128)	(0.107)	(0.183)	(0.169)	(0.129)
−0.3	0.2	−0.179	0.149	0.000	−0.127	0.098	−0.002	0.050	−0.050	−0.001
		(0.270)	(0.281)	(0.040)	(0.237)	(0.256)	(0.041)	(0.196)	(0.211)	(0.086)
−0.3	−0.3	−0.085	0.062	−0.001	−0.049	0.033	0.003	0.118	−0.056	−0.000
		(0.149)	(0.157)	(0.025)	(0.118)	(0.138)	(0.027)	(0.131)	(0.117)	(0.087)
−0.3	−0.8	−0.028	0.024	−0.001	−0.013	0.022	−0.000	0.181	−0.012	0.001
		(0.105)	(0.073)	(0.019)	(0.091)	(0.070)	(0.022)	(0.138)	(0.065)	(0.114)

Among the three estimates of d in each row, the one with the least bias is underlined.
All simulations were based on 500 replications of a sample size of 100.

Table 1B. Simulation of the ARFIMA (0, *d*, 1) model

True		CSS			Mean			Median		
d	θ	d	θ	μ	d	θ	μ	d	θ	μ
0.3	0.9	0.005	−0.018	−0.029	−0.048	−0.037	−0.005	−0.046	−0.034	−0.029
		(0.123)	(0.055)	(1.564)	(0.101)	(0.070)	(0.801)	(0.100)	(0.068)	(0.819)
0.3	0.5	−0.045	0.021	−0.055	−0.047	0.020	0.014	−0.050	0.023	−0.003
		(0.123)	(0.119)	(0.736)	(0.117)	(0.108)	(0.613)	(0.111)	(0.108)	(0.623)
0.3	−0.3	−0.138	0.123	−0.018	−0.140	0.127	−0.011	−0.108	0.097	0.014
		(0.212)	(0.221)	(0.311)	(0.199)	(0.213)	(0.290)	(0.190)	(0.209)	(0.318)
0.3	−0.8	−0.398	0.359	0.006	−0.307	0.279	−0.008	−0.075	0.086	0.002
		(0.357)	(0.347)	(0.087)	(0.334)	(0.338)	(0.090)	(0.272)	(0.249)	(0.123)
0.	0.9	−0.038	−0.018	−0.002	−0.047	−0.021	−0.005	−0.033	−0.021	0.002
		(0.104)	(0.058)	(0.259)	(0.099)	(0.060)	(0.187)	(0.091)	(0.060)	(0.208)
0.	0.5	−0.062	0.037	0.011	−0.055	0.023	0.005	−0.036	0.023	−0.008
		(0.116)	(0.112)	(0.150)	(0.109)	(0.112)	(0.148)	(0.094)	(0.110)	(0.179)
0.	−0.3	−0.139	0.123	0.006	−0.145	0.132	−0.004	−0.021	0.020	−0.003
		(0.202)	(0.213)	(0.071)	(0.186)	(0.190)	(0.068)	(0.204)	(0.229)	(0.099)
0.	−0.8	−0.317	0.304	0.001	−0.165	0.157	0.002	0.105	0.023	0.002
		(0.342)	(0.337)	(0.021)	(0.296)	(0.287)	(0.024)	(0.191)	(0.134)	(0.096)
−0.3	0.9	−0.039	−0.012	−0.002	−0.033	−0.017	−0.006	0.026	−0.017	−0.002
		(0.100)	(0.056)	(0.061)	(0.093)	(0.056)	(0.066)	(0.088)	(0.059)	(0.115)
−0.3	0.5	−0.056	0.022	−0.003	−0.043	0.023	0.002	0.032	−0.009	−0.002
		(0.119)	(0.112)	(0.046)	(0.110)	(0.110)	(0.048)	(0.104)	(0.114)	(0.088)
−0.3	−0.3	−0.127	0.122	0.002	−0.080	0.080	−0.001	0.305	−0.246	0.004
		(0.206)	(0.217)	(0.023)	(0.180)	(0.204)	(0.025)	(0.280)	(0.266)	(0.089)
−0.3	−0.8	−0.112	0.150	−0.000	0.015	0.061	−0.001	0.309	0.016	−0.005
		(0.243)	(0.214)	(0.011)	(0.183)	(0.142)	(0.015)	(0.182)	(0.068)	(0.101)

Among the three estimates of *d* in each row, the one with the least bias is underlined.
All simulations were based on 500 replications of a sample size of 100.

Table 1C. Simulation of the ARFIMA (1, d, 1) model

True			CSS				Mean				Median			
d	ϕ	θ	d	ϕ	θ	μ	d	ϕ	θ	μ	d	ϕ	θ	μ
0.3	0.5	0.2	−0.205	0.056	0.109	0.050	−0.331	0.157	0.112	−0.048	−0.294	0.135	0.116	0.045
			(0.350)	(0.342)	(0.161)	(1.398)	(0.287)	(0.274)	(0.137)	(1.018)	(0.285)	(0.291)	(0.148)	(1.039)
0.3	0.2	0.5	−0.258	0.177	0.043	−0.017	−0.302	0.216	0.039	0.015	−0.294	0.217	0.033	−0.045
			(0.379)	(0.387)	(0.127)	(1.051)	(0.355)	(0.383)	(0.125)	(0.809)	(0.321)	(0.350)	(0.126)	(0.806)
0.3	−0.2	−0.5	−0.215	−0.074	0.269	0.005	−0.223	−0.066	0.266	−0.002	−0.108	−0.049	0.152	0.001
			(0.258)	(0.252)	(0.345)	(0.190)	(0.245)	(0.246)	(0.334)	(0.175)	(0.227)	(0.203)	(0.327)	(0.213)
0.3	−0.5	−0.2	−0.094	−0.039	0.125	−0.003	−0.109	−0.036	0.128	0.001	−0.077	−0.023	0.084	0.006
			(0.228)	(0.148)	(0.316)	(0.280)	(0.190)	(0.146)	(0.269)	(0.233)	(0.184)	(0.155)	(0.277)	(0.257)
0.	0.5	0.2	−0.362	0.185	0.129	−0.009	−0.328	0.163	0.124	0.005	−0.238	0.107	0.095	−0.010
			(0.289)	(0.285)	(0.143)	(0.256)	(0.270)	(0.276)	(0.145)	(0.233)	(0.261)	(0.282)	(0.144)	(0.259)
0.	0.2	0.5	−0.322	0.241	0.042	−0.004	−0.291	0.222	0.033	−0.000	−0.197	0.132	0.038	−0.009
			(0.352)	(0.370)	(0.125)	(0.183)	(0.303)	(0.340)	(0.123)	(0.185)	(0.280)	(0.330)	(0.133)	(0.205)
0.	−0.2	−0.5	−0.223	−0.084	0.287	−0.002	−0.193	−0.057	0.234	−0.002	0.121	−0.073	−0.035	−0.002
			(0.227)	(0.218)	(0.335)	(0.044)	(0.210)	(0.230)	(0.325)	(0.043)	(0.289)	(0.160)	(0.306)	(0.095)
0.	−0.5	−0.2	−0.122	−0.039	0.134	−0.004	−0.108	−0.029	0.128	−0.003	0.075	−0.016	−0.045	0.004
			(0.192)	(0.142)	(0.280)	(0.053)	(0.172)	(0.151)	(0.264)	(0.055)	(0.225)	(0.142)	(0.319)	(0.104)
−0.3	0.5	0.2	−0.284	0.135	0.110	−0.001	−0.208	0.078	0.104	0.002	−0.057	−0.035	−0.081	−0.006
			(0.277)	(0.291)	(0.154)	(0.080)	(0.270)	(0.296)	(0.159)	(0.078)	(0.254)	(0.311)	(0.179)	(0.103)
−0.3	0.2	0.5	−0.186	0.121	0.043	0.001	−0.154	0.095	0.038	0.001	−0.002	−0.032	0.039	0.006
			(0.275)	(0.351)	(0.146)	(0.063)	(0.241)	(0.319)	(0.141)	(0.061)	(0.217)	(0.297)	(0.152)	(0.106)
−0.3	−0.2	−0.5	−0.128	−0.067	0.192	−0.000	−0.060	−0.050	0.128	−0.001	0.496	−0.146	−0.252	−0.005
			(0.235)	(0.205)	(0.312)	(0.014)	(0.221)	(0.204)	(0.308)	(0.018)	(0.264)	(0.127)	(0.201)	(0.100)
−0.3	−0.5	−0.2	−0.086	−0.031	0.110	0.001	−0.028	−0.015	0.041	0.000	0.452	−0.023	−0.366	0.003
			(0.203)	(0.151)	(0.284)	(0.019)	(0.177)	(0.140)	(0.264)	(0.022)	(0.335)	(0.123)	(0.333)	(0.097)

Among the three estimates of d in each row, the one with the least bias is underlined.
All simulations were based on 500 replications of a sample size of 100.

Table 2. Simulation of the ARFIMA (1, 0.3, 1) model with known mean

True			CSS		
d	ϕ	θ	d	ϕ	θ
0.3	0.5	0.2	−0.063 (0.268)	−0.035 (0.332)	0.081 (0.189)
0.3	0.2	0.5	−0.085 (0.255)	0.047 (0.310)	0.021 (0.142)
0.3	−0.2	−0.5	−0.003 (0.255)	−0.061 (0.188)	0.066 (0.330)
0.3	−0.5	−0.2	0.029 (0.198)	−0.009 (0.143)	−0.016 (0.294)

All simulations were based on 500 replications.

ARFIMA(1, 0.3, 1) process are a useful starting point for the investigation of the impact of estimating μ.

Table 2 presents results for the same model, conditional on μ being known and with a sample size of 100. The magnitude of the bias drops to an order that is quite similar to those reported in Sowell's (1992a) Monte Carlo study. The contrast between Tables 2 and 1C offers the strongest evidence yet for the argument that estimating μ substantially increases the degree of bias in the other parameter estimates.

Table 3 gives Monte Carlo results based on a larger sample size of 300; μ is again assumed unknown and is estimated. Comparing Tables 3 and 1C indicates a considerable reduction in the bias. Clearly, the small sample bias is substantially reduced as the sample size increases. In particular, the estimate of the fractional differencing parameter d experiences more than a 40 percent reduction in the bias. In three out of the four cases the reduction is more than 50 percent.

In contrast to the large bias in estimating d and the ARMA parameters, the bias of the estimates of μ is reasonably small. When $d > 0$, the SRMSE of the μ estimates are usually quite large due to the slower convergence rate of $T^{1/2-d}$ as mentioned earlier. It is surprising that large SRMSE do not necessarily imply a large bias in the estimates of μ. These results confirm the assertion of Yajima (1988) and Samarov and Taqqu (1988) that the efficiency of the sample mean and the MLE of μ is about the same when $d > -0.3$.

5 Conclusion

The estimation of ARFIMA processes is likely to be an important activity for economists and area of research for econometricians for some time to come. As

Table 3. Simulation of the ARFIMA (1, 0.3, 1) model based on the sample size 300

True			CSS				Mean				Median			
d	ϕ	θ	d	ϕ	θ	μ	d	ϕ	θ	μ	d	ϕ	θ	μ
0.3	0.5	0.2	<u>−0.123</u>	0.060	0.057	0.022	−0.188	0.114	0.057	−0.025	−0.176	0.103	0.059	−0.088
			(0.256)	(0.236)	(0.100)	(1.149)	(0.236)	(0.215)	(0.089)	(0.753)	(0.242)	(0.226)	(0.094)	(0.773)
0.3	0.2	0.5	<u>−0.107</u>	0.088	0.010	−0.037	−0.109	0.089	0.009	−0.057	−0.124	0.106	0.005	0.010
			(0.240)	(0.261)	(0.080)	(0.773)	(0.215)	(0.237)	(0.084)	(0.620)	(0.214)	(0.245)	(0.086)	(0.631)
0.3	−0.2	−0.5	−0.066	−0.032	0.092	0.003	−0.079	−0.019	0.094	−0.005	<u>−0.050</u>	−0.020	0.065	−0.002
			(0.169)	(0.107)	(0.212)	(0.155)	(0.150)	(0.108)	(0.191)	(0.145)	(0.154)	(0.102)	(0.195)	(0.151)
0.3	−0.5	−0.2	−0.031	−0.013	0.039	0.009	−0.044	−0.014	0.059	0.000	<u>−0.031</u>	−0.007	0.036	0.001
			(0.125)	(0.083)	(0.186)	(0.183)	(0.107)	(0.087)	(0.165)	(0.186)	(0.104)	(0.079)	(0.152)	(0.198)

Among the three estimates of d in each row, the one with the least bias is underlined.
All simulations were based on 500 replications.

indicated in our results, the assumption of μ being known is far from innocuous. The estimation of μ in small sample sizes corrupts the CSS estimates of the other parameters. One corollary of our results is that estimation of ARFIMA models for small samples, e.g., T less than 150, should only be attempted with extreme caution. The resulting bias will be sufficiently large to make inference extremely unreliable. A useful check of the specification of the ARFIMA model in small sample cases would be to use all three estimates of μ (the CSS, the sample mean, as well as the sample median). Radically different estimates of the other parameters are likely to suggest a specification problem.

The CSS estimator appears to be a useful technique for quite general ARFIMA models in moderate to large samples but can possess substantial small-sample bias. The CSS estimator is of interest since it can be extended to more complicated models with non-normal conditional densities and time-dependent heteroskedasticity of the ARCH type. Some applications in this context are reported in Baillie, Chung and Tieslau (1992).

Appendix

In this appendix we show that setting the initial values $y_0, y_{-1}, y_{-2}, \ldots$ to zero is immaterial in examining the asymptotic distribution of the CSS estimator in the simple fractionally integrated white-noise ARFIMA(0, d, 0) model. Similar results for ARMA processes and univariate random walks are given by Pierce (1971) and Phillips (1987), respectively.

As indicated in the text, the ARFIMA(0, d, 0) model

$$(1 - L)^d y_t = \varepsilon_t \ ,$$

has the infinite moving average and autoregressive representations, respectively,

$$y_t = \psi(L)\varepsilon_t \qquad \text{and} \qquad \pi(L)y_t = \varepsilon_t \ ,$$

where

$$\psi(L) \equiv \sum_{j=0}^{\infty} \psi_j L^j \qquad \text{and} \qquad \pi(L) \equiv \sum_{j=0}^{\infty} \pi_j L^j \ .$$

If we assume $y_0 = y_{-1} = y_{-2} = \cdots = 0$, then these infinite-series representations will be truncated as follows:

$$y_t = \psi^*(L)\varepsilon_t \qquad \text{and} \qquad \pi(L)^* y_t = \varepsilon_t \ ,$$

where

$$\psi^*(L) \equiv \sum_{j=0}^{t} \psi_j L^j \qquad \text{and} \qquad \pi^*(L) \equiv \sum_{j=0}^{t} \pi_j L^j \ ,$$

since $\pi^*(L)\psi^*(L) = 1$, which is the truncated version of the fact $\pi(L)\psi(L) = 1$. Note that $\pi^*(L)\psi^*(L) = 1$ is due to the equalities $\sum_{j=0}^{t} \pi_j \psi_{t-j} = 0$, for all $t > 0$, which are in turn due to the equality $\pi(L)\psi(L) = 1$. Furthermore, if we compare the derivatives of ε_t with respect to d that are based on the three alternative forms $(1 - B)^d y_t$, $\pi(B)y_t$ and $\psi^{-1}(B)y_t$ of ε_t, we find

$$\sum_{k=0}^{j} \frac{\partial \psi_k}{\partial d} \pi_{j-k} = \frac{1}{j} = -\sum_{k=0}^{j} \frac{\partial \pi_k}{\partial d} \psi_{j-k} , \qquad \text{for} \qquad j = 1, 2, \ldots \tag{A1}$$

The computation of the CSS estimator of d is based on minimizing the CSS function $S(d)$ or, equivalently, by solving the first-order condition

$$\frac{\partial S(d)}{\partial d} = \frac{1}{\sigma^2} \sum_{t=1}^{T} \varepsilon_t \frac{\partial \varepsilon_t}{\partial d} = 0 . \tag{A2}$$

With the initial conditions $y_0 = y_{-1} = y_{-2} = \cdots = 0$, the derivative of ε_t with respect to d in (A2) is

$$\frac{\partial \varepsilon_t}{\partial d} = \frac{\partial \pi^*(L)}{\partial d} y_t = \frac{\partial \pi^*(L)}{\partial d} \psi^*(L)\varepsilon_t \equiv \tau(L)\varepsilon_t ,$$

and, by (A1), we have

$$\begin{aligned} \tau(L) &\equiv \frac{\partial \pi^*(L)}{\partial d} \psi^*(L) = \sum_{j=1}^{t-1} \sum_{k=1}^{j} \frac{\partial \pi_k}{\partial d} \psi_{j-k} L^j + \sum_{j=t}^{2t-2} \delta_{jt} L^j \\ &= -\sum_{j=1}^{t-1} \frac{1}{j} L^j + \sum_{j=t}^{2t-2} \delta_{jt} L^j , \end{aligned}$$

where

$$\delta_{jt} \equiv \sum_{k=j-(t-1)}^{t-1} \frac{\partial \pi_k}{\partial d} \psi_{j-k} , \qquad \text{for} \qquad j = t, \ldots, 2(t-1) .$$

Now, given that the expectation of the first-order condition (A1) is zero:

$$E\left[\frac{\partial S(d)}{\partial d}\right] = \frac{1}{\sigma^2} E\left[\sum_{t=1}^{T} \varepsilon_t \frac{\partial \varepsilon_t}{\partial d}\right] = \frac{1}{\sigma^2} \sum_{t=1}^{T} E[\varepsilon_t \tau(B)\varepsilon_t] = 0 .$$

then the CSS estimator $\hat{d}$ converges almost surely to the true value of d under standard regularity conditions. We now show the asymptotic variance of $\hat{d}$ is the same as that of the MLE, which is $6/\pi^2$. Consider the expectation of the second-order derivative of $S(d)$:

$$\begin{aligned} E\left[\frac{\partial^2 S(d)}{\partial d^2}\right] &= \frac{1}{\sigma^2} E\left[\sum_{t=1}^{T} \left(\frac{\partial \varepsilon_t}{\partial d}\right)^2 + \sum_{t=1}^{T} \varepsilon_t \frac{\partial^2 \varepsilon_t}{\partial d^2}\right] = \frac{1}{\sigma^2} \sum_{t=1}^{T} E\left(\frac{\partial \varepsilon_t}{\partial d}\right)^2 \\ &= \frac{1}{\sigma^2} \sum_{t=1}^{T} E[\tau(B)\varepsilon_t]^2 = \frac{1}{\sigma^2} \sum_{t=1}^{T} E\left[-\sum_{j=1}^{t-1} \frac{1}{j} B^j \varepsilon_t + \sum_{j=t}^{2t-2} \delta_{jt} B^j \varepsilon_t\right]^2 \end{aligned}$$

$$= \frac{1}{\sigma^2} \sum_{t=1}^{T} \left[\sum_{j=1}^{t-1} \frac{1}{j^2} E(\varepsilon_{t-j}^2) + \sum_{j=t}^{2t-2} \delta_{jt}^2 E(\varepsilon_{t-j}^2) \right]$$

$$= \sum_{t=1}^{T} \left[\sum_{j=1}^{t-1} \frac{1}{j^2} + \sum_{j=t}^{2t-2} \delta_{jt}^2 \right] = \sum_{t=1}^{T} (T - t) \frac{1}{t^2} + o(T) .$$

So $\lim_{T \to \infty} \frac{1}{T} E\left[\frac{\partial^2 S(d)}{\partial d^2} \right] = \sum_{t=1}^{\infty} \frac{1}{t^2} = \frac{\pi^2}{6}$, which is the inverse of the asymptotic variance of $\hat{d}$.

References

Agiakloglou, Newbold P, Wohar M (1992) Bias in an estimator of the fractional differencing parameter. Journal of Time Series Analysis, forthcoming

Baillie RT, Chung CF, Tieslau MA (1992) The long memory and variability of inflation: A reappraisal of the friedman hypothesis. Michigan State University Working Paper 9102

Box GEP, Jenkins GM (1976) Time series analysis: forecasting and control, second edition, Holden-Day San Francisco

Cheung YW, Diebold FX (1993) On maximum-likelihood estimation of the differencing parameter of fractionally integrated noise with unknown mean. Journal of Econometrics, forthcoming

Diebold FX, Rudebusch GD (1989) Long memory and persistence in aggregate output. Journal of Monetary Economics 24:189–209

Diebold FX, Rudebusch GD (1991) Is consumption too smooth? Long memory and the deaton paradox. The Review of Economics and Statistics 73:1–9

Engel RF (1982) Autoregressive conditional heteroscedasticity with estimates of the variance of United Kingdom inflations. Econometrica 50:987–1008

Fox R, Taqqu MS (1986) Large sample properties of parameter estimates for strongly dependent stationary gaussian time series. Annals of Statistics 14:517–532

Geweke J, Porter-Hudak S (1983) The estimation and application of long memory time series models. Journal of Time Series Analysis 4:221–238

Granger CWJ (1980) Long memory relationships and the aggregation of dynamic models. Journal of Econometrics 14:227–238

Granger CWJ (1981) Some properties of time series data and their use in econometric model specification. Journal of Econometrics 16:121–130

Granger CWJ, Joyeux R (1980) An introduction to long memory time series models and fractional differencing. Journal of Time Series Analysis 1:15–39

Hosking JRM (1981) Fractional differencing. Biometrika 68:165–176

Hosking JRM (1984). Modeling persistence in hydrological time series using fractional differencing. Water Resources Research 20:1898–1908

Li WK, McLeod AI (1986) Fractional time series modeling. Biometrika 73:217–221

Newbold P (1974) The exact likelihood function for a mixed autoregressive-moving average process. Biometrika 61:423–426

Phillips PCB (1987) Time series regression with a unit root. Econometrica 55:277–301

Pierce DA (1971) Least squares estimation in the regression model with autoregressive-moving average errors. Biometrika 58:299–312

Samarov A, Taqqu MS (1988) On the efficiency of the sample mean in long-memory noise. Journal of Time Series Analysis 9:191–200

Shea GS (1989) Ex-post rational price approximations and the empirical reliability of the present-value relation. Journal of Applied Econometrics 4:139–159
Shea GS (1991) Uncertainty and implied variance bounds in long-memory models of the interest rate term structure. Empirical Economics 16:287–312
Sowell FB (1992a) Maximum likelihood estimation of stationary univariate fractionally integrated time series models. Journal of Econometrics 53:165–188
Sowell FB (1992b) Modelling long-run behavior with the fractional ARIMA model. Journal of Monetary Economics 29:277–302
Taqqu MS (1975) Weak convergence to fractional brownian motion and to the Rosenblatt process. Zeitschrift Wahrscheinlichkeitstheorie verw. Gebiete 31:287–302
Yajima Y (1988) On estimation of A regression model with long-memory stationary errors. Annals of Statistics 16:791–807

GPSR Compliance

The European Union's (EU) General Product Safety Regulation (GPSR) is a set of rules that requires consumer products to be safe and our obligations to ensure this.

If you have any concerns about our products, you can contact us on ProductSafety@springernature.com

In case Publisher is established outside the EU, the EU authorized representative is:

Springer Nature Customer Service Center GmbH
Europaplatz 3
69115 Heidelberg, Germany

Kolibri 360 GmbH
Ferdinand-Jühlke-Straße 7
99095 Erfurt, Deutschland
produktsicherheit@kolibri360.de